STUDY GUIDE

Philip Kotler
Northwestern University

Gary Armstrong
University of North Carolina

Rob Warren
University of Manitoba

PRINCIPLES OF MARKETING

Fourth Canadian Edition

Philip Kotler
Northwestern University
Gary Armstrong
University of North Carolina
Peggy Cunningham
Queen's University

Prentice Hall Canada Inc.
Scarborough, Ontario

© 1999 Prentice-Hall Canada Inc., Scarborough, Ontario
Pearson Education

Prentice-Hall, Inc., Upper Saddle River, New Jersey
Prentice-Hall International (UK) Limited, London
Prentice-Hall of Australia, Pty. Limited, Sydney
Prentice-Hall Hispanoamericana, S.A., Mexico City
Prentice-Hall of India Private Limited, New Delhi
Prentice-Hall of Japan, Inc., Tokyo
Simon & Schuster Southeast Asia Private Limited, Singapore
Editora Prentice-Hall do Brasil, Ltda., Rio de Janeiro

ISBN 0-13-973660-3

Acquisitions Editor: Mike Ryan
Production Editor: Kelly Dickson
Editorial Assistant: Sherry Torchinsky
Production Coordinator: Jane Schell

3 4 5 03 02 01 00

Printed and bound in Canada.

Visit the Prentice Hall Canada Web site! Send us your comments, browse our catalogues, and
more. **www.phcanada.com** Or reach us through e-mail at
phcinfo_pubcanada@prenhall.com

A CIP catalogue record for this book is available from the National Library of Canada.

Contents

PREFACE

The purpose of this Study Guide is to help students learn and apply the concepts and ideas presented in the Fourth Canadian Edition of Kotler, Armstrong and Cunningham, *Principles of Marketing*.

The Study Guide should be viewed as a supplement rather than as a substitute for the text. The objectives are to allow the student to focus on the key terms and main topics of each chapter, demonstrate an understanding of the material through self-testing with multiple-choice and true-false questions and apply the concepts by analysing brief cases in marketing.

The Study Guide is divided into three sections. The first section is divided into 22 chapters with each chapter corresponding to a chapter in the text. Each chapter contains:

• Chapter Overview
• Chapter Objectives
• Chapter Topics
• Chapter Summary
• Key Terms
• Multiple Choice Questions
• True / False Questions
• Applying Terms and Concepts
• Answers

The second section of the Study Guide provides outlines for research papers and/or class projects. These activities are designed to reinforce learning which has taken place throughout the course. They are intended to be a practical application of the marketing theories presented in the text. Specific guidelines concerning topics, length, due date, method of presentation, grading and so on, will be provided by the course instructor.

The third section of the Study Guide contains information about selected careers in marketing. Its purpose is to demonstrate the great variety of employment opportunities which exist within the discipline of marketing. Information is also provided about trade associations and professional publications which will allow the student to gain additional information about various careers in marketing.

Studying Marketing

To better appreciate marketing and its role within the organization and society, the student is encouraged to personalize marketing by considering it from three perspectives: the consumer, the marketer and the member of society. The student is also encouraged to periodically review the various topics studied in marketing to develop a greater appreciation of their inter-relatedness. The intent of this course is to have the student realize that the topics are not separate and disjointed but rather, flow together in a synergistic fashion. With this knowledge, the student will appreciate the importance of marketing and how it interacts and coordinates with the other business functions.

This conceptual view of marketing will reinforce the need for a societal marketing orientation, providing a greater opportunity for consumer satisfaction and the achievement of organizational and societal objectives.

Chapter 1

Marketing in a Changing World

Chapter Overview

Today's successful companies share a strong focus on and a heavy commitment to marketing. Modern marketing seeks to attract new customers by promising superior value, and to keep current customers by delivering satisfaction. Sound marketing is critical to the success of all organizations, whether large or small, for-profit of non-profit, domestic or global.

Many people view marketing as only selling or advertising. But marketing combines many activities – marketing research, product development, distribution, pricing, advertising, personal selling and others – designed to sense, serve and satisfy customer needs while meeting the organization's goals. Marketing operated within a dynamic global environment. Rapid changes can quickly make yesterday's winning strategies obsolete. In the next century, marketers will face many new challenges and opportunities. To be successful, companies will have to be strongly market focused.

Chapter Objectives

1. Define Marketing and discuss its core concepts.
2. Discuss marketing management and examine how marketers manage demand and build profitable customer relationships.
3. Compare the five marketing management philosophies.
4. Analyse the major challenges facing marketers heading into the next century

Chapter Topics

What it marketing?
- Needs, Wants, Demands
- Products and Services
- Value, Satisfaction and Quality
- Exchange, Transactions, and Relationships
- Markets
- Marketing

Marketing Management
- Demand Management
- Building Profitable Customer Relationships

Marketing Management Philosophies
- The Production Concept
- The Product Concept
- The Selling Concept
- The Marketing Concept
- The Societal Marketing Concept

Marketing Challenges into the Next Century
- Growth of Non-Profit Marketing
- The Information Technology Boom
  - The Internet
- Rapid Globalization
- The Changing World Economy
- The Call for More Ethics and Social Responsibility
- The New Marketing Landscape

Chapter Summary

1.   Marketing and its role in the economy.

Marketing is a social and managerial process by which individuals and groups obtain what they need and want through creating and exchanging products and values with others. Economic roles include: meeting needs, wants and demands; creating products; creating value and satisfaction; facilitating exchanges; transactions; and mutually beneficial relationships; developing markets; meeting societal needs; increasing consumer choice, and providing fair profiles.

2.   The five marketing management philosophies.

Production Concept: consumers favour products that are available and highly affordable
Product Concept: consumers favour products that offer most values, performance, innovative features
Selling Concept: consumers will not normally buy enough products on their own
Marketing Concept: delivering needs and wants more efficiently than competition
Societal Marketing Concept: company determines customer's needs and wants and society's best interest

3.   The major forces now changing the marketing landscape and challenging marketing strategy.

A growth in non-profit marketing seems to meet new needs. Rapid globalization marked by geographic dispersion of purchasing, manufacturing and marketing activities. A changing world economy marked by a decline in real buying power and the increase in two-income households in the US. Increased demand for social responsibility including more ethical business practices and more attention to the environmental consequences of business decisions. A new marketing landscape characterised by extremely rapid change.

4.   The marketing management concept.

Marketing management is the analysis, planning, implementation and control of programs designed to create, build, and maintain beneficial exchanges with target buyers for the purpose of achieving organizational objectives. Marketing management seeks to manage demand efficiently and effectively so as to help consumers obtain value in their transactions with the company at a profit.

5.   The relationship between value, satisfaction and quality.

Customer value is the difference between the value of customer gains from owning and using a product and the costs of obtaining it. Satisfaction depends on a product's perceived performance in delivering value relative to the buyer's expectations. Quality, especially in the form of TQM is a company's commitment to constant improvement. Satisfaction comes from delighting and surprising customers with more quality, which heightens their perceived sense of value. Such practices are the only formula for long term success.

Key Terms

Customer Value   (pg. 11)
Customer Satisfaction (pg. 11)
Demands   (pg. 8)
Demarketing   (pg. 15)
Exchange   (pg. 12)
Internet   (pg. 22)
Market   (pg. 13)
Marketing   (pg. 7)
Marketing Concept   (pg. 18)
Marketing Management   (pg. 14)

Needs   (pg. 7)
Product   (pg. 9)
Product Concept   (pg. 17)
Production Concept   (pg. 16)
Relationship Marketing   (pg. 12)
Selling Concept   (pg. 17)
Societal Marketing Concept (pg. 19)
Total Quality Management   (pg. 11)
Transaction   (pg. 12)
Wants   (pg. 7)

Multiple Choice Questions

1-1   Multiple

The basic part(s) of the human makeup consist of:

1. Social needs
2. Physical needs
3. Psychological needs
4. 1, 2
5. All of the above

1-2   Multiple

Ogo lives in a small rural community in Tanzania. Resources are scarce, therefore in order to satisfy his families needs he will:

1. Try to reduce their desires
2. Try to reduce their needs
3. Satisfy their needs with what is available
4. Find or develop objects that will satisfy their needs
5. 1 and 3

1-3   Multiple

The importance of physical goods lies in

1. The satisfaction of owning them
2. The satisfaction they provide
3. The benefits they provide
4. The desires they satisfy
5. None of the above

1-4   Multiple

Fabiana is looking for a new microwave. She is on a limited budget, but values quality and performance above price. Which of the following concepts will she apply in choosing the appropriate microwave?

1. Customer value
2. Consumer preference
3. Product quality
4. Product value
5. Customer Satisfaction

4

1-5   Multiple

Which of the following systems of commerce allows a society to produce much more than it would with any alternative system?

1. Transaction
2. Exchanging
3. Relationship marketing
4. Open markets
5. All of the above

1-6   Multiple

Guida's 15-year-old car has just broken down and she has vowed it is the last time. This Saturday she will go car shopping and purchase a new car. She has been saving for the past 3 years for this. She will pay cash for her new car. This form of purchase is known as:

1. Transaction
2. Exchanging
3. Relationship marketing
4. Markets
5. Bartering

1-7   Multiple

The buyers in a market send _____ and _____ to the sellers in the industry.

1. Communication and money
2. Products/services and information
3. Products/services and money
4. Money and information
5. Communication and products/services

1-8   Multiple

Marketing management involves:

1. Managing customer relationships
2. Managing supplier relationships
3. Managing demand
4. 1 and 2
5. 1 and 3

1-9   Multiple

Grand Beach is always overcrowded on the May long weekend, as it is the first weekend
of the summer. Everybody wants to have a good time, making Grand Beach the party
location in Manitoba. Park officials could use which of the following techniques to
reduce the overcrowding situation?

1. Marketing management
2. Demand management
3. Demarketing
4. Negative marketing
5. None of the above

1-10   Multiple

Companies operating under which philosophy run the risk of focusing too narrowly on
developing and advertising the product, and fail to produce enough to meet the newly
increased demand?

1. Production concept
2. Product concept
3. Marketing concept
4. Societal Marketing concept
5. Selling concept

1-11   Multiple

Non-profit organizations spend a lot of money promoting their organization to the public.
They are sometimes more concerned with receiving donations than with providing the
best service. They are applying which type of company philosophy?

1. Production concept
2. Product concept
3. Marketing concept
4. Societal Marketing concept
5. Selling concept

1-12   Multiple

Societal Marketing concept argues the pure marketing concept overlooks the possible
conflicts between _____ and _____.

1. Short-term wants and short-term welfare
2. Short-term needs and long-term welfare
3. Short-tern wants and long-term welfare
4. Long-term wants and long-term welfare
5. Long-term wants and short-term welfare

1-13   Multiple

The social and managerial process by which individuals and groups obtain what they need and want through creating and exchanging products and value with others is called:

1. Commerce
2. Economics
3. Sales
4. Marketing
5. Purchasing power

1-14   Multiple

The term "goods and services" distinguish:

1. Products from the support mechanisms for them
2. Physical products from intangible ones
3. Expensive items from inexpensive items
4. Products that meet needs versus products that satisfy wants
5. 1 and 3

1-15   Multiple

_____ is the analysis, planning, implementation, and control of programs designed to create, build and maintain beneficial exchanges with target buyers for the purpose of achieving organizational objectives.

1. Demand management
2. Marketing management
3. Sales management
4. Corporate management
5. Consumer management

1-16   Multiple

Which of the following concepts takes an "inside-out" perspective?

1. The marketing concept
2. The product concept
3. The selling concept
4. The societal marketing concept
5. The production concept

1-17   Multiple

With the expansion of jet travel to every country, fax machines and the Internet are characteristic of what new challenge to marketing?

1.   Rapid globalization
2.   The changing world economy
3.   The call for more socially responsible marketing
4.   The micro-chip revolution
5.   1 and 2

1-18   Multiple

The fact many Canadian households need both spouses to work to maintain the buying power of a single-wage earner from a generation ago is characteristic of:

1.   The new world order
2.   The "yuppie" consumption syndrome
3.   The changing world economy
4.   The inflationary spiral of the 1970s
5.   Rapid globalization

1-19   Multiple

When a merchant appears in a central location called a marketplace, the total number of transactions required to accomplish a given volume of exchange:

1.   Increases
2.   Decreases
3.   Remains the same
4.   Fluctuates over time
5.   Unable to determine from the information given

1-20   Multiple

Programs designed to constantly improve the quality of products, service, and marketing processes fall under which of the following concepts?

1.   Customer satisfaction
2.   Customer value
3.   The exchange process
4.   Total quality management
5.   All of the above

1-21   Multiple

Which of the following entities is not considered a product entity?

1.   Person
2.   Place
3.   Organization
4.   Ideas
5.   All of the above are considered product entities

1-22   Multiple

Which of the following situations provide potential marketing opportunities for firms in the next century?

1.   Changing customer values and orientations
2.   Economic stagnation
3.   Environmental decline
4.   Increased global competition
5.   All of the above provide opportunities

1-23   Multiple

Which of the following companies would definitely not set up shop on the Internet?

1.   Jim's Fix-it Centre
2.   Carl's Roofing and Plumbing
3.   IGA
4.   Canadian Airlines
5.   All of the above would probably set up shop on the Internet

1-24   Multiple

Most large marketing companies like Coca-Cola and Nike do a lot of marketing research to understand their customers and be able to cater to their needs. Which of the following questions is not usually answered after they have conducted their marketing research?

1.   Why
2.   What
3.   Where
4.   How
5.   All of them are answered

1-25   Multiple

The marketing concept of the firm is very important to its survival. The focus of the marketing concept is:

1.   Market
2.   Integrated marketing
3.   Customer needs
4.   Profits through customer satisfaction
5.   Providing value

1-26   Multiple

Which philosophy in business is typically practised when marketing unsought goods?

1.   The marketing concepts
2.   The selling concept
3.   The production concept
4.   The product concept
5.   The societal marketing concept

1-27   Multiple

Looking for growth markets in other countries, such as Coca-Cola and Pepsi have done, is characteristic of which trend?

1.   Rapid globalization
2.   The need for increased profits
3.   The slow growth rate of the North American Market
4.   The increasing ethnic diversity of senior managers in major corporations
5.   All of the above

1-28   Multiple

Basic needs such as food, clothing, and safety refer to:

1.   Social needs
2.   Physical needs
3.   Physical wands
4.   Individual needs
5.   Social wants

1-29   Multiple

A (n) _____ consists of a trade of values between parties.

1.   Sale
2.   Exchange
3.   Transaction
4.   Market
5.   Barter

1-30   Multiple

The _____ holds that achieving organizational goals depends on determining the needs, wants of target markets and delivering the desired satisfaction more effectively and efficiently than the competition.

1.   Production concept
2.   Product concept
3.   Selling concept
4.   Marketing concept
5.   Societal marketing concept

True/False Questions

1-1   True/False

Needs are states of perceived depravation.

1-2   True/False

Customer satisfaction is the extent to which a product's perceived performance matches a buyer's expectations.

1-3   True/False

Exchange is the core concept of marketing.

1-4   True/False

Exchange marketing is part of the larger idea of relationship marketing.

1-5   True/False

Each nation's economy and the whole world's economy consist of simple interacting sets of markets linked through exchange processes.

1-6   True/False

It costs more than four times as much to attract a new customer than it does to keep an existing customer satisfied.

1-7   True/False

In today's highly competitive marketplace, companies cannot afford to lose money on one transaction if it helps to cement a profitable long-term customer relationship

1-8   True/False

The goal of the marketing concept is to build customer satisfaction into the very fabric of the firm.

1-9   True/False

Companies are not only trying to sell more of their locally produced goods in international markets, but they are also buying more components and supplies locally.

1-10   True/False

The World Wide Web has given companies access to millions of new customers at a fraction of the cost of print and television advertising despite the huge costs of setting up a web page.

1-11   True/False

Marketing myopia occurs when sellers are so taken with their products they focus only on existing wants and lose sight of underlying customer needs.

1-12   True/False

To qualify as an economic exchange, the buyer must offer the seller money for a product or service.

1-13   True/False

The societal marketing concept holds the organization should determine the needs, wants and interests of target markets.

1-14   True/False

The changing world economy is the primary reason for the emergence of "hybrid products," where design, material purchases, manufacture, and marketing may all take place in different counties.

1-15   True/False

Although related, marketing management and demand management are very different activities.

1-16   True/False

A market is a set of actual, not potential, buyers of a product.

1-17   True/False

Consumers favour products that are available and highly affordable is the central tenet of the production concept.

1-18   True/False

The selling concept holds the organization should determine the needs, wants of consumers and undertake large-scale selling efforts.

1-19   True/False

Ironically, markets are not among the core marketing concepts identified in the text.

1-20   True/False

A new car, a car cleaner, and a car wash are all considered products.

Applying Terms and Concepts

To determine how well you understand the materials in this chapter, read each of the following brief cases and then respond to the questions that follow. Answers are given at the end of this chapter.

Case #1   Handyman Hardware and Lumber[1]

Thomas Steenburgh began Handyman Stores in 1979 after determining a huge do-it-yourself market existed for hardware and building supplies. His research showed as plumbers, electricians, carpenters, and others began charging more in the mid-70s, many homeowners decided to do their own repairs and remodelling. And if their work wasn't quite perfect, homeowners could at least take satisfaction in knowing they had done the work themselves and that they had saved money. Steenburgh's research was consistent with the findings of the Do-it-Yourself Research Institute, based in Indianapolis, which estimated that do-it-yourself sales would grow from $6.4 billion in 1970 to $63.5 billion in 1990, thereafter increasing approximately 8% per year.

Steenburgh's concept of retailing was to stock a wide variety of name-brand hardware and building supplies in what is essentially a warehouse. He spends virtually no money on fixtures and allows customers to use handcarts to select their own merchandise, which they bring to a centralized checkout area. The stores are open from 7 a.m. to 10 p.m., Monday through Saturday. Handyman's main form of advertising consists of flyers and inserts in local newspapers. When a Handyman Store is opened in a city, its prices are reduced to a minimum. The usual practice is to post a local competitor's catalogue or flyer at the store and offer the customer the same or comparable goods for 20% less. Prices are kept low because Handyman buys direct from the manufacturer and sells for cash or approved cheque only. It also saves money because its stores serves as its own warehouse; each store is between 75,000 and 100,000 sq. ft. What merchandise does not fit on a shelf or rack is stacked on the floor, sometimes up to the ceiling.

One area where Steenburgh will not skimp is personnel. Since 85% of his sales are to do-it-yourselfers, he typically hires 30 to 40 salespeople for each store and trains them in do-it-yourself tasks. These salespeople liberally dispense free Handyman how-to pamphlets and practical advice on projects from start to finish.

Steenburgh's philosophy of selling quality products at a low price with good advice has served Handyman well. Sales per square foot have average between $250 and $275 at each of its 19 store with projected profits this year of $22 million.

---

[1] *Principles of Marketing*, 3rd Edition, Kotler, Armstrong, Warren (Prentice Hall) – pg. 7.

1.   What type of people are involved in marketing activities at Handyman Stores?

_____

_____

_____

_____

2.   How do each of the above people contribute to the marketing activities?

_____

_____

_____

_____

3.   How Does Steenburgh implement marketing management in his stores?

_____

_____

_____

_____

4.   What product(s) is Handyman selling to its consumers?

_____

_____

_____

_____

5.   Identify Handyman's marketing philosophy and list the reasons for your decision.

_____

_____

_____

_____

Case #2   First Nations Cola

Mike Birch is from Cross Lake, Manitoba, a small isolated reserve community located 850 km north of Winnipeg. The only way to reach the reserve in the summer was by airplane and in the winter, by a winter road. Mike decided since there was only one store in town, and it charged above average prices, many needs were not being met. He decided to bring in a trailer to sell soft drinks, chips and chocolate bars. His most successful product was the soft drinks, because Aboriginal consume them at 4 times the national consumption rate. He realized this was an issue on his reserve, it must also be an issue on other reserves. Mike, therefore, decided to start First Nations Cola so Aboriginal people could have a beverage to call their own. Since its inception, his company has expanded to cover not only reserves, but also urban centres like Winnipeg. He also entered the international market by exporting to Europe and bottling in the US under license. He went after the European market because of their fascinations with the Aboriginal culture. This is an excellent example of how an entrepreneur saw an unmet need, capitalized on it and made a profitable business.

1. In your opinion, why was this a good opportunity to capitalize upon?

_____

_____

_____

_____

2. Describe the profitable customer relationship.

_____

_____

_____

_____

3. Describe the marketing philosophy you feel Mike Birch used.

_____

_____

_____

_____

4. What new potential markets should Mike Birch investigate?

_____

_____

_____

_____

Case #3   Coca Cola International[2]

The Coca-Cola Company is the world's leading soft-drink maker and sells its brands in more than 200 countries. In fact, Coca-Cola outsells Pepsi three to one overseas with the largest growth occurring in Latin America and Asia. Both Coca-Cola and Pepsi are concentrating on the Asian market as it holds almost half of the world's population and the growth opportunities are tremendous. However, Pepsi will find it difficult to compete against Coca-Cola in these markets because Coca-Cola invested heavily in bottling plants and has demonstrated they understand local market needs and marketing tactics. Coca-Cola has used its resources and creativity to become a very profitable multinational company.

1.   Which marketing management philosophy is Coca-Cola using? Why has it been so successful for them?

    _____

    _____

    _____

    _____

2.   What do you believe the primary need is being satisfied by Coca-Cola?

    _____

    _____

    _____

    _____

3.   Do you believe this move into Asia and Latin America is socially responsible? Why or why not?

    _____

    _____

    _____

    _____

---

[2] *Principles of Marketing*, 4th Edition, Kotler, Armstrong, Cunningham (Prentice Hall) – pg. 25.

Case #4   Pet Insurance Company of America[3]

George Smrtic founded the Pet Insurance Company of America (PICA) three years after the death of his shetland collie, Priscilla. It seems that the 11 year old Priscilla developed heart and lung trouble and rather than spend the estimated $1,200 for treatment he had Priscilla put to sleep.

Smrtic reasoned that since Americans are inclined to insure themselves and many of their possessions, they might also be inclined to insure their pets. Especially since pets are seen by many as an integral part of the family – in some cases more loyal, obedient and loving than certain family members.

Smrtic researched the concept of pet insurance and found there are in excess of 110 million dogs and cats in approximately 65 million households. He also found that Americans spend $15 billion a year on pets for everything from air-conditioned dog houses to designer clothing, to toys, to vacations and more recently, beefy flavoured beverages and ice cream treats. Smrtic's research, including data collected from the American Veterinary Society, pet owners, and individual veterinarians, indicated that dog owners spend $95 per year on veterinary care while cat owners spend $78 per year. Smrtic also found that not only are people's attitudes toward pets changing, but also that increasingly sophisticated and expensive medical treatments including chemotherapy, cataract operations and heart pacemakers are now available.

The basic policies, which are underwritten by the Black Hawk Data Group of Dallas, sell for $49 with a $300 deductible clause. For $90 per year, the deductible falls to $100. Each policy insures the pet against catastrophic illness and/or accident. Not covered are routine procedures such as examinations, office visits, inoculations and neutering.

The policies currently available only on dogs and cats are sold only through veterinary offices with the veterinarian acting as an agent for PICA.

Sales to date have been excellent with over 70,000 policies providing $3,000,000 of coverage on approximately 100,000 dogs and cats. Competition from tow other firms is minimal in that the market is expanding by 20-30 percent per year. PICA, which is licensed in 47 states, expects to begin offering policies on pets other than dogs and cats within a year.

1. What is the marketing concept used by PICA?

    _____

    _____

    _____

    _____

---

[3] *Principles of Marketing*, 3rd Edition, Kotler, Armstrong, Warren (Prentice Hall) – pg. 9.

2. The product provided my PICA is an intangible item. Why is it still considered a product?

_____

_____

_____

3. How would PICA expand its insurance products to other pets?

_____

_____

_____

4. What type of business transfer would an insurance policy qualify as?

_____

_____

_____

5. How could PICA use the Internet to expand their business? Are there any concerns with this mode of media for PICA?

_____

_____

_____

_____

Case #5   Changes Come to the Soviet Union[4]

The shortages of consumer goods in the former Soviet Union were legendary. Meat, poultry, detergents, toilet paper, razor blades, gasoline, automobiles, fashionable clothing and decent housing were in chronic short supply. An ordinary citizen would wait in line an average of two hours each day to buy what was available. Over a lifetime, that amounted to five years wasted standing in line. The Soviet currency, the ruble, until recently, was virtually worthless in international trade because it was not freely exchangeable with world currencies. This along with restrictive trade policy severely limited the average citizen's access to foreign goods.

It was easy to assume that the reason so few consumer goods were available was that soviet leaders simply decoded to devote more of the nation's resources to military

---

[4] *Principles of Marketing*, 3rd Edition, Kotler, Armstrong, Warren (Prentice Hall) – pg. 11.

production and less to the production of consumer goods. But the problem was more complex that that and was partly based on how decision were made in the USSR.

In our capitalistic society with its market-directed economy, the public has the major say about what gets produced because they "vote" with their dollars. If people like a product, they will buy more of it. The manufacturers will quickly make more of it because they want to make money, and the only way to make money is to give the public what it wants.

Things didn't work that way in the Soviet Union. The Soviets had a planned economy which meant that central planners in Moscow decided what it was the people want, or should want, and then ordered it produced. Decisions that were made in the market placed in the United States were made by central planners in the Soviet Unions. Sometimes the central planners were right; more often they were wrong. When they were wrong, shortages occurred and a black-market arose to allocate the scarce goods and services.

In an effort to address certain problem within the Soviet Union, former President Mikhail Gorbachev instituted two revolutionary policies, Perestroika (Economic Restructuring) and Glasnost (openness and political democracy). Glasnost allowed the Soviet citizens the opportunity to say what was on their minds while Perestroika allowed economic reform.

Government officials realised that the satisfaction of consumer needs wants and demands, and the flexibility to accommodate changing market conditions was critical to raising the standard of living of the Soviet people. Government officials also realized that the average Soviet citizen has long enjoyed considerable security with guaranteed employment, health care, schooling and housing. But the movement to a more market directed economy would exact a considerable price in the form of lower security, higher inflation, unemployment and crime, and the need to institute unemployment and welfare programs.

These are problems that the former republic, now a collection of independent states, are grappling with.

1.   What are the main characteristics of a market directed economy?

_____

_____

_____

_____

2. What role does marketing play in providing customer satisfaction in a market directed economy?

_____

_____

_____

_____

3. How does a market-directed economy differ from a planned economy?

_____

_____

_____

_____

4. Identify the types of goods and services resulting from the decisions made by government officials in a market-directed economy. Explain why they cannot easily be made in the marketplace?

_____

_____

_____

_____

5. In the new companies in the Soviet Union wanted to start a relationship-marketing program, what would be their main focus?

_____

_____

_____

_____

Multiple Choice Answers

1. Correct Answer: 4   Reference: pg. 7
2. Correct Answer: 5   Reference: pg. 7
3. Correct Answer: 3   Reference: pg. 10
4. Correct Answer: 1   Reference: pg. 11
5. Correct Answer: 2   Reference: pg. 12
6. Correct Answer: 1   Reference: pg. 12
7. Correct Answer: 4   Reference: pg. 13
8. Correct Answer: 5   Reference: pg. 14
9. Correct Answer: 3   Reference: pg. 15
10. Correct Answer: 1   Reference: pg. 17
11. Correct Answer: 5   Reference: pg. 17
12. Correct Answer: 3   Reference: pg. 19
13. Correct Answer: 4   Reference: pg. 7
14. Correct Answer: 2   Reference: pg. 10
15. Correct Answer: 2   Reference: pg. 14
16. Correct Answer: 3   Reference: pg. 18
17. Correct Answer: 1   Reference: pg. 23
18. Correct Answer: 3   Reference: pg. 26
19. Correct Answer: 2   Reference: pg. 13
20. Correct Answer: 4   Reference: pg. 12
21. Correct Answer: 5   Reference: pg. 10
22. Correct Answer: 5   Reference: pg. 20

23.	Correct Answer:	5	Reference:	pg. 23
24.	Correct Answer:	1	Reference:	pg. 9
25.	Correct Answer:	3	Reference:	pg. 18
26.	Correct Answer:	2	Reference:	pg. 17
27.	Correct Answer:	1	Reference:	pg. 24
28.	Correct Answer:	2	Reference:	pg. 7
29.	Correct Answer:	3	Reference:	pg. 12
30.	Correct Answer:	4	Reference:	pg. 19

True/False Answers

1. FALSE   Reference: pg. 7   Topic: Needs, Wants, and Demands

2. TRUE   Reference: pg. 11   Topic: Value, Satisfaction, and Quality

3. TRUE   Reference: pg. 12   Topic: Exchange, Transactions, and Relationships

4. FALSE   Reference: pg. 12   Topic: Exchange, Transactions, and Relationships

5. FALSE   Reference: pg. 13   Topic: Markets

6. TRUE   Reference: pg. 14   Topic: Building Profitable Customer Relationships

7. FALSE   Reference: pg. 16   Topic: Marketing Highlight 1-2

8. TRUE   Reference: pg. 18   Topic: The Marketing Concept

9. FALSE   Reference: pg. 24   Topic: Rapid Globalization

10. TRUE   Reference: pg. 22   Topic: The Internet

11. TRUE   Reference: pg. 17   Topic: The Product Concept

12. FALSE   Reference: pg. 12   Topic: Exchange, Transactions, and Relationships

13. TRUE   Reference: pg. 19   Topic: The Societal Marketing Concept

14. FALSE   Reference: pg. 26   Topic: The Changing World Economy

15. FALSE   Reference: pg. 14   Topic: Marketing Management

16. FALSE   Reference: pg. 13   Topic: Markets

17. TRUE   Reference: pg. 17   Topic: The Production Concept

18. FALSE   Reference: pg. 17   Topic: The Selling Concept

19. FALSE   Reference: pg. 7   Topic: Marketing Defined

20. TRUE   Reference: pg. 10   Topic: Products and Services

Applying Terms and Concepts Answers

Case #1   Handyman Hardware and Lumber:

Question #1
- Handyman
- Store personnel
- Customers

Question #2
- Handyman – the store sells what is advertises, they live up to their name of quality products and provide all the services they say they do, also the profits from the store pay for the advertisements in the papers and flyers
- Store personnel – they sell their expertise and knowledge and obviously suggest products the store carries in order to help someone complete the task at hand
- Customers – if they are satisfied with the service and products they received at Handyman's and they are content with the finished job, they will tell others of their experiences and suggest that they go to Handyman's for any required home repair projects

Question #3
- Steenburgh knows it is very important to have customer loyalty. For this reason his marketing plan is to provide quality products at low prices. This is evident in the marketing strategy of showing the competitors' prices and beating them, also the no frills atmosphere lets consumers know that they are not spending money on unnecessary things so they get the lowest price. He ensures his staff is very knowledgeable and qualified to be a "professional" in their departments so consumers get quality service and a complete experience

Question #4
- Hardware and building supplies
- How-to-pamphlets
- Free how-to-advice
- They are selling a complete package so they can be a one-stop-shop destination location which will give them a competitive advantage over other stores

Question #5
- The market concept
- The key to Steenburgh's success is determining the needs and wants of target markets and delivering the desired satisfaction more effectively and efficiently than competitors
- Low prices, quality products, name brand merchandise, convenient hours, large selection, free advice and knowledge, how-to pamphlets

Case #2   First Nations Cola:

Question #1
- Aboriginals had a greater than average consumption rate
- The local convenience stores were charging high prices
- They could identify with this cola and therefore customer loyalty would not be difficult to maintain
- Many companies would not fly products into reserves because of the expense

Question #2
- They can identify with the product as it was started and is run by an Aboriginal person
- Their logo is Aboriginal
- The product has a similar taste to the national brands, so this is a minor issue

Question #3
- First Nations Cola uses the Marketing Concept as they see a need and try to satisfy it by making it available to all reserves
- They market the product as Aboriginal and people feel pride in the product and are extremely loyal
- The customers are obviously satisfied as the company is growing and moving into new markets.

Question #4
- Europe and capitalize on their fascination with First Nations' Culture
- The US reserves and Aboriginal Peoples
- Australia and South America have many Aboriginal people; these could be very profitable markets.

Case #3   Coca Cola International:

Question #1
- The Selling Concept
- The organization has taken on a major promotion effort
- There is a huge potential market in Asia and Latin America so Coca-Cola must get loyal customers now, they are selling an image that will maintain loyalty

Question #2
- The primary need is an image, not the drink
- This is seen as a "cool" product, which is a treat. Disposable income in these countries is not very high; therefore this is a luxury item which sends a certain image to those around you.

28

Question #3
- It is for the reason that you are providing a country with a good product that satisfies a needs
- It could not be if Coca-Cola is bottling product in these plants at sub-standard working conditions and wages.
- It could not be if the marketing would convince the people that coke is very important that they must buy it rather that a meal
- It is because it is bringing joy and contentment to the peoples of these countries

Case #4   Pet Insurance Company of America:

Question #1
- Marketing Concept
- Smrtic has identified a need and a want and has been able to provide it to consumers in a more efficient and effective manor, as he has a lower deductible and is planning on expanding coverage to other pets and not limiting it to dogs and cats

Question #2
- A product can be a tangible or intangible item
- Intangible items are referred to as services and are just as important as a product as it satisfies needs and wants in a way that satisfies customers

Question #3
- PICA could expand its service to other pets through veterinarians, pet stores, or even flyers to communities where pets are predominant, like the suburbs
- As PICA is growing, they now have more income being generated, therefore they can spend more on advertising and would probably be beneficial to them to start a television of radio campaign to make consumers aware of their services, and to convince them that a pet is just as important as a family member, and therefore should be insured

Question #4
- It would be considered a transaction
- It involves a trade between two parties that involves at least 2 things of value, and agreed-upon conditions – money for financial coverage at the necessary time
- The agreement only covers certain amount of conditions and they are known at the time of signing and paying for the agreement

Question #5
- They could build a web page so consumers can look and see what PICA is all about
- They could provide all necessary logistical information on the web page so consumers know how to contact them
- They could also use vets home pages and have links to their web site to increase exposure and the chances that their ads will be seen
- Issuing policies over the Internet is not possible as people must understand the terms and conditions of the agreement before they sign

Case #5   Change Comes to the Soviet Union:

Question #1
- The people have a major say in what gets produced because they "vote" with their money
- If they like a product they will buy more of it and manufacturers will make more
- The only way for a manufacturer to make money is to provide what consumers want and are willing to buy
- Supply and demand are allowed to interact
- Competition helps to increase the quality of a product and reduce process

Question #2
- Consumers have the opportunity to get what they want, when they want it and where they want it
- They use the above to obtain and use goods and services
- They also acquire knowledge about these goods and services

Question #3
- In a planned economy the government decides what to produce, who will produce it, when and where it will be produced and the prices they will charge
- In a market directed economy, these decision are made as a result of the profit motive, supply and demand, competition and the pursuit of consumer satisfaction

Question #4
- Government officials in a market driven economy make decision about
  - National defence
  - Police and fire protection
  - Primary education
  - Welfare
  - Pollution control
- These decisions are made by the government because people in the marketplace would not be interested in really buying or paying for the above services

Question #5
- Def'n: The process of creating, maintaining, and enhancing strong, value-laden relationships with customers
- Reliable amounts of products
- Constant priccs
- Assortment of products
- Information where you can get more products

Chapter 2

Strategic Planning and the Marketing Process

Chapter Overview

Strategic planning sets the stage for the rest of the company planning. Marketing contributes to strategic planning and the overall plan defines marketing's role in the company. Although formal planning offers a variety of benefits to companies, not all companies use it or use it well. Many discussions of strategic planning focus on large corporations; however, small business also can benefit greatly from sound strategic planning.

Chapter Objectives

1. Explain company-wide strategic planning and its four steps.
2. Discuss how to design business portfolios and growth strategies.
3. Explain functional planning strategies and assess marketing's role in strategic planning.
4. Describe the marketing process and the forces that influence it.
5. List the marketing management functions, including the elements of a marketing plan.

Chapter Topics

Strategic Planning
- Defining the Company Mission
- Setting Company Objectives and Goals

Designing the Business Portfolio
- Analyzing the Current Business Portfolio
  - The Boston Consulting Group Approach
  - The General Electric Approach
- Developing Growth Strategies
- Planning Functional Strategies
- Strategic Planning and Small Business

The Marketing Process
- Target Consumers
  - Market Segmentation
  - Market Targeting
  - Market Positioning
- Marketing Strategies for Competitive Advantage
- Developing the Marketing Mix

Managing the Marketing Effort
- Marketing Analysis
- Marketing Planning
- Marketing Implementation
- Marketing Department Organization
- Marketing Control
- The Marketing Environment

Chapter Summary

1. The strategic planning process and the four steps of strategic planning.

    Strategic planning is defined as the process of developing and maintaining a strategic fit between the organization's goals and capabilities and its changing marketing opportunities.

    The four steps in the strategic planning process includes:
    1. Defining the company mission;
    2. Setting company objectives and goals;
    3. Designing the business portfolio;
    4. Planning marketing and other related strategies.

2. Comparing and contrasting the BCG and GE portfolio matrix models and their limitations.

    The BCG consists of Stars, high-growth high-share; Cows, low-growth high-share; Questions Marks, low-share high-growth; Dogs, low-share low-growth. Strategies include build, hold, harvest, or divest. The GE Planning Grid consists of two dimensions: industry attractiveness and business strength. Dimensions are an index rather than a single measure. BCG may rely too much on market stare while GE Grid may rely too much on formal planning.

3. The marketing management process and the forces that influence it.

    The marketing management process involves helping each business unit of the company reach its strategic objectives in relation to creating value for target consumers while fulfilling company goals. Factors influencing the process are target consumers (central), marketing mix decisions, planning, implementation, analysis and control procedures, and micro and macro environmental forces.

4. The sections of the marketing plan, their strategic function and what each section contains.

    Marketing plans should have eight sections. The executive summary provides a brief overview of key points. Current marketing situation presents relevant background. Threats and opportunities identify factors affecting the product. Objectives and issues define share, profit, and sales goals. Marketing strategy presents the broad approach. Action programs specify how to proceed. Budgets give P/L estimates. Controls measure plan progress.

5.	The marketing implementation process and how companies implement, organize, and control their marketing efforts.

Marketing implementation turns strategies into plans and actions specifying who, where, when and how. It requires an action program, an organization structure, decision and reward systems, human resources planning, and fit with the company culture. Controls must provide objective feedback measures for all these areas.

Key Terms

Business Portfolio	(pg. 44)
Cash Cows	(pg. 44)
Diversification	(pg. 47)
Dogs	(pg. 45)
Growth-Share Matrix	(pg. 44)
Market Development	(pg. 47)
Market Penetration	(pg. 47)
Market Positioning	(pg. 54)
Market Segment	(pg. 52)
Market Segmentation	(pg. 52)
Market Targeting	(pg. 53)
Marketing Audit	(pg. 63)
Marketing Control	(pg. 62)

Marketing Implementation	(pg. 59)
Marketing Process	(pg. 49)
Marketing Mix	(pg. 55)
Marketing Strategy	(pg. 59)
Mission Statement	(pg. 41)
Portfolio Analysis	(pg. 44)
Product Development	(pg. 47)
Product/Market Expansion Grid	(pg. 47)
Question Marks	(pg. 45)
Stars	(pg. 44)
Strategic Business Unit (SBU)	(pg. 44)
Strategic Planning	(pg. 41)

Multiple Choice Questions

2-1   Multiple

Strategic planning is useful to all organizations because it:

1. Encourages management to think systematically
2. Forces management to sharpen its objectives and policies
3. Helps with performance standards for control
4. Helps the company to anticipate and respond quickly to environmental changes
5. All of the above

2-2   Multiple

A clear _____ acts as an invisible hand that guides people in the organization so that they can work independently and yet collectively toward overall organizational goals.

1. Company objective
2. Company goal
3. Mission statement
4. Business portfolio
5. Vision

2-3   Multiple

Mission statements should be:

1. Specific, realistic, motivating
2. Specific, realistic, simplistic
3. Realistic, motivating, simplistic
4. Motivating, simplistic, specific
5. None of the above

2-4   Multiple

Which of the following is a good objective for a company?

1. Increase our market share
2. Increase our market share by 15% over the next 2 years
3. Increase our market share by 15%
4. Increase our market share over the next 2 years
5. Increase our market share indefinitely over the next 2 years

2-5   Multiple

André owns a fishing, tackle and grocery store. Sales in the fishing equipment have been booming, however, the store merchandise is not moving and there is substantial waste. He decides to drop the grocery products to concentrate on the fishing and tackle trade. André has used _____ to make this decision.

1. Strategic business unit
2. Business portfolio
3. Portfolio analysis
4. Strategic business planning
5. Clarify company goals and objectives

2-6   Multiple

Procter & Gamble is a large multinational organization specializing in many different products. As can be expected it is comprised of many different strategic business units (SBU). Which of the following would qualify as a SBU?

1. Beauty products division
2. Bounty towels
3. South American division
4. 1 and 3
5. All of the above

2-7   Multiple

_____ often require heavy investment to finance their rapid growth.

1. Stars
2. Cash cows
3. Question marks
4. Dogs
5. New products

2-8   Multiple

Which of the following in NOT a problem with a matrix approach to strategic planning?

1. They provide little direction with respect to future planning
2. They can be time consuming
3. They can be costly to implement
4. They can be misleading with respect to consumer value
5. They can be difficult to define

2-9   Multiple

Reebok is developing many new products for different segments of the market. They have especially designed a new marketing campaign for seniors and children. Which quadrant of the product/market expansion grid are they focusing on?

1. Market penetration
2. Markct dcvclopment
3. Product development
4. Product expansion
5. Diversification

2-10   Multiple

Perfect Balance is a small accounting company with limited resources but a huge potential to succeed and grow in the future if they focus their efforts correctly. They have decided it is in their best interest to limit the amount of customers they serve by limiting their services provided. They are focusing on:

1. Market segmentation
2. Market segments
3. Market positioning
4. Market targeting
5. Markct strategies

2-11   Multiple

In the past 3 years, the city of Winnipcg has been flooded with new bagel stores opening up on every corner. These new stores are following the _____ approach to a marketing strategy.

1. Market-follower
2. Market-leader
3. Market-nicher
4. Market-challenger
5. Market-penetrator

2-12   Multiple

Through _____ the company turns the strategic and marketing plan into actions that will achieve the company's strategic objectives.

1. Analysis
2. Implementation
3. Planning
4. Control
5. Managing

2-13   Multiple

Which of the following is NOT a marketing department organization?

1. Functional
2. Geographic
3. Product management
4. Division
5. Market management

2-14   Multiple

Typically, answers to the questions, "Who is our customer?" "What is our business?" and "What should our business be?" are found in which of the following?

1. The product concept
2. The company mission statement
3. The company goals and objectives
4. The organizational culture
5. The personnel manual

2-15   Multiple

Which of the following in not a component of industry attractiveness under the GE portfolio planning system?

1. Market size
2. Market growth rate
3. Amount of competition
4. Relative market share
5. None of the above

2-16   Multiple

All the following statements about formal portfolio planning tools are true except:

1. It is sometimes difficult to measure market share and market growth
2. Portfolio approaches classify current businesses not future ones
3. Portfolio approaches alleviate the need for manager's to use their judgement in determining what resources to give each SBU
4. Formal planning approaches can lead management to place too much emphasis on market-share
5. None of the above

2-17   Multiple

In terms of business functions, the marketing department seeks to take the consumer's point of view. But this can create conflicts with other departments. Problems marketing create for other departments include:

1. Increased production costs
2. Disrupted production schedules
3. Increased inventories
4. 1 and 2
5. All of the above

2-18   Multiple

To successfully communicate and deliver the company's desired position to the consumer the company:

1. Must emphasize advertising in support of its positioning strategy
2. Must focus its promotional efforts on personal selling
3. Must place its greatest efforts on producing the desired product efficiently
4. Must focus the entire marketing program in support of the chosen positioning strategy
5. Must split the focus between the personal selling and product efficiency

2-19   Multiple

One limitation of the perspective taken by the "4 P's" is:

1. They exclude such controllable variables as the economy, competition, and government regulation
2. They represent the seller's view of the marketing tools used to influence buyers, not the view of the consumers
3. They are impossible to apply to a new product
4. They exclude the most important "P" in business, profits
5. They cannot be adaptable to different geographic regions

2-20   Multiple

When you are starting a small business or you currently own a small business, all the following situations can be remedied or even prevented by developing and actually implementing a sound strategic plan except:

1.   You have taken on too much debt
2.   Your growth is exceeding your production capacity
3.   Your engineering design is not stable and does not meet industry standards
4.   If you are losing market share to a competitor with a lower price
5.   All of the above can be solved with a proper strategic plan

2-21   Multiple

Which of the following is not considered a step in the process by which small firms create their strategic plans?

1.   Identify the major elements of the business environment
2.   Purchase all necessary resources in order to compete successfully
3.   Describe the mission of the organization in terms of its nature and function
4.   Develop a set of long-term objectives that will identify what the organization will become in the future
5.   Identify the major driving force that will direct the organization in the future

2-22   Multiple

In a solid marketing plan, all the following areas are covered in the current market situation except:

1.   Information about the market
2.   A product review
3.   A review of the competition
4.   A review of the distribution
5.   All of the above are covered

2-23   Multiple

Ideally the best company mission statements will be:

1.   Product oriented
2.   Production oriented
3.   Market oriented
4.   Employee oriented
5.   Company oriented

2-24   Multiple

In setting marketing objectives to reach goals, which of the following is true?

1.   Increasing sales is a better strategy than increasing profits
2.   Marketing strategies must be developed to support marketing objectives
3.   Increasing profits is best achieved by reducing costs
4.   Increasing profits is a better strategy that increasing sales
5.   Customer satisfaction is the priority, not sales of profits

2-25   Multiple

Under the BCG growth-share matrix, the market growth rate provides:

1.   A measure of market attractiveness
2.   A measure of the company's strength in the market
3.   The primary information for investment/divestiture decisions
4.   A measure of profitability for all products
5.   None of the above

2-26   Multiple

Heinz has decided their new hot dog sauce division has not been performing well and is using too many resources. They decide to phase this SBU out and use the resources to develop a new product. This move would be considered a _____ strategy.

1.   Build
2.   Harvest
3.   Hold
4.   Divest
5.   Product

2-27   Multiple

The General Electric strategic business-planning grid evaluates business on the basis of:

1.   Macro and Micro environmental factors
2.   Market share and growth ratings
3.   Industry attractiveness and business strength
4.   Profit margins and demographic trends
5.   Tangible and intangible products

2-28   Multiple

Nike has just introduced into the market its first ever orthopedic sandal for seniors or people with arthritis. This situation is considered:

1.   Product development
2.   Market penetration
3.   Market development
4.   Diversification
5.   None of the above

2-29   Multiple

Nike has decided to bring back the "flip-flop" sandal. They will cater their advertising to seniors, as this is a comfortable shoe that is easy to put on. This situation is considered:

1.   Product development
2.   Market penetration
3.   Market development
4.   Diversification
5.   None of the above

2-30   Multiple

Levi's realizes they have very different markets with very different needs, characteristics and behaviours. The process of dividing up the different markets is referred to as:

1.   Demand forecasting
2.   Market segmentation
3.   Market targeting
4.   Market positioning
5.   Market segments

True/False Questions

2-1   True/False

Strategic planning in not useful at all in a fast changing environment.

2-2   True/False

Because long-range plans encompass many years into the future, they only need to be revised every 3 years.

2-3   True/False

Market definitions of a business are better than product or technological definitions.

2-4   True/False

Missions statements are best when guided by almost and impossible dream.

2-5   True/False

The purpose of strategic planning is to identify ways in which the company can best use its strengths to tale advantage of attractive opportunities in the environment.

2-6   True/False

Market penetration, market development, product development and market expansion are the four different quadrants in the product/market expansion grid.

2-7   True/False

Some marketing managers may find that it is their objective to hold existing sales with a smaller marketing budget, or it may be to reduce demand.

2-8   True/False

In positioning its product, a company first identifies its possible weaknesses, which they can improve on, to build their competitive position.

2-9   True/False

Designing competitive marketing strategies begins with a thorough competitor analysis.

2-10   True/False

The marketing mix consists of product, place, performance, and promotion.
2-11   True/False

Marketers must continually plan their analysis, implementation and control activities.

2-12   True/False

Successful marketing implementation depends on how well the company blends the five elements – action programs, organization and structure, total quality management, company culture and the pay scale.

2-13   True/False

The strategic business-planning grid plots SBUs in terms of industry attractiveness and business strength.

2-14   True/False

Diversification often involves buying new businesses unrelated to the company's current products and markets.

2-15   True/False

The company's mission needs to be turned into detailed supporting objectives for only the top level of management

2-16   True/False

The BCG growth-share matrix plots relative market share to industry attractiveness.

2-17   True/False

Whereas most small ventures start out with extensive business and marketing plans used to attract potential investors, strategic planning often falls by the wayside once the business gets going.

2-18   True/False

Advertising refers to the activities surrounding the communication of a company's offer and its efforts to persuade target customers to buy.

2-19   True/False

Turning marketing strategies into specific day-to-day, month-to-month activities is the concern of the marketing implementation function.

2-20   True/False

Hiring a consultant is an element of a successful implementation program.

Applying Terms and Concepts

To determine how well you understand the materials in this chapter, read each of the following brief cases and then respond to the questions that follow. Answers are given at the end of this chapter.

Case #1   Cyberdesk

The Cyberdesk is an ergonomic, stylish computer desk created to fill deficiencies in the marketplace for computer furnishings. The market for computer desks, like the rest of the home computer industry, is growing rapidly as the PC becomes a part of people's everyday lives. Currently, products offered by establishing furniture manufacturers leave a great deal of room for improvement regarding features and style. Through superior design, Cyberdesk seeks to penetrate the growing computer furnishings market.

Cyberdesk will be structured in the form of a "virtual company," under which it will perform the functions of design, distribution, and sales, while outsourcing production to an independent manufacturer. The production process will flow through a "pull-system," whereby manufacturers will commence production based upon Cyberdesk receiving a confirmed customer order. Upon completion of production, the product will be shipped directly to the customer. This system minimizes working capital requirements by minimizing investment in inventory, and by allowing a framework by which purchases from manufacturers can be financed – namely by securing financing with receivables. Through strong cooperation with suppliers, sound working capital management policies, and intense sales efforts, Cyberdesk will be able to effectively compete in the marketplace and achieve high profitability.

Cyberdesk will require a little in the way of overhead and capital investment, and will be funded initially through $50,000 in equity from the four founders and a $50,000 loan from the Business Development Corporation. Due to the nature of the organization, with its low initial investment and overhead requirements, all sales over a marginal break-even point (1,500 units in year 1) contribute directly to profit and strong returns.

The Cyberdesk will offer superior features, quality, ergonomics and a style to those who place a value on these qualities. Thus, Cyberdesk's marketing effort will target home and small office users, professionals, and enthusiasts. This will be accomplished by achieving floor space with high-end furniture and computer retailers. As well, an Internet home page and advertisements in appropriate personal computer magazines will be utilized to generate dales and product awareness. Subsequent sales efforts will seek to penetrate the market by focusing on national office furniture retailers in Canada and the United States, and by pursuing opportunities to design customized desks for computer manufacturers.

1.   What do you believe would be a good mission statement for this company?

_____

_____

_____

_____

2.   Which developing growth strategy is Cyberdesk using? Do you believe that it is the appropriate one?

_____

_____

_____

_____

3.   What are the 2 different segments that Cyberdesk is trying to attract? Are they different?

_____

_____

_____

_____

4.   List some of the places where Cyberdesk should display and sell their product.

_____

_____

_____

_____

5.   What do you believe could be some barriers to entry for Cyberdesk to enter this new market?

_____

_____

_____

_____

<u>Case #2</u>   On-Line Data Corporation[1]

The On-Line Data Corporation produces and sells minicomputers. Its highly diversified customers are found in the consumer, governmental, and institutional areas. The firm's marketing department is now organized along functional lines, but management is considering adopting some other organizational format in order to remedy a sales decline it feels is at least partially attributable to its organizational approach.

1.   What types of organizational problems would you expect a firm like On-Line Data to encounter as a result of utilizing a functional approach in its marketing?

_____

_____

_____

_____

2.   Briefly evaluate each of the following organizational formats in light of the firm's product/market situation and likely requirements.

A.   Geographic Organization

_____

_____

_____

B.   Product Management Organization

_____

_____

_____

C.   Market Management Organization

_____

_____

_____

---

[1] *Principles of Marketing*, 3rd Edition, Kotler, Armstrong, Warren (Prentice Hall) – pg. 31.

D.   Product/Market Management Organization

_____

_____

_____

3.   On the basis of the analysis above, which organizational format would you recommend?

_____

_____

_____

_____

Case #3   Don Seville Rum

In 1859, Don Jorge Seville began distilling and selling rum in Kingston, Jamaica. Initially, the townspeople carried his rum away in pails and tubs. Later, when Don Jorge began to bottle the rum, he had the labels marked with the likeness of a seagull, to assist illiterates in identifying his brand.

The seagull is still on each bottle of Don Seville Rum, and the company is now run by descendants of Don Jorge. The rum's secret formula hasn't changed, but just about everything else about the company has. Seville is now a worldwide operation with sugar cane plantations in Jamaica and bottling plants in Puerto Rico and Martinique, ocean-going cargo ships based in Trinidad, office buildings, warehouses and advertising agencies in Mexico and the USA, and a trucking firm in Spain. While most operations were somehow originally connected with the production and distribution of the rum, others, such as the development of a 124-acre luxury resort on the island of Antigua, are totally unrelated. The 11 semi-autonomous firms making up the Seville empire have sales estimated at $1 billion.

Don Seville is the world's largest selling rum, with an estimated 60 percent of the market. In the United States, Don Seville accounts for 75 percent of total rum sales. Although, impressive, Miguel Serrales, a great-great-grandson of the founder, has found the sales and profitability figures to be disappointing. While hard liquor sales in the USA decreased by 4.5 percent in recent years, rum sales increased by 2.3 percent. In view of this trend, Serrales had hoped that sales and profitability would have been higher. However, Serrales noted that increased competition from two firms, who promoted their product as premium rums, have recently begun to erode Don Seville's sales.

After considerable study, Serrales ordered the development and ultimate distribution of Caribe as Seville's own entry into the premium rum market.

Caribe will sell for $3 more per bottle than Don Seville. Projected sales this year are for 85,000 cases of Caribe and 7.6 million cases of Don Seville.

In 1978, Seville engaged in a promotional campaign designed to increase the public's awareness of rum. It was at this time that a change was taking place in American drinking habits. Drinkers switched from heavier whiskeys to lighter spirits such as rum. By 1990, rum accounted for 9.2 percent of the distilled spirits consumed in the USA compared to 2.1 percent twelve years earlier. It was during this period of time that sales of Don Seville rum increased dramatically.

_____1. The symbol of a seagull, which appears on each bottle of Don Seville rum, is an example of a brand. The brand should be considered part of which element of the marketing mix?

    A.   product

    B.   promotion

    C.   place

    D.   price

    E.   both (A) and (B)

_____2. The development of the luxury resort by Seville on the island of Antigua is an example of:

    A.   market development.

    B.   product development.

    C.   market penetration.

    D.   diversification.

    E.   both (A) and (C)

_____3. When Seville introduced Caribe rum to compete in the premium market, it was engaged in:

    A.   market penetration.

    B.   market development.

    C.   product development.

    D.   diversification.

    E.   none of the above

____4. The various businesses making up the Seville Organization are known as its:

    A.   business portfolio.

    B.   strategic plan.

    C.   company mission.

    D.   marketing concept.

    E.   marketing mix.

____5. Using the Boston Consulting Group approach to portfolio analysis, Don Seville Rum would be considered a(n):

    A.   star.

    B.   cash cow.

    C.   question mark.

    D.   dog.

    E.   none of the above

Case #4   Barth Enterprises

William Barth started Barth Chevrolet in 1974 after having worked as a sales manager for two other dealerships. He had a simple philosophy of meeting his customers personal transportation needs at a fair price. Barth Chevrolet was a success, so much so that he eventually opened dealerships which cover General Motors full range of automobiles and pick-up trucks. Barth opened a Pontiac/Buick/GMC Dealership in 1978 and an Oldsmobile/Cadillac Dealership in 1984. Barth's latest dealership was a Saturn Franchise opened in 1992. Each dealership sells new and used automobiles, vans, pick-up trucks and sport utility vehicles. Lease and rental programs are available for customers who do not wish to purchase vehicles outright.

Also part of the Barth Transportation Network is a Honda Motorcycle and all terrain vehicle (ATV) center opened in 1991. With the exception of the motorcycle shop, now run by Barth's 28 year old son—a motorcycle enthusiast and main impetus for the shop—Barth engaged in careful and extensive research to identify customer needs, wants and demands and their relative satisfaction with existing dealerships. Research in each case indicated considerable consumer dissatisfaction with existing dealerships. This led Barth to start the Chevrolet and Saturn Dealerships from scratch, but he acquired the other dealerships by buying out the previous owner. Barth pioneered the now-common practice of free shuttle service for service customers, a free loaner if the work takes more than one full day, a service department open from 7 a.m. to 9 p.m. on weekdays and to 5 p.m. on Saturdays. Additionally, each dealership has a fully stocked park department for the do-it-yourself and local service stations.

Sales at each dealership have increased steadily despite the periodic downturns in the automotive industry. Barth attributes this success to his philosophy of treating customers fairly and to a pricing strategy of selling vehicle for an average of 10% over invoice. Sales per dealership have averaged 2,000 vehicles per year as opposed to the industry average of 975. Profitability has averaged 18% before taxes. Barth sets realistic quotas for each dealership and then allows his dealership managers considerable flexibility in achieving the goal. A liberal profit sharing plan and autonomous dealership management have resulted in a successful organization controlling 46% of the local market.

The motorcycle franchise, however, is not as successful as the auto dealerships. Although it is marginally profitable, the operation experienced only 2% increase in sales last year, while the market expanded by 12%. The shop currently controls less than 10% of the local market.

1.   Using portfolio analysis, characterize and evaluate each of the following:

     motorcycle/atv dealership

     _____

     _____

     _____

     auto dealership

     _____

     _____

     _____

2.   Comment on Barth's strategic planning related to the automotive dealerships

     _____

     _____

     _____

Multiple Choice Answers

1. Correct Answer: 5   Reference: pg. 40

2. Correct Answer: 3   Reference: pg. 41

3. Correct Answer: 1   Reference: pg. 42

4. Correct Answer: 2   Reference: pg. 43

5. Correct Answer: 3   Reference: pg. 44

6. Correct Answer: 5   Reference: pg. 44

7. Correct Answer: 1   Reference: pg. 44

8. Correct Answer: 4   Reference: pg. 46

9. Correct Answer: 1   Reference: pg. 47

10. Correct Answer: 4   Reference: pg. 53

11. Correct Answer: 1   Reference: pg. 54

12. Correct Answer: 2   Reference: pg. 59

13. Correct Answer: 4   Reference: pg. 61

14. Correct Answer: 2   Reference: pg. 41

15. Correct Answer: 4   Reference: pg. 45

16. Correct Answer: 3   Reference: pg. 46

17. Correct Answer: 5   Reference: pg. 48

18. Correct Answer: 4   Reference: pg. 54

19. Correct Answer: 2   Reference: pg. 56

20. Correct Answer: 3   Reference: pg. 49

21. Correct Answer: 2   Reference: pg. 51

22. Correct Answer: 5   Reference: pg. 58 Table 2-2

23.	Correct Answer:	3	Reference:	pg. 41
24.	Correct Answer:	2	Reference:	pg. 43
25.	Correct Answer:	1	Reference:	pg. 44
26.	Correct Answer:	4	Reference:	pg. 45
27.	Correct Answer:	3	Reference:	pg. 46
28.	Correct Answer:	1	Reference:	pg. 47
29.	Correct Answer:	3	Reference:	pg. 47
30.	Correct Answer:	2	Reference:	pg. 52

True/False Answers

1.   FALSE   Reference: pg. 40   Topic: Strategic Planning
2.   FALSE   Reference: pg. 41   Topic: Strategic Planning
3.   TRUE   Reference: pg. 42   Topic: Defining the Company Mission
4.   TRUE   Reference: pg. 42   Topic: Defining the Company Mission
5.   TRUE   Reference: pg. 44   Topic: Analysing the Current Business Portfolio
6.   FALSE   Reference: pg. 47   Topic: Developing Growth Strategies
7.   TRUE   Reference: pg. 48   Topic: Marketing's Role in Strategic Planning
8.   FALSE   Reference: pg. 54   Topic: Market Positioning
9.   TRUE   Reference: pg. 54   Topic: Marketing Strategies for Competitive Advantage
10. FALSE   Reference: pg. 55   Topic: Developing the Marketing Mix
11. TRUE   Reference: pg. 57   Topic: Managing the Marketing Effort
12. FALSE   Reference: pg. 59   Topic: Marketing Implementation
13. TRUE   Reference: pg. 45   Topic: The General Electric Approach
14. TRUE   Reference: pg. 47   Topic: Developing Growth Strategies
15. FALSE   Reference: pg. 43   Topic: Setting Company Objectives and Goals
16. FALSE   Reference: pg. 45   Topic: The Boston Consulting Group
17. TRUE   Reference: pg. 49   Topic: Strategic Planning and Small Business
18. FALSE   Reference: pg. 57   Topic: Developing the Marketing Mix
19. TRUE   Reference: pg. 59   Topic: Marketing Implementation
20. FALSE   Reference: pg. 59   Topic: Marketing Implementation

Applying Terms and Concepts Answers

Case #1   Cyberdesk:

Question #1
- To continually design and distribute functional, ergonomic, stylish computer desks that meets the needs and desires of home and office computer users.

Question #2
- Product Development
- They are offering a new or modified product to current market segments. There is no company that specializes in computer desks; therefore they are filling a need.
- This is a new company with very little capital and exposure, therefore they must focus on their product in order to make a name for themselves and become profitable. This is the best strategy for that.

Question 3
- The two different target markets are: enthusiastic professionals and home and small office computer users.
- They are different because the home computer markets want a functional affordable desk that will meet their needs, the professionals, will probably be looking to spend a little more money and they will be wanting more amenities than the first group.

Question #4
- Office Supply Stores
- Computers Stores
- Home Furnishing Stores
- Home Depot and Revy Stores
- Over the Internet
- Trade and Computer Magazines

Question #5
- Economies of scale
- Intense competition for retail space
- Large capital investment required to enter the manufacturing industry
- Establishing distribution channels
- Many competitors

<u>Case #2</u>   <u>On-Line Data Corporation:</u>

Question #1
- They have probably experienced inadequate planning for specific products and/or markets
- Some of the products have been stressed while others have been neglected
- Functional rivals may inhibit coordination efforts

Question #2
A.   Geographic
- Generally used by a firm selling national products
- On-Line is not affected by geographic lines and to become a national company may be too expensive right now

B.   Product Management
- Used by firms producing and selling a variety of products and brands
- Usually used by another layer of management to correct any shortcomings of another management team

C.   Market Management
- Used by firms that sell a line of products to a diverse set of markets
- Good when customers fall into groups with distinct buying patters or product preferences

D.   Product/Market Management
- Large companies that produce many different products for many different people in many different areas
- Assures each function receives its share of management attention
- Can be costly and reduce management flexibility

<u>Case #3</u>   <u>Don Seville Rum:</u>

1.   A

2.   D

3.   C

4.   A

5.   A

<u>Case #4</u>   <u>Barth Enterprises:</u>

1.   The motorcycle/atv dealership should be classified as a dog. It is a low growth, low
         market share business. It is marginally profitable and does not hold much promise to be a
         great source of cash.

         Barth needs to determine what role the dealership should play in his business portfolio.
         Divesting himself of it may make sense from a financial standpoint. However, there may
         be other considerations such as family interests which might lead Barth to allow it to
         remain.

         The auto dealerships appear to be cash cows. The overall market is not expanding greatly.
         However, Barth controls a substantial share of the market. The dealerships produce a
         significant cash flow as indicated by the 18% profit margin. The strategy Barth may
         decide to build on his market share by investing even further in the industry. This may be
         achieved by acquiring additional dealerships, marketing program vehicles and/or by
         consolidating his operations into the now popular auto super store.

2.   Barth has adopted the marketing concept where customer interests determine (or at least
         influence) company plans. His product and service offerings as well as his growth and
         profitability can be attributed to philosophy or customer sovereignty and mutual gain.

Chapter 3

The Global Marketing Environment

Chapter Overview

Companies must constantly watch and adapt to the marketing environment in order to seek opportunities and ward off threats. The marketing environment comprises all the actors and forces influencing the company's ability to transact business effectively with its target markets.

Chapter Objectives

1. Describe the environmental forces that affect the company's ability to serve its customers.
2. Explain how changes in the demographic and economic environments affect marketing decisions.
3. Identify the major trends in the firm's natural and technological environments.
4. Explain the key changes in the political and cultural environments.
5. Discuss how companies can react to the marketing environment.

Chapter Topics

The Company's Microenvironment
- The Company
- Suppliers
- Marketing Intermediaries
- Customers
- Competitors
- Publics

The Company's Macroenvironment
- Demographic Environment
  - Changing Age Structure of the Canadian Population
  - The Changing Family
  - Geographic Shifts in Population
  - A Better-Educated and More White-Collar Population
  - Increasing Diversity

- Economic Environment
  - Changes in Income
  - Paradoxes of the New Economy
  - Changing Consumer Spending Patters
- Natural Environment
  - Shortages of Raw Materials and Increased Pollution
- Technological Environment
  - Fast Pace of Technological Change
  - High R&D Budgets
- Political Environment
  - Legislation Regulating Business
- Cultural Environment
  - Persistence of Cultural Values
  - Shifts in Secondary Cultural Values

Responding to the Marketing Environment

Chapter Summary

1.   The environmental forces that affect the company's ability to serve its customers.

Companies are constrained by micro- and macroenvironmental forces. Microenvironmental forces include company departments, suppliers, marketing intermediaries, customers, competitors, and various publics. Macroenvironmental forces include demographics, economic, natural, technological, political, and cultural forces.

2.   The effect of changes in the demographic and economic environments on marketing management decisions.

Changes in the demographic environment that affect marketing decisions are the changing age structure of the Canadian population, the changing Canadian family, geographic shifts in population, a better educated and more white collar workforce, and increasing ethnic and racial diversity. Economic trends include changes in income and income distribution, and changes in consumer spending patterns.

3.   The major trends in the firm's natural and technological environments.

Trends in the natural environment include shortages of raw materials, increased cost of energy, increased pollution, and government intervention in natural resource management. Trends in the technological environment include the fact pace of technological change, high R & D budgets, concentration on minor improvements, and increased regulation by government agencies.

4.   The key changes that occur in the political and cultural environments.

Changes in the political environment include legislation regulating business, changing government agency enforcement, the growth of public responsible actions. Changes in the cultural environment include the persistence of cultural values, shifts in secondary cultural values, and people's views of themselves, others, organizations, society, nature and the universe.

5.   The significance of cultural values to marketers.

Marketers should remain alert to shifting cultural values in order to spot developing threats of opportunities and to help ensure that their marketing strategies reflect the relevant culture's values. Cultural values may be reflected in the political-legal environment and in the competitive environment. Firms that engage in international marketing may have to learn how to deal with completely different cultures.

Key Terms

Baby boom   (pg. 83)   Marketing environment   (pg. 77)
Cultural environment (pg. 97)   Marketing intermediaries   (pg. 78)
Demography (pg. 80)   Microenvironment   (pg. 77)
Economic environment   (pg. 90)   Natural environment (pg. 93)
Engel's laws (pg. 93)   Political environment (pg. 95)
Environmental mgmt perceptive (pg. 102) Public   (pg. 79)
Macroenvironment   (pg. 77)   Technological environment (pg. 94)

Multiple Choice Questions

3-1   Multiple

A very large towel supplier for Wal-Mart has just burned down, they have outstanding orders to fill, however, and Wal-Mart must find another supplier to fill them. This situation affects which of the following environments for Wal-Mart?

1.   Marketing environment
2.   Microenvironment
3.   Microenvironment
4.   Customer environment
5.   Competitor environment

3-2   Multiple

Which of the following is not a marketing intermediary?

1.   Resellers
2.   Physical distribution firms
3.   Marketing services agencies
4.   Financial intermediaries
5.   Internet providers

3-3   Multiple

This group's image of the company really affects a company's buying patterns and behaviours.

1.   Financial publics
2.   Citizen action publics
3.   General public
4.   Government publics
5.   Internal publics

3-4   Multiple

The single most important demographic trend in Canada is:

1.   The changing age structure of the population
2.   The increasing amount of urban dwellers
3.   The increasing amount of immigration in the last few years
4.   The increasing amounts of women in the workforce
5.   The increasing amount of divorces in the country

3-5   Multiple

Hong Kong is known as a (n) _____ and China is known as a (n) _____

_____.

1.   economic environment, agricultural environment
2.   subsistence economy, self-sustaining economy
3.   industrial economy, self-sustaining economy
4.   industrial economy, subsistence economy
5.   first world economy, second world economy

3-6   Multiple

In the early 1990s Canada was faced with a recession. The carefree spending days of the late 80s were non-existent, as people became very conscious of how they spent their money. Marketers had to change the focus of their advertising to:

1.   Price sensitive marketing
2.   Value marketing
3.   Quality marketing
4.   Performance marketing
5.   Prestige marketing

3-7   Multiple

Ernst Engel studied how people shifted their spending as their incomes rose. Even though this research was done over a century ago, others have confirmed his findings. Which of the following is not a change in spending patterns despite and increase in income?

1.   Percentage spent of food declines
2.   Percentage spent on housing remains the same
3.   Percent spent on saving increases
4.   Percent spent on leisure activities increases
5.   Percent spent of food increases

3-8   Multiple

Which of the following is not considered a trend in the natural environment?

1.   Shortages of raw materials
2.   Increased cost of energy
3.   Increased pollution
4.   Government intervention in resource management
5.   All are considered a trend in the natural environment

3-9   Multiple

Business practices have been enacted for many reasons. Which of the following is not one of those reasons?

1.   To protect the economic interest of the government of Canada
2.   To protect companies from each other
3.   To protect the consumers from unfair business practices
4.   To protect the interests of society against unrestrained business behaviour
5.   All of the above are good, viable reasons

3-10   Multiple

The 90s will see a marked change in the way society defines success, with achievements such as a happy family life and service to one's community replacing money as the measure of worth. This statement is a belief about:

1.   People's views of themselves
2.   People's views of the universe
3.   People's views of others
4.   People's views of society
5.   People's views of nature

3-11   Multiple

The adoption and adherence to professional codes of ethics among businesses reflects which trend in the political environment?

1.   Legislation regulating business
2.   The persistence of cultural values
3.   Changing government agency enforcement of existing laws regulating business
4.   The increased emphasis on ethics and socially responsible actions
5.   Societal pressures to do so

3-12   Multiple

In most economies this is the largest single market.

1.   Industrial market
2.   Consumer market
3.   Reseller market
4.   Government market
5.   Retail market

3-13   Multiple

Shareholders would be considered part of which of the following?

1.   Internal public
2.   Local public
3.   Financial public
4.   Media public
5.   General public

3-14   Multiple

The set of laws and regulations guiding commerce and that limit business for the good of society as a whole is called:

1.   Public policy
2.   Consumer protection
3.   Public interest group action
4.   Social responsibility
5.   Legislation

3-15   Multiple

Alex De Nobel decides to volunteer at a local senior's centre. This is a reflection of which cultural trend?

1.   People's views of themselves
2.   People's views of others
3.   People's views of organizations
4.   People's views of nature
5.   People's views of the universe

3-16   Multiple

Vansco Electronics recently introduced a global positioning system for use in tractors so that agricultural producers know their location within 10 metres. The idea behind this innovation is to help producers apply fertilizer and other chemicals more efficiently. Vansco is involved in the:

1.   Demographic environment
2.   Economic environment
3.   Technological environment
4.   Natural environment
5.   Agricultural environment

3-17   Multiple

Bell Canada's monthly newsletter meets the needs of which of the following publics?

1.   Financial
2.   Media
3.   Citizen-action
4.   Internal
5.   General

3-18   Multiple

Which of the following countries has had the higher population growth in the last few years?

1.   Mexico
2.   Japan
3.   Hong Kong
4.   China
5.   Canada

3-19   Multiple

Which of the following countries has the highest GNP per capita?

1.   Australia
2.   Japan
3.   Hong Kong
4.   Canada
5.   USA

3-20   Multiple

The Canadian province with the highest percentage increase in population from 1991-94 was:

1.   Ontario
2.   Quebec
3.   British Columbia
4.   Yukon & North West Territories
5.   Alberta

3-21   Multiple

Which of the following would not be classified as a regional difference with respect to product usage patterns?

1.   Newfoundlanders think they are the hardest working Canadians
2.   British Columbians express the greatest love for reading
3.   Quebecers are less likely to use no-name products
4.   Montrealers eat more deep brown beans than other Canadians
5.   All of the above would classify as regional differences

3-22   Multiple

Imperial Oil teamed with the Toronto Hospital for Sick Children have sponsored a campaign to reduce preventable children's accidents, which is the leading killer of children. This act is considered:

1.   Cause-related marketing
2.   Charitable donations
3.   Tax reduction incentive
4.   Good-will marketing
5.   None of the above

3-23   Multiple

What would be considered the third largest industry in Canada

1.   Forestry
2.   Fishery
3.   Car manufacturing
4.   Agriculture
5.   None of the above

3-24   Multiple

Which of the following statements about the marketing environment is (are) true?

1.   The marketing environment offers the company opportunities
2.   The marketing environment contains threats to the company
3.   The marketing environment required the company conduct research and use intelligence systems to monitor changes
4.   1 and 2
5.   All of the above

3-25   Multiple

A new "Burger Heaven" wants to open up in rural Ontario. Before this can happen, the management must establish all the marketing intermediaries they will require. Which of the following is not considered one?

1.   Suppliers
2.   Physical distribution firms
3.   Financial intermediaries
4.   Marketing service firms
5.   All of the above are considered marketing intermediaries

3-26   Multiple

The Manitoba Steel Association (MSA) purchases old cars and metal parts from auto wrecking lots from across Canada. They melt this metal down and make steel to use in casing. MSA is an example of the:

1.   Consumer market
2.   Business market
3.   Industrial market
4.   Supplier market
5.   Reseller market

3-27   Multiple

Shifts in secondary cultural values, such as the belief you should get married at an early age, can be expressed through which of the following?

1.   People's views of themselves
2.   People's views of others
3.   People's views of organizations
4.   All of the above
5.   None of the above

3-28   Multiple

McDonalds's construction of "Ronald McDonald Houses" for families to stay while their children are in the hospital shows support for which public?

1.   Media
2.   Citizen-action
3.   Local
4.   General
5.   Internal

3-29   Multiple

Wal-Mart uses many of its employees as models for their television and print ads. This type of tactic is used to appeal to which type of public?

1.   Local
2.   Internal
3.   General
4.   Citizen-action
5.   Media

3-30   Multiple

If we were to make up a village of 1,000 people who would represent the entire population of the world and its characteristics, which of the following would NOT be true?

1.   There would be 520 women and 480 men
2.   About 1/3 of our people would have access to clean, safe drinking water
3.   The woodlands would be decreasing rapidly and the wastelands would be increasing rapidly
4.   Only 500 of the 100 people would control 75% of the village's wealth
5.   All the above are true

True/False Questions

3-1   True/False

Demographics, economics, natural, technological, political and cultural factors affect the marketing environment.

3-2   True/False

Top management is part of the company's internal environment and can be grouped in with all other functional areas of a company.

3-3   True/False

Reseller organizations frequently have enough power to dictate terms or even shut the manufacturer out of large markets.

3-4   True/False

It is sufficient for a company to simply adapt to the needs of target consumers to be successful.

3-5   True/False

Seniors value information in advertising materials and claims based on impulse.

3-6   True/False

The United Nations reported Toronto is the world's most multicultural city.

3-7   True/False

Upper class consumers' spending patterns are affected by the current economic events, as they are major consumers of luxury goods.

3-8   True/False

Many companies are investing a large amount of their R & D budget on new innovations, to develop new technologies and products to be profitable in the future.

3-9   True/False

Even the most liberal advocates of free-market economies agree the system works best with at least some regulation.

3-10   True/False

Marketers through good, effective advertisement have a good chance of changing core beliefs and even a better chance at changing secondary beliefs.

3-11   True/False

Companies who hire lobbyists to influence legislation affecting their industries and stage media events to gain favourable press coverage are taking an environmental management perspective to their business.

3-12   True/False

Consumer organizations and environmental groups are considered part of the company's general public.

3-13   True/False

The "baby boom" refers to the growth in population that occurred between World War I and World War II.

3-14   True/False

The technological environment is perhaps the most dramatic force now shaping the nature of the marketplace.

3-15   True/False

A growing population means growing human needs to satisfy which definitely means growing market opportunities.

3-16   True/False

Today, people in charge of new product development always consider the opinions of ethnic groups when developing their product concepts.

3-17   True/False

For decades, many analysts predicted advances in technology would create a leisure generations. Their predictions have come true as people do have more time on their hands they use for leisure.

3-18   True/False

Instead of opposing regulations, marketers should help develop solutions to the material and energy problems facing the world.

3-19   True/False

One of the major potential problems with cause-related marketing is charitable corporate donation support will shift towards visible, popular, and low-risk charities – those with more substantial market appeal.

3-20   True/False

Neighbourhood residents and community organizations belong to the general public.

Applying Terms and Concepts

To determine how well you understand the materials in this chapter, read each of the following brief cases and then respond to the questions that follow. Answers are given at the end of this chapter.

Case #1   Barnes Coal Company[1]

The Barnes Coal Company has been in operation since 1872 and is the second largest producer of anthracite coal within the United States. The majority of its holdings are in northeastern Pennsylvania with major production in the Williamsport, Scranton, and Hazleton areas. The bulk of Barnes's production is sold to out-of-state buyer and moves through the Philadelphia and Erie ports. The Lehigh Valley and Pennsylvania Central Railroads are the prime movers of the coal to these ports of entry.

This year Scott Barnes, President of Barnes Coal Company, fought passage of the state law, which required that all mining companies in Pennsylvania to reclaim mine land. All land according to the bill must be covered with no less than six inches of topsoil, whether or not the topsoil was evident prior to mining. Enforcement of this law will be by the Pennsylvania Soil and Water Conservation Commission.

Barnes attributed passage of the bill to pressure brought on the state legislators in Harrisburg by the Pennsylvanian Beautification Society (PBS). The PBS is a private group interested in promoting tourism and preserving wildlife throughout the beautification and reforestation of Pennsylvania.

Barnes expects the price of coal to increase by 8% if the costs associated with compliance are passed onto buyers. Production would likely decrease as buyers shift their purchasing to mines from Ohio, Kentucky, Illinois and West Virginia.

1.   The Lehigh Valley and Pennsylvania Central Railroads are example of what type of marketing intermediaries? What is their responsibility?

_____

_____

_____

_____

---

[1] *Principles of Marketing*, 3rd Edition, Kotler, Armstrong, Warren (Prentice Hall) – pg. 49.

2.   What are the implications of coal being a non-renewable resource for Barnes Coal Company with respect to the marketing environment?

_____

_____

_____

3.   What type of public is the Pennsylvanian Beautification Society? How do they have their voices heard with respect to their issues?

_____

_____

_____

4.   Does Barnes have a choice as to how they will fund this project? Should the consumers really pay for it?

_____

_____

_____

5.   What would be the effect on all of society if the government did not intervene and enact legislation to protect society from unrestrained business behaviour?

_____

_____

_____

Case #2   Borden Eagle Brand

Eagle Brand SCM was developed in the mid-1800s as a result of many babies dying from drinking the milk of diseased cows. In response to this, Mr. Borden developed a process to preserve milk that was patented in 1956.

Eagle Brand SCM was first sold as baby formula door-to-door on milk trucks. During the Civil War, Eagle Brand provided troops with the much-needed supply of milk, and during WWII, women started using this milk as a sweetener for their coffee as well as in baking products. Now the Eagle Brand SCM is commonly used in many desserts.

Borden is one of the largest and most successful food marketers in the US. Sales increased from $5 billion in 1986 to $7.2 billion in 1988. Borden like any other company, is fighting hard to compete in the very competitive market. The challenge with this product is that Eagle Brand SCM is not consumed on its own, rather it is used to make other products. For this reason, Borden has advertised its products in many women's magazines. Often recipes for delicious desserts are seen in the ad with slogans such as "Easy to make, hard to resist."

Unfortunately for Borden, the amount of "from-scratch" baking has decreased dramatically in the last few years. Also the turn to a healthy lifestyle has caused many people to cut out many of the delicious desserts which Eagle Brand SCM makes. There has also been intense competition from Carnation, which has introduced a very similar product.

These circumstances have caused Borden to conduct a review of the current product strategy for Eagle Brand SCM and to explore new strategies for it. The goal is to continue the brand as a major, profitable product in the portfolio of Borden products. In other words, the issue is how to increase sales of a product that may be maturing in the product life cycle and is facing new competition on a price basis.

1.   How can consumer awareness of the product and its benefits be increased?

_____

_____

_____

_____

2.   How can repeat use be increased and sustained?

_____

_____

_____

_____

3.   What form and sources of information should be used?

_____

_____

_____

_____

4.   What promotional tools and strategies will be most effective?

_____

_____

_____

_____

5.   Who do you believe Borden's' target market is for Eagle Brand SCM?

_____

_____

_____

_____

Case #3:   The Bank of Calgary

The Bank of Calgary is just one of the lending agencies in the Province of Alberta, Canada, which is faced with a perplexing problem. During the late 1970s and early 1980s the Athabasca Tar Sands, with estimated reserves of 300 billion barrels of crude oil, were being developed. Thousands of new jobs were created in mining, refining, distribution, construction, and support services, with the majority of workers settling in the Edmonton area. Most of these workers scorned apartment living and eagerly sought to buy homes. Many viewed home ownership as an integral part of living, along with marriage, work, and raising a family. Property values skyrocketed as lenders, including the Bank of Calgary, eagerly sought to meet the needs of future homeowners. Mortgage rates stabilized in the 17 to 19 percent range. Prospects for the region remained promising while the tar sands were in production.

Today, however, the economy of Alberta is in a deep slump, in part because of a downturn in the oil and gas industry. Hundreds had their jobs eliminated outright, thousands were placed on indefinite furlough, and many others accepted reduced wages which just covered their absolute necessities.

Economic growth in the area has slowed dramatically, while real estate prices plummeted by over 50 percent in two years. Many homeowners now owe more on their mortgages than they can sell their homes for. So even if they could sell their homes, they wouldn't get enough to pay off their loans.

The problem for the lenders has been compounded by the Scoff Realty Company, which has developed a unique plan to assist the beleaguered homeowners. Scott will buy the house from the homeowner for $1 and assume the unpaid mortgage. But Scoff Realty never makes any mortgage payments, and leases the house back to the former homeowner for substantially less than the monthly mortgage payment. The former homeowner has a relatively inexpensive place to stay for the approximately nine months it takes the bank to foreclose on the property, while Scoff makes easy profit.

The lender can't sue the property owner or Scott Realty because a Depression Era law on the books prevents lenders from suing anyone to recover their losses. Specifically, if Calgary forecloses on a piece of property and in turn sells it for less than the outstanding loan, it can't sue anyone to make up the loss.

Scoff Realty sees itself as helping unfortunate property owners who were caught in the escalation of land prices. They reason that the Bank of Calgary is unlikely to suffer much because as a $2 billion financial institution, it can easily absorb the estimated $1.5 million lost to date. And as for the homeowners, they seem to do well; after paying a low rent on their former home, they usually are able to save enough to make a down payment on another home.

1.   The oil extracted from the Athabasca Tar Sands is an example of _____ resource.

2.   The Depression Era law that protects property owners as detailed in this case is part of the _____ environment.

3.   The decrease in the income of the workers mentioned in this case is part of the _____ environment.

4.   The fact that most of the workers in the Edmonton area bought a house indicates that home ownership is a _____ belief and not easily changed.

Case #4:   Martin Marietta

Martin Marietta — the company that was big in the aerospace and defense industries and which became even bigger after its merger with Lockheed — is also big into aggregate. That's rocks, gravel and sand to the uninitiated. What is one of the nation's largest defense and space contractors doing in the aggregate business? Making money!

The market for aggregate is enormous. The amount used each year equates to approximately nine tons per American citizen. That is 50 pounds of aggregate needed per person per day. And just as the demand for aggregate is likely to increase, so is the price.

Aggregate is used for roads, driveways, concrete foundations and cement blocks. It is used in roofing and gardens. It is a decorative material replacing lawns in desert communities and as walkways and borders around shrubs. It is used in poultry feed and as a scrubbing agent in coal fired power plants. The list of uses of sand, gravel and rock is almost endless.

Make no mistake, aggregate is not rare. In fact, it is found just about everywhere. What makes aggregate increasingly valuable is the lack of government permission to expand existing pits or to open new pits. As existing pits run low on reserves (supply) local state and federal permits to expand become difficult to obtain. Environmentalists, as well as local residents, have blocked hundreds of proposed pits and some are seeking to close existing pits. The blasting vibration, dust, noise, danger and damage to local roads as well as the general unsightliness of the pits make them unpopular.

People don't want gravel pits and mines in their neighborhood. Therefore, it has to be brought in by truck, by rail and even by ship to coastal communities. This adds significantly to the cost. So while the actual cost of the material is quite low at the mine, the delivered cost can be quite high. By one estimate the cost of aggregate doubles for every 30 miles it must be transported by truck.

It is difficult to obtain a permit and those firms that do receive them have virtually a monopoly in the immediate area. One pit in an area may be bad - two are decidedly worse. This plays into the hands of major producers who have the financial resources needed to ensure the years it may take to obtain the needed permits. After several recent acquisitions, Martin Marietta became the nation's second largest aggregate producer just behind Vulcan Materials Co. of Birmingham, Alabama.

1.   Identify the major elements in Martin Marietta's macroenvironment and explain how they might impact the company.

_____

_____

_____

2.   Identify the major elements in Martin Marietta's macroenvironment and explain how they might impact the company.

_____

_____

_____

Sources: "Business is Boring: Some Companies Really Dig Aggregate," *Wall Street Journal* March 1, 1995, M. Charles, p. 1.

Multiple Choice Answers

1.   Correct Answer: 2   Reference: pg.77

2.   Correct Answer: 5   Reference: pg. 78

3.   Correct Answer: 3   Reference: pg. 79

4.   Correct Answer: 1   Reference: pg. 82

5.   Correct Answer: 4   Reference: pg. 90

6.   Correct Answer: 2   Reference: pg. 92

7.   Correct Answer: 5   Reference: pg. 93

8.   Correct Answer: 5   Reference: pg. 93

9.   Correct Answer: 1   Reference: pg. 96

10.   Correct Answer: 2   Reference: pg. 101

11.   Correct Answer: 4   Reference: pg.96

12.   Correct Answer: 2   Reference: pg. 78

13.   Correct Answer: 3   Reference: pg. 79

14.   Correct Answer: 1   Reference: pg. 96

15.   Correct Answer: 2   Reference: pg. 99

16.   Correct Answer: 3   Reference: pg. 94

17.   Correct Answer: 4   Reference: pg. 79

18.   Correct Answer: 1   Reference: pg. 81 (Table 3-1)

19.   Correct Answer: 2   Reference: pg. 81 (Table 3-1)

20.   Correct Answer: 4   Reference: pg. 88 (Table 3-2)

21.   Correct Answer: 5   Reference: pg. 98

22.   Correct Answer: 1   Reference: pg. 100

23.	Correct Answer:	5	Reference:	pg. 101
24.	Correct Answer:	5	Reference:	pg. 77
25.	Correct Answer:	1	Reference:	pg. 78
26.	Correct Answer:	2	Reference:	pg. 79
27.	Correct Answer:	4	Reference:	pg. 99
28.	Correct Answer:	3	Reference:	pg. 79
29.	Correct Answer:	2	Reference:	pg. 80
30.	Correct Answer:	4	Reference:	pg. 82

True/False Answers

1.	FALSE	Reference:	pg. 77	Topic: Chapter Introduction
2.	TRUE	Reference:	pg. 78	Topic: Figure 3-1
3.	TRUE	Reference:	pg. 78	Topic: Marketing Intermediaries
4.	FALSE	Reference:	pg.79	Topic: Competitors
5.	FALSE	Reference:	pg. 86	Topic: Changing Age Structure of the Canadian Population
6.	TRUE	Reference:	pg. 89	Topic: Increasing Diversity
7.	FALSE	Reference:	pg. 92	Topic: Paradoxes of the New Economy
8.	FALSE	Reference:	pg. 95	Topic: High R&D Budgets
9.	TRUE	Reference:	pg. 95	Topic: Legislation Regulating Business
10.	FALSE	Reference:	pg. 98	Topic: Persistence of Cultural Values
11.	TRUE	Reference:	pg. 102	Topic: Responding to the Marketing Environment
12.	FALSE	Reference:	pg. 80	Topic: Publics
13.	FALSE	Reference:	pg. 83	Topic: Changing Age Structure of the Canadian Population

14.	TRUE	Reference:	pg.94	Topic:	Technological Environment
15.	FALSE	Reference:	pg. 82	Topic:	Demographic Environment
16.	TRUE	Reference:	pg. 91	Topic:	Marketing Highlight 3-3
17.	FALSE	Reference:	pg. 92	Topic:	Paradoxes of the New Economy
18.	TRUE	Reference:	pg. 94	Topic:	Shortages of Raw Materials and Increased Pollution
19.	TRUE	Reference:	pg. 100	Topic:	Marketing Highlight 3-5
20.	FALSE	Reference:	pg. 80	Topic:	Publics

Applying Terms and Concept Answers

Case #1   Barnes Coal Company:

Question #1
- They are considered physical distribution firms who are responsible to transport the manufacturer's product to the retailers or the customers

Question #2
- Because coal is a non-renewable resource, it is a sought-after product
- Marketing efforts are minimal as usually the demand exceeds the supply; therefore, consumers come to you looking for products, instead of you looking for consumers for your products

Question #3
- The PBS is a citizen action public
- They lobby the government and educate the public on different issues
- By lobbying the government and pressing them to pass legislation, they get their voices heard and their concerns are addressed
- They work because there is safety in numbers, the more voices that are heard, the better the chance of action

Question #4
- Barnes can fund this project in a number of different ways, dip into the company's savings, take out a bank loan, cut costs to be able to pay for it or charge consumers more for the product
- Because it is a non-renewable resource, it would not be unheard of if the price of coal went up
- Consumers may switch suppliers for a while, but because demand exceeds supply, Barnes will not have to worry about selling their product

Question #5
- Legislation intervenes on behalf of society to ensure that businesses do not take advantage of their position because they have the capital to do it
- If there were no legislation, then the waters would all be polluted, many species would be extinct, we all would be breathing bad air, etc.
- Businesses like many humans like to get away with all they can, legislation is there to protect the silent minorities, the public

Case #2   Borden Eagle Brand:

Question #1
- Increase advertising using different mediums like television, newspaper and radio
- Have samples available at supermarkets of products made with Eagle Brand so people can realize how good it is
- Provide free recipes with a purchase of Eagle Brand so people can try it

Question #2
- Once people use Eagle Brand and enjoy it, they will be looking for more exciting recipes to use it in
- Have an Eagle Brand cookbook published and either people have to send in 15 Eagle Brand wrappers to get it, or they can pay for it
- Perhaps send out new recipe books every few years to keep people interested in the product and wanting to try new recipes

Question #3
- Television
- Newspapers
- Magazines
- In-store displays
- Billboards

Question #4
- Coupons will entice people to try it the first time
- Group purchasing will encourage people to buy more than one can at a time
- Provide a small recipe book (i.e., 5) with the purchase of 2 or more cans etc.

Question #5
- Older people are our target market as they have more time to cook from scratch
- If our recipes are really easy, then anyone with a family or who likes to entertain guests with delicious dessert ideas.

Case # 3:   The Bank of Calgary

   1.   finite nonrenewable

   2.   political

   3.   economic

   4.   core

1.

The Company -

Officials, within the Martin Marietta Organization, are enthusiastically pursuing new sources of supply. This commitment, along with an expanding market, should allow the company to pursue its marketing strategy while generating profits.

Suppliers and Marketing Intermediaries -

Martin Marietta must work with their various suppliers of equipment and materials as well as their marketing intermediaries including resellers, physical distribution firms, marketing services agencies and financial intermediaries to ensure a profitable operation. Proper selection of suppliers and marketing intermediaries becomes increasingly important as competition and public concerns increase.

Customers -

The company needs to monitor its customer markets closely. Consumer, business, reseller and government markets all present an opportunity. Martin Marietta must study the markets closely to understand the needs of each market and then decide how best to satisfy them.

Competitors -

The marketing concept states that to be successful, a company must provide greater customer value and satisfaction than its competitors. Thus marketers must do more than simply adapt to the needs of target consumers. They also must gain strategic advantage by positioning their offerings against competitors' offerings against competitors' offerings in the minds of customers.

Publics -

There are seven different types of publics that have an actual or potential interest in or impact on an organization's ability to achieve its objectives.

Anticipating and reacting to the financial, media, government citizen action, local, general and internal publics becomes increasingly important when there is opposition to the operation of the gravel pits. Strategies need to be developed which address and alleviate concerns thereby allowing the company to more effectively implement its marketing strategy.

2.

The Demographic Environment –	Given the Geographic shifts in population, Martin Marietta needs to anticipate where growth will take place and work to secure the permits necessary to expand or open the aggregate pits necessary to supply the required materials.
The Natural Environment –	Concerns of environmentalists need to be considered for their potential impact on the firm and its ability to serve its customers. Land reclamation and beautification programs are expensive but increasingly important considerations in obtaining needed permits.
The Political Environment –	The political environment consists of laws, government agencies and pressure groups that influence and limit organizations and individuals within society. The fact that it may take years to obtain the needed permits and appease the various publics, indicates that Martin Marietta must be cognizant of the various groups and their concerns. They must also be willing to work with the elements of the political environment to promote understanding and ultimately a mutually beneficial relationship.

Chapter 4

Marketing Research and Information Systems

Chapter Overview

In today's complex and rapidly changing environment, marketing managers need more and better information to make effective and timely decisions. Fortunately, this greater need for information has been matched by the explosion of information technologies for supplying information. Using new technologies such as small but powerful computers, videoconferencing, the Internet, and a host of other advances, companies can now handle great quantities of information – sometimes even too much. Yet marketers often complain they lack enough of the right kind of information of have an excess of the wrong kind. In response, many companies are now studying their managers' information needs and designing information systems to satisfy those needs.

Chapter Objectives

1. Explain the importance of information to the company.
2. Define the marketing information system and discuss its parts.
3. Outline the four steps in the marketing research process.
4. Compare the advantages and disadvantages of various methods of collecting information.
5. Discuss the special issues some marketing researchers face, including public policy and ethics issues.

Chapter Topics

The Marketing Information System
- Assessing Information Needs
- Developing Information
  - Internal Data
  - Marketing Intelligence
  - Marketing Research
  - Information Analysis
- Distributing Information

The Marketing Research Process
- Defining the Problem and Research Objectives
- Developing the Research Plan
  - Determining Specific Information Needs

- Gathering Secondary Information
- Planning Primary Data Collection
- Presenting the Research Plan
- Implementing the Research Plan
- Interpreting and Reporting the Findings
- Other Marketing Research Considerations
  - Marketing Research in Small Business and Non-Profit Organizations
  - International Marketing Research
  - Public Policy and Ethics in Marketing

Chapter Summary

1.   The importance of information to the company.

Marketing managers need timely, reliable, and relevant information in order to make decisions that will enhance the company's ability to compete successfully in the marketplace and increase customer value relative to the competition. Information is important but must be balanced between manager needs and what is feasible to offer. Too much information can overwhelm managers just as surely as too little information can lead to poor decisions.

2.   The marketing information system and its parts.

A marketing information system (MIS) consists of people, equipment, and procedures to gather, sort, analyze, and distribute needed, timely, and accurate information to marketing decision makers. Its four parts consist of developing information components, information system components, marketing managers, and the marketing environment. The MIS links all elements in a useable form.

3.   The four steps in the marketing research process.

The four steps in the marketing research process are defining the problem and the research objectives; developing the research plan; implementing the research plan; and, interpreting and reporting the findings.

4.   The different kinds of information a company might use.

A company might use secondary data information or primary data information. Secondary data consists of information that already exists somewhere, having been collected for another purpose. Primary data consists of information collected for the specific purpose at hand.

5.   Comparing the advantages and disadvantages of various methods of collecting information.

Advantages: Mail questionnaires—collect large amounts of information, low cost, more homes, no interview bias. Telephone—best for quick collection, flexible, sample control, response rates. Personal—individual or group, flexible, focus.
Disadvantages: Mail—not flexible, low response rates. Telephone—cost higher, interview bias. Personal—costs and sampling problems.

Key Terms

Casual research   (pg. 122)
Descriptive research   (pg. 122)
Experimental research(pg. 130)
Exploratory research (pg. 122)
Focus-group interviewing   (pg. 131)
Internal databases   (pg. 116)
Marketing information systems (MIS)
(pg. 114)

Marketing intelligence   (pg. 117)
Marketing research   (pg. 120)
Observational research   (pg. 127)
On-line databases   (pg., 126)
Primary data   (pg. 124)
Secondary data   (pg. 124)
Single-source data systems   (pg. 128)
Survey research   (pg. 130)

Multiple Choice Questions

4-1   Multiple

Which of the following is not a step in the MIS process?

1.   Develop needed information
2.   Provide necessary recommendations
3.   Information analysis
4.   Assess information needed
5.   Distribute information

4-2   Multiple

A locally owned lawn care store recently invested a substantial amount of money in developing a database for its customers. This database contains information on customer demographics, psychographics and buying behaviour. This database tool is classified as a _____ type of information development.

1.   Marketing intelligence
2.   Marketing research
3.   Information analysis
4.   Internal data
5.   Marketing environment

4-3   Multiple

A.C. Neilson of Canada gather and sells bimonthly data information on brand shares, retail prices, percentage of stores stocking an item and percent of stores that have run out of the item. This type of tool is classified as a _____ type of information development.

1.   Marketing intelligence
2.   Marketing research
3.   Information analysis
4.   Internal data
5.   Marketing environment

4-4   Multiple

Which of the following steps is the hardest in the research process?

1.   Implementing the research plan and collecting and analyzing the data
2.   Interpreting and reporting the findings
3.   Defining the problem and research objectives
4.   Developing the research plan for collecting information
5.   All the above are equally difficult

4-5   Multiple

The people who have developed Ponds beauty products have seen a steady decline in sales due to the increased advertising of Oil of Olay. The marketing personnel would like to know what effect dropping the price of their products by 15% would have on sales. This type of research would be classified as:

1.   Exploratory research
2.   Casual research
3.   Descriptive research
4.   Cause-and-effect research
5.   Market research

4-6   Multiple

Which of the following is not considered a source of secondary data?

1.   Government publications
2.   Periodicals and books
3.   On-line data
4.   Commercial data obtained from another company
5.   Telephone survey data conducted by your company

4-7   Multiple

Wal-Mart is very interested to know the effect floor greeters have on their customers. In the US the greeters are seen very positively, as the tiles leading to the greeters are very worn down. They will conduct the same test here in Canada to see how they perceive the greeters. This type if primary data collecting is known as:

1.   Single-source data research
2.   Survey research
3.   Experimental research
4.   Observational research
5.   Marketing research

4-8   Multiple

Which of the following types of primary data collection tries to gather information of cause-and-effect relationships?

1.   Single-source data research
2.   Survey research
3.   Experimental research
4.   Observational research
5.   Marketing research

4-9   Multiple

Which of the following contact methods is the quickest, provides flexibility, has fairly high response rates and allows for a greater amount of sample control?

1.   Mail questionnaires
2.   Telephone interviews
3.   Personal interviewing
4.   Individual interviewing
5.   Group interviewing

4-10   Multiple

Which of the following contact methods can be higher in cost than some; time consuming because the respondents may want to get off topic and it is difficult to get back on track; may exhibit interviewer bias and to save time the interviewer may skip some questions and fill the answers in themselves?

1.   Mail questionnaires
2.   Telephone interviews
3.   Personal interviewing
4.   Individual interviewing
5.   Group interviewing

4-11   Multiple

Which of the following is NOT part of designing a sample group?

1.   Where should the survey be conducted
2.   Who should be chosen
3.   How many people should be surveyed
4.   How should the people in the survey be chosen
5.   All the above are part of designing a sample group

4-12   Multiple

Open-end questions are especially useful in what type of research?

1.   Observational research
2.   Survey research
3.   Experimental research
4.   Marketing research
5.   Exploratory research

4-13   Multiple

Researchers are responsible to provide many services to management. Which of the following does management not appreciate?

1.   Providing complex numbers and statistical analysis of findings
2.   Interpreting findings
3.   Drawing conclusions
4.   Reporting findings to management
5.   All the above are appreciated by management

4-14   Multiple

International research presents many problems or difficulties for companies. These difficulties include all the following except:

1.   Markets often vary greatly in their levels of economic development, cultures, customs, and buying patterns
2.   In many foreign markets, the international researcher has a difficult time finding good secondary data
3.   It is often very difficult to collect primary data as the tools available in North America are lacking in other countries
4.   People in other countries are not as intelligent and sophisticated as those in North America; therefore, questionnaires and research methods used here would not be appropriate in other parts of the world
5.   It is often very difficult to reach people in order to collect data as many countries' systems of distribution are not as sophisticated as those of North America

4-15   Multiple

Internal data can be used for all the following except:

1.   Targeting segments of existing customers for special product and service offers
2.   Providing on-the-spot answers to customer questions
3.   Obtaining information on market share
4.   Analyzing daily sales performance
5.   All the above are used

4-16   Multiple

Choosing between doing survey research and experimental research is decided at which step in the marketing research process?

1.   Defining the problem
2.   Setting the research objectives
3.   Developing the research plan
4.   Implementing the research plan
5.   None of the above

4-17   Multiple

Sara works for Quality Specialty Products in Toronto. Each day she downloads the previous day's sales figures to decide which products to keep and which to drop. Sara is engaged in what area of MIS?

1.   Internal records
2.   Information analysis
3.   Marketing intelligence
4.   Marketing research
5.   Providing recommendations

4-18   Multiple

Raphael's job is to make sure the people interviewed during a survey meet a certain profile. He is involved in which area of primary data collection planning?

1.   Sampling plans
2.   Screening process
3.   Research approaches
4.   Contact methods
5.   Research instruments

4-19   Multiple

Shania finds the best secondary data information on foreign markets is available from *The Economist's Country Reports*. These reports are published annually and cost up to $5,000 per country. This is an example of what type of secondary data?

1.   Internal sources
2.   Government publications
3.   On-line sources
4.   Periodicals and books
5.   Commercial data

4-20   Multiple

Information found in a company's internal database would include which of the following:

1.   The accounting departments' records on financial statement
2.   The manufacturing departments' records on production schedules
3.   The marketing departments' records on customer demographics and buying behaviour
4.   The customer service departments' records on customer satisfaction
5.   All of the above could be found in a database

4-21   Multiple

US Industrial Outlook provides projections of industrial activity by industry and includes data on production, sales, shipments and employment. This type of data source is considered:

1.   Internal
2.   Commercial
3.   International
4.   Governmental
5.   Internet

4-22   Multiple

All the following are problems with secondary data sources except:

1.   The needed information may not exist
2.   The data is fairly expensive to obtain
3.   The data found may not be relevant
4.   The data found may not be usable
5.   The data alone is not sufficient by itself

4-23   Multiple

There have been many studies done to determine a basic characteristic of Internet users. Which of the following characteristic of Internet users was NOT found to be common:

1.   Are better educated
2.   Are on average younger than the average consumer
3.   Are usually male
4.   Are on average single or recently married
5.   Are more affluent

4-24   Multiple

When every member of a population has a known and equal chance of being selected for a study, this is known as a _____ type of sample.

1.   Simple random sample
2.   Stratified random sample
3.   Convenience sample
4.   Judgement sample
5.   Probable random sample

4-25   Multiple

A scale that rates some attribute from "poor" to "excellent" is known as a (n) _____ type of closed-ended question.

1.   Dichotomous
2.   Likert scale
3.   Rating scale
4.   Semantic differential
5.   Intention-to-buy scale

4-26   Multiple

"What is your opinion of Canadian Airlines?" is an example of a (n) _____ type of open-ended question.

1.   Word association
2.   Sentence completion
3.   Picture completion
4.   Completely unstructured
5.   Story completion

4-27   Multiple

Which of the following is a common problem facing marketers when using information gathered from internal data?

1.   It may be out of date
2.   It is too ordinary to be of much use
3.   It may be incomplete or in the wrong form for marketing needs
4.   It is too easily accessible to other areas of the company
5.   All the above are common problems

4-28   Multiple

Which, if any, of the following is NOT a typical source of marketing intelligence?

1.   Company executives
2.   Competitors
3.   Purchasing agents
4.   Consumers
5.   All the above are sources

4-29   Multiple

A simple definition of _____ is it is the function linking the consumer, customer, and public to the marketer through information.

1.   Marketing intelligence
2.   Marketing research
3.   The marketing information system
4.   Marketing control
5.   Marketing segmentation

4-30   Multiple

Marcel has noticed fewer customers are stopping at his store in the mall. He has a hunch about the reason but thinks he needs a little preliminary information before acting. Which type of research should Marcel use?

1.   Exploratory research
2.   Investigative research
3.   Descriptive research
4.   Correlational research
5.   Observational research

True/False Questions

4-1 True/False

Marketing Information Systems begin with marketing managers and end with a joint effort of all managers in all functional areas.

4-2 True/False

The MIS must watch the marketing environment to provide decision-makers with information they should have to make key marketing decisions.

4-3 True/False

By itself information has no worth; its value comes from its use.

4-4 True/False

Internal records can be accessed more quickly than other information sources, but because all the people involved are more expensive than other information sources.

4-5 True/False

A radio station wants to know what type of people listen to their station, how many, how long they listen each day and where they listen, to decide what their target market is. This type of information would be classified as marketing research.

4-6 True/False

Solutions to the type of marketing mix, designing sales territories and sales-call plans and a forecast of future new-product sales is a function of the Marketing Research step in developing information.

4-7 True/False

Marketing information has no value until managers use it to make better marketing decisions.

4-8 True/False

The University of Manitoba wants to know how many students it can potentially expect to enroll in Year 1 for the upcoming year. They decide to look at the number of graduating students in all of Manitoba for this year obtained from the Manitoba High School Association's database. They will then use a pre-assigned number as to how many will attend a post-secondary institution, obtained from a recently published article in the

Winnipeg Free Press. Of this number, they have calculated about 58% will attend the U of M, which is based on a yearly average of the past 10 years. This type of data is known as primary research.

4-9   True/False

Experimental research is the approach best suited for gathering descriptive information.

4-10   True/False

Focus group interviewing has become one of the major marketing research tools for gaining insight into consumer thought and feelings.

4-11   True/False

"What is your income to the nearest hundred dollars?" is an example of a closed-ended question.

4-12   True/False

A written proposal is especially important when the research project is large and complex, or when many different departments inside the firm carry it out.

4-13   True/False

The data-collection phase of the marketing research process is generally the most expensive and the most subject to error.

4-14   True/False

The marketing research techniques discussed in this chapter are only appropriate for large companies with large budgets. Small businesses and non-profit organizations are not able to perform marketing research because of lack of resources.

4-15   True/False

In practice, a good MIS system can supply all the information manager's requests.

4-16   True/False

Descriptive research gathers preliminary information that will help define the problem and suggest research hypothesis.

4-17   True/False

The main drawbacks of personal interviewing are costs and sampling problems.

4-18   True/False

Key customers are not a source which keep companies informed about their competitors and their products.

4-19   True/False

The Internet provides a quick and inexpensive access to rich assortment of intelligence information.

4-20   True/False

When multiple-source data systems are properly used, they can provide marketers with fast and detailed information about how their products are selling, who is buying them, and what factors affect purchases.

Applying Terms and Concepts

To determine how well you understand the materials in this chapter, read each of the following brief cases and then respond to the questions that follow. Answers are given at the end of this chapter.

Case #1   Hogan's Shoe Store[1]

Robert Hogan is the founder of Hogan's Shoe Store located in the business district of Brandon, Manitoba. Hogan's has been in business since 1952, and its past success has been attributable to personalized service combined with quality leather footwear offered at reasonable prices. Richard Hogan, the owner's son, assumed control of the store when his father retired two years ago. Richard immediately implemented several changes, including, a shift in the store's promotion, favouring radio advertising and an increase in the store's inventory by 10%.

Sales at Hogan's have increased an average of 5% in each of the past 2 years; however, net profit has decreased slightly. According to industry data, shoe stores similar to Hogan's experienced an average increase in sales of 12% and an average increase in net profit of 8% during the same period.

After causally speaking with the store manager, salesperson, and several customers, Hogan concluded that the declining profits could be attributed to the low inventory turnover resulting from the prices charged.

In an effort to increase the store's profitability, Hogan contacted Mary Collin, a distributor for the Hozelton brand of footwear. Although the Hozelton line is constructed of man-made materials; it has a good reputation in the business. Collins assured Hogan Hozelton quality was comparable to his existing line and the retail prices would be lower than of his current merchandise. Collins also stated that Hozelton would be willing to grant advertising allowances equal to 10% of Hogan's advertising budget to a maximum of $400, whichever was lower.

Hogan is seriously considering Collin's proposal, however, he in unsure how his customers will react if he begins to substitute Hozelton for his established line.

1.   List the type of internal reports which might prove useful to Hogan in his situation.

_____

_____

_____

_____

2. List some possible external secondary sources of information which might prove useful to Hogan

_____

_____

_____

_____

3. Since Hogan is unsure of his exact problem, which type of research would you recommend?

_____

_____

4. Do you feel Hogan needs to collect additional secondary data before he makes a decision?

_____

_____

_____

_____

5. List possible reasons for the decrease in the store's profitability during the past 2 years.

_____

_____

_____

_____

Case #2   Angus Reid Group[2]

Angus Reid Group is a marketing research group that conducts and analyzes results for many different companies around the world. They perform research on many different products in a variety of industries. An example of this is the Food and Beverage division.

Packaged food and beverage is one of the most dynamic categories in Canada. The emergence of large volume retailers, endless product choices and the inroads of store brands have made it one of the most competitive. The marketers who success will be armed with an accurate understanding of the motivations and commitments of consumers.

---

[1] *Principles of Marketing*, 3rd Edition, Kotler, Armstrong, Warren (Prentice Hall) – pg. 69.
[2] Information taken from the Angus Reid Web Site.

Marketing research performed by Angus Reid Group touches every stage of the product cycle: New Product Development, Product marketing Strategies and Product evaluation. Here are a few examples of their research.

- A North American beverage manufacturer was interested in new market niche opportunities. A US segmentation study revealed two largely ignored consumer segments
- A large package dairy products manufacturer brought us a problem: from a number of alternative concepts, which new product combination would have been the most favourable market impact? Result: a new brand of cheese
- A national manufacturer was faced with three alternative packaging options. Angus Reid research helped choose the winning design.

1. What type of research models and techniques would you use for new product development?

    _____

    _____

    _____

    _____

2. What type of research models and techniques would you use for product marketing strategies?

    _____

    _____

    _____

    _____

3. What type of research models and techniques would you use for product evaluation?

    _____

    _____

    _____

    _____

4. Do you believe it is beneficial for large companies to outsource their marketing research to companies like Angus Reid?

    _____

    _____

    _____

    _____

5.   What other companies or industries might benefit from this service?

_____

_____

_____

_____

Case #3   Margaret Gorman

Margaret Gorman was reading the *Wall Street Journal* when she came upon an article with the headline "'TV Networks Turning to Comedies as They Frantically Search for Hits." The article went on to say that fluffy comic programming was being "shipped" up after last season's flings with gumshoes, doctors, lawyers, and oil-drenched soap operas produced one of the most dismal 23 weeks in television history. "All they want now is sitcoms," says a veteran TV writer. The networks were depending on the old, reliable laugh to produce some new hits and reverse the decline in share of viewers during prime time.

Gorman had just formed her own TV company to produce TV programs for the networks and independent stations. After reading this article, Gorman was convinced that this was an excellent opportunity to produce a nonviolent, nonsex adventure series for TV. She believed that something different from standard fare would stand a good chance of getting high ratings. Gorman planned to dramatize important historical events, and at the beginning, middle, and end of each program a group of history professors would discuss causes and effects of the event. To verify her belief that this kind of program would have broad appeal, she had developed a plan for a survey of the university community in which she lived. She wanted to do a good job of research so that she could use the results to help convince network and station executives that the new program would capture the mass market, which she believed was now saturated with comedy; but she did not want violence or sex as an alternative.

Gorman spent a considerable amount of money to secure a computer-generated random sample of telephone numbers of both professors and students — making sure she had proportionate representation from both groups. She designed a questionnaire (shown below) and hired twenty students to do the telephone interviewing at $2 per completed interview. Each interviewer was given a batch of questionnaires and telephone numbers and told to go home and start at the top of the list of numbers. Calls were to be made between 9 a.m. and 4 p.m. If contact could not be established on the first call, the interviewer was to make up to nine more calls to the same number at different times between 9 a.m. and 5 p.m. in an effort to reach the originally selected respondent. If the respondent could not be reached or refused to cooperate, the interviewer was to move on to the next name on the list and continue in this fashion until twenty questionnaires had been completed.

After two days of interviewing, Gorman was not sure how to evaluate the situation. Mary and Bill, two interviewers, completed twenty calls the first day, but all the others were having difficulty — they had many refusals, partially completed interviews, not-at-home respondents, busy numbers, changed or not working numbers, and so on. They seemed to be confused, and their questionnaires were often improperly filled out or unusable. Gorman was considering assigning to Mary and Bill some of the number's given to other interviewers.

Gorman's Questionnaire

1. What is your income? _____

2. What is your sex? Male _____ Female _____ Bisexual _____

3. What is your age? _____

4. What kind of education do you have?_____

5. Is your race white or other?   W _____   O _____

6. Are you religious?   Yes _____   No _____

7. Most people feel that TV is bad and are watching less. Do you agree?
   Yes _____   No _____

8. Do you watch a lot of TV?   Yes _____   No _____   Sometimes _____

9. Do you think we should encourage criminal depravity by showing a lot of violence and sex on TV?   Yes _____   No _____

10. Do you agree with most people that most TV programs are not intellectually stimulating?   Yes   No

11. Do you think we can have interesting and intellectually stimulating programs without a lot of violence and sex?   Yes   No

12. What is the least popular television program among your friends?

   _____

13. What's your general opinion of TV programming — that is, what do you dislike about it, and how can it be improved?

   _____

   _____

1.   What were the fundamental weaknesses in Gorman's marketing research plan?

      _____

      _____

      _____

      _____

      _____

      _____

      _____

      _____

2.   What should be done to improve Gorman's marketing research plan?

      _____

      _____

      _____

      _____

      _____

      _____

      _____

Case #4   Carlson's Supermarkets

Bud Carlson, owner of a small chain of supermarkets headquartered in Minneapolis, Minnesota, was surveying his company's financial statements when he noticed what he considered disturbing information. Dog and cat food sales dropped an additional 8% on top of last years 11% drop.

Carlson pondered his situation and figured he either needed to get out of pet food sales altogether or to expand his offerings considerably. According to a recent article he read in *American Demographics Magazine*, supermarkets held a 95% share of the market in the early 1980s; while in the mid '90s, their share of the market was hovering around 10%.

According to the article, three changes in the pet products industry were responsible for the shift. The first involved super premium pet foods which were originally only sold through veterinarians and pet stores. The new foods claimed to offer a healthier alternative to traditional pet food. In time, pet owners concerned about their pet's nutrition and health began to buy the super premium food in increasingly greater quantities.

The second challenge was posed by mass marketers such as Target, Wal-Mart and K Mart. A wide array of pet products along with discount prices on pet food resulting from volume purchasing, attracted buyers in significant numbers. Pet owners slowly shifted their buying behaviour from the supermarkets to the mass merchandisers further eroding market share.

The most recent assault has come from pet food superstores. These outlets offers lower prices and a wider variety of pet foods, toys, accessories, clothing and furniture than even the mass merchandisers. And as an added twist, pets are welcome to join their owners as they peruse store offerings.

Two weeks later, a disgruntled Carlson began his senior staff meeting by stating "Carlson Supermarkets has experienced another drop in pet food sales and the problem is we are losing sales to those discount stores, and I want to know what we are going to do about it."

1. If Carlson authorizes a marketing research project to investigate the decline in pet food sales, the article he mentioned as well as the company's financial statements would be considered secondary data and would be reviewed as part of the research plan. What is secondary data and what are the relative advantages and disadvantages of its review as part of a research project?

    _____

    _____

    _____

    _____

    _____

    _____

2. Explain why Carlson was mistaken when he stated "... the problem is we are losing sales to those discount stores ..."

    _____

    _____

    _____

    _____

    _____

    _____

    _____

Source: "Reigning Cats and Dogs" *American Demographics,* April 1995, p. 10.

Multiple Choice Answers

1. Correct Answer: 2 Reference: pg. 114

2. Correct Answer: 4 Reference: pg. 116

3. Correct Answer: 1 Reference: pg. 117

4. Correct Answer: 3 Reference: pg. 122

5. Correct Answer: 2 Reference: pg. 122

6. Correct Answer: 5 Reference: pg. 125

7. Correct Answer: 4 Reference: pg. 127

8. Correct Answer: 3 Reference: pg. 130

9   Correct Answer: 2 Reference: pg. 131

10. Correct Answer: 2 Reference: pg. 131

11. Correct Answer: 1 Reference: pg. 134

12. Correct Answer: 5 Reference: pg. 135

13. Correct Answer: 1 Reference: pg. 137

14. Correct Answer: 4 Reference: pg. 141

15. Correct Answer: 3 Reference: pg. 116

16. Correct Answer: 3 Reference: pg. 124

17. Correct Answer: 2 Reference: pg. 21

18. Correct Answer: 1 Reference: pg. 134

19. Correct Answer: 5 Reference: pg. 125

20. Correct Answer: 5 Reference: pg. 116

21. Correct Answer: 3 Reference: pg. 126

22. Correct Answer: 2 Reference: pg. 127

23.	Correct Answer:	4	Reference:	pg. 133
24.	Correct Answer:	1	Reference:	pg. 134 (Table 4-5)
25.	Correct Answer:	3	Reference:	pg. 133
26.	Correct Answer:	4	Reference:	pg. 133
27.	Correct Answer:	3	Reference:	pg. 116
28.	Correct Answer:	5	Reference:	pg. 117
29.	Correct Answer:	2	Reference:	pg. 120
30.	Correct Answer:	1	Reference:	pg. 122

True/False Answers

1.	FALSE	Reference:	pg. 114	Topic:	The Marketing Information System
2.	TRUE	Reference:	pg. 115	Topic:	Assessing Information Needs
3.	TRUE	Reference:	pg. 115	Topic:	Assessing Information Needs
4.	FALSE	Reference:	pg. 116	Topic:	Internal Records
5.	TRUE	Reference:	pg. 119	Topic:	Marketing Research
6.	FALSE	Reference:	pg. 120	Topic:	Information Analysis
7.	TRUE	Reference:	pg. 120	Topic:	Distributing Information
8.	FALSE	Reference:	pg. 123	Topic:	Gathering Secondary Information
9.	FALSE	Reference:	pg. 127	Topic:	Planning Primary Data Collection
10.	TRUE	Reference:	pg. 130	Topic:	Contact Methods
11.	FALSE	Reference:	pg. 132	Topic:	Research Instruments
12.	FALSE	Reference:	pg. 134	Topic:	Presenting the Research Plan
13.	TRUE	Reference:	pg. 134	Topic:	Implementing the Research Plan

14.	FALSE	Reference:	pg. 135	Topic:	Marketing Research in Small Businesses and Non-Profit Organizations
15.	FALSE	Reference:	pg. 114	Topic:	Assessing Information Needs
16.	FALSE	Reference:	pg. 122	Topic:	Defining the Problem and Research Objectives
17.	TRUE	Reference:	pg. 131	Topic:	Contact Methods
18.	FALSE	Reference:	pg. 118	Topic:	Marketing Highlight 4-1
19.	TRUE	Reference:	pg. 119	Topic:	Marketing Highlight 4-1
20.	FALSE	Reference:	pg. 129	Topic:	Marketing Highlight 4-3

Applying Term and Concepts Answers

Case #1   Hogan's Shoe Store:
Question #1
- Operating and sales expenses
- Sales reports
- Inventory records
- Invoices
- Accounts receivable
- Balance sheets
- Profit and loss statements

Question #2
- Industry surveys
- Government publications
- Business periodicals
- Trade association information

Question #3
- Exploratory research
- This is marketing research which gathers preliminary information that will help better define problems and suggest hypotheses

Question #4
- Yes – the information collected is inadequate and unreliable
- His sample was far too small
- He spoke to these people in a casual manor, not a scientific one
- There was no patterning to his questions

Question #5
- Change in advertising medium
- Change in population characteristics
- Increased competition
- Increased operating expenses
- Change in salespeople
- Change in product price
- Downturn in local economy

Case #2　　　　Angus Reid Group:

Question #1
- Brand maps based on lifestyle and segmentation models
- Identify potential gaps in the market
- Future niches for new entries
- Idea generation sessions
- Concept tests to help refine product strategies, packaging and brand names

Question #2
- Models ranging from quasi-experimental customer tests to in-home placement
- Examine impact of alternative marketing
- Packaging and pricing scenarios for a broad range of packaged goods

Question #3
- Tracking studies to help evaluate product performance in the marketplace
- Plot changes in consumer perceptions
- Information useful in targeting further product enhancements

Question #4
- Unbiased research and interpretation of results
- May be cheaper as in-house resources are not being used
- They are specialists, therefore information may be more accurate
- Can focus on the implementation plan if the results

Question #5
- Drug stores
- Hardware stores
- Clothing and shoe stores
- Grocery stores
- Etc.

1.   There was an inadequate review of secondary data related to the research project.

      The respondents who made up the sample may not be representative of the intended target market. Gorman stated she wanted the programming to have broad appeal; yet her sample was very narrowly defined — students and professors with telephones who were available between 9 a.m. and 5 p.m.

      The questionnaire was poorly designed. There were too few questions used to gather data on which to draw conclusions and make decisions. The sequencing of the questions was wrong. Some questions were too vague and others were very leading. The questions were biased and would undoubtedly result in answers and opinions that support Gorman's beliefs.

      The interviewers were inadequately trained and supervised. There is the potential for interviewer bias. There was no verification of interviews conducted by Mary and Bill — their results should be suspect given their high completion rate relative to the other interviewers.

2.   Gorman needs to have a better understanding of the situation she faces and therefore needs a better review of the secondary data. This will assist her in defining the "problem" and setting her research objective.

      The sampling plan needs to be carefully analyzed. Gorman needs an appropriate sample unit and sample size. She needs to use an appropriate sampling procedure. There is some question as to whether her current sample plan is appropriate.

      The current questionnaire needs to be discarded and a new one constructed. Questions should be placed in the proper sequence. That is, the demographic and biographic questions should be placed at the end of the questionnaire. A variety of open-end questions seeking the respondent's opinions should be meshed with the closed-end questions. The questions should not be vague or leading. The questionnaire should also be pretested to identify and correct problems which may skew the results.

      The interviewers need to be properly trained and monitored as they gather data. This would help to minimize interviewer bias and help ensure the collection of reliable and accurate data.

      Gorman may also wish to conduct personal interviews and/or group interviews (focus-group interviews) to complement the telephone interviews. Personal interviewing has several drawbacks, but the advantages may very well offset those disadvantages and yield very significant information.

1.   Secondary data consists of information that already exists, having been collected for another purpose. It is typically reviewed in a research project, because it helps the researcher understand better the situation to be studied. Its relative advantages are that it usually can be obtained more quickly and at lower cost than primary data.

Secondary data can also present problems. The needed information may not exist. Even when data can be found, it might not be very usable. The research must evaluate secondary information carefully to make certain it is relevant (fits research project needs), accurate (reliably collected and reported), current (up to date enough for current decisions), and impartial (objectively collected and reported).

Secondary data provide a good starting point for research and often help to define problems and research objectives. In most cases, however, the company must also collect primary data.

2.   The first step in the marketing research process is often the hardest step. It is defining the problem and research objective. The problem is not that Carlson is losing sales to the mass marketers, rather, the decline in sales is a symptom of the problem. That is, something is causing the decline in sales. The question Carlson needs to ask is "Why are sales declining?" When that question is answered — perhaps after conducting exploratory research — Carlson can develop strategies to address the decline.

Chapter 5

Consumer Markets and Consumer Buying Behaviour

Chapter Overview

The Canadian Consumer Market consists of about 29 million people who consume billions of dollars worth of goods and services each year, making it one of the most attractive consumer markets in the world. The world consumer market consists of more than 5 billion people. Consumers around the world vary greatly in age, income, education level, and tastes. Understanding how these differences affect consumer buying behaviour is one of the biggest challenges marketers face.

Chapter Objectives

1. Define the consumer market and construct a simple model of consumer buyer behaviour.
2. Name the four major factors influencing consumer buyer behaviour.
3. List and understand the stages in the buyer decision process.
4. Describe the adoption and diffusion process for new products.

Chapter Topics

Model of Consumer Behaviour

Characteristics Affecting Consumer Behaviour
- Cultural Factors
  - Culture
  - Subculture
  - Social Classes
- Social Factors
  - Groups
  - Family
  - Roles and Status
- Personal Factors
  - Age and Life-Cycle Stage
  - Occupation
  - Economic Situation
  - Lifestyle
  - Personality and Self-Concept

- Psychological Factors
  - Motivation
  - Perception
  - Learning
  - Beliefs and Attitudes

Consumer Buying Roles

Types of Buying Decision Behaviour
- Complex Buying Behaviour
- Dissonance-Reducing Buying Behaviour
- Habitual Buying Behaviour
- Variety Seeking Buying Behaviour

The Buyer Decision Process
- Need Recognition
- Information Search
- Evaluation of Alternatives
- Purchase Decision
- Postpurchase Behaviour

The Buyer Decision Process for New Products
- Stages in the Adoption Process
- Individual Differences in Innovativeness
- Influence of Product Characteristics on Rate of Adoption

Consumer Behaviour Across International Borders

Chapter Summary

1.   The consumer market and the elements of a simple model of buying behaviour as identified in the text.

The consumer market is made up of all the final consumers of products and services combined. A simple model of consumer behaviour consists of the 4 Ps (Product, Place, Price, Promotion) and Environmental Forces, the Buyer's Black Box (buyer characteristics, buyer decision processes), and Observable Choices (product, brand, dealer, purchase timing, and purchase amount).

2.   The major social factors that influence consumer buying behaviour.

Social factors include small groups, family, and social roles and status. Groups can be membership (primary, secondary) or reference or aspirational. Opinion leaders exert influence within reference groups.

Family or orientation (parents and procreation (spouse and children) also influence buying behaviour. Roles are expected activities and status is the esteem granted to the person performing roles by society.

3.   The four major psychological factors that affect the buying process.

Psychological factors include motivation, perception, learning, and beliefs and attitudes. A motive is a drive sufficiently pressing to direct the person to seek satisfaction. Perception is influence by selective retention, attention, and distortion. Learning arises from changes in behaviour due to experience and occurs through the interplay of drives, stimuli, cues, responses, and reinforcement. Beliefs are descriptive attitudes endure.

4.   The stages in the consumer adoption process for new products.

New product adoption stages include awareness, interest, evaluation, trial and adoption.

5.   The four types of behaviour associated with different types of buying situations.

Four types of buying behaviour include complex buying behaviour, dissonance-buying behaviour, variety-seeking buying behaviour, and habitual-buying behaviour.

Key Terms

Adoption process   (pg. 183)
Alternative evaluation (pg. 179)
Attitude   (pg. 172)
Belief   (pg. 172)
Brand image   (pg. 180)
Cognitive dissonance (pg. 181)
Complex buying behaviour   (pg. 175)
Consumer buying behaviour (pg. 155)
Consumer market   (pg. 155)
Culture   (pg. 156)
Dissonance-reducing buying behaviour(pg. 175)
Group   (pg. 163)
Habitual buying behaviour   (pg. 175)
Information search   (pg. 177)

Learning   (pg. 172)
Lifestyle   (pg. 166)
Motive   (pg. 169)
Need Recognition   (pg. 177)
New Product (pg. 183)
Opinion leaders   (pg. 163)
Perception   (pg. 171)
Personality   (pg. 168)
Postpurchase behaviour   (pg. 181)
Psychographics   (pg. 166)
Purchase decision   (pg. 180)
Social classes (pg. 161)
Subculture   (pg. 157)
Variety-seeking buying behaviour   (pg. 176)

Multiple Choice Questions

5-1   Multiple

Which of the following does not comprise the marketing and other stimuli section of the Model for Buying Behaviour?

1.   Product
2.   Price
3.   Promotion
4.   Politics
5.   All of the following

5-2   Multiple

Cristina has been looking for a new VCR for a long time. She is interested in purchasing a fairly high-tech VCR as she has a top of the line television. The great salesman at Future Shop has convinced her the Zenith DVD 500 is the best value for her dollar. Cristina decides to go with this VCR and makes the purchase. Cristina used all the steps in the buyer's response except:

1.   Product choice
2.   Brand choice
3.   Purchase amount
4.   Dealer choice
5.   All of the above

5-3   Multiple

Canadians live in a very time poor society. To help Canadians increase their leisure time, all the following are convenience goods and services, except _____, which help them accomplish this goal.

1.   Microwave ovens
2.   Fast food
3.   Catalogue industry
4.   Gas lawn mowers
5.   Automatic tellers

5-4   Multiple

Canada is a very multi-cultural country with very distinctive and significant ethnic markets. Which of the following does not belong to the three largest ethnic Canadian markets?

1.   Ukrainian
2.   Italian
3.   German
4.   Chinese
5.   All of the above do not belong to the top three

5-5   Multiple

The Canadian market is maturing, which is a very important issue marketers must address. Which of the following is (are) characteristic of this age group, which comprises people currently aged 50 and older?

1.   Possess 2/3 of the countries disposable income
2.   Represent 25% of the population
3.   Comprise 1/3 of the heads of households
4.   Possess 3/5 of the countries disposable income
5.   1,2,3,

5-6   Multiple

Marketers have found seniors are a significant market, who have both time and money on their hands. All the following would be very profitable for companies if they marketed them to seniors except:

1.   Exotic travel
2.   Home physical-fitness products
3.   Financial services
4.   Health foods
5.   All of the above

5-7   Multiple

Which of the following class structure meet these criteria? They tend to be active in social and civic affairs and buy for themselves and their children they symbols of status, such as expensive homes, swimming pools and cars.

1.   Upper Uppers
2.   Lower Uppers
3.   Upper Middles
4.   Middle Class
5.   Working Class

5-8   Multiple

Which of the following class structures meet these criteria? They perform unskilled work but they manage to present a picture of self-discipline and maintain some effort of cleanliness.

1.   Lower Lowers
2.   Upper Lowers
3.   Working Class
4.   Middle Class
5.   Upper Middles

5-9   Multiple

Social classes show distinct product and brand preferences in the following areas except:

1.   Clothing choices
2.   Home furnishings
3.   Food choices
4.   Leisure activities
5.   Automobiles

5-10   Multiple

All new and old engineers must belong to the Engineering Association of each province. This type of group would be considered a:

1.   Aspirational group
2.   Reference groups
3.   Primary membership group
4.   Secondary membership group
5.   Membership group

5-11   Multiple

The importance of group influence varies across products and brands. However, group influence tends to be the strongest in which of the following situations?

1.   The product is visible to others
2.   The products are bought and used privately
3.   The product could be a reflection of your profession
4.   The product are bought publicly but used privately
5.   None of the above

5-12   Multiple

Which of the following would not be considered a group in the middle-aged stage of the life cycle?

1.   Single
2.   Married without children
3.   Single with children
4.   Married with children
5.   Divorced without children

5-13   Multiple

The VALS2 is a tool used to classify people into different lifestyles. Which category would Stephan, a 25 year-old male who buys goods and services based on his views of the world, and is very content with minimal resources?

1.   Fulfilleds
2.   Achievers
3.   Strugglers
4.   Strivers
5.   Believers

5-14   Multiple

Which of the following is not considered a psychological factor?

1.   Motivation
2.   Self-concept
3.   Perception
4.   Learning
5.   Beliefs and attitudes

5-15   Multiple

Maslow's hierarchy of needs encompasses five distinct needs. The need for a sense of belonging and love falls under which category?

1.   Physiological needs
2.   Safety needs
3.   Social needs
4.   Esteem needs
5.   Self-actualization needs

5-16   Multiple

Many people perceive situations differently. This is a very difficult challenge for marketers. Paula is watching television and has probably seen 50 different ads. Currently she is not in the market for anything so when she sees the commercials, none of them really sink in. In this situation, marketers must really try to differentiate their ads from others in order to combat _____
_____:

1.   Selective distortion
2.   Selective retention
3.   Selective perception
4.   Selective attention
5.   Selective recording

5-17   Multiple

Sven and Inga just got married and realize they need to buy a new car. Inga's father was a car dealer and mechanic and so Inga is very well educated in cars and their functions. Sven has Inga collect the necessary information to make an informed decision. Inga comes back with 3 different alternatives and they both decide on the car. They purchase the car at the local dealer that Saturday, as both of them need to use the car the upcoming week. Which of the following roles did Sven not partake in?

1.   Initiator
2.   Influencer
3.   Decider
4.   Buyer
5.   Sven contributed to all of these roles

5-18   Multiple

Hen Wee does the grocery shopping for her family every week. She usually purchases Dad's oatmeal cookies but this time, she decided to buy the new Duncan Heinz oatmeal cookies for change. This purchase does not require too much involvement, as there are few differences between brands. She is practising this type of buying behaviour.

1.   Complex buying behaviour
2.   Dissonance-reducing buying behaviour
3.   Habitual buying behaviour
4.   Variety seeking buying behaviour
5.   New Product buying behaviour

5-19   Multiple

Brent is walking home from school and he passes a McDonald's. His stomach is rumbling so he decides to stop in and looks at some menu items before choosing a large fries and drink. He eats his snack there and on the rest of his journey he is content, as the food was very satisfying. Which of the following steps, if any did Brent omit in his buyer decision process?

1.   Information search
2.   Evaluation of alternatives
3.   Need recognition
4.   Purchase decisions
5.   None of the above

5-20   Multiple

Evaluation of alternatives is a very important step in the buyer decision process. Which of the following is not a consideration at this step?

1.   Product attributes
2.   Degrees of importance
3.   Brand attitudes
4.   Total product satisfaction
5.   All of the above

5-21   Multiple

Rachel has heard about a new hand held computerized agenda from a friend of hers who bought one three months earlier. She is always losing her pens and therefore misses appointments because she cannot write them down. This new product would solve many of her problems. She decided to go to the corner computer store in the mall and talk to a sales agent there. She is sold right away on one of the three different choices, and takes one home and start inputting all her data to this new agenda that afternoon. Which of the stages in the adoption process, if any, did Rachel miss?

1.   Adoption
2.   Trail
3.   Evaluation
4.   Awareness
5.   None of the above

5-22   Multiple

In the above example, Rachel would be considered a:

1.   Laggard
2.   Late Majority
3.   Early Majority
4.   Early adopter
5.   Innovator

5-23   Multiple

The new hand held computerized agenda is considered a new product. Many characteristics will determine the rate of its adoption into today's society. These new agendas are easily portable and can be shown to many different people with ease. This characteristic is known as:

1.   Communicability
2.   Divisibility
3.   Complexity
4.   Compatibility
5.   Relative Advantage

5-24   Multiple

The type of purchase for which group influence is strongest is:

1.   Convenience purchases
2.   Consumptive purchases
3.   Conspicuous purchases
4.   Conventional purchases
5.   Collective purchases

5-25   Multiple

Hank relies on his parents for advice on all his major purchases and to help pay his bills. His father is the breadwinner in the family and his mom stays at home to care for his 2 younger sisters. Hank belongs to which social class?

1.   Middle class
2.   Lower uppers
3.   Upper lowers
4.   Lower lowers
5.   Working class

5-26   Multiple

Brand image is formed from which of the following concepts associated with alternative evaluation?

1.   Product attributes
2.   Degrees of importance
3.   Brand beliefs
4.   Utility function
5.   Brand attitudes

5-27   Multiple

Regarding customer satisfaction, which of the following statements is true?

1.   Dissatisfied customers tend to behave much like satisfied customers
2.   Bad word of mouth travels farther and faster than good word of mouth
3.   Dissatisfied customers tell fewer people about their experiences than do satisfied customers
4.   Dissatisfied customers complain to the company in large numbers
5.   Satisfied customers will always come back and tell their friends

5-28   Multiple

While driving home from work, Lucy hears a radio commercial for a new gym next door to her office. Being interested in fitness and a gym closer to work, she decides to seek out further information. She is at which stage in the new product adoption process?

1.   Awareness
2.   Interest
3.   Evaluation
4.   Trial
5.   Adoption

5-29   Multiple

Janiqua got to test drive a new fuel-efficient car that ran on propane. Janiqua's trial qualifies as which of the following characteristics?

1.   Relative advantage
2.   Communicability
3.   Compatibility
4.   Divisibility
5.   Complexity

5-30   Multiple

Tradition meant something to Alfred and he didn't see much need to buy something "new."
Alfred is in which of the following groups?

1.   Innovators
2.   Early Majority
3.   Late Majority
4.   Late Adopters
5.   Laggards

True/False Questions

5-1   True/False

The company who really understands how consumers will respond to different product features, prices, and advertising has only a moderate advantage over its competitors.

5-2   True/False

Cultural factors influence the broadest and deepest influence on consumer behaviour.

5-3   True/False

Canadians expect all government institutions, but not necessarily businesses, to honour their core values.

5-4   True/False

Despite the increasing number of immigrants to Canada in the last few years, consumers from ethnic groups still represent one of the slowest-growing markets in Canada.

5-5   True/False

Seniors are a growing market segment in Canada. Most of them are healthy and active, and they have many of the same needs and wants as the younger consumers.

5-6   True/False

In recent years, marketers have adjusted to the fact the Net is a means of one-way communications between the consumer and a vendor, much the same as the traditional advertising.

5-7   True/False

All countries, including Canada, have a very rigid social class. The lines between the social classes are fixed and rigid; people cannot move to a higher class or fall down to a lower class.

5-8   True/False

Manufacturers of products and brands subject to strong group influence must determine how to reach the opinion leaders in the relevant reference group instead of marketing to the general public.

5-9   True/False

Groups and peers have surpassed the family in recent years, as the strongest influence of buying behaviour, in today's consumer markets.

5-10   True/False

The basic self-concept premise is people's possessions contribute to their identities, but do not reflect them.

5-11   True/False

Learning changes an individual's behaviour arising from experience. The following make up and contribute to the entire learning process: needs, stimuli, cues and responses.

5-12   True/False

Marketers are interested in the beliefs people formulate about specific products and services, because these beliefs comprise product and brand images that affects buying behaviour.

5-13   True/False

The buying decision process is a very thorough and complete process to purchasing value-added products. Despite this fact, in more routine purchases, consumers often skip or reverse some of these stages.

5-14   True/False

Generally the consumer receives the most information about a product from public sources, those controlled by the marketer.

5-15   True/False

Consumers will vary as to the attributes they consider relevant and they will pay the most attention to those attributes connected with their needs.

5-16   True/False

Two factors can come between the intention to buy and the purchase decision. These two factors are attitudes of others and expected situational factors.

5-17   True/False

In international situations, marketers must decide the degree they will adapt their marketing to various cultures and their needs, but the products can be homogeneous.

5-18   True/False

Middle class people serve as a reference group for other to the extent that their consumption decisions are imitated by other classes.

5-19   True/False

The life-style concept, when used carefully, can help a marketer understand changing consumer values and how they affect buying behaviour.

5-20   True/False

Motivation research is based upon Freudian psychological principles.

Applying Terms and Concepts

To determine how well you understand the materials in this chapter, read each of the following brief cases and then respond to the questions that follow. Answers are given at the end of this chapter.

Case #1   Line-Haul Jeans[1]

Mike Ianari is a Line Haul (long-distance) truck driver for Richards Express, based in Thompson, Manitoba. Ianari recently saw an advertisement in *Overdrive Magazine* about a new type of blue jeans called "Line-Haul." "Line-Hauls" are made of stretch denim, cut wider in the seat and thighs and have oversized back pockets. The advertisement indicated unlike tighter fitting designer jeans, Line Hauls at $39.95, were loose fitting, had plenty of stretch, and felt comfortable the first time worn. At 6'4" and 245 pounds Ianari reason that these prewashed, preshrunk jeans would be ideal.

Ianari, remembering the advertisement, was determined to buy a pair of these jeans on his next trip through Winnipeg, the city with STOP 55 Truck Stops, which sold them exclusively, were located. Ianari was even more determined to buy a pair of these jeans after he began noticing that the "Line Haul" label was acquiring quite a following amoung his fellow drivers. Many truckers are now wearing "Line Haul" caps, T-shirts, vests and belt buckles featuring the brand's "Tractor with Cab Over" emblem.

1.   Which marketing stimuli can be identified in the case?

_____

_____

_____

_____

2.   Which reference group would Ianari most likely be influenced by to purchase "Line Haul" jeans?

_____

_____

_____

_____

---

[1] *Principles of Marketing*, 3rd Edition, Kotler, Armstrong, Warren (Prentice Hall) – pg. 97.

3. Ianari's purchasing of the jeans would satisfy which need or needs according to Maslow's theory of motivation?

_____

_____

_____

_____

4. Which selective perceptual process was evident when Ianari remembered that information which supported his attitude and beliefs about "Line Haul" jeans?

_____

_____

_____

_____

5. Ianari just loves these new jeans and has decided he will never wear any other type of jeans. Which psychological factor most likely accounts for his change in his behaviour?

_____

_____

_____

_____

Case #2   Product Placement in Movies

Product placement in movies has become an acceptable means of advertising. The movie this is most predominant in is *Happy Gilmore*. You may feel like you are watching commercials while watching this movie. If you ask people who have seen this movie, almost all of them will remember that Happy Gilmore was the spokesperson for Subway. By advertising in the movies, consumers associate the product with the movie therefore making retention of information more probable and a purchase more likely.

1. How does product placement help with the need recognition stage of the buyer decision process (BDP)?

_____

_____

_____

_____

2.   How does product placement help with the information search stage of the BDP?

_____

_____

_____

_____

3.   How does product placement help with the postpurchase stage of the BDP?

_____

_____

_____

_____

4.   Do you believe learning takes place as a result of product placements in movies?

_____

_____

_____

_____

5.   With what type of buying behaviour would this type of advertisement be most useful for?

_____

_____

_____

_____

Case #3   The Dawsons

Jeff and Margaret Dawson, after 15 years of marriage and two children, decided this past winter to purchase a power boat. Their income had increased to the point where a $16,000 to $21,000 expenditure was within reason. This boat was a lifelong dream for them. Their only previous experience with boats was a 14-ft Starcraft fishing boat with a 15 hp Mercury outboard motor. Their next purchase was to be in the 20- to 24-ft range with an inboard motor. The prime uses of this boat were to be for water-skiing, fishing, and leisurely motoring on the Finger Lakes of central New York where they lived.

The Dawsons wanted to stay with a Starcraft/Mercury combination if possible. They were disappointed to find, upon attending the Northeast Boat Show at the New York State Fairgrounds in Syracuse, that Starcraft did not produce a boat which suited them. Mercury engines, however, were available in a variety of sizes and price ranges.

Mr. Dawson's reason for wishing to stay with a Mercury engine was his past experience with his outboard motor. In the 14 years he had owned the motor he had had virtually no problems with it. Dawson's fishing friends who owned Johnson and Evinrude motors, however, seemed to experience an abnormally high (compared to Mercury) number of problems, several of which involved major expenditures.

The Dawsons collected literature from exhibitors at the boat show as they viewed a wide variety of boat and motor combinations.

At the boat show, Mercury was introducing a new 210 hp V8 engine. Mercury promoted its new engine as unique because it was the only engine on the market rated at 210 hp, and it introduced V8 cylinder design instead of the more traditional V4 and V6 designs. Dawson was impressed by the information in the literature on this new engine. Fuel consumption, speed, and ease of maintenance were reasonable. Mercury's price, however, was several hundred dollars more than the competition's.

Later, in speaking with his friends about what he had seen at the show, Dawson's friends cautioned him about the potential danger of buying an engine the first year it was produced. They felt it would take a year or two to work the bugs out of the new engine. Although an 8 cylinder engine was common in offshore racing boats, it was still unusual in this horsepower range and motor style for the sport market.

After reviewing the literature from the boat show and visiting several marinas where they spoke with sales representatives and took boats out for a "test drive," the Dawsons decided on a 22-ft craft made by Invader Industries. The boat could be equipped with either a 200 hp Volvo engine or the new 210 hp Mercury. Without hesitation, Dawson ordered the boat with the Mercury. Although they had spent more than they had planned, the Dawsons felt their purchase would be a source of considerable pride and enjoyment.

_____1. Identify the major cultural theme that played a role in the Dawson's decision to purchase a power boat.

    A.   leisure time

    B.   health

    C.   youthfulness

    D.   informality

    E.   social

_____2. Dawson's fishing friends are an example of a(n) _____ group.

    A.   primary

    B.   secondary

    C.   aspirational

    D.   dissociative

    E.   normal

_____3. Which need or needs, according to Maslow's theory of motivation, would be satisfied by Dawson's purchase of the 22-ft Invader power boat?

    A.   social

    B.   esteem

    C.   self-actualization

    D.   only (A) and (B)

    E.   all of the above

_____4. Which selective process was evident when Dawson remembered information about Mercury motors which supported his attitudes and beliefs?

    A.   selective attention

    B.   selective distortion

    C.   selective retention

    D.   selective regression

    E.   selective intention

Caesar Gonzales played tennis. He had played the game since high school and now he was 50 years old. He still thought he was 25, but after three vigorous sets, he felt like 75. So 50 just about summed, or averaged, it all up. His eyes were slower in focusing and seemed not to pick up the character of opponents' shots as rapidly as they used to. He often probed for volleys, and his ground strokes were not as accurate and powerful as they once were. And he could not cover the court as quickly as he had a mere five years ago.

Caesar had all but resigned himself to his fate when he became aware of a new type of racket — an oversized, clumsy-looking instrument. He observed a few older players and inept younger players using it on the courts. At first he viewed the object with disdain; then he saw some professional players on TV using the racket. Next Caesar played a tournament match against a fellow he thought he could dispatch with ease and lost, much to his chagrin. The opponent had used an oversized racket.

After pondering these circumstances, Caesar decided to investigate the oversize tennis racket to see what it might have to offer. He had heard of the first large racket, the Prince, but he knew there were other brands and styles. Caesar looked through all the tennis magazines for ads or articles about the rackets; he visited a sporting goods store and examined several different styles and brands of oversized rackets; he talked with tennis instructors and people he saw playing with the racket.

As this point Caesar began to identify various characteristics of each racket style and brand and decided which was most important to him. Some obvious characteristics were size, weight, and price. These he had noted or speculated about from the very first time he saw an oversized racket. After investigating, he knew that other factors were equally or more important: balance, power, control, and ease of handling. Caesar concluded that he ought to try some rackets that met most of his minimum requirements, and he borrowed five from a Sporting goods store.

He had decided that to be acceptable, a racket should have a certain minimum level of power, control, and ease of handling. After playing with each racket, Caesar narrowed his choice to two. He had a slight preference for racket A, but it had a price of $235 and Caesar had only $100 to spend. Racket B was not quite as desirable but could be purchased for $99. Caesar decided to buy racket B.

As he stood in the sporting goods store making a decision, one of Caesar's friends passed by and said: "Well, old boy, are you going to buy one of these old man's rackets? I didn't know you were that old." "Just looking. Curious about these things, you know," was Caesar's reply. "Sounds fine. Give me a ride home and we'll talk about it." Caesar walked out with his friend without buying the racket.

Caesar spent the rest of the day and evening ruminating on the purchase of the racket. He could visualize the guffaws and scoffing that he would have to bear when he showed up with the giant racket. Finally he decided that the racket would improve his game more than enough to compensate for any jocularity it might generate. The next day he bought the oversized racket.

_____1. Gonzales progressed through which stages in the buying decision process?

    A.   need recognition, information search, evaluation of alternatives, purchase decision

    B.   need recognition, limited problem solving, information search, evaluation of alternatives, purchase decision

    C.   awareness, interest, evaluation, trial, adoption

    D.   need recognition, information search, purchase decision dissonance

    E.   awareness, interest, evaluation, trial, dissonance

_____2. If Gonzales did pass through the need recognition stage, at what point was it?

    A.   when he realized he could not play as well as in the past

    B.   when he lost the tournament match

    C.   when he first saw older players using the large racket

    D.   either or both (A) and (B)

    E.   none of the above

_____3. At what point did awareness of the product occur?

    A.   when he realized he could not play as well as in the past

    B.   when he lost the tournament match

    C.   when he first saw older players using the large racket

    D.   when he first saw professional players on TV using the racket

    E.   both (B) and (D)

_____4. Gonzales obtained most of his information from:

    A.   personal sources.

    B.   public sources.

    C.   commercial sources.

    D.   experimental sources.

    E.   private sources.

_____5. At what point in the decision process was Gonzales when he assigned importance weights to product attributes?

    A.   interest

    B.   information search

    C.   trial

    D.   evaluation of alternatives

    E.   consideration

_____6. The appearance of Gonzales' friend in the store:

    A.   was an unanticipated situational factor.

    B.   shifted Caesar's ideas.

    C.   altered Caesar's importance weights.

    D.   altered Caesar's beliefs about racket B.

    E.   none of the above

_____7. Gonzales postponed the purchase of the racket because:

    A.   the attitudes of others and perceived risks.

    B.   unanticipated situational factors and perceived performance.

    C.   unconfirmed expectations and situational factors.

    D.   reduced expectancy values and altered beliefs.

    E.   cognitive dissonance.

Multiple Choice Answers

1.	Correct Answer:	5	Reference:	pg. 155
2.	Correct Answer:	3	Reference:	pg. 155
3.	Correct Answer:	4	Reference:	pg. 157
4.	Correct Answer:	1	Reference:	pg. 158
5.	Correct Answer:	5	Reference:	pg. 159
6.	Correct Answer:	5	Reference:	pg. 159
7.	Correct Answer:	2	Reference:	pg. 162
8.	Correct Answer:	2	Reference:	pg. 162
9.	Correct Answer:	3	Reference:	pg. 163
10.	Correct Answer:	4	Reference:	pg. 163
11.	Correct Answer:	1	Reference:	pg. 163
12.	Correct Answer:	3	Reference:	pg. 165
13.	Correct Answer:	5	Reference:	pg. 166
14.	Correct Answer:	2	Reference:	pg. 169
15.	Correct Answer:	3	Reference:	pg. 171
16.	Correct Answer:	4	Reference:	pg. 171
17.	Correct Answer:	2	Reference:	pg. 174
18.	Correct Answer:	4	Reference:	pg. 175
19.	Correct Answer:	1	Reference:	pg. 176
20.	Correct Answer:	3	Reference:	pg. 180
21.	Correct Answer:	2	Reference:	pg. 183

22.	Correct Answer:	4	Reference:	pg. 184
23.	Correct Answer:	1	Reference:	pg. 184
24.	Correct Answer:	3	Reference:	pg. 163
25.	Correct Answer:	5	Reference:	pg. 162
26.	Correct Answer:	3	Reference:	pg. 180
27.	Correct Answer:	2	Reference:	pg. 181
28.	Correct Answer:	1	Reference:	pg. 183
29.	Correct Answer:	3	Reference:	pg. 184
30.	Correct Answer:	5	Reference:	pg. 184

True/False Answers

1.	FALSE	Reference:	pg. 155	Topic: Model of Consumer Behaviour
2.	TRUE	Reference:	pg. 156	Topic: Cultural Factors
3.	FALSE	Reference:	pg. 157	Topic: Culture
4.	FALSE	Reference:	pg. 158	Topic: Subculture
5.	TRUE	Reference:	pg. 159	Topic: Subculture
6.	FALSE	Reference:	pg. 161	Topic: Subculture
7.	FALSE	Reference:	pg. 163	Topic: Social Class
8.	TRUE	Reference:	pg. 163	Topic: Groups
9	FALSE	Reference:	pg. 164	Topic: Family
10.	FALSE	Reference:	pg. 168	Topic: Personality and Self-Concept
11.	FALSE	Reference:	pg. 172	Topic: Learning
12.	TRUE	Reference:	pg. 172	Topic: Beliefs and Attitudes
13.	TRUE	Reference:	pg. 176	Topic: The Buyer Decision

14.	FALSE	Reference:	pg. 178	Topic:	Information Search
15.	TRUE	Reference:	pg. 179	Topic:	Evaluation of Alternatives
16.	FALSE	Reference:	pg. 180	Topic:	Purchase Decision
17.	FALSE	Reference:	pg. 186	Topic:	Consumer Behaviour Across International Borders
18.	FALSE	Reference:	pg. 162	Topic:	Table 5-2
19.	TRUE	Reference:	pg. 166	Topic:	Lifestyle
20.	TRUE	Reference:	pg. 169	Topic:	Motivation

Applying Terms and Concepts Answers

<u>Case #1</u>   <u>Line Haul Jeans:</u>

Question #1
- Product   -   The jeans
- Place   -   STOP 55 Truck Stops where they are sold
- Price   - $39.95
- Promotion -   The advertisement in *Overdrive Magazine*

Question #2
- Primary Group

Question #3
- Physiological need for comfort and social need for belongingness and the need to identify with his fellow truckers

Question #4
- Selective retention

Question #5
- Learning
- Changes in an individual's behaviour arising from experience

<u>Case #2</u>   <u>Product Placement in Movies:</u>

Question #1
- People are watching a movie, and realize that they need the product
- If the movie is enjoyable, they will be in a good mood and therefore actually act on the need impulse

Question #2
- The information may be provided in the context of the movie, Happy Gilmore tells the audience why he likes subway
- However, most products are just displayed and no information about them is given

Question #3
- The more people see their products in the movies, the more they are content with the purchase, therefore this reinforces their buying behaviour and decisions

Question #4
- No real learning takes place with product placement, instead motivation to purchase the product may occur
- Beliefs and attitudes may also be formed depending on the extent to which the product is displayed in the movie

Question #5
- Habitual buying behaviour like soft drinks, junk food and fast food items
Non-complex items are also frequently used in this type of advertising medium

Case #3	The Dawsons
1.	A
2.	A
3.	E
4.	C

Case #4	Caesar Gonzales
1.	A
2.	D
3.	C
4.	C
5.	D
6.	A
7.	A

Chapter 6

Business Markets and Business Buyer Behaviour

Chapter Overview

Business markets and consumer markets are alike in some key ways. For example, both include people in buying roles who make purchase decisions to satisfy needs. Business markets, however, differ in many ways from consumer markets. For one thing, the business market is enormous, far larger than the consumer market. Within Canada alone, the business market includes more than one million organizations that annually purchase billions of dollars worth of goods and services.

Chapter Objectives

1. Define the business market and explain how business markets differ from consumer markets.
2. Identify the major factors that influence business buyer behaviour.
3. List and define the steps in the business buying-decision process
4. Compare the institutional and government markets and explain how institutional and government buyers make their buying decisions.

Chapter Topics

Business Markets
- Characteristics of Business Markets
    - Market Structure and Demand
    - Nature of the Buying Unit
    - Types of Decisions and the Decision Process
- Model of Business Buyer Behaviour

Business Buyer Behaviour
- Major Types of Buying Situations
- Participants in the Business Buying Process
- Major Influences on Business Buyers
    - Environmental Factors
    - Organizational Factors

- Interpersonal Factors
- Individual Factors
- The Business Buying Process
  - Problem Recognition
  - General Need Description
  - Product Specification
  - Supplier Search
  - Proposal Solicitation
  - Supplier Selection
  - Order-Routine Specification
  - Performance Review

Institutional and Government Markets
- Institutional Markets
- Government Markets

Chapter Summary

1.   How business markets differ from consumer markets.

Main differences include market structure and demand, nature of the buying unity, and types of decisions and decision processes. Business markets are geographically concentrated and have derived, inelastic, and fluctuating demand. Buying is more professional and involves more people. Decisions are more professional and involve more people. Decisions are more complex, more formalized, and the buyer and seller are more dependent upon one another.

2.   The major factors that influence business buyer behaviour.

There are four major influences. Environmental elements are level of primary demand, economic outlook, cost of money, supply conditions, technological change, political/regulatory change, competitive developments. Organizational elements are authority, status, empathy, and persuasiveness. Individual elements are age, education, job position, personality, and risk attitudes.

3.   The stages in the business buying decision process, and their definitions.

Stages include problem recognition, general need description, product specification, supplier search, proposal solicitation, supplier selection, order routine specification, performance review.

4.   The three major types of buying situations.

Straight rebuy is a reorder without any modifications. A modified rebuy involves some changes in product specifications, prices, terms, and suppliers. New task buying occurs when a company buys a product or service for the first time. In such cases, greater risk or cost will lead to a larger number of decision participants and a greater information search effort.

5.   The unique aspects of how institutional and government buyers make their buying decisions.

Institutional buyers are schools, hospitals, prisons and other organizations. Many institutions have low budgets and captive patrons. Government buying may be coordinated by a special agency and the buying process may be scrutinized by various publics. Governments may be influenced by non-economic decision criteria. Government buying practices can be complex, have too much paperwork, bureaucracy, regulation, low prices, and other factors.

Key Terms

Business markets   (pg. 199)
Business buying process   (pg. 199)
Buyers   (pg. 204)
Buying centre (pg. 204)
Deciders   (pg. 204)
Derived demand   (pg. 200)
Gatekeepers   (pg. 204)
General need description   (pg. 210)
Government market   (pg. 214)
Influencers   (pg. 204)
Institutional market   (pg. 214)
Modified rebuy   (pg. 203)

New Task   (pg. 203)
Order-routine specification   (pg. 212)
Performance review   (pg. 212)
Problem recognition   (pg. 209)
Product specification   (pg. 210)
Proposal solicitation   (pg. 211)
Straight rebuy   (pg. 203)
Supplier search   (pg. 210)
Supplier selection   (pg. 211)
Systems buying   (pg. 203)
Users   (pg. 204)
Value Analysis   (pg. 210)

Multiple Choice Questions

6-1   Multiple

Business buying involves a more professional purchasing effort in which of the following areas?

1.   Marketing structure and demand
2.   Nature of the buying unit
3.   Types of decisions
4.   The decision process
5.   None of the above

6-2   Multiple

A drop in the price of leather will not cause shoe manufacturers to buy more leather. This is considered what type of demand structure?

1.   Inelastic
2.   Elastic
3.   Fluctuating
4.   Stagnating
5.   Indifferent

6-3   Multiple

The business buying process tends to be more formal than the consumer buying process. Large business purchases require all the following except:

1.   Detailed product specification
2.   Written purchase orders
3.   Careful supplier searches
4.   Formal approval
5.   All of the above

6-4   Multiple

Buying centres and buying decisions in a business are influenced by the following forces except:

1.   Internal organizational
2.   Interpersonal
3.   Intrapersonal
4.   Individual
5.   External environment

6-5   Multiple

There are four major questions in the business buyer behaviour model. These questions include all the following except:

1.   What buying decisions do business buyers make?
2.   Who participates in the buying process?
3.   What are the major influences on buyers?
4.   Who are the buyers responsible to in the buying process?
5.   How do business buyers make their buying decisions?

6-6   Multiple

In which of the following do the "In" suppliers try to maintain product and service quality?

1.   Straight rebuy
2.   Modified rebuy
3.   New task buying
4.   Systems buying
5.   All of the above

6-7   Multiple

In a new task buying situation, a buyer must concentrate on all the following issues except:

1.   Product specifications
2.   Price limits
3.   Payment terms
4.   Order quantities
5.   All of the above

6-8   Multiple

Teresa works at a cross stitching shop where she provides her patrons with the specifications on different patterns and gives out information to help her customers evaluate alternatives. Teresa is considered a (n):

1.   User
2.   Influencer
3.   Buyer
4.   Decider
5.   Gatekeeper

6-9   Multiple

Many international companies participate in business buying. In a recent study _____ was found to have the highest amount of team buying – there was more than one person involved in each purchase decision.

1.   United States
2.   Canada
3.   France
4.   Sweden
5.   Germany

6-10   Multiple

Business buyers are heavily influenced by factors in the current and expected economic environment. These factors include all the following except:

1.   Level of primary demand
2.   Economic outlook
3.   Level of secondary demand
4.   The cost of money
5.   All of the above

6-11   Multiple

Wanda works as a purchasing agent for Motorola. The company has been moving towards _____ as Wanda is dealing with fewer, and higher level buyers. She believes this system is much easier to work with and helps the company save money.

1.   Centralized buying
2.   Upgraded purchasing
3.   National account sales force
4.   Electronic data interchange
5.   Long-term contracts

6-12   Multiple

Just-in-time production has grown in recent years as companies realize the great effects it has on profitability. Just-in-time production encompasses all the following concepts except:

1.   Vendor-managed inventory systems
2.   Value analysis
3.   Total quality management
4.   Flexible manufacturing
5.   Employee self-management

6-13   Multiple

Jacinta has worked for Maple Rock Foods for over a year. Maple Rock Foods has had a bad year and they need a change. The CEO has suggested the purchasing department streamlines its activities, or look to new solutions. All the following would be stages of the buying process for Jacinta in this new task buy except:

1.   General need description
2.   Supplier search
3.   Proposal solicitation
4.   Order routine specification
5.   All of the above

6-14   Multiple

Che Lau has operated his own potting business for the last 5 years. He has established very good relations with a major supplier of peat moss and potting soil. There are relatively few changes in his orders as this purchase is considered a straight rebuy. From the following, which stage must Che Lau perform every time?

1.   Product specification
2.   Problem recognition
3.   Proposal solicitation
4.   General need description
5.   None of the above

6-15   Multiple

Choosing a supplier is a long and tedious process, however, finding the right supplier provides tremendous benefits. There are many important characteristics to look for in a supplier. Which of the following is NOT considered to be among these characteristics?

1.   Quality products and service
2.   Reasonable prices
3.   On-time delivery
4.   Ethical corporate behaviour
5.   Honest communication

6-16   Multiple

Among the primary factors helping a company choose the correct supplier, there are also secondary factors, which could be just as important. Which of the following characteristics is not an important secondary factor?

1.   Repair and servicing capabilities
2.   Technical aid and advice
3.   Presence of an EDI system
4.   Performance history
5.   All of the above are important

6-17   Multiple

Institutional markets are different from business and consumer markets in many ways. All the following are considered institutional markets except:

1.   Schools
2.   Hospitals
3.   Prisons
4.   Recreational facilities
5.   Nursing homes

6-18   Multiple

Dealing with the government can be a long drawn-out process. There are many people involved and unless the business seller knows the following, except _____ they may not be successful.

1.   Be able to locate the key decision makers
2.   Identify the factors that affect buying behaviour
3.   Knows someone in the government who can help them build a relationship with the buyers
4.   Understand the buying decision process
5.   All of the above are helpful and necessary

6-19   Multiple

Governments require companies to submit bids for their proposals and projects, and then select the lowest bidder. However, governments sometimes buy on a negotiated contract basis if all the following are true except:

1.   Major R&D costs are involved
2.   There is high risk
3.   In cases where little competition exists
4.   It is a straight rebuy situation
5.   All of the above would qualify for a negotiated contract

6-20   Multiple

Although the government is quite a different business entity than "private" business, their buyers are affected by the same factors as consumer and business buyers. These factors include all the following except:

1.   Political
2.   Environmental
3.   Organizational
4.   Interpersonal
5.   Individual

6-21   Multiple

As stated before, government is usually different from "private" companies. Examples of issues businesses have in dealing with the government include all the following except:

1.   Bureaucracy
2.   Regulations
3.   Rapid decision marking
4.   Frequent shifts in procurement personnel
5.   All of the above

6-22   Multiple

Sellers and buyers can use _____ as a tool to help secure a new contract.

1.   General need description
2.   Product specification
3.   Value analysis
4.   Product analysis
5.   None of the above

6-23   Multiple

Terrence and Phillip have worked as Wal-Mart buyers for the past 2 years. They graduated from university together and underwent their company training together. They are both good friends and accomplished buyers. Their style of buying is slightly different however. Terrence is very in-depth in his analysis of proposals, while Phillip is more interested in the relationship aspect of the proposal. These differences can be attributed to:

1.   Interpersonal factors
2.   Organizational factors
3.   Environmental factors
4.   Individual factors
5.   None of the above

6-24   Multiple

The buying centre is a fundamental part of the business buying process. One role not found in the buying centre is:

1.   Users
2.   Gatekeepers
3.   Infuencers
4.   Buyers
5.   All roles are found in the buying centre

6-25   Multiple

All the following are differences in market structure and demand between consumer and business markets except:

1.   Business markets are more geographically concentrated
2.   Business markets have fewer numbers of buyers
3.   Business markets have derived demand
4.   Business markets have more elastic demand
5.   All of the above are true

6-26   Multiple

When consumer demand increased slightly, but leads to a large increase in business market demand, we can say that the business market is experiencing:

1.   Fluctuating demand
2.   Geographic demand
3.   Elastic demand
4.   Inelastic demand
5.   Offsetting demand

6-27   Multiple

Which of the following statements about buying centres is/are true?

1.   The buying centre is not a fixed and formally identified unit within the buying organization
2.   Buying centre roles can be assumed by different people for different purchases
3.   In some cases, one person may assume all the buying centre roles
4.   Only 1 and 2
5.   All of the above

6-28   Multiple

Factors such as supplier reputation for repair and servicing capabilities are important criteria for evaluation at which stage in the business buying decision process?

1.   Problem recognition
2.   Supplier selection
3.   Product specification
4.   Value analysis
5.   Proposal solicitation

6-29   Multiple

From your knowledge of buying situations, which two stages of the business buying process can always be expected to be completed for new task, modified rebuy, and straight rebuy?

1.   Problem recognition and product specification
2.   General need description and proposal solicitation
3.   Product specification and performance review
4.   General need description and supplier selection
5.   Problem recognition and supplier selection

6-30   Multiple

Gina is the Executive Assistant to Ang Lee, Vice President of Purchasing for Radenko Industries. Gina fills which buying centre role?

1.   Gatekeeper
2.   Influencer
3.   Buyer
4.   Decider
5.   User

True/False Questions

6-1   True/False

Business markets are much larger than consumer markets.

6-2   True/False

Business demand is desired demand.

6-3   True/False

Business marketers may roll up their sleeves and work closely with their customers during all stages of the buying process.

6-4   True/False

The greater the cost or risk, the fewer the number of participants involved in the decision process.

6-5   True/False

Systems selling is a key business marketing strategy for holding accounts, but it is not successful for winning accounts.

6-6   True/False

Purchasing agents often have the authority to prevent salespersons from seeing users of deciders.

6-7   True/False

The buying centre is a fixed and formally identified unit within the buying organization.

6-8   True/False

A buying centre is only composed of people from one firm.

6-9   True/False

Business buyers actually respond to both economic and personal factors.

158

6-10   True/False

When competing products differ greatly, business buyers are more accountable for their choices and pay more attention to economic factors.

6-11   True/False

Business buyers are increasingly seeking short-term contracts with suppliers.

6-12   True/False

In advertising to business customer, marketers often alert customers to potential problems, and show how their products provide solutions.

6-13   True/False

A supplier's primary task is to get listed in major buying directories, and a secondary task is to build a good reputation in the marketplace.

6-14   True/False

Many buyers prefer to limit their numbers of suppliers to ensure high-quality, and reliable service. They are reluctant to increase suppliers because the risks outweigh the benefits.

6-15   True/False

Blankct contracting leads to more single-source buying and to buying more items from that source.

6-16   True/False

Low budgets and captive patrons characterize many institutional markets.

6-17   True/False

Although institutional marketers have special needs, many marketers use the same divisions to meet the special characteristics and needs of institutional buyers.

6-18   True/False

Government organizations are not concerned with the issue of domestic or foreign supplier. Their major concern is the lowest bid.

6-19   True/False

On an open-bid basis, advertising and personal selling makes no difference in winning a bid.

6-20   True/False

By showing buyers a better way to make an object, outside sellers can turn a straight rebuy situation into a new task situation.

Applying Terms and Concepts

To determine how well you understand the materials in this chapter, read each of the following brief cases and then respond to the questions that follow. Answers are given at the end of this chapter.

Case #1   Trade Shows

Tradeshows are increasingly popular in the business market industry. Tradeshows are places where businesses go to see all the products and companies that could help manufacture their products, supply them with products, or sell their products. Participants in tradeshows have an advantage in that the attendees are there looking for something. For example, a home renovations tradeshow attracts potential customers who want to renovate their homes, but it will also attract many retailers and wholesalers to the show, because they are looking to stock their shelves with the latest products. Many large companies buy all their merchandise for the upcoming year at tradeshows; therefore they are a very powerful marketing opportunity for businesses.

1.   List three ways on which a tradeshow could capitalize on the characteristics of a business market.

_____

_____

_____

2.   What types of buying situations can be found at a tradeshow?

_____

_____

_____

3.   Which members of a buying centre would you expect to attend a tradeshow?

_____

_____

_____

_____

4. Which steps of the business buying process would you expect a tradeshow to influence?

_____

_____

_____

_____

5. Do you believe a tradeshow is a viable and profitable way for business markets to sell their products?

_____

_____

_____

_____

Case #2   Buffalo Express[1]

Darin Cosentino, executive vice-president of Buffalo Express, recently completed negotiations with the Black Eagle Paper Company of Montreal, Quebec, to be the exclusive transportation company moving Black eagle newsprint roll paper into the United States.

Buffalo could easily handle the projected annual volume of 50,000 tonnes with its current fleet of trailers; however, Cosentino believed a special trailer might better haul this high-density, high-weight freight. He authorized Eric Moore, director of operations, to organize a committee to investigate the problem.

Moore's committee posed the problem to representatives of the major trailer manufacturers, including Fruehauf, Intercontinental Truck body, Great Dane, and Trailmobile. Buffalo has purchased hundreds of trailers from each of these manufacturers in building its fleet of 1,500 trailers, but this was the first time it wanted a manufacturer to modify its product specification to meet the needs of a single shipper.

Each manufacturer supplied a written proposal for the project, with most simply offering their standard trailer with a reinforced frame to handle the weight. Intercontinental, however, sent a sales representative who presented information on a unique trailer design called the Wedge. The Wedge was similar to a standard trailer, with two important differences: first, the front of the trailer was 20 cm lower than the rear; and second, instead of traditional rectangular shape, the sides of the trailer in the front were slightly tapered to form a less blunt front end--hence the name Wedge.

---

[1] *Principles of Marketing*, 3rd Edition, Kotler, Armstrong, Warren (Prentice Hall) – pg. 115.

The trailer was in compliance with Transport Canada Regulations, specifying a length of no more than 15 metres of a width exceeding 3 metres. The Wedge with a reinforced frame could easily carry the 20,000-22,000 kg load without difficulty. Additionally, the aerodynamics of the Wedge was projected to decrease fuel consumption by 1 litre per 100 km.

Moore's committee reviewed each manufacturer's proposal regarding trailer design, capacity, price, delivery date, warranty, and construction. After some deliberation, the contract for 25 trailers was awarded to Intercontinental.

1. What type of buying situation did Buffalo create with Intercontinental and why?

_____

_____

_____

_____

2. The demand for trailers was based on the demand for roll paper, which in turn was based on the consumer demand for newspapers. What type of demand is exemplified by the demand for trailers and roll paper and why?

_____

_____

_____

_____

3. What is the main type of influence on business buying illustrated in Buffalo's business decision to haul Black Eagle's paper? Why?

_____

_____

_____

4. What other types of influences or factors did the buying committee respond to?

_____

_____

_____

_____

5.   Why was personal selling important in this case?

_____

_____

_____

_____

Case #3   For McMurray Community College

McMurray Community College is one of seven community colleges in Alberta. Located in the city of Fort McMurray, it is a two-year school which offers degrees in variety of programs including business administration, engineering science, mathematics, liberal arts, the natural sciences, and telecommunications. The college also offers certificates in the occupational trades of industrial electricity, automotive mechanics, industrial machining, and drafting.

Carl Palmer, the coordinator of occupational education at the college was faced with the need to acquire two additional vertical milling machines for the industrial machining program in which there had been a substantial increase in enrollment in recent years. After consulting with Vincent Barone, the dean of instruction, the administration decided that the college would apply for a provincial grant, which if received, would allow the college to purchase the machine tools.

Since the college had not purchased such equipment since 1989, an ad hoc committee was formed to gather the appropriate information and write the grant proposal. The committee was composed of Palmer, Michael Whyte, an instructor of industrial machining, and Lisa Klein, the college's assistant business manager. In gathering information the committee met with the department's advisory council, made up of area employers, to learn their opinions as to which makes and models of machine tools were used in their machine shops and which might meet the college's needs. The committee also attended the Northwestern Tool Show held in Seattle, Washington, where members spoke with manufacturers' representatives and also gathered brochures on various pieces of equipment.

The committee learned that a general price increase of 10 percent was expected by most manufacturers on February 1. The committee realized it Would not receive final notification of the grant until April 1, but decided that the price increase would not affect the decision to purchase any equipment, even if additional funds had to come from the college.

The committee applied for the grant and also developed the set of specifications for the milling machine that would meet the school's needs. The specification sheets indicated that the firm awarded the contract must supply a machine equal to or better than a Bridgeport series one vertical mill, with the college reserving the right to reject any or all bids. The specification sheets, which also stipulated that the machines must be delivered and set up at the college by August 1, were then distributed to all interested parties that had responded to the invitation to bid notice placed in area newspapers.

Supplier	Manufacturer	Price per Machine (CDN)
Langley Brothers	Jet	$12,995
J and B Industrial Supply	Bridgeport	16,750
Belros Corporation	Enterprise	13,750
Yukon Supply	Bridgeport	16,250
U. T. A.	Savrin	14,950

After careful consideration, the committee rejected the Jet, Enterprise, and Savrin milling machines as not meeting specifications. The committee awarded the bid to Yukon Supply.

_____1. Identify the type of demand faced by Fort McMurray Community College when it decided to place an order for the two milling machines after the price was scheduled to increase.

    A.   derived demand

    B.   inelastic demand

    C.   latent demand

    D.   full demand

    E.   elastic demand

_____2. Identify the type of demand faced by Fort McMurray Community College when it made a decision to purchase two additional milling machines due to an increase in enrollment in the machine trades program.

    A.   derived demand

    B.   inelastic demand

    C.   latent demand

    D.   full demand

    E.   elastic demand

_____3. The buying process used by Fort McMurray Community College is an example of _____ buying.

    A.   value analysis

    B.   negotiated contract

    C.   open bid

    D.   open-to-buy

    E.   top-down

_____4. Identify the type of buying situation faced by Fort McMurray Community College. Provide justification for your answer.

Case #4:   Quality Croutons

Ray Kroc, the founder of McDonald's, as we know it, believed in sharing his good fortune — not only with his employees, stockholders, and store owners, but also with his suppliers. As McDonald's grew, so too did the company's need for organizations to supply it with food, paper products, and equipment.

It might have been natural for McDonald's to acquire control of their various suppliers to ensure consistency and dependability. As McDonald's expanded horizontally, they could have grown vertically as well. But Ray Kroc did not want it that way. Instead, he chose to use outside suppliers of the needed products and services. McDonald's requires some products to be made to their specifications, but other items they purchase are the same as those available in a local supermarket.

Many of the McDonald's suppliers are internationally known companies such as Tyson, Kraft, Hunt's, Gortons, Coca Cola, Sara Lee, Vlasic, and McCormick. Others are very small operations whose major business — and in some cases, survival — is dependent upon McDonald's. One such firm is Quality Croutons, based in Chicago, Illinois. Quality Croutons supplies approximately 80 percent of the croutons used in McDonald's salads.

George Johnson and David Moore were contacted by the Business Development Group of McDonald's to set up the business. McDonald's was interested in having a minority-owned company supply their croutons. Backed by McDonald's, Johnson and Moore had little trouble arranging the needed financing to start the company, even though neither man had any expertise in the banking business. Although McDonald's is still the company's major customer, Quality Croutons has supplied a variety of other firms since their organization in 1986.

Interestingly, many suppliers conduct business with McDonald's on nothing more than a handshake. Suppliers' products are monitored for consistency through periodic inspection, and if the desired quality is lacking, the agreement can be terminated. But if quality is maintained, so is the relationship. The fact that agreements aren't terminated very often is a testament not only to the careful selection of suppliers by McDonald's but also to their genuine desire to have relationships succeed. If, for example, a supplier is experiencing difficulty providing McDonald's with the proper volume of a high-quality product, McDonald's management will work with the supplier to correct the problem rather than simply drop them.

Obviously, the choice of a particular supplier is most critical. Supplier selection involves the senior vice president/chief purchasing officer, the director of purchasing, and other members of management, including representatives from research and development and the business development group. Occasionally, McDonald's chooses suppliers who have sought out a business relationship with them; at other times, McDonald's seeks out existing companies that are in a position to become suppliers. If a suitable existing firm cannot be found, McDonald's will help entrepreneurs establish a business, as they did with Quality Croutons, to provide them with their needed products and services.

1. Explain the concept of derived demand as it applies to Quality Croutons and McDonald's.

_____

_____

_____

_____

2. Explain the concept of inelastic demand as it applies to McDonald's buying of croutons.

_____

_____

_____

_____

Source: John B. Clark. *Marketing Today: Successes, Failures and Turnarounds.* 2nd Edition, Prentice Hall, 1991. ABC News Business World Broadcast, 3/12/89.

Multiple Choice Answers

1.	Correct Answer:	2	Reference:	pg. 200
2.	Correct Answer:	1	Reference:	pg. 200
3.	Correct Answer:	5	Reference:	pg. 201
4.	Correct Answer:	3	Reference:	pg. 202
5.	Correct Answer:	4	Reference:	pg. 203
6.	Correct Answer:	1	Reference:	pg. 203
7.	Correct Answer:	5	Reference:	pg. 203
8.	Correct Answer:	2	Reference:	pg. 204
9.	Correct Answer:	4	Reference:	pg. 205
10.	Correct Answer:	3	Reference:	pg. 206
11.	Correct Answer:	1	Reference:	pg. 206
12.	Correct Answer:	5	Reference:	pg. 208
13.	Correct Answer:	5	Reference:	pg. 210 (Table 6-2)
14.	Correct Answer:	1	Reference:	pg. 210 (Table 6-2)
15.	Correct Answer:	2	Reference:	pg. 211
16.	Correct Answer:	5	Reference:	pg. 211
17.	Correct Answer:	4	Reference:	pg. 214
18.	Correct Answer;	3	Reference:	pg. 214
19.	Correct Answer:	4	Reference:	pg. 214
20.	Correct Answer:	1	Reference:	pg. 215
21.	Correct Answer:	3	Reference:	pg. 215

22.	Correct Answer:	3	Reference:	pg. 210
23.	Correct Answer:	4	Reference:	pg. 209
24.	Correct Answer:	5	Reference:	pg. 204
25.	Correct Answer:	4	Reference:	pg. 200
26.	Correct Answer:	1	Reference:	pg. 200
27.	Correct Answer:	5	Reference:	pg. 204
28.	Correct Answer:	2	Reference:	pg. 211
29.	Correct Answer:	3	Reference:	pg. 210
30.	Correct Answer:	1	Reference:	pg. 204

True/False Answers

1.   TRUE   Reference: pg. 199   Topic: Business Markets

2.   FALSE   Reference: pg. 200   Topic: Market Structure and Demand

3.   TRUE   Reference: pg. 201   Topic: Types of Decisions and the Decision Process

4.   FALSE   Reference: pg. 203   Topic: Major Types of Buying Situations

5.   FALSE   Reference: pg. 204   Topic: Major Types of Buying Situations

6.   TRUE   Reference: pg. 204   Topic: Participants in the Business Buying Process

7.   FALSE   Reference: pg. 204   Topic: Participants in the Business Buying Process

8.   FALSE   Reference: pg. 205   Topic: Participants in the Business Buying Process

9.   TRUE   Reference: pg. 206   Topic: Major Influences on Business Buyers

10.   TRUE   Reference: pg. 206   Topic: Major Influences on Business Buyers

11.   FALSE   Reference: pg. 208   Topic: Organizational Factors

12.   TRUE   Reference: pg. 210   Topic: Problem Recognition

13.   FALSE   Reference: pg. 210   Topic: Supplier Search

14.   FALSE   Reference: pg. 211   Topic: Supplier Selection

15.   TRUE   Reference: pg. 212   Topic: Order-Routine Specification

16.   TRUE   Reference: pg. 214   Topic: Institutional Markets

17.   FALSE   Reference: pg. 214   Topic: Institutional Markets

18.   FALSE   Reference: pg. 214   Topic: Government Markets

19.   TRUE   Reference: pg. 215   Topic: Government Markets

20.   TRUE   Reference: pg. 210   Topic: Product Specification

Applying Terms and Concepts Answers

<u>Case #1</u>   <u>Tradeshows:</u>

Question #1
- Business customers are more geographically centred, therefore attending a tradeshow in a good location, could be very successful for a company
- Business purchasing involves more buyers, therefore many buyers will attend tradeshows and more sales will be completed
- Business buyers often buy directly from producers, which is the whole idea of a tradeshow

Question #2
- Straight rebuy
- Modified rebuy
- New task
- System buying

Question #3
- Users
- Influencers
- Buyers
- Deciders

Question #4
- Problem recognition
- Product specification
- Supplier search
- Proposal solicitation
- Supplier selection
- Order-routine specification

<u>Case #2</u>   <u>Buffalo Express:</u>

Question #1
- Buffalo created a modified rebuy situation because they wanted to modify product specifications before their purchase.

Question #2
- Derived demand is exemplified as the business demand ultimately comes from the demand for consumer goods.
- Consumer purchases drive the need to produce and/or deliver the product.

Question #3
- The organizational influence on business buying is illustrated because Buffalo's decision to contract with Intercontinental was based on their client's needs as well as their suppliers capacities.
- The buying committee had their own organizational objectives to fulfill.

Question #4
- Economic
- Environmental (regulations and laws)

Question #5
- Personal selling was imperative in this case because it was what distinguished Intercontinental from its competitors.

The Wedge product along with personal selling persuaded the buying committee that the Wedge was the trailer best suited for their purposes.

Fort McMurray Community College

1.   B

2.   A

3.   C

4.   The administrative and instructional staff of Fort McMurray Community College faced a purchasing decision that involved the gathering of considerable information from a variety of sources. This information included machine manufacturers' distributors, machine specification and capabilities, delivery dates, prices, machine setup, and so on. The buying process was conducted over several months. Also, the college had not purchased such a machine in some years and was unlikely to purchase additional machinery in the near future. Therefore, although this approximated the new-task buying process used by business firms, technically, Fort McMurray Community College used the open bid buying process.

<u>Quality Croutons</u>

1.   Derived demand means that the demand for the organizational product — in this case croutons — comes from the consumer demand for salads with various toppings. In essence if there was no demand for salads in McDonald's Restaurants, there would be no demand for croutons.

2.   Total demand for croutons is not much affected by price changes, especially in the short run. A drop in the price of croutons due to lower material costs, improved productivity though automation or improved distribution facilities is not likely to result in McDonald's purchasing much more. McDonald's buys what they need to meet consumer demand. If several suppliers were used and one became a lower cost supplier, McDonald's might shift buying among the suppliers, but total crouton purchases by McDonald's would remain approximately the same.

Chapter 7

Market Segmentation, Targeting, and positioning for Competitive Advantage

Chapter Overview

Organizations selling to consumer and business markets recognize that they cannot appeal to all buyers in those markets or at least not to all buyers in the same way. Buyers are too numerous, too widely scattered and too varied in their needs and buying practices. Therefore, most companies are moving away from mass marketing. Instead they practice target marketing- identifying market segments, selecting one or more of them, and developing products and marketing mixes tailored to each. In this way, sellers can develop the right product for each target market and adjust their prices, distribution channels, and advertising to reach the target markets efficiently.

Chapter Objectives

1. Define the three steps of target marketing: market segmentation, market targeting, and market positioning.
2. List and discuss the major levels of market segmentation and bases for segmenting consumer and business markets.
3. Explain how companies identify attractive market segments and choose a market-coverage strategy.
4. Explain how companies can position their products for maximum competitive advantage in the marketplace.

175

Chapter Topics

Markets

Market Segmentation
- Levels of Market Segmentation
    - Mass Marketing
    - Segment Marketing
    - Niche Marketing
    - Micromarketing
- Bases for Segmenting Consumer Markets
    - Geographic Segmentation
    - Demographic Segmentation
        - Age and Life-Cycle Stage
        - Gender
        - Income
    - Psychographic Segmentation
        - Social Class
        - Lifestyle
        - Personality
    - Behavioural Segmentation
        - Occasions
        - Benefits Sought
        - User Status
        - Usage Rate
        - Loyalty Status
    - Using Multiple Segmentation Bases
- Segmenting Business Markets
- Segmenting International Markets
- Requirements for Effective Segmentation

Market Targeting
- Evaluating Market Segments
    - Segment Size and Growth
    - Segment Structural Attractiveness
    - Company Objectives and Resources
- Selecting Market Segments
    - Undifferentiated Marketing
    - Differentiated Marketing
    - Concentrated Marketing
    - Choosing a Market-Coverage Strategy

Positioning for Competitive Advantage
- Positioning Strategies
- Choosing and Implementing a Positioning Strategy
    - Identifying Possible Competitive Advantages
        - Product Differentiation
        - Services Differentiation
        - Personnel Differentiation
        - Image Differentiation
    - Selecting the Right Competitive Advantages
        - How Many Differences to Promote
        - Which Differences to Promote
    - Communicating and Delivering the Chosen Position

Chapter Summary

1.   The definitions of market segmentation, market targeting, and market positioning.

Market segmentation is the process of dividing a market into distinct groups of buyers with different needs, characteristics, or behaviour who might require separate products or marketing mixes. Market targeting is evaluating each segment's attractiveness and deciding which segments to enter. Market positioning is the setting of the competitive position and creating a detailed marketing mix.

2.   The major bases for segmenting consumer and business markets.

The major bases for segmenting consumer markets are geographic, demographic, psychographic, and behavioural. The major bases for segmenting business markets are demographics, operating variables, purchasing approaches, situational factors, and personal characteristics.

3.   How companies identify attractive market segments and choose a market-coverage strategy.

Segment attractiveness depends upon desirable segment size and growth, current and potential competitors, threat of substitutes, power of buyers, and the power of suppliers. Market-coverage can include undifferentiated, differentiated, and concentrated strategies.

4.   The four characteristics of effective market segmentation.

Market segments must have measurability (in terms of size, purchasing power, and clear profiles), accessibility (can be effectively reached and served), substantiality (large or profitable enough), and actionability (can design programs for attracting customers effectively).

5.   How companies can position their products for maximum competitive advantages in the marketplace.

Competitive advantage (Porter) offers consumers a superior value for the price. Differentiation is the key to competitive advantage. A product's position is the view customers have of its value. Positions can be differentiated by product attributes, services, personnel, or image characteristics.

Key Terms

Age and life-cycle segmentation (pg. 234)

Behavioural segmentation   (pg. 234)

Benefit segmentation   (pg. 235)

Competitive advantage   (pg. 248)

Concentrated marketing   (pg. 246)

Demographic segmentation   (pg. 230)

Differentiated marketing   (pg. 245)

Gender segmentation (pg. 232)

Geographic segmentation   (pg. 230)

Income segmentation (pg. 233)

Individual marketing (pg. 227)

Intermarket segmentation   (pg. 240)

Local marketing   (pg. 227)

Market positioning   (pg. 225)

Market segmentation (pg. 225)

Market targeting   (pg. 225)

Micromarketing   (pg. 227)

Niche marketing   (pg. 226)

Occasion segmentation   (pg. 234)

Product position   (pg. 247)

Psychographic segmentation (pg. 233)

Segment marketing   (pg. 226)

Target market (pg. 242)

Undifferentiated marketing   (pg. 242)

178

Multiple Choice Questions

7-1   Multiple

Sprite has begun a new marketing campaign to attract the world's youth to their product. They are focusing on being individual and drinking something because you want to drink it, not because somebody tells you to. Sprite is practising:

1.   Market segmentation
2.   Market targeting
3.   Target marketing
4.   Market positioning
5.   Direct targeting

7-2   Multiple

Markets consist of many different buyers and these buyers differ in many different ways. Which of the following would not be considered a buyer difference?

1.   Needs
2.   Wants
3.   Locations
4.   Buying attitudes
5.   All of the above

7-3   Multiple

When Coca-Cola first came into the market, they tried to promote their drink to every one hoping it would be enough to gain reasonable market share. This type of promotional strategy is considered:

1.   Niche marketing
2.   Segment marketing
3.   Macromarketing
4.   Mass marketing
5.   Micromarketing

7-4   Multiple

Wal-Mart and Sears have similar merchandise in their stores; however, they do not sell or promote snowblowers in Texas and they do not sell lawn mowers in Canada in January. This type of marketing would be considered:

1.   Niche marketing
2.   Segmented marketing
3.   Macromarketing
4.   Mass marketing
5.   Micromarketing

7-5   Multiple

Mass customization is the ability to prepare on a mass basis individually designed products and communication to meet each customer's requirements. All the following help the progress of mass customization except:

1.   Detailed databases
2.   Call display
3.   Robotics production
4.   E-mail
5.   Internet

7-6   Multiple

Consumer markets can be segmented in various ways. The population density distribution of an area, urban, suburban and rural, is classified as which of the following?

1.   Geographic
2.   Demographic
3.   Psychographic
4.   Behavioural
5.   1 and 2

7-7   Multiple

Samia comes from a large family. She has 4 brothers and 2 sisters. It was quite difficult for her to really express herself in such an environment. Through her childhood she learned to fend for herself and to really push herself hard if she wanted something in life. Samia is an achiever and now, after completing her Bachelor of Commerce degree, she is a financial analyst for Procter & Gamble and very proud of her achievements. This characteristic of Samia is considered a:

1.   Geographic
2.   Demographic
3.   Psychographic
4.   Behavioural
5.   3 and 4

7-8   Multiple

All markets can be segmented into different user statuses. Which of the following would not be considered a user status?

1.   Non-user
2.   Post-user
3.   Ex-user
4.   Potential User
5.   First-time user

7-9   Multiple

Rodrigo loves Lays potato chips. Out of the last 10 times he visited the store he purchased Lays 9 times and he got Lays and Old Dutch once. This routine of always purchasing Lays is an example of which trait?

1.   Brand loyalty
2.   Indifference
3.   Low price
4.   Habit
5.   All of the above

7-10   Multiple

Marketers are using _____ in an effort to identify smaller, better defined target groups.

1. Behavioural segmentation
2. Psychographic segmentation
3. Demographic segmentation
4. Multiple segmentation
5. Geographic segmentation

7-11   Multiple

Many studies have been done and they have found the affluent people of Quebec do not travel as much as affluent people from other provinces in Canada, however, when they do travel they prefer Latin America as their destination. This type of segmentation would be considered:

1.   Demographic
2.   Psychographic
3.   Geodemographic
4.   Geographic
5.   Psychodemographic

7-12   Multiple

Market segmentation for businesses are slightly different than those for consumer markets. The decision to focus on companies whose people and values are similar to your company would be considered a part of which of the following variables?

1.   Demographic
2.   Operating variables
3.   Purchasing approaches
4.   Situational factors
5.   Personal characteristics

7-13   Multiple

Business buying behaviour is very closely related to the benefits derived from a purchase. Connie owns a small convenience store and is very knowledgeable about her competitors, offerings and is always ready to switch suppliers for a better price, even if it means loosing some service. Connie's business buying behaviour would be considered:

1.   Transaction buying
2.   Bargain hunting
3.   Relationship buying
4.   Programmed buying
5.   1 and 2

7-14   Multiple

The world market can be segmented in many different ways. The most common way would be through economic factors, as this is easy to measure. Currently there exists a group called the G7. Which of the following countries would not be considered part of this group.

1.   France
2.   Canada
3.   Japan
4.   Spain
5.   Germany

7-15   Multiple

There are many ways you can segment markets. Bush Pilots Inc. identified seven major market segments, however its staff was too small to develop separate marketing programs for each. Bush Pilots Inc. has a problem with:

1.   Measurability
2.   Actionability
3.   Accessibility
4.   Substantiality
5.   All of the above

7-16   Multiple

Segmenting markets is only useful if the evaluation of such segments leads to concrete marketing plans and eventually sales. In evaluating different market segments, companies must consider all of the following except:

1.   Segment size
2.   Segment growth
3.   Segment purchasing power
4.   Segment structural attractiveness
5.   Company objectives

7-17   Multiple

Which of the following business segments are knowledgeable about competitor's offerings, view packaging as moderately important and receive a small discount?

1.   Programmed buyers
2.   Relationship buyers
3.   Transaction buyers
4.   Bargain hunters
5.   Price conscious buyers

7-18   Multiple

Dyson in a manufacturer of kitchen utensils. They researched their markets thoroughly and they segmented their markets according to certain characteristics. They found the market segment of DINK's (dual income no kids) was not only a growing segment, but it was also large enough to help their company grow and prosper. However, over the last few months they have been having troubles. They know their planning and research was not the problem, so it must be all of the following except:

1.   Aggressive competitors
2.   Substitute products
3.   Power of sellers
4.   Powerful suppliers
5.   All of the following

7-19   Multiple

_____ marketing relies on mass distribution and advertising and aims to give the product a superior image in people's minds.

1.   Differentiated
2.   Concentrated
3.   Mass
4.   Undifferentiated
5.   Unilateral

7-20   Multiple

Russell Stover's is a growing chocolate shop with limited resources. It has a very unique product and the owners know they can be a profitable company with the right approach to marketing. Which marketing strategy would you recommend for them?

1.   Concentrated
2.   Differentiated
3.   Unilateral
4.   Undifferentiated
5.   Mass

7-21   Multiple

Many factors need to be considered when choosing a market-coverage strategy. Some of these factors include all the following except:

1.   Product variability
2.   Product's stage in the life cycle
3.   Supplier variability
4.   Market variability
5.   Competitors marketing strategy

7-22   Multiple

Competitive advantage is fundamental to the success of a company. Which of the following would not be a means on which a company or market can be fundamentally differentiated?

1.   Product
2.   Price
3.   Personnel
4.   Services
5.   Image

7-23   Multiple

TaiTai's is a new oriental cloth embroidery company that has experienced phenomenal growth in the last few years. The do have a distinct competitive advantage; however, they have failed to position the company well and therefore people are only vaguely familiar with their services or do not really know anything special about it. TaiTai's has performed which of the following positioning errors?

1.   Over-positioning
2.   Confused positioning
3.   Reluctant positioning
4.   Under-positioning
5.   2 and 4

7-24   Multiple

Not all brand differences are meaningful or worthwhile. A difference is worth establishing to the extent that it satisfies the following criteria except:

1.   Superior
2.   Distinctive
3.   Affordable
4.   Profitable
5.   All of the above

7-25   Multiple

Market segmentation by quality, service, or economy would be an example of behavioural segmentation by:

1.   Purchase occasion
2.   Benefits sought
3.   User status
4.   User rate
5.   Loyalty status

7-26   Multiple

Dividing markets by categories such as none, medium, strong, or absolute would be examples of which type of behavioural segmentation?

1.   User rate
2.   User status
3.   Loyalty status
4.   Purchase occasion
5.   Benefits sought

7-27   Multiple

In terms of the purchasing approach segmentation for business markets, focus on centralized organizations would be an example of which kind of segmentation?

1.   Power structure
2.   Nature of existing relationships
3.   General purchase policies
4.   Purchasing function
5.   Purchasing criteria

7-28   Multiple

A focus on the urgency for delivery or service as the basis for segmenting business markets is an example of segmentation by:

1.   Demographics
2.   Situational factors
3.   Operating variables
4.   Purchasing approaches
5.   Personal characteristics

7-29   Multiple

Consumers who enjoy skydiving, bungee jumping and white water rafting could all be grouped using this segmentation variable.

1.   Geographic
2.   Demographic
3.   Psychographic
4.   Behavioural
5.   Personal

7-30   Multiple

Punjabi is responsible for market targeting at Chapters Book Sellers. Chapters is looking at entering the Regina market within the next year. Punjabi is currently in Regina to visit current competitors and learn if Barnes and Noble is considering the Regina market. Punjabi's work at Chapters contributes to which area of marketing targeting?

1.   Assessing segment structural attractiveness
2.   Undifferentiated marketing strategy
3.   Differentiated marketing strategy
4.   Choosing a market coverage strategy
5.   Concentrated marketing

True/False Questions

7-1   True/False

Companies who scatter their marketing approach are practising the "shotgun" approach, while those who can focus on the buyer who has greater purchasing interest are practising the "rifle" approach.

7-2   True/False

Because buyers have unique needs and wants, each buyer is potentially a separate market.

7-3   True/False

The proliferation of advertising and distribution channels has made it much easier to practise the "one-size-fits-all" marketing strategy.

7-4   True/False

Market segments are usually small identifiable groups within a market.

7-5   True/False

Niches are becoming more common in today's society. Niches are normally smaller and usually attract only one or a few competitors.

7-6   True/False

A marketer is only required to segment the market according to one variable to find the best view of the market structure.

7-7   True/False

Geographic variables are easier to measure than other variables.

7-8   True/False

Marketers can use stereotypes when using age and life-style segmentation as it makes their jobs much easier and fairly reliable.

188

7-9   True/False

Young adults want ads to tell them about the company and the product, and then leave it up to them to decide whether or not they like the company and its product.

7-10   True/False

Many marketers believe that behaviour variables are the best starting point for building market segments.

7-11   True/False

Market share leaders will focus on attracting potential users, whereas smaller firms will focus on attracting current users away from the market leader.

7-12   True/False

International geographic segmentation assumes that nations close to one another will have very different traits and behaviours.

7-13   True/False

A company's economic structure shapes its population's product and service needs and, therefore, the marketing opportunities it offers.

7-14   True/False

There are many ways to segment markets, and they are all equally effective.

7-15   True/False

The largest, fastest-growing segments are always the most attractive ones for every company.

7-16   True/False

If a segment fits the company's objectives, then the company will seek the skills and resources needed to succeed in that segment.

7-17   True/False

Companies should enter segments only where it can offer superior value and gain advantages over competitors.

7-18   True/False

Rapid advances in computer and communications technology are allowing many large mass marketers to act more like concentrated marketers.

7-19   True/False

Consumers position products only with the help of marketers.

7-20   True/False

A company can create an image through the events it sponsors.

Applying Terms and Concepts

To determine how well you understand the materials in this chapter, read each of the following brief cases and respond to the questions that follow. Answers are given at the end of this chapter.

Case #1   Eldin Incorporated[1]

Marjorie Miele, a former vice-president of marketing at General Dynamics of England, was often dismayed at the clutter on her desk. The paperwork was bad enough, she reasoned, but the telephone, calculator, and rolodex file only contributed to the lack of order.

Miele informally researched the problem and found that she was not alone in her thoughts about the need to have a more organized desk. She left General Dynamics to start Eldin Incorporated. After engaging in a formal research project where she studied the office equipment needs of executives, Miele found a definite need for a desktop organizer. Her solution to the problem was the Mark 3 Execusystem.

The Mark 3 Incorporated the more cumbersome office devices into a single unit. The system, which looked like a desk blotter had a built-in digital clock with alarm and calendar. Other components of the Mark 3 included a radio, calculator, computerized file system, and a telephone with an automatic dialer. The telephone was a "hands-free" model with a "mute" button, ideal for those conference calls where occasional privacy was needed while conferring with other people in the office. The Mark 3 was 60 x 100 cm, weighed 6 kilograms, and was made of black leather with nickel trim.

The profile of potential customers included the following characteristics: college educated, married, male , age 35-49, title of vice president or director, and income over $100,000 a year.

The selling price of the Mark 3 was $685.00 and she calculated her first year break-even point to be 425 units. The potential demand was many times this number as she planned to market the product using mail-order world wide utilizing *The Globe and Mail* and *The Financial Post* to advertise. Competition at this level was nonexistent. While many companies produced executive desk products, not one had the features of the Mark 3.

---

[1] *Principles of Marketing*, 3rd Edition, Kotler, Armstrong, Warren (Prentice Hall) – pg. 154.

1. Miele determined the market segment was large enough to be served at a profit. Which requirement does this market meet for effective market segmentation? Why?

_____

_____

_____

_____

2. The customer profile developed by Miele is made up of demographic characteristics. Define demographic segmentation.

_____

_____

_____

_____

3. Which market coverage strategy is Miele pursuing? Explain.

_____

_____

_____

_____

4. Miele had designed the Mark 3 to provide those benefits identified and desired by her intended target market. Which basic variable has she used in segmenting this market? Why?

_____

_____

_____

_____

5. There are several stages of marketing such as segmentation, or positioning. At which stage of marketing is Eldin Incorporated operating? Explain.

_____

_____

_____

_____

Case #2   Crew Toothpaste

Michel Joudrey, a chemist by trade, began mixing his own toothpaste three years ago after being bothered by sensitive teeth and sore gums. He had tried commercially available toothpastes especially formulated for sensitive teeth, but he found that even the most popular pastes — Sensodyne and Promise — were of little help. He began to neglect his dental hygiene and in time his teeth also became stained from coffee and tobacco.

As his teeth and gums became increasingly sensitive, Joudrey tried a number of folk remedies. He was surprised to find that aloe, a gel extracted form the Aloe Vera plant, was quite effective in reducing pain during brushing. Looking for a more convenient method of application, Joudrey formulated his own toothpaste by combining aloe with flavoring and most of the other ingredients found in regular toothpaste. Jedra also added a polishing agent to help his toothpaste brighten teeth.

Joudrey passed samples of his paste to friends who had similar dental complaints. Based upon their very favourable responses. Joudrey, at the age of 54, retired from his position at DuPont Research Laboratories to devote his energies to promoting his toothpaste, which we called "Crew."

After designing an attractive package, Joudrey ordered 400,000 tubes and cartons and hired a company to manufacture and pack the toothpaste. Without benefit of an advertising budget or the blessing of the Canadian Dental Association, Joudrey began to call on wholesalers who serviced drugstore chains and supermarkets. He also called on the health and beauty aid buyers of discount department stores. Distributors at first were hesitant to stock the product, but after reviewing the testimonials Joudrey produced, they agreed to handle Crew if he would advertise it and agree to buy back any unsold tubes.

Crew sells for $3.89 for a 150 ml tube, about twice as much as other "sensitive teeth" toothpastes. Crew is intended for those people who have sensitive teeth, canker sores, fever blisters, or sensitive gums and/or stained teeth.

To almost everyone's amazement, Crew is selling well. Crew is currently stocked in over 700 stores in Ontario and Quebec, including such well-known chains as Shoppers Drug Mart, Pharmasave and Jean Coutu.

Research conducted by Joudrey indicates that most customers prefer Crew over Sensodyne because of Crew's polishing agent, which brightens their teeth without irritation. Customers do admit, however, that they do occasionally buy Sensodyne because of its lower cost.

Although Joudrey had recently begun to make a profit on his investment, he decided to spend the money on advertising. His new campaign will stress Crew's superiority to Sensodyne, the leader of the market.

_____1. Michel Joudrey was practicing which philosophy of marketing?

    A.   mass marketing

    B.   product-differentiated marketing

    C.   selling differentiated marketing

    D.   target marketing

    E.   market penetration

_____2. The loyalty status of Crew's customers may be used to segment the market. Loyalty status is an example of _____ segmentation.

    A.   behavioristic

    B.   psychographic

    C.   demographic

    D.   geographic

    E.   socialistic

_____3. The placement of Crew toothpaste in 700 stores indicates that which requirement for effective segmentation has been met?

    A.   substantiality

    B.   measurability

    C.   accessibility

    D.   actionability

    E.   marketability

_____4. Which market coverage alternative is Joudrey pursuing?

    A.   concentrated marketing

    B.   differentiated marketing

    C.   undifferentiated marketing

    D.   mass marketing

    E.   hybrid marketing

Case #3   The Colliers

Linda and Miles Collier have decided to bottle and market their own shampoo. They want
to distribute this first variety as widely as possible and have therefore, avoided labeling it
"natural" or "organic," even though it is. If this brand is successful, they would like to
experiment with other formulas for more specialized varieties of shampoos.

_____1. At this stage, Linda and Miles are practicing what kind of marketing?

    A.   concentrated marketing

    B.   test marketing

    C.   differentiated marketing

    D.   undifferentiated marketing

    E.   hybrid marketing

_____2. Linda maintains that a shopper selects shampoo with one of two possible
       objectives in mind: one is to get hair very clean and shiny; the other is to
       condition and protect. If Linda and Miles were to produce and market shampoos
       according to this distinction, they would have segmented the market on the basis
       of:

    A.   age.

    B.   buyer readiness.

    C.   benefits.

    D.   social class.

    E.   income.

____3. Miles insists that their first step in product differentiation should be to manufacture shampoos for dry, normal, and oily hair types. He maintains that teenagers prefer shampoo for oily hair and thinks that the oily hair segment can even be defined as the 15-to 17-year old age group. If Miles and Linda decide to target a market segment defined in this way, the segment will be useful because it will have all of the following qualities except:

    A.   measurability.

    B.   actionability.

    C.   originality.

    D.   accessibility.

    E.   marketability.

____4. Sometimes Linda tells Miles that she would like to work exclusively with herbs and wildflowers and devote their resources to capturing a dominant share of the "natural and organic" market segment. If Linda and Miles were to do this, they would be practicing:

    A.   concentrated marketing.

    B.   differentiated marketing.

    C.   environmental marketing.

    D.   undifferentiated marketing.

    E.   hybrid marketing.

Multiple Choice Answers

1. Correct Answer: 3   Reference: pg. 225
2. Correct Answer: 1   Reference: pg. 225
3. Correct Answer: 4   Reference: pg. 227
4. Correct Answer: 5   Reference: pg. 227
5. Correct Answer: 2   Reference: pg. 228
6. Correct Answer: 1   Reference: pg. 231 (Table 7-1)
7. Correct Answer: 3   Reference: pg. 231 (Table 7-1)
8. Correct Answer: 2   Reference: pg. 235
9. Correct Answer: 5   Reference: pg. 237
10. Correct Answer: 4   Reference: pg. 237
11. Correct Answer: 3   Reference: pg. 237
12. Correct Answer: 5   Reference: pg. 238 (Table 7-3)
13. Correct Answer: 1   Reference: pg. 239
14. Correct Answer: 4   Reference: pg. 240
15. Correct Answer: 2   Reference: pg. 241
16. Correct Answer: 3   Reference: pg. 241
17. Correct Answer: 2   Reference: pg. 228
18. Correct Answer: 3   Reference: pg. 242
19. Correct Answer: 4   Reference: pg. 244
20. Correct Answer: 1   Reference: pg. 246
21. Correct Answer: 3   Reference: pg. 247

22.	Correct Answer:	2	Reference:	pg. 248
23.	Correct Answer:	4	Reference:	pg. 251
24.	Correct Answer:	5	Reference:	pg. 252
25.	Correct Answer:	2	Reference:	pg. 231
26.	Correct Answer:	3	Reference:	pg. 231
27.	Correct Answer:	4	Reference:	pg. 238
28.	Correct Answer:	2	Reference:	pg. 238
29.	Correct Answer:	3	Reference:	pg. 233
30.	Correct Answer:	1	Reference:	pg. 247

True/False Answers

1. TRUE   Reference: pg. 225   Topic: Markcts

2. TRUE   Reference: pg. 225   Topic: Levels of Segmentation

3. FALSE   Reference: pg. 226   Topic: Mass Marketing

4. FALSE   Reference: pg. 226   Topic: Niche Marketing

5. TRUE   Reference: pg. 227   Topic: Niche Marketing

6. FALSE   Reference: pg. 230   Topic: Bases for Segmenting
                                                  Consumer Markets

7. FALSE   Reference: pg. 230   Topic: Demographic Segmentation

8. FALSE   Reference: pg. 232   Topic: Age and Life-Cycle Stage

9. TRUE   Reference: pg. 232   Topic: Age and Life-Cycle Stage

10. TRUE   Reference: pg. 234   Topic: Behavioural Segmentation

11. TRUE   Reference: pg. 235   Topic: User Status

12. FALSE   Reference: pg. 239   Topic: Segmentation of International
                                                  Markets

13. TRUE   Reference: pg. 240   Topic: Segmentation of International
                                                  Markets

14. FALSE   Reference: pg. 240   Topic: Requirements for Effective
                                                  Segmentation

15. FALSE   Reference: pg. 242   Topic: Segment Size and Growth

16. FALSE   Reference: pg. 242   Topic: Company Objectives and
                                                  Resources

17. TRUE   Reference: pg. 242   Topic: Company Objectives and
                                                  Resources

18. TRUE   Reference: pg. 246   Topic: Concentrated Marketing

19. FALSE   Reference: pg. 247   Topic: Positioning for Competitive
                                                  Advantage

20. TRUE   Reference: pg. 251   Topic: Image Differentiation

Applying Terms and Concepts Answers

Case #1   <u>Eldin Incorporated:</u>

Question #1
- This market meets the substantiality requirement for effective segmentation because the market is large and profitable enough to consider and serve.

Question #2
- Demographic segmentation consists of dividing the market into groups based on variables such as age, gender, family size, income, occupation, education, religion, race, and nationality.
- Demographic variables are often used because they are more easily measured than other variables.

Question #3
- Miele is pursuing a concentrated marketing strategy.
- Miele has chosen to pursue a large share of one or a few submarkets, instead of pursuing a small share of a large market.
- Concentrated marketing can help establish a strong market position (or a niche) because of its greater knowledge of the segments' needs and the special reputation it acquires.

Question #4
- Miele has isolated and satisfied the behavioural variable (needs) of her intended target market.
- This is evident as she has satisfied such concerns as: user status, usage rate, and benefits sought.

Question #5
Eldin Incorporated is operating at the target marketing stage because Miele (the seller) is identifying market segments, selecting these segments, and developing products and marketing mixes to tailor the needs of her target market.

<u>Case #2 Crew Toothpaste</u>	<u>Case #3 The Colliers</u>
1. D	1. D
2. A	2. C
3. C	3. C
4. A	4. A

Chapter 8

Product and Services Strategies

Chapter Overview

A product is more than a set of tangible features. In fact, many marketing offers consist of combinations of both tangible goods and services. Offerings range from pure tangible goods at one extreme to pure services at the other. Each product or service offered to customers can be viewed on three levels. The core product consists of the problem-solving benefits consumers seek when they buy a product. The actual product exists around the core and includes the quality level, features, design, brand name, and packaging. The augmented product is the actual product plus the various services and benefits offered with it, such as warranty, free delivery, installation and maintenance.

Chapter Objectives

1. Define the product and the major classifications of products and services.
2. Describes the roles of product and service branding, packaging, labelling, and product support services.
3. Explain the decisions that companies make when developing product lines and mixes.
4. Identify the four characteristics that affect the marketing considerations that services require.
5. Discuss the additional marketing considerations that services require.

Chapter Topics

What is a Product?
- The Product-Service Continuum
- Levels of Product

Product Classifications
- Consumer Products
- Industrial Products
- Organizations, Persons, Places and Ideas

Individual Product Decisions
- Product Attributes
  - Product Quality
  - Product Features
  - Product Design
- Branding
  - Brand Equity
  - Brand Name Selection
  - Brand Sponsor
    - Manufacturers Brands vs. Private Brands
    - Licensing
    - Co-Branding
  - Brand Strategy
    - Line Extensions
    - Brand Extensions
    - Multibrands
    - New Brands
- Packaging
- Labelling
- Product Support Services

Product Line Decisions
- Stretching Downward
- Stretching Upward
- Stretching Both Ways
- Filling in the Product Line

Product Mix Decisions

Services Marketing
- Nature and Characteristics of a Service
  - Intangibility
- Marketing Strategies for Service Firms
- The Service-Profit Chain
  - Managing Service Differentiation
  - Managing Service Quality
  - Managing Productivity

International Product and Services Marketing

Chapter Summary

1.   The definition of PRODUCT and the major classifications of consumer and industrial products.

A product is anything that can be offered to a market for attention, acquisition, use, or consumption and that might satisfy a want or need. Products can be classified as durable, non-durable, and services. Consumer classifications include convenience, shopping, speciality, and unsought. Industrial classifications are material & parts, capital items, supplies & services.

2.   The roles of product packaging and labelling.

Packaging refers to the design and producing of a container or wrapper for the product. The packaging concept states what the package should be or do for the product. Packages at least protect and, hopefully, promote and distinguish the product. Labelling at least identifies and perhaps grades, describes, and promotes the product.

3.   Brand equity.

Powerful brands have equity. Brand equity combines high brand awareness with brand preference and loyalty to create value in and of itself. The credibility of brand equity becomes a marketable product commodity in itself. Over time, brand equity can be the enduring asset of a company as it reliably provides continuing customer equity.

4.   The definition of service and the four characteristics that affect the marketing of a service.

A service is any activity or benefit that one party can offer to another that is essentially intangible and does not result in the ownership of anything. The four characteristics of services are intangibility, inseparability, variability, and perishability.

5.   How persons are marketed.

Person marketing consists of activities undertaken to create, maintain, or change attitudes or behaviour toward particular people. The objective of person marketing is to create a celebrity whose name generates attention, interest, and action. Key aspects of celebrity are durability life-cycle patterns (standard, overnight, comeback, and meteor) and scope (the geographic range of their celebrity).

Key Terms

Actual product (pg. 266)
Augmented product   (pg. 266)
Brand (pg. 273)
Brand equity   (pg. 274)
Brand extension   (pg. 280)
Capital items (pg. 269)
Co-branding   (pg. 279)
Consumer products   (pg. 267)
Convenience products (pg. 267)
Core product   (pg. 266)
Industrial marketing   (pg. 268)
Interactive marketing (pg. 291)
Internal marketing   (pg. 291)
Line extension (pg. 279)
Manufacturers brand   (pg. 277)
Materials and parts   (pg. 268)
Multibranding (pg. 280)
Packaging   (pg. 281)

Packaging concept   (pg. 281)
Private brand (pg. 277)
Product   (pg. 265)
Product design   (pg. 271)
Product line   (pg. 284)
Product mix   (pg. 286)
Product quality   (pg. 271)
Product support services   (pg. 283)
Service   (pg. 265)
Service inseparability (pg. 290)
Service intangibility   (pg. 290)
Service perishability (pg. 290)
Service variability   (pg. 290)
Shopping products   (pg. 267)
Slotting fees   (pg. 277)
Specialty products   (pg. 268)
Supplier and services (pg. 269)
Unsought products   (pg. 268)

Multiple Choice Questions

8-1   Multiple

Which of the following is not considered a product?

1.   A Sony CD Player
2.   A Terri Clark concert
3.   A GMC Truck
4.   Advice from an attorney
5.   All of the above are products

8-2   Multiple

Products include more than just tangible goods. Broadly defined products include everything except:

1.   Ideas
2.   Persons
3.   Thoughts
4.   Places
5.   Organizations

8-3   Multiple

Monique decides to go and visit her sister in Montreal for the week. She books her flight with Air Canada. Their flight leaves at 10:30 am and will arrive in Montreal at 2:45 pm local time. She will be fed on the plane and will be provided with reading material and music. This experience is considered:

1.   A service with accompanying goods
2.   A hybrid offer
3.   A tangible good with accompanying services
4.   An intangible goods with accompanying services
5.   None of the above

8-4   Multiple

Which of the following five characteristics does an actual product not posses?

1.   Quality level
2.   Features
3.   Brand name
4.   Image
5.   Packaging

8-5   Multiple

Warranties on parts and service, free lessons, and quick repair services are all considered part of the _____.

1.   Core benefit
2.   Core service
3.   Augmented product
4.   Actual product
5.   Core product

8-6   Multiple

An umbrella purchased during a rainstorm is a (n):

1.   Staple product
2.   Impulse product
3.   Necessary product
4.   Emergency product
5.   2 and 4

8-7   Multiple

_____ products are bought less frequently and more consideration goes into each purchase.

1.   Consumer
2.   Shopping
3.   Convenience
4.   Specialty
5.   Unsought

8-8   Multiple

Raquel and Paulo just had a baby and it is time for them to buy life insurance. The purchase of life insurance is considered a _____ product.

1.   Consumer
2.   Shopping
3.   Convenience
4.   Specialty
5.   Unsought

8-9   Multiple

Which of the following is not considered a group of industrial products?

1.   Final consumer feedback
2.   Materials and parts
3.   Capital items
4.   Suppliers and services
5.   All of the above

8-10   Multiple

Fax machines, desks and garbage cans would be considered:

1.   Capital items
2.   Manufactured materials
3.   Accessory equipment
4.   Fixed equipment
5.   Supplies

8-11   Multiple

Small motors, small tires and castings would be considered:

1.   Component materials
2.   Manufactured material
3.   Natural products
4.   Component parts
5.   Supplies

8-12   Multiple

In recent years, marketers have broadened the concept of a product to include all other "marketable entities" not already included. All the following except _____ have been added to the list as they were not previously considered.

1.   Services
2.   Organizations
3.   Persons
4.   Places
5.   Ideas

8-13   Multiple

Motor clubs, oil companies, hotels, and government agencies have all pitched in to help with:

1.   Social marketing
2.   Tourism marketing
3.   Place marketing
4.   Business site marketing
5.   All of the above

8-14   Multiple

Sedco has made a commitment to its employees and its consumers their products will be free from defects and reliable. This promise is a result of:

1.   Product quality
2.   Performance quality
3.   Conformance quality
4.   Total quality management
5.   1 and 3

8-15   Multiple

All the following questions help a company identify new features and decide which ones to add to their product except:

1.   What is your frequency of use of our product?
2.   How do you like the product?
3.   Which specific features of the product do you like the most?
4.   Which features could we add to improve the product?
5.   All the above are useful

8-16   Multiple

Pietro is assigned the task of developing a design for P&G's new product that they will launch this fall. Pietro knows there are many benefits of a good design. These benefits include all the following except:

1.   It can attract attention
2.   It can improve product performance
3.   It can obtain better shelf space in retail outlets
4.   It can cut production costs
5.   It can give a product a strong competitive advantage in the target market

8-17   Multiple

Professional marketers have many distinctive skills. Among these skills is their ability to do everything except:

1.   Create brands
2.   Cannibalize competitors brands
3.   Maintain brands
4.   Protect brands
5.   Enhance brands

8-18   Multiple

A consumer's view of a brand is very important to the future success of a company. Everything is considered part of the brand except:

1.   A name
2.   A term
3.   A symbol
4.   An idea
5.   A design

8-19   Multiple

Well engineered, well built, high resale value, durable and high prestige are considered product _____.

1.   Attributes
2.   Benefits
3.   Values
4.   Personality
5.   None of the above

8-20   Multiple

Brands vary in the amount of power and value they have in the market place. P&G's Tide laundry detergent has a large amount of power in the market place because of everything except:

1.   Brand loyalty
2.   Name awareness
3.   Deep corporate pockets
4.   Perceived quality
5.   Channel relationships

8-21   Multiple

A high level of brand equity provides a company with many competitive advantages.
Which of the following is not considered to be one of these advantages?

1.   Brand awareness
2.   Bargaining leverage with resellers
3.   Brand loyalty
4.   Launch lines are easier to establish
5.   Economies of scale

8-22   Multiple

When General Mills and Hershey's joined forces to create Reese's Peanut Butter Puffs
cereal, they engaged in _____.

1.   Store branding
2.   Co-branding
3.   Licensed branding
4.   Distributor branding
5.   Private branding

8-23   Multiple

Store brands like Presidents Choice, Safeway Select and Our Compliments are becoming
a very popular household items. Currently __ % of Canadian households buy at least
some store brands.

1.   50
2.   80
3.   100
4.   75
5.   65

8-24   Multiple

_____ gives a new product instant recognition and faster acceptance.

1.   Line extension
2.   Multibranding
3.   New brands
4.   Brand extension
5.   Product extension

8-25   Multiple

Packaging a container of shampoo and conditions includes everything but:

1.   The actual container holding the shampoo
2.   The plastic wrap covering the bottle of shampoo together with the conditioner
3.   The large cardboard box used to ship the shampoo from the manufacturer to the retailer
4.   The labelling on the bottle of shampoo
5.   All the above are considered part of packaging

8-26   Multiple

Mercedes-Benz realized the market for their luxury cars has been decreasing over the last few years. To counter this trend, they will introduce a new more affordable car backed by their high quality guarantee, during the 2000 model year. This new car is a product line decision to:

1.   Stretch downward
2.   Stretch Upward
3.   Stretch both ways
4.   Fill in the product line
5.   Grab more market share

8-27   Multiple

The quality of a service depends on who provides it as well as when, where and how the service is delivered. These issues are considered a (n) _____ characteristic of services.

1.   Intangible
2.   Inseparable
3.   Variable
4.   Perishable
5.   Personable

8-28   Multiple

The service-profit chain consists of five links. The first chain in that link is:

1.   Satisfied and loyal customers
2.   Healthy service profits and growth
3.   Greater service value
4.   Satisfied and productive service employees
5.   Internal service quality

8-29   Multiple

Interactive marketing is the marketing process between _____ and _____.

1.   Customers, company
2.   Company and employees
3.   Employees and employees
4.   Employees and customers
5.   Companies and companies

8-30   Multiple

Many people judge the quality of service on five different dimensions. Which of the following is not considered one of these?

1.   Credibility
2.   Empathetic
3.   Reliable
4.   Responsive
5.   Valuable

True/False Questions

8-1   True/False

Services are a form of product that consist of activities, benefits and satisfaction.

8-2   True/False

A hybrid offer is one that consists of 75% goods and 25% service.

8-3   True/False

Today most competition occurs at the actual product level.

8-4   True/False

When buying specialty products and services, consumers spend considerable time and effort in gathering information and making comparisons.

8-5   True/False

The distinction between a consumer product and an industrial product is based on the purpose for which the product is bought.

8-6   True/False

In the end, marketing is about an idea.

8-7   True/False

One of a company's main objectives is to offer the highest possible performance quality level.

8-8   True/False

The ultimate goal of total quality is to improve consumer value.

8-9   True/False

Being one of the first producers to introduce a needed and valued new feature is one of the most effective ways to compete.

8-10   True/False

Features consumers value little in relation to cost should be added, as this is very profitable for the company.

8-11   True/False

A brand is a seller' promise to deliver consistently a specific set of features, benefits, and services to buyers.

8-12   True/False

Since retailing is more concentrated in Canada than in the US, store brands are more powerful.

8-13   True/False

A major drawback of brand extensions is each brand might obtain only a small market share, and none may be very profitable.

8-14   True/False

Some marketers have considered packaging as the fifth "P" along with place, price, promotion and product.

8-15   True/False

Companies keen on high, short-term profitability generally carry longer lines consisting of selected items.

8-16   True/False

The product mix dimensions of width, length, depth and quality provide the handles for defining to company's product strategy.

8-17   True/False

A service provider's task is to make the service tangible in one or more ways.

8-18   True/False

The perishability of a service is a problem even when demand is steady.

8-19   True/False

To the extent that customers view the service of different providers as similar, they care less about the provider than the price.

8-20   True/False

The key is to exceed the customer's service-quality expectations in order to succeed as a service company.

Applying Terms and Concepts

To determine how well you understand the materials in this chapter, read each of the following brief cases and then respond to the questions that follow. Answers are given at the end of this chapter.

Case #1   Martha Hamel[1]

Martha Hamel was in her third year of high school when her father lost his job. His employer was closing the carpet manufacturing plant in Windsor, where he worked as a weaver. Martha's father, George, had spent 29 years working at the plant and at the age of 53, was looking for a new job. His employer had moved south to Mexico with its cheaper labour and more favourable tax structure. George was offered an opportunity to move south with his employer, but family concerns made that option unworkable. George decided he would make the best of his situation but without much of a formal education, and other manufacturing plants in the area either closing or downsizing, his prospects were not promising.

Martha never forgot the effect the plant closing had on her father. This once proud and fiercely independent man was suddenly racked by self-doubt. His sense of self-worth was shaken and his ability to provide for his family uncertain. George shielded his family from most of the problem but the strain was evident. George ultimately did land a position with another firm, but Martha decided she would do what she could to take control over her life, so she would have greater flexibility than he had. Control for Martha meant a university education. Eight years later, Martha had earned a B.Comm (Accounting) from Laurier, an MBA in Marketing from Queen's and a Chartered Accountant designation.

1.   A university degree is an example of what type of product?

    _____

    _____

2.   When Martha chose to pursue an education, she ultimately realized the product she was buying existed on three levels. Explain how a university degree exists on each of the following levels.
    a. core product:

    _____

    _____

    _____

---

[1] *Principles of Marketing*, 3rd Edition, Kotler, Armstrong, Warren (Prentice Hall) – pg. 174.

b. actual product:

_____

_____

_____

c. augmented product:

_____

_____

_____

_____

3. Discuss the implications of your answer to the final question, for university administrators.

_____

_____

_____

_____

Case #2   Woodstock '94[2]

Woodstock '94 – Three days of peace, love and music, not to mention cash machines, metal detectors, corporate sponsor, the Eco Village, the Peace Patrol, mud and 2,800 overflowing portable toilets. It wasn't quite the same as the original Woodstock held some 25 years earlier, but then it couldn't be.

For three days in August 1994, approximately a quarter of a million people descended on an 840 acre site in Saugerties, New York. The mainly white, middle class crowd came to the 25th anniversary of the Woodstock Music and Art Fair originally held in Bethel, New York. Such diverse groups as the Band, Red Hot Chili Peppers, Blind Melon, Salt-n-Pepa, Bob Dylan, Joe Cocker and the Cranberries were among the 50 bands invited to entertain the fair goers. Corporate sponsors, such as Pepsi, Apple Computers and Haagen-Daz were also there, promoting their wares and subsidizing the event.

---

[2] *Principles of Marketing*, 3rd Edition, Kotler, Armstrong, Warren (Prentice Hall) – pg. 422.

The Eco Village – reportedly there to educate the masses about the environment – seemed more about making money than education. The private security force dubbed the "Peace Patrol" reinforced the 550 State Troopers enforcing the ban on alcohol and drugs, while maintaining order.

Where the original concert didn't even have an official T-shirt, Woodstock '94 seemed decidedly mainstream. Blatant commercialism caused some idealistic musicians to boycott the event. But most seemed genuinely glad to have been invited--besides the better paid acts reportedly received $350,000 plus a share of the royalties. Promoters of Woodstock'94 reportedly filed a multi-million dollar lawsuit against rival promoters who wanted to stage an event called Bethel '94—a concert on the site of the original event. Two concerts, commemorating the same event in the same general area, at the same time, would be bad for business.

Some complained the event should have been called Greenstock, not Woodstock. But Woodstock'94 cost $42 million, more than ten times the cost of the original concert. It takes money to stage such a colossal event. This is not to suggest the organizers sold out completely. Other corporate sponsors including alcohol and tobacco companies were politely turned away. Even though profits would have been higher, and ticket prices lower.

Apparently, the commercialism wasn't too much of a deterrent. Over 250,000 people paid the $190 ticket price (compared to the $25 price for the original event) for three days of music, camping, camaraderie, and parking. And by some estimates, that was a bargain.

Note: All figures are in Canadian dollars

1. Briefly explain how the promotion of Woodstock '94 might deal with the following characteristics of their offerings.
    a. Intangibility:

    _____

    _____

    _____

    _____

    b. Inseparability:

    _____

    _____

    _____

    c. Variability:

_____

_____

_____

d. Perishability:

_____

_____

_____

2.   How does the experience of Woodstock'94 constitute a service?

_____

_____

_____

_____

Case #3   Ajax Supermarkets

Several Ajax supermarkets have been located in upper-class neighbourhoods throughout the Toronto area for over 35 years. Ajax enjoys an excellent reputation for a wide range of high-quality, high-priced, difficult-to-find food items, and it caters almost exclusively to the upper-income market segment. The number of supermarkets in the Toronto area has been increasing steadily, and Ajax has experienced a slowing in its growth trend. Dollar sales are up significantly, but unit volume is only slightly ahead of last year in most of the Ajax locations in established neighbourhoods, and profit margins have been squeezed.

Management is considering a number of alternatives as possible remedies. One of these is the establishment of the Ajax brand name on several product lines. Ajax has carried only the highest-quality national brands in the past, and there is some question in the minds of two members of the management committee about whether the use of a private label would be appropriate in Ajax's prestige stores. Another possibility under review is the addition of generic lines. During the last meeting of the management committee it was pointed out that the lower prices of generics have a strong appeal to consumers during inflationary times. The attraction is even stronger during recessions when there is high unemployment. Furthermore, profit margins on the generics could be expected to be about the same as the current average, with only slightly reduced quality that would be barely detectable by consumers.

_____1. The alternatives being considered deal with:

   A.   brand repositioning.

   B.   product line stretching.

   C.   the depth of the product line.

   D.   brand extension decisions.

   E.   both (A) and (C)

_____2. If the generic labels are added, this would be a(n):

   A.   augmentation of the core product.

   B.   blanket family name.

   C.   downward stretch in the product line.

   D.   widening of the product line.

   E.   none of the above

_____3. The decision to add or not to add generics concerns not only quality considerations, but also considerations regarding the:

   A.   core product offered by Ajax.

   B.   consistency of the product line.

   C.   products that must be deleted to make room for the new line.

   D.   classification of the generic line.

   E.   breadth of the product line.

_____4. What is the proper decision for Ajax regarding the addition of generic products?

   A.   Add them — this will broaden its market.

   B.   Adding generics is a line-filling decision that will not broaden the market but will create an opportunity to sell more to the existing market.

   C.   Generics should increase sales, but will not add much to profit margins.

   D.   The addition of generics is a bad idea because it may damage the company's prestige reputation.

   E.   none of the above

_____5. The addition of a private brand with the Ajax label would:

    A.   damage the quality image Ajax has built over many years.

    B.   offer the company an opportunity to capitalize on its reputation and widen profit margins.

    C.   only reduce profit margins even further.

    D.   attract another market segment.

    E.   both (A) and (C)

Case #4   Irish Shoes

James O'Donovan is president of Irish Shoes, a Kelowna, BC distributor of specialty athletic shoes. Three years ago O'Donovan was a centre for the University of British Columbia Thunderbirds. He spent two seasons at that position until serious foot and ankle injuries ended his career. It seems that the constant running, jumping, and dead stops placed excessive pressure on his back, legs, and feet. This ultimately resulted in permanent damage which surgery could not correct.

In discussing his problems with Dr. H. N. Woofe, a prominent Canadian podiatrist, O'Donovan learned that the type of difficulty he suffered was quite common, although usually not so severe, in the athletic community. Collegiate tennis, basketball, and football players, in addition to track and field athletes, were very susceptible to the problem. Dr. Woofe also mentioned that amateur joggers were also coming to her complaining of foot and leg problems.

With Dr. Woofe and her two partners providing technical advice and financial backing, O'Donovan developed a unique athletic shoe. The sole of the shoe contains a polyurethane pad, partially filled with mineral oil. There is sufficient resilience within the pad to prevent it from bursting on impact from the foot as the wearer runs and jumps. The pads essentially act as shock absorbers, significantly reducing impact and so pressure on the legs, feet, and back.

O'Donovan called his creation the Irish Shoe. To further distinguish it from the inevitable competitors, he designed a symbol of an eagle in flight, and had it made as a blue rubber implant into the sole of the shoe.

The shoe sells for $140, about the price of other quality shoes; its acceptance has been phenomenal. In only six months, O'Donovan has nearly sold out his initial factory runs of 5,000 pairs. He has since placed another order for 2,000 pairs from his manufacturer in Italy. Irish shoes are distributed throughout Canada — although on a very limited basis in all provinces — by independent shoe stores. Store managers indicate that it is not unusual for shoe store patrons to drive over 160 kilometres to a store which stocks the shoes and to ask for them by name.

Although the shoe was originally intended for athletes, distributors have noted that approximately 60 percent of sales have been to nonathletes. In fact, senior citizens are the most avid fans of the shoe. This has O'Donovan and the podiatrists working on designs for shoes more appropriate for work settings and leisure activities.

_____1. The comfort provided by the Irish Shoe is an example of a _____ product.

    A.   core

    B.   augmented

    C.   tangible

    D.   intangible

    E.   actual

_____2. The shoe itself is an example of a(n) _____.

    A.   nondurable good

    B.   durable good

    C.   service

    D.   intangible

    E.   convenience

_____3. The fact that customers drive many kilometres to a store which carries the shoe and ask for it by name indicates that this shoe has achieved _____ goods status for those customers.

    A.   convenience

    B.   homogeneous shopping

    C.   heterogeneous shopping

    D.   specialty

    E.   unsought

____4. The Blue Eagle implant, which has come to symbolize Irish Shoes, is an example of:

A.　　brand.

B.　　brand name.

C.　　brand mark.

D.　　trademark.

E.　　both (A) and (C)

____5. Irish Shoes is an example of a _____ brand.

A.　　manufacturer

B.　　private

C.　　national

D.　　dealer brand

E.　　both (B) and (D)

Case #5　　　Madame Zorba

Madame Zorba, a former fortuneteller, has just opened Yellowknife's first complete occult science centre. Madame offers a complete line of paranormal services. In addition to palmistry, tarot readings, and crystal ball gazing, interested customers can have their aura analyzed, engage in seances, receive training in astral projection, test their powers of ESP, or sample any number of the more exotic occult practices.

Madame Zorba has invested in an unusually nice facility housing a large staff and supported by the best equipment. She expects to enjoy a brisk business, with clientele drawn from "widely diverse socio-economic strata." Like any other businessperson, she is concerned about how best to market her rather unusual "product."

____1. Briefly explain how Madame Zorba might deal with each of the following characteristics which will affect her marketing program:

A.　　Intangibility

B.　　Inseparability

C.　　Variability

D.　　Perishability

223

_____2. Madame Zorba should be classified as providing a(n) _____-_____ service.

_____3. Since the client's presence is necessary in the performance of this service, Madame Zorba is correct to invest in impressive facilities and equipment.

A.   True   B.   False

_____4. Madame Zorba's clients are most likely to purchase the services to meet a(n) _____ need, although some clients will purchase for _____ reasons.

_____5. At present, Madame Zorba has little or no competition. What will be the major concern of her marketing program after she opens her business?

Case #6   Tours of the Darkside

Dr. Sheila Aniston, a prominent social critic and professor at the University of Toronto, recently introduced a three-credit hour undergraduate course, Soc. 365 -Deviant Subcultures. The course allows students to observe the underbelly of society and is popularly known as "Tours of the Darkside."

The course begins with readings and lectures on sociology and urban history, the class structure, subcultures and deviance. The class takes an unusual twist when the students travel into Toronto's famed "Yonge Street." The tours allow students to observe behaviour typically considered unacceptable and to understand how it thrives and coexists with "polite" society. Interviews with area residents and patrons are included in the tours. Aniston prohibits cameras and tape recorders to preserve the desired anonymity and cooperation of interviewees.

Following these experiences, students are assigned a research paper wherein they analyze the motivations of the more respectable patrons who use and have come to depend upon the area's existence. The paper also allows the student to consider the adaptive skills necessary for area residents to survive and in fact thrive in that environment. The student must also evaluate the role played by the area in a larger socioeconomic society.

Aniston, who has studied this area for six years, expects to publish her findings next year.

_____1. The University of Toronto allows only Dr. Aniston to teach and supervise the tours associated with Soc. 365. This suggests the _____ of the course.

A. variability

B. inseparability

C. perishability

D. intangibility

E. substantiality

_____2. The people interviewed and the behaviours observed on a given tour are unique and differ from one to another. This suggests the _____ of the tours associated with Soc. 365.

A. variability

B. inseparability

C. perishability

D. intangibility

E. substantiality

_____3. To protect the anonymity and to entice the cooperation of area interviewees; Dr. Aniston prohibits tape recorders and cameras on the tours. This lack of an actual, unbiased record (film and recording) of the tour would suggest the _____ of the experience.

A. variability

B. inseparability

C. perishability

D. intangibility

E. substantiality

_____4. Dr. Aniston is never sure what the students will experience (see, hear, smell, etc.) on a given tour before it occurs. This suggests the _____ of the experience.

A. variability

B. inseparability

C. perishability

D. intangibility

E. substantiality

Multiple Choice Answers

1.	Correct Answer:	5	Reference:	pg. 265
2.	Correct Answer:	3	Reference:	pg. 265
3.	Correct Answer:	1	Reference:	pg. 266
4.	Correct Answer:	4	Reference:	pg. 266
5.	Correct Answer:	3	Reference:	pg. 266
6.	Correct Answer:	4	Reference:	pg. 267
7.	Correct Answer:	2	Reference:	pg. 267
8.	Correct Answer:	5	Reference:	pg. 268
9.	Correct Answer:	1	Reference:	pg. 268
10.	Correct Answer:	3	Reference:	pg. 269
11.	Correct Answer:	4	Reference:	pg. 269
12.	Correct Answer:	1	Reference:	pg. 269
13.	Correct Answer:	2	Reference:	pg. 270
14.	Correct Answer:	5	Reference:	pg. 271
15.	Correct Answer:	1	Reference:	pg. 271
16.	Correct Answer:	3	Reference:	pg. 272
17.	Correct Answer:	2	Reference:	pg. 273
18.	Correct Answer:	4	Reference:	pg. 273
19.	Correct Answer:	1	Reference:	pg. 274
20.	Correct Answer:	3	Reference:	pg. 274
21.	Correct Answer:	5	Reference:	pg. 274

22.	Correct Answer:	2	Reference:	pg. 276
23.	Correct Answer:	3	Reference:	pg. 277
24.	Correct Answer:	4	Reference:	pg. 279
25.	Correct Answer:	5	Reference:	pg. 281
26.	Correct Answer:	1	Reference:	pg. 285
27.	Correct Answer:	3	Reference:	pg. 290
28.	Correct Answer:	2	Reference:	pg. 291
29.	Correct Answer:	4	Reference:	pg. 291
30.	Correct Answer:	5	Reference:	pg. 293

True/False Answers

1.   TRUE   Reference: pg. 265   Topic: What is a Product?

2.   FALSE   Reference: pg. 266   Topic: The Product-Service
                                                   Continuum

3.   FALSE   Reference: pg. 267   Topic: Levels of Products

4.   FALSE   Reference: pg. 267   Topic: Consumer Products

5.   TRUE   Reference: pg. 268   Topic: Industrial Products

6.   TRUE   Reference: pg. 270   Topic: Organizations, Persons,
                                                   Places and Ideas

7.   FALSE   Reference: pg. 271   Topic: Product Quality

8.   TRUE   Reference: pg. 271   Topic: Product Quality

9.   FALSE   Reference: pg. 271   Topic: Product Features

10. FALSE   Reference: pg. 271   Topic: Product Features

11. TRUE   Reference: pg. 274   Topic: Branding

12. TRUE   Reference: pg. 277   Topic: Brand Sponsor

13. FALSE   Reference: pg. 280   Topic: Multibrands

14. TRUE   Reference: pg. 281   Topic: Packaging

15. FALSE   Reference: pg. 284   Topic: Product Line Decisions

16. FALSE   Reference: pg. 287   Topic: Product Mix Decisions

17. TRUE   Reference: pg. 290   Topic: Intangibility

18. FALSE   Reference: pg. 290   Topic: Intangibility

19. TRUE   Reference: pg. 292   Topic: Managing Service
                                                   Differences

20. TRUE   Reference: pg. 293   Topic: Managing Service Quality

Applying Terms and Concepts Answers

Case #1   Martha Hamel:

Question #1
• Specialty product

Question #2
a. The core product identifies what the customer is really buying. In this situation Martha is acquiring the means to control her professional life. Her education will give her the flexibility to pursue a variety of opportunities as she wishes. Her degrees will provide significant earning potential and personal as well as professional satisfaction. Martha's education also provided her with specific technical skills, which have enhanced her decision making, and communication skills. Her conceptual and human skills were also more developed as a result of her education. Martha might say the prestige associated with her graduation from the various colleges is also part of the core product.

b. The actual product would be the degrees earned from each university. The university name and reputation and level of degree would further identify her accomplishment.

c. The augmented product would be the variety of services and activities provided by the colleges and universities, which enhanced her educational experience. These might have included, counseling, financial aid, library, computer facilities, housing, placement, clubs and organizations, social and cultural event (concerts, speakers and sporting events.) These services and activities add quality, texture and variety and are designed to enrich the educational experience.

Question #3
• University administrators must realize they are selling a product, just as their competition is doing.
• When student choose to attend a particular school, they are really buying a total product.
• The more administrators understand what students really need, want, and demand, the more they will be able to offer these prospective students and distinguish themselves from the competition.

Case #2   Woodstock '94:

Question #1

a. *Intangibility* – means that the services cannot be seen, tasted, heard, felt or smelled before they are bought. Organizers gave festival goers an idea of what to expect by announcing the preparations that had taken place. Preparations included offsite parking with shuttle buses, camping areas, a ban on drugs and alcohol, the list of performers and the number of portable toilets along with a host of others. References to the original gathering also gave attendees a sense of what to expect.

   But neither organizers nor attendees knew exactly what to expect prior to the concert. Advanced preparations and the actual event would still be affected by external uncontrollables such as weather.

b. *Inseparability* – means that services cannot be separated from their providers. Because the customer is also present the service is provided, the outcome is affected by both the provider and the customer.

   This meant that to some extent, the success of the concert would be dependent on the behaviour of the concertgoers as well as that of the performer, vendors, security force and the organizers. So collectively they, along with other publics, created the event.

c. *Variability* – means that the quality of the services depends on who provides the service as well as when, where and how they are provided.

   Concert organizers hope to instill confidence in potential attendees by providing information about the concert and their preparations. The suggestion was that a less organized concert would be less enjoyable.

d. *Perishability* – means that services cannot be stored for later use. The point was that one had to be there to truly experience the event. Although there were numerous news broadcasts from Saugerties, MTV televised some of the festival, there was pay per view on cable and there would be the inevitable CD and film, nothing compared to actually being present at the concert.

   The sights, sounds, smells, and tastes cannot be totally captured or recreated during or after the event. Once the event is over—it is over, the experience cannot be recreated. Even another concert—Woodstock '94 compared to Woodstock '69—cannot recreate the events each becomes its own happening.

Question #2
- Woodstock'94 is an activity (or event) that is essentially intangible and does not result in the ownership of anything. The event is not tied to a physical product.

Case #3 Ajax Supermarkets	Case #4 Irish Supermarkets
1. B	1. A
2. C	2. B
3. A	3. D
4. D	4. E
5. B	5. E

Case #5   Madame Zorba

1. A. *Intangibility*- Madame Zorba should emphasize the benefits of her services. Testimonials from respected customers would be helpful.

   B. *Inseparability* - Madame Zorba should carefully select and personally train her staff. Their experiences, training, and credentials should be matched to their services and publicized.

   C. *Variability*- Madame Zorba should establish and enforce training and service standards to ensure as much uniformity of quality as possible.

   D. *Perishability*- Madame Zorba should consider reservation systems and increased customer participation.

2. people based

3. True

4. personal, business

5. To present an image of professionalism and credibility for both her services and her staff.

1.   B

2.   A

3.   C

4.   D

Chapter 9

New-Product Development and Life-Cycle Strategies

Chapter Overview

Organizations must develop effective new product and service strategies. Their current products face limited life spans and must be replaced by newer products. But new products can fail – the risks of innovation are as great as the rewards. The key to successful innovation lies in a total-company effort, strong planning, and a systematic new-product development process.

Chapter Objectives

1. Explain how companies find and develop new-product ideas.
2. List and define the steps in the new-product development process.
3. Describe the stages of the product life cycle.
4. Describe how marketing strategies evolve during the product's life cycle.

Chapter Topics

New-Product Development Strategy
- The New-Product Development Process
- Idea Generation
- Idea Screening
- Concept Development and Testing
  - Concept Development
  - Concept Testing
- Marketing Strategy Development
- Business Analysis
- Product Development
- Test Marketing
  - Standard Test Markets
  - Controlled Test Markets
  - Simulated Test Markets
  - Test Marketing Business Products
- Commercialization
- Speeding Up New-Product Development

Product Life-Cycle Strategies
- Introduction Stage
- Growth Stage
- Maturity Stage
- Decline Stage

Chapter Summary

1.   The steps in new-product development.

Steps include idea generation, idea screening, concept development and testing, marketing strategy development, business analysis, product development, test marketing, and commercialization. At each level, go/no-go decisions become increasingly more specific.

2.   How companies find and develop new product ideas.

Major new sources of new product ideas include internal sources (sales force, employees), customers, competitors, distributors and suppliers, and the general public or societal trends.

3.   The stages of the product life cycle.

The stages of the product life cycle include product development, introduction, growth, maturity and decline.

4.   How the marketing strategy changes during a product's life cycle.

As products are prepared to launch, marketers must choose the initial positioning carefully. Strategies must decide between short-term and long-term profits, especially market pioneers. During introduction, strategy focuses on awareness and acceptance of basic product. Growth attracts competitors and more features. In maturity, strategy looks to modifying the market, product, or mix. Decline forces choices on dropping or continuing a weak product.

5.   Distinguishing between the sequential product development and simultaneous product development processes.

In sequential product development, each functional area of the company works on the new product and sends its completes work to the next division. In simultaneous product development, each functional area provides on-going (or real-time or on-line) feedback that is incorporated into the design, production, and marketing planning stage. Simultaneous design is organizationally more complicated but reduces total development and improves quality.

Key Terms

Business analysis   (pg. 320)
Commercialization   (pg. 323)
Concept testing   (pg. 318)
Decline stage (pg. 332)
Fads   (pg. 328)
Fashion   (pg. 328)
Growth stage (pg. 329)
Idea generation   (pg. 314)
Idea screening (pg. 317)
Introduction stage   (pg. 328)
Marketing strategy development
      (pg. 319)

Maturity stage (pg. 330)
New-product development   (pg. 313)
Product concept   (pg. 318)
Product development (pg. 320)
Product life cycle (PLC)   (pg. 327)
Sequential product
      development (pg. 325)
Simultaneous product
      development (pg. 325)
Style   (pg. 328)
Test marketing   (pg. 321)

Multiple Choice Questions

9-1   Multiple

Given the rapid changes in all the following except _____ companies must
develop a steady stream of new products and services.

1.   Consumer tastes
2.   Technology
3.   Competition
4.   Maturing markets
5.   All the above

9-2   Multiple

When companies talk about new products and services, they may be talking about all the
following except:

1.   Original products
2.   Product revival
3.   Product improvements
4.   Product modifications
5.   New brands

9-3   Multiple

New products are a necessity for survival in today's very competitive environment.
Unfortunately, many new products fail. Which of the following would not be a reason for
this phenomenon?

1.   The market size may have been overestimated
2.   The actual product was not designed as well as it should have been
3.   The product was incorrectly placed in the market
4.   The product was priced too high
5.   The product was over-advertised

9-4   Multiple

A new product may have many rolls in a company. Among them are:

1.   Help the company remain an innovator
2.   To defend the company's market share
3.   To cannibalize the competition
4.   Only 1 and 2
5.   All of the above

9-5   Multiple

A recent survey of product managers found that of 100 proposed new ideas, _____ begin the product development process, ____ survive the development process, ____ reach the marketplace and only _____ eventually reach their business objectives.

1.   50,25,10,5
2.   43,18,9,3
3.   39,17,8,1
4.   24,14,7,2
5.   18,13,7,1

9-6   Multiple

New-product ideas come from a variety of places. Which of the following does not fit into the top five major sources of new product ideas?

1.   Internal sources
2.   Trade magazines
3.   Competitors
4.   Suppliers
5.   Consumers

9-7   Multiple

The purpose of succeeding stages in the new-product development process is to _____ the number of products introduced.

1.   Reduce
2.   Increase
3.   Hold constant
4.   Improve
5.   1 and 4

9-8   Multiple

Many companies require executives to submit a short write-up about any new product they want the committee to review. Basic information is needed for this write-up, and all the following information would be required except:

1.   Consumer perception
2.   Market size
3.   Development time and costs
4.   Manufacturing costs
5.   All of the above

9-9   Multiple

Once the committee receives all the proposals for new products, they would probably ask the following questions except:

1.   Is the product truly useful for consumers and society?
2.   Is it good for our particular company?
3.   Does it mesh well with company strategies and objectives?
4.   Is the competition developing something similar?
5.   Do we have the people, resources and skills to succeed?

9-10   Multiple

A _____ is a detailed version of the idea stated in meaningful consumer terms.

1.   Product development
2.   Concept testing
3.   Product concept
4.   Concept development
5.   Concept testing

9-11   Multiple

The marketing strategy development statement consists of many parts. The _____ _____ part describes the target market, and the sales, market share and profit goals for the first few years.

1.   First
2.   Second
3.   Third
4.   Fourth
5.   In all of the above

9-12   Multiple

The planned long-run sales goals, the profit goals and the marketing mix strategy are all described in the _____ stage of the marketing strategy statement.

1.   First
2.   Second
3.   Third
4.   Fourth
5.   In all of the above

9-13   Multiple

The business analysis stage of new-product development is a very crucial step. After preparing the sales forecast for the new product, management is able to estimate the costs and profits for all the following except:

1.   Marketing
2.   Competition
3.   R&D
4.   Accounting
5.   Manufacturing

9-14   Multiple

The product development stage of the new-product development process calls for a large investment of both time and money. Developing a successful prototype can take:

1.   Days
2.   Weeks
3.   Months
4.   Years
5.   All of the above

9-15   Multiple

At the _____ stage of the new-product development process, the product and marketing program are introduced into more realistic market settings.

1.   Marketing program
2.   Commercialization
3.   Marketing strategy development
4.   Test marketing
5.   Concept development and testing

9-16   Multiple

Janice has been asked by her boss to develop a marketing plan for Campbell Soup's new baby formula soups. Which of the following would not be part of this marketing program?

1.   Positioning strategy
2.   Advertising
3.   Financing
4.   Distribution
5.   Branding

9-17   Multiple

In the following type of test marketing, the results are used to forecast national sales and profits, discover potential problems and fine-tune the marketing program.

1.   Controlled
2.   Standard
3.   Simulated
4.   Multiple
5.   All of the above

9-18   Multiple

Controlled test marketing take less time than standard test marketing and usually cost less. However, there are some downfalls in using this strategy. Which of the following would not be included?

1.   Companies are not able to control important variables in the testing
2.   The small cities used may not be representative of society as a whole
3.   The panel consumers may not be representative of society as a whole
4.   It allows the competitors to get a look at the new product
5.   All of the above

9-19   Multiple

Simulated test marketing is the fastest and easiest type of testing a new product. They are used widely and often used as _____.

1.   Post-test markets
2.   Multiple-test markets
3.   Preliminary markets
4.   Pre-test markets
5.   Joint-test markets

9-20   Multiple

Business markets and consumer markets vary is certain ways. It would be logical to assume that the way a new product is test marketed would also vary somewhat. All the following are acceptable ways to test market business products except:

1.   Product-use tests
2.   Tradeshows
3.   Simulated test markets
4.   Standard test markets
5.   All of the above

9-21   Multiple

Suet Mai works for Nabisco. Their new bed time snack has passed all the stages in the new-product development process and is now at the commercialization stage. It is Suet Mai's job to ensure this product passes this stage. When launching a new product, the company must first decide on:

1.   Introduction timing
2.   Where to launch the new product
3.   The planned market roll-out for the product
4.   The financing required for the product
5.   The reception the new product will receive in the marketplace

9-22   Multiple

To get their new products to market more quickly, many companies are adopting a faster, team-oriented approach called _____ product development.

1.   Sequential
2.   Simultaneous
3.   Congruent
4.   Concurrent
5.   Successive

9-23   Multiple

Teams of different departments are all pitching in to help new products progress along the new-product development process with greater speed. The different people involved in this process come from all the following departments except:

1.   Supplier
2.   Finance
3.   Manufacturing
4.   Legal
5.   All of the above

9-24   Multiple

In the product life cycle, the stage which is characterized as a period of rapid market acceptance and increasing profits, is the _____ stage.

1.   Product development
2.   Introduction
3.   Growth
4.   Maturity
5.   Decline

9-25   Multiple

The _____ have the longest life cycles as their products stay in the mature stages of the life cycle for a long time.

1.   Product forms
2.   Product classes
3.   Brand classes
4.   Fashions
5.   Fads

9-26   Multiple

Victorian homes, casual clothing and abstract art are all considered:

1.   Fashion
2.   Fad
3.   Product class
4.   Style
5.   None of the above

9-27   Multiple

Because the market is not ready for product refinements at this stage, the company and its few competitors produce basic versions of the product.

1.   Introduction
2.   Product development
3.   Maturity
4.   Decline
5.   Growth

9-28   Multiple

At this stage in the product life cycle, educating the market remains a goal, but now the company also needs to meet the competition.

1.   Introduction
2.   Product development
3.   Maturity
4.   Decline
5.   Growth

9-29   Multiple

At the maturity stage of the life cycle, the company has an opportunity to prolong the life of its products in many ways. When a company tries to _____ the company is trying to increase the consumption of the current product.

1.   Modify the product
2.   Modify the marketing mix
3.   Modify the line extensions
4.   Modify the market
5.   Modify the target market

9-30   Multiple

Carrying a weak product can be very costly to a firm. The following are all problems with carrying a weak product except:

1. A weak product may take too much manager's time
2. A weak product often requires frequent price adjustments
3. A weak product takes advertising and salesforce attention away from "healthy" products
4. A weak product may delay searching for new products
5. All of the above

True/False Questions

9-1 True/False

Innovation is risky.

9-2 True/False

New products continue to fail at a disturbing rate. One recent study estimated new consumer packaged products fail at a rate of 60%.

9-3 True/False

One study found the number one success factor in new products is a unique, superior product; one with high quality, new features and low in price.

9-4 True/False

The search for new-product ideas should be systematic rather than haphazard.

9-5 True/False

Companies can watch competitor's ads and other communications for clues about their new products.

9-6 True/False

The purpose of idea generation is to create a list of good, quantifiable ideas.

9-7 True/False

The product idea rating process promotes a more systematic product idea evaluation and basis for discussion – however, it is not designed to make the decision for management.

9-8 True/False

An attractive idea is already considered a product concept.

9-9 True/False

For concept tests, a word or picture description is not sufficient, physical presentation of the product must be used.

9-10   True/False

Many firms routinely test new-product concepts with consumers before attempting to turn them into actual new products.

9-11   True/False

Once management has decided on its product concept, it can evaluate the business attractiveness of the proposal.

9-12   True/False

Prior to the product development stage, the product may have existed as only a word description, a drawing or perhaps a crude mockup.

9-13   True/False

The product development stage usually calls for a huge jump in investment.

9-14   True/False

The prototype must have the required functional features and also convey the intended physical characteristics of the proposed new product.

9-15   True/False

When the costs of developing and introducing the new product are low, or when management is already confident about the new product, the company may do little or no test marketing.

9-16   True/False

Competitors often do whatever they can to make test market results hard to read, for example, they will lower their prices in the test market area so consumers will buy their products, or they will purchase all the competitors products to skew the results.

9-17   True/False

Many companies are shifting to quicker and cheaper controlled and standard test-marketing methods.

9-18   True/False

Test marketing gives management the information needed to make a final decision about whether to launch the new product.

9-19   True/False

In rapidly changing industries facing increasingly shorter product life cycles, the rewards of fast and flexible product development are minimized by the risks.

9-20   True/False

Using the product life-cycle concept to develop a marketing strategy can be difficult because strategy is both a cause and a result of the product's life cycle.

Applying Terms and Concepts

To determine how well you understand the materials in this chapter, read each of the following brief cases and then respond to the questions that follow. Answers are given at the end of this chapter.

Case#1   Oat Bran[1]

Everyone seems to be selling it, and we've all heard it over and over again that oat bran can lower cholesterol levels. But a study detailed in the *New England Journal of Medicine* says it's not necessarily so. This prompts the question: Is oat bran good for your health or not?

Judging by the number of new oat bran cereals introduced in the last few years, cereal manufacturers suggest the answer is yes. Kellogg, with approximately 40 percent of the ready-to-eat cereal market, recently introduced Heartwise, Common Sense Oatbran, S.W. Graham, Nut and Honey, Crunch Biscuits, Oatbake, and Golden Crunch Mueslix for health-conscious consumers. General Mills, holding a 27 percent share of the market, introduced Benefit; Ralston Purina with 5 percent of the market, has put out Oatbran Options; Nabisco, with 6 percent of the market, has introduced Wholesome and Harty, a hot breakfast cereal; and Quaker Oats Company, with 8 percent of the market, has brought out a new ready-to-eat version of its Quaker Oatbran. (It should be noted that Heartwise and Benefit also contain an exotic grain called psyllium, which like oat bran, is being hailed as a cholesterol reducer, and that S.W. Graham is made from whole-wheat flour, both ingredients are aimed at health-conscious consumers.)

Consider the impact the oat bran mania has had on one cereal alone. General Mills' Cheerios is now the most popular cereal in the United States, having replaced Kellogg's Frosted Flakes. Cheerios gained a startling 3.1 percentage points in market share (from 6.2 to 9.9 percent) with each percentage point worth $66 million in revenues. General Mills has benefited enormously from the oat bran craze—more so than Kellogg, because while 20 percent of Kellogg's cereals are made with oats, 40 percent of General Mills cereals are.

Oat Bran is a manufacturer's dream come true. Consumers love it—not for the taste, but because research suggested you could eat it and reduce your cholesterol level and your chances of getting heart disease. Cereal makers loved it for the profits to be made, and farmers loved it because it increased the demand for their grain. The demand for oat bran increased by 800 percent in 1988 alone, and the growth has been sustained. In 1989, sales of all oat bran products totaled over $1 billion. It seems that high-fiber food is the hottest craze to hit supermarket shelves in years.

---

[1] *Principles of Marketing*, 3rd Edition, Kotler, Armstrong, Warren (Prentice Hall) – pg. 192.

There is now some evidence that rice bran and corn bran have cholesterol-reducing properties. Although this evidence is preliminary and far from conclusive, it might stimulate the market for these grains as well.

But what of the oat bran study reported in the *New England Journal of Medicine*, which concluded that "Oat-bran has little cholesterol-lowering effect and that high-fiber and low-fiber dietary grain supplements reduce serum cholesterol levels about equally, probably because they replace dietary fats." Dr. Timothy Johnson of *ABC News* makes these points: (1) a low-fat diet is extremely important in lowering cholesterol, and the extent to which oat bran contributes to this is debatable; (2) despite the criticism raised by the *New England Journal of Medicine* study of some of the hype about oat bran, it is a nutritious food worth eating in moderation; (3) the benefit of grain fiber, both soluble and insoluble, on the gastrointestinal tract is considerable –perhaps decreasing the risk of several ailments, including colon cancer.

So the answer to the question posed appears to be: If consumers substitute oat and oat bran products for cheese and eggs and other foods that are high in cholesterol, they will succeed in lowering their cholesterol level—but through the substitution effect rather than through any independent cholesterol-lowering benefit from oat bran.

1.   What typically happens during the market maturity stage of the product life cycle?

_____

_____

_____

_____

2.   Explain how cereal manufacturers could modify the market, the product or the marketing mix to stimulate sales during the market maturity stage of the product life cycle.
      a. The market:

_____

_____

_____

_____

      b. The product:

_____

_____

_____

_____

c. The marketing mix:

_____

_____

_____

_____

3.   If oat bran is found to have no unique ability to lower cholesterol levels, what is
        likely to happen to those products whose main attribute is oat bran?

_____

_____

_____

Case #2   Scented Disc Player

The House of Butler, a perfume maker and subsidiary of the William Schwab
Corporation, is selling a device it calls "The Newest Horizon in Home Entertainment."
The device is called the Scented Disc Player.

The player, which costs about $25, is a box about the size of a portable radio (30 cm
wide, 35 cm long, and 8 cm high). The discs are scented pads nearly identical in size to a
45 RPM record. When slipped into the player, a scent is given off as the disc is heated.
Each "play" lasts about two minutes, but the aroma from the play may linger for as long
as an hour.

The company currently offers 50 scents, including Spring Garden, Ocean Mist, Spruce,
Locker Room, and Arousal. Butler believes that virtually any scent can be reproduced and
plans to introduce many more as the market builds. A long-play disc can give up to 100
plays and cost approximately $7, while a short-play disc costs $2, but gives only 15 plays.
Butler has been working on the device for three years. It acquired the rights to the player
from an inventor who wishes to remain anonymous.

After significant development work in the laboratory, the device was introduced on a trial
basis in June 1994 in three markets. Information gathered from these markets in
Winnipeg, St. John's and Sudbury, which led Butler to decide on the final selling price,
promotional campaign, and distribution strategy. Information from these markets also led
to development of the long-play disc.

The company is limiting distribution of the player to 300 stores this fall so it won't be treated as a fad. It is now in national distribution and is currently being sold in Such stores as Eaton's and The Bay. Sales at this point are relatively low and profits are negligible as Butler builds its distribution system and heavily promotes the device. Competition currently is nonexistent and Butler expects to turn a profit in the upcoming Christmas selling season.

____1. The idea for the Scented Disc Player came from:

A.   internal source.

B.   customers.

C.   competition.

D.   suppliers.

E.   another source.

____2. The Scented Disc Player is currently in the _____ stage of its life cycle.

A.   introduction

B.   growth

C.   maturity

D.   decline

E.   market modification

____3. The Scented Disc Player is an example of a product _____. (class or form)

____4. The introduction of the long-playing disc is an example of:

A.   product modification.

B.   market modification.

C.   commercialization.

D.   concept development.

E.   test marketing.

250

_____5. The introduction of the Scented Disc Player in the Idaho, Louisiana, and Georgia markets is an example of:

    A.   commercialization.

    B.   business analysis.

    C.   product development

    D.   market testing.

    E.   market penetration.

Case #3   Lunenberg Yacht

Howard Nelson, a sailing enthusiast and crew member on the Defiant Racing Yacht, recently completed work on what he calls "A New Concept in Racing." His new AC-4 is a one-person, 15-foot fiberglass sailboat that is a one-fourth, scale version of the traditional racing yachts that compete in the Americas' Cup races.

His craft, which is suitable for sailors of all ages and levels of experience, is the result of four years of design and test work by his company, Lunenberg Yacht, located in Lunenberg, NS. The boat features a semi-horizontal cockpit which allows the sailor to steer via a foot lever, leaving hands free to work the sail control lines, which are conveniently placed in front of the helmsman. Another unique feature of the AC-4 is that Boom swing is not a problem on this lightweight boat (250 kg plus 160 kg of removable ballast), as only the sailor's head is above deck.

Nelson pooled ideas from amateur and experienced sailors as well as from dealer/distributors and design engineers before arriving at the final version of the AC-4. After significant testing in the laboratory and in the field for stability, safety, ease of handling, and positioning of the rigging, Nelson produced and sold a limited number of boats this summer at Hancock's Marina in Halifax, Nova Scotia, to gauge customer and dealer reaction.

Based on the success of the Hancock Marina experience, he plans to introduce the boat to marina dealers at the Montreal Boat Show in March. He has also determined that with a selling price of $4,800 on a cost of $3,900, his break-even point will be 200 boats, assuming his current fixed and variable costs do not change appreciably. Sales projections, however, are for a minimum of 250 boats in the coming year. Nelson has further determined that if demand begins to exceed his productive capability of 300 boats per year, the price of the AC4 will be raised to $5,400.

_____1. The testing of the AC-4 in the laboratory and field for stability, safety, ease of handling and positioning of rigging is an example of _____ testing.

    A.   functional

    B.   consumer

    C.   market

    D.   concept

    E.   viability

_____2. When Nelson decided to introduce the AC-4 to marina owners at the Montreal Boat Show in March, he decided on the _____ step in the new product development process.

    A.   market test

    B.   commercialization

    C.   product development

    D.   market strategy

    E.   market development

_____3. Lunenberg Yacht was engaged in _____ when the AC-4 was sold on a limited basis at Hancock's Marina in Halifax, Nova Scotia, the summer before introduction at the Montreal Boat Show.

    A.   concept testing

    B.   product development

    C.   consumer testing

    D.   market testing

    E.   idea screening

_____4. The review of estimated sales, costs, break-even, and profit projections are part of the _____ stage of the new product development process.

    A.   market strategy development

    B.   market analysis

    C.   concept analysis

    D.   business analysis

    E.   commercialization

_____5. The AC-4 is currently in the _____ stage of its life cycle.

    A.   market modification

    B.   growth

    C.   introduction

    D.   product modification

    E.   marketing-mix modification

Multiple Choice Answers

1.   Correct Answer: 4   Reference: pg. 313

2.   Correct Answer: 2   Reference: pg. 313

3.   Correct Answer: 5   Reference: pg. 314

4.   Correct Answer: 4   Reference: pg. 314

5.   Correct Answer: 3   Reference: pg. 314

6.   Correct Answer: 2   Reference: pg. 315

7.   Correct Answer: 5   Reference: pg. 317

8.   Correct Answer: 1   Reference: pg. 317

9.   Correct Answer: 4   Reference: pg. 317

10.   Correct Answer: 3   Reference: pg. 318

11.   Correct Answer: 1   Reference: pg. 319

12.   Correct Answer: 3   Reference: pg. 320

13.   Correct Answer: 2   Reference: pg. 320

14.   Correct Answer: 5   Reference: pg. 320

15.   Correct Answer: 4   Reference: pg. 321

16.   Correct Answer: 3   Reference: pg. 321

17.   Correct Answer: 2   Reference: pg. 322

18.   Correct Answer: 1   Reference: pg. 322

19.   Correct Answer: 4   Reference: pg. 323

20.   Correct Answer: 3   Reference: pg. 323

21.   Correct Answer: 1   Reference: pg. 323

22.	Correct Answer:	2	Reference:	pg. 325
23.	Correct Answer:	5	Reference:	pg. 327
24.	Correct Answer:	3	Reference:	pg. 327
25.	Correct Answer:	2	Reference:	pg. 327
26.	Correct Answer:	4	Reference:	pg. 328
27.	Correct Answer:	1	Reference:	pg. 329
28.	Correct Answer:	5	Reference:	pg. 329
29.	Correct Answer:	4	Reference:	pg. 330
30.	Correct Answer:	5	Reference:	pg. 332

True/False Answers

1. TRUE   Reference: pg. 313   Topic: New-Product Development Strategy
2. FALSE   Reference: pg. 314   Topic: New-Product Development Strategy
3. FALSE   Reference: pg. 314   Topic: New-Product Development Strategy
4. TRUE   Reference: pg. 314   Topic: Idea Generation
5. TRUE   Reference: pg. 315   Topic: Idea Generation
6. FALSE   Reference: pg. 317   Topic: Idea Screening
7. TRUE   Reference: pg. 318   Topic: Idea Screening
8. FALSE   Reference: pg. 318   Topic: Concept Development and Testing
9. FALSE   Reference: pg. 319   Topic: Concept Testing
10. TRUE   Reference: pg. 319   Topic: Concept Testing
11. FALSE   Reference: pg. 320   Topic: Business Analysis
12. TRUE   Reference: pg. 320   Topic: Product Development
13. TRUE   Reference: pg. 320   Topic: Product Development
14. FALSE   Reference: pg. 321   Topic: Product Development
15. TRUE   Reference: pg. 321   Topic: Test Marketing
16. TRUE   Reference: pg. 322   Topic: Standard Test Markets
17. FALSE   Reference: pg. 322   Topic: Standard Test Markets
18. TRUE   Reference: pg. 323   Topic: Commercialization
19. FALSE   Reference: pg. 327   Topic: Speeding Up New-Product Development
20. TRUE   Reference: pg. 328   Topic: Product Life-Cycle Strategy

Applying Terms and Concepts Answers

<u>Case#1</u>   <u>Oat Bran:</u>

Question #1
- During the market maturity stage of the product life cycle, sales typically slow down because many producers are selling the product.
- Overcapacity leads to greater competition.
- Competitors begin marking down prices and increasing their advertising and sales promotions.
- They may also increase their research and development budgets to find better versions of the product.
- Usually, these steps lead to a drop in profits, and some of the weaker competitors withdraw.

Question #2
a. Through market modification, the manufacturer tries to increase the consumption of the product by looking for new users and market segments. The firm would also look for ways to increase usage among current customers, or it might reposition the brand to appeal to a larger or faster-growing market segment—in this case, health-conscious consumers.
b. Using product modification, the manufacturer could increase the amount of oat bran in its cereal to attract new users and more usage.
c. Marketing-mix modification means the manufacturer would try to improve sales by changing one or more marketing-mix elements. Prices could be cut to attract new users and competitors' customers. A new advertising campaign highlighting changes in the product and/or new research could be launched. Aggressive sales promotion—trade deals, coupons, gifts, and contests—could be used. The company could also seek new distribution channels, such as mass merchandisers, to move the product.

Question #3
- If oat bran is found to have no unique ability to lower cholesterol levels, what is likely to happen to those products whose main attribute is oat bran?
- It is likely that certain brands of cereal will quickly move through the growth and maturity stages of the product life cycle to the sales decline stage.
- Sales and profits will continue to decline; competition will be reduced as some firms pull their product from the market; and the minimal amounts will be spent to promote the product, which will remain essentially unchanged.
- The strategic focus will be on improving productivity in view of a low cash flow.
- Eventually, many of the brands of cereal could be pulled from the market.

Case #2 Scented Disc Player:		Case #3 Lunenberg Yacht:	
1.	E	1.	A
2.	A	2.	B
3.	Form	3.	D
4.	A	4.	D
5.	D	5.	C

Chapter 10

Pricing Considerations and Approaches

Chapter Overview

Price can be defined narrowly as the amount of money charged for a product or service, or more broadly as the sum of the values consumers exchange for the benefits of having and using the product or service. Despite the increased role of non-price factors in the modern marketing process, price remains an important element in the marketing mix. It is the only element in the marketing mix that produces revenue; all other elements represent costs. Price is also one of the most flexible elements of the marketing mix. Unlike product features and channel commitments, price can be raised or lowered quickly. Even so, many companies are not good at handling pricing – pricing decisions and price competition are major problems for many marketing executives. Pricing problems often arise because prices are too cost oriented, not revised frequently enough to reflect market changes, not consistent with the rest of the marketing mix, or not varied enough for differing products, market segments, and purchase occasions.

Chapter Objectives

1. Identify and define the internal factors affecting a firm's pricing decisions.
2. Identify and define the external factors affecting pricing decisions, including the impact of consumer perceptions of price and value.
3. Contrast the three general approaches to setting prices.

Chapter Topics

Factors to Consider when Setting Prices
- Internal Factors Affecting Pricing Decisions
  - Marketing Objectives
  - Marketing-Mix Strategy
  - Costs
    - Types of Costs
    - Costs at different levels of production
    - Costs as a function of production experience
  - Organizational Considerations

- External Factor Affecting Pricing Decisions
  - The Market and Demand
    - Pricing in different types of markets
    - Consumer perceptions of price and value
    - Analyzing the price-demand relationship
    - Price elasticity of demand
  - Competitors' Costs, Prices, and Offers
  - Other External Factors

General Pricing Approaches
- Cost-Based Pricing
  - Cost-Plus Pricing
  - Breakeven Analysis and Target Profit Pricing
- Value-Based Pricing
- Competition-Based Pricing
  - Going-Rate Pricing
  - Sealed-Bid Pricing

Chapter Summary

1.   How marketing objectives affect pricing decisions.

Marketing objectives are among the internal company factors affecting price. Common objectives include survival that sets a low price. Current profit maximization sets a high price to meet current financial outcomes rather than long-term performance. Market-share leadership seeks the dominant market share through low prices to gain low-cost advantages. Product quality leadership sets high prices for superior products and high R & D.

2.   How costs affect pricing decisions.

Costs set the floor for price. Costs include variable costs that vary directly with the level of production and fixed costs that remain constant. Total costs are the sum of both. Costs can also be influenced by experience curves that lower cost as production becomes more efficient. Companies must estimate demand for each level of price considered and set the price that makes best use of the companies resources.

3.   Factors outside the company that affect pricing decisions.

Several external factors affect price. The nature of the market (pure competition, monopolistic, oligopolistic, pure monopoly) describes the number of buyers and sellers in a market. The competition and its resource also affect price. Demand elasticity and economic, social, and political factors must also be considered.

4.   The price-demand relationship and its affect on pricing decisions.

Each price a company might charge leads to a difficult level of demand expressed as the demand curve. Generally, the more a product costs the lower its level of demand although consumer perceptions of value for many premium goods are exceptions. Price elasticity can also affect price. If demand is inelastic, then changes in price won't affect demand. The less elastic the demand, the more it pays for the seller to raise the price.

5.   The three general pricing approaches.

Cost-plus pricing adds a standard mark-up to the cost of the product. Breakeven analysis and target profit pricing are common cost-oriented methods. Buyer-based or perceived-value pricing uses buyers' perceptions of value, not the seller's cost as the key to pricing. Competition-based pricing focuses on competitive prices over seller costs. Two forms are going-rate pricing that matches the competition and sealed-bid that tries to anticipate their price.

Key Terms

Breakeven Pricing   (pg. 354)
Cost-plus pricing   (pg. 353)
Demand curve   (pg. 351)
Experience curve   (pg. 351)
Experience curve   (pg. 348)
Fixed cost   (pg. 346)
Going-rate pricing   (pg. 358)
Monopolistic competition   (pg. 349)
Oligopolistic competition   (pg. 350)

Price   (pg. 343)
Price elasticity   (pg. 352)
Pure competition   (pg. 349)
Pure monopoly   (pg. 351)
Sealed-bid pricing   (pg. 358)
Total costs   (pg. 346)
Value-based pricing   (pg. 355)
Value pricing (pg. 356)
Variable costs (pg. 346)

Multiple Choice Questions

10-1   Multiple

Internal factors affecting pricing include all of the following except:

1.   Marketing objectives
2.   Marketing-mix strategy
3.   Costs
4.   Organization
5.   All of the above

10-2   Multiple

Companies set _____ as their major objective if they are troubled by too much capacity, heavy competition, or changing consumer wants.

1.   Survival
2.   Current profit maximization
3.   Market-share leadership
4.   Product-quality leadership
5.   Price leadership

10-3   Multiple

Companies interested in _____ set their prices as low as possible.

1.   Survival
2.   Current profit maximization
3.   Market-share leadership
4.   Product-quality leadership
5.   Price leadership

10-4   Multiple

If a product is positioned on non-price factors, which of the following not affect price?

1.   Quality
2.   Promotion
3.   Distribution
4.   Value
5.   All of the above

10-5   Multiple

Rent, heat and interest costs are considered what types of cost?

1.   Fixed
2.   Variable
3.   Total
4.   Expendable
5.   Predictable

10-6   Multiple

Management must decide who within the organization sets prices. Which of the following groups of people would set prices in an organization?

1.   Top management
2.   Division managers
3.   Product line managers
4.   Salespeople
5.   All of the above

10-7   Multiple

Not everybody in an organization actually sets the prices; however, many people influence the pricing strategies used. Who among the following would not have any influence in setting a pricing strategy?

1.   Sales managers
2.   Production managers
3.   Packaging managers
4.   Finance managers
5.   Accountants

10-8   Multiple

There are many external factors affecting a pricing strategy. Which of the following does not influence the pricing strategy?

1.   Nature of the market
2.   Demand
3.   Competition
4.   Supply
5.   Environmental elements

10-9   Multiple

Whereas costs set the lower limit of prices, the _____ and _____ set the upper limit.

1.   Market, demand
2.   Market, supply
3.   Consumers, market
4.   Consumers, demand
5.   Consumers, supply

10-10 Multiple

Under _____ competition, no single buyer of seller has much effect on the going market price.

1.   Monopolistic
2.   Pure
3.   Oligopolistic
4.   Pure monopoly
5.   Competitive

10-11 Multiple

In a purely competitive market, all the following play little or no role except:

1.   Marketing research
2.   Product development
3.   Advertising
4.   Sales promotion
5.   All the above play no role

10-12 Multiple

In _____ competition, a company is never sure it will gain anything permanent through a price cut.

1.   Monopolistic
2.   Pure
3.   Oligopolistic
4.   Pure monopoly
5.   Competitive

10-13 Multiple

A pure non-regulated monopoly is free to price whatever level they feel the market will bear. However, they do not always charge the full price for a number of reasons. One reason they do not consider is:

1. A desire not to attract competition
2. A desire to be perceived as socially responsible
3. A desire to penetrate the market faster
4. A fear of government regulation
5. All of the above are reasons

10-14 Multiple

The _____ curve shows the number of units the market will buy in a given period of time, at the different prices that might be charged.

1. Supply
2. Price
3. Market
4. Demand
5. Profit

10-15 Multiple

The price elasticity of demand equation divides _____ by _____

1. % change in quantity demanded, % change in price
2. % change in quality supplied, % change in price
3. % change in price, % change in quantity supplied
4. % change in price, % change in quantity demanded
5. % change in quantity demanded, % change in quantity supplied

10-16 Multiple

Nicolette is an up and coming executive for Nesbitt Burns. She is very happy with her promotion, as it has considerably increased her level of disposable income. She has become much less price sensitive. Which of the following is not an additional for her being price sensitive?

1. The products she buys are unique
2. The products she buys are high in quality
3. The products she buys are usually gifts
4. The products she buys are prestigious
5. The products she buys are exclusive

10-17 Multiple

Canon wants to introduce a new colour printer. To help them decide whether or not they are operating at a cost advantage or disadvantage, Canon needs to _____ its costs against its competitor's costs.

1.   Compare
2.   Contrast
3.   Match
4.   Benchmark
5.   Analyze

10-18 Multiple

Companies set prices by selecting a general pricing approach that includes all of the following factors except:

1.   Cost-based approach
2.   Supplier-based approach
3.   Buyer-based approach
4.   Competition-based approach
5.   All of the above are factors

10-19 Multiple

The equation for unit costs is the following:

1.   Fixed costs + (variable costs/units sales)
2.   Unit sales + (fixed costs/variable costs)
3.   Variable costs + (fixed costs/unit sales)
4.   Fixed costs + (unit sales/variable costs)
5.   Variable costs + (unit sales/fixed costs)

10-20 Multiple

The _____ pricing strategy is used by utility companies, which are constrained to make a fair return on their investment.

1.   Breakeven
2.   Target profit
3.   Cost-plus
4.   Value-based
5.   Value

10-21 Multiple

The equation for breakeven volume is the following:

1.   Fixed cost/(variable costs-price)
2.   Fixed cost/(price-variable cost)
3.   Variable cost/(price-fixed cost)
4.   Variable cost/(fixed cost-price)
5.   Price/(variable cost-fixed cost)

10-22 Multiple

In many business-to-business marketing situations, the pricing challenge is to find ways to adjust the value of the company's marketing offer to escape price competition and justify higher price margins. This is especially true for which of the following products?

1.   Consumer
2.   Industrial
3.   Convenient
4.   Commodity
5.   Manufactured

10-23 Multiple

In _____ industries that sell a commodity such as steel, paper or fertilizer, firms typically charge the same price.

1.   Pure competition
2.   Monopolistic
3.   Monopoly
4.   Consumer
5.   Oligopolistic

10-24 Multiple

Companies are not free to do exactly what they want. In setting prices, a company's short-term sales, market share, profit goals, as well as the ability of the vulnerable to afford them may have to be tempered by _____. If consumers do not approve, they will not buy.

1.   Social concerns
2.   Government
3.   Resellers
4.   Economic conditions
5.   1 and 2

10-25 Multiple

Common mistakes companies make when it comes to pricing include:

1.   Pricing is too cost oriented
2.   Prices are not revised often enough to reflect market changes
3.   Pricing does not take the rest of the marketing mix into account
4.   Only 1 and 3
5.   All of the above

10-26 Multiple

Pricing to cover variable costs and some fixed costs, as in the case of automobile dealerships that sell below total costs, is typical of which of the following pricing objectives.

1.   Current profit maximization
2.   Product-quality leadership
3.   Survival
4.   Market-share leadership
5.   Price leadership

10-27 Multiple

Companies that price products to enhance current financial results rather than long-run performance are using which of the following pricing objectives?

1.   Survival
2.   Product-quality leadership
3.   Market-share leadership
4.   Current profit maximization
5.   Price leadership

10-28 Multiple

Which, if any, of the following are not reasons why sellers use markup pricing?

1.   Because it simplifies the pricing process
2.   Because it is based ultimately on demand for the product
3.   Because it reduces price competition when all firms in an industry use it
4.   Because many people fee it is fairer to both buyers and sellers than other forms of pricing
5.   None of the above

10-29 Multiple

When a coffee shop in an airport and a fine restaurant in a luxury hotel charge different prices for the same meal to customers who find the atmosphere in the hotel worth the difference, we can say this pricing method is being used.

1.   Cost-based pricing
2.   Going-rate pricing
3.   Value-based pricing
4.   Sealed-bid pricing
5.   Prestige pricing

10-30 Multiple

If the percentage change in a product's demand is greater than the percentage change in price, we say that demand is:

1.   Elastic
2.   Weak
3.   Inelastic
4.   Unitary
5.   Indifferent

True/False Questions

10-1   True/False

If the company has selected its target market and positioning carefully, then its marketing-mix strategy, including price, will be fairly straightforward.

10-2   True/False

Pricing strategy is largely determined by decisions on market segmentation.

10-3   True/False

Prices have no bearing on keeping the loyalty and support of resellers or avoiding government intervention.

10-4   True/False

Companies often make their pricing decisions first and then base other marketing-mix decisions on the prices they want to charge.

10-5   True/False

Target costing starts with an ideal selling price and targets, or controls, costs, to ensure this price is met.

10-6   True/False

The best strategy is to charge the lowest price, rather than differentiating the marketing offer to make it worth a higher price.

10-7   True/False

Costs set the floor price the company can charge for its product.

10-8   True/False

To price wisely, management needs to know how its costs vary with different levels of production.

10-9   True/False

An aggressive pricing strategy might give the product a superior image.

10-10 True/False

Both consumers and industrial buyers balance the price of a product or service against the benefits of using it.

10-11 True/False

Buyers may see differences in sellers' products, but are not willing to pay different prices for them.

10-12 True/False

A government monopoly has the flexibility and power to pursue a variety of pricing objectives.

10-13 True/False

Pricing decisions, like other marketing-mix decisions, must be supplier oriented.

10-14 True/False

Usually, the higher the price of a product, the lower the demand of that product is.

10-15 True/False

For prestige goods like perfume, the demand curve sometimes slopes up meaning the higher the price, the more the demand.

10-16 True/False

The simplest pricing method is cost-plus pricing.

10-17 True/False

Mark up pricing only works if that price actually brings in the expected level of profits.

10-18 True/False

Value-based pricing uses the seller's cost as well as the user's perceptions of value as the key to pricing.

10-19 True/False

A company using value-based pricing must find what values buyers assign to different competitive offers.

10-20 True/False

More and more marketers have adopted the value pricing strategies as it is based on the right combination of quality and goods and services at a fair price.

Applying Terms and Concepts

To determine how well you understand the materials in this chapter, read each of the following brief cases and then respond to the questions that follow. Answers are given at the end of this chapter.

Case #1   Polar Plate Incorporated

Polar Plate is an innovative retractable block heater extension cord located between a vehicle's bumper and licence plate. The re-innovation of a flawed past product allows Polar Plate to satisfy existing demand for this convenient product.

By offering a high-quality product with superior components, Polar Plate positions itself as a convenience item targeting "baby boomers" in the automotive aftermarket. Through the efforts for the founding members, Polar Plate will find a place in automotive part stores where it can be made available to automobile enthusiasts and hobbyists. The convenient features will be communicated to consumers as a hassle-free-time-saving device. Finally, Polar Plate will have a place at service stations as part of their options in different winterization packages.

Currently, traditional extension cords are the only alternative in the marketplace. These products require the user to manually attach the cord to the block heater and then into an active outlet. Polar Plate's features and benefits will help to avoid the traditional scenarios including stolen cords, damage to vehicles resulting from hanging extension cords off mirror or antenna, and lost cords from individuals driving away forgetting their vehicles were plugged in. Polar Plate's sturdy construction, and retractable mechanism provide solutions for the hardships associated with traditional extension cords and block heater use.

1.   What characteristics would Polar Plate's target market have?

_____

_____

_____

_____

2.   What benefits of Polar Plate could be promoted to help price the product at a premium?

_____

_____

_____

_____

3. Polar Plate's fixed costs are $100,000, variable costs are $12.50 and they expect to sell 9,000 in the first year. What is the unit cost?

_____

_____

_____

_____

4. If Polar Plate sells its product for $30.00, what is the breakeven volume?

_____

_____

_____

_____

5. Do you believe value-based pricing could work in this situation? Why or why not?

_____

_____

_____

_____

Case #2   Scott Refining Company

The Scott Refining Company had been producing gasoline from the same refinery in Leduc, Alberta for over fifteen years, but the outlook over the near term was grim, and something had to be done soon. The members of the executive committee o] Scott were involved in a heated discussion about price policy.

During the past four months, the gasoline industry had been engaged in a price war in the provinces of Alberta, Saskatchewan, and Manitoba. Prices had declined to the point where refiners were breaking even — at best. Industry prices had gone down by over 9 percent, but gasoline sales volume had gone up only 4 percent.

The Sunpower Oil Company, one of Scott's competitors, had experienced sales gains of over 10 percent, but this extra litreage was the result of luring away competitors' dealers by offering even lower prices than those offered to established Sunpower dealers. Scott experienced a 4.8 percent gain in gasoline sales, while prices had declined 8 percent as a result of the price war. Part of Scott's price decline had been offset by lower average production costs as the plant moved from 87 percent to 96 percent of rated capacity. The competition's costs, however, had either remained stable or increased because all were operating at near rated capacity prior to the price war.

Clifford Cole, one member of Scott's executive committee, suggested getting together with some of the competitors to see if they couldn't reach some kind of agreement to stop this cut-throat competition and set prices at a reasonable level. Linda Klein, another member, said she thought the company ought to set a resale (retail) price for its own dealers and refuse to sell to them if they cut prices below this level. Several other solutions were offered, but after several hours the meeting was adjourned without any decision.

_____1. The price elasticity of gasoline demand for the industry during the past four months was:

    A.   very elastic.

    B.   slightly elastic.

    C.   inelastic.

    D.   declining substantially.

    E.   remaining constant.

_____2. The price elasticity of demand for Scott Gasoline during the past four months was:

    A.   very elastic but not as much as that of the industry.

    B.   slightly elastic.

    C.   inelastic.

    D.   positive.

    E.   both (A) and (D)

_____3. The decline in Scott's production costs was probably a result of:

    A.   lower variable costs.

    B.   the experience curve.

    C.   lower total costs.

    D.   spreading fixed costs offer greater volume.

    E.   higher variable costs.

_____4. Regarding the pricing practices of Sunpower Oil Company:

    A.   Scoff should consider doing the same thing.

    B.   Scoff should not meet Sunpower prices if Sunpower offers a lower price to a Scoff dealer because matching competitors' prices is illegal.

    C.   it is probably illegal unless Sunpower can show lower costs in serving the dealers who get lower prices.

    D.   it is probably legal because sellers can lower their prices to whomever they wish.

    E.   both (A) and (D)

_____5. The suggestion that several competitors get together to set a "reasonable" price is:

    A.   probably illegal per se.

    B.   probably an acceptable practice as long as no small competitors are injured.

    C.   legal because firms can raise prices whenever they want to, with whomever they wish to.

    D.   illegal unless all parties to the agreement are selling below cost.

    E.   both (A) and (C)

Case #3   Ronica Camera Company

The Ronica Camera Company was at one time a leader in the development of a 35 mm single lens reflex (S.L.R.) camera. Ten to twelve years ago, they enjoyed an excellent reputation as they pioneered features which have since become industry standards. Today, however, the Ronica Camera Company is no longer an industry leader but rather is seen by consumers as simply just another camera company.

Ronica's latest entry into the highly competitive field of 35 mm S.L.R. cameras is the Ronica XG-2. This camera was designed to compete with the Canon AE-6, Rollei SL 35-C, Yashica FR-2, and Vivitar XV-4.

The XG-2 features a shutter speed of 4 to 1/1,000 seconds with automatic aperture and shutter control, ASA range from 12-1,600 split range view-finder, microprism, automatic film loading, and hot shoe provision for flash attachment. (These features, however, are common to most 35 mm S.L.R.'s).

The suggested retail selling price for the XG-2 is $480. However, like its competitors' prices, the discount price is only about 75 percent of the suggested retail price. Ronica did not discount its prices in the past, but has now found this to be a necessity as consumers became increasingly price sensitive. Also, like its competitors, the XG-2 is not sold through discount department stores where consumers display little brand loyalty. Ronica has used the standard industry markup of 25 percent of cost in calculating its suggested retail price. The discounted selling price, however, just covers the costs associated with producing and selling the XG-2.

Ray Walsh, Ronica's president, is concerned about the long-term viability of the company. He was especially disturbed to hear that the Japanese and Germans are both expected to introduce new, lightweight (less than 400 grams) cameras with electronic circuitry designed to provide an even greater range of features. The selling price of these new cameras is expected to be comparable to the discounted price of existing S.L.R.'s.

1.   Which type of market situation is the Ronica Camera Company facing?

    _____

2.   The pricing objective for the Ronica XG-2 is probably

    _____

3.   The fact that Ronica Camera Company is using an industry standard markup gives indication that the company is using _____ pricing.

4.   Identify the type of demand curve that the Ronica Camera Company is facing, as well as the factors which have led you to this conclusion.

    _____

    _____

    _____

    _____

    _____

    _____

Case #4   Perfume

It seems $20 or so a mililitre isn't too high a price to pay to feel good about yourself — or so the marketers of perfumes hope.

There are over 700 different brands of perfume on the market, with new brands introduced each year. Celebrities such as Cher, Sophia Loren, Jane Seymour, Elizabeth Taylor, and Linda Evans are spokespersons for brands they hope women will enjoy. Even designers and high-profile stores have been getting in on the act.

Marketers hope that when a consumer buys a perfume, she will adopt it as her own. The right perfume can help a woman feel feminine and attractive, independent and confident, special and with a more positive outlook. So is $20/ml too much to spend to feel good about yourself? Many consumers believe the benefits are well worth the price.

But consumers might be surprised to learn that the cost of producing many perfumes is actually quite low. The ingredients might cost $1, with a similar amount going for the bottle and package. The sales representative might receive an additional $1, with the balance of the sales price split between the retailer and the producer of the brand.

The makers of Obsession spent $17 million to launch their perfume, while it cost an estimated $10 million to promote Poison. The high profile of glamorous celebrities and organizations such as Giorgio's helps promote an image of prestige. The high price enhances the image.

1.   Explain the nature of the demand curve for a prestige product as it applies to more expensive perfumes.

    _____

    _____

    _____

    _____

    _____

2. Assuming perfume marketers are in monopolistic competition, discuss the relative freedom they have in pricing.

_____

_____

_____

_____

_____

3. Discuss the elasticity of demand facing marketers of more expensive perfumes.

_____

_____

_____

_____

4. What factors are likely to influence the price elasticity of demand for perfume?

_____

_____

_____

_____

Sources: "France's BIC Bets U.S. Consumers Will Go for Perfume on the Cheap," *The Wall Street Journal,* January 12, 1989, p. B 4; "$22 Million Campaign Urges: Spritz Your BIC," *Advertising Age,* February 20, 1989, pp. 3-69; "Will $4 Perfume Do the Trick for BIC?", *Business Week,* June 20, 1988, pp. 89-92; "BIC Begins Campaign for New Perfume Line," *The New York Times,* March 20, 1989, p. 9; and "Of Flicks and Flickers," *Financial World,* January 10, 1989, pp. 60-61. "BIC Markets Perfume," *ABC News Business World Broadcast,* March 5, 1989.

Multiple Choice Answers

1. Correct Answer: 5 Reference: pg. 343

2. Correct Answer: 1 Reference: pg. 344

3. Correct Answer: 3 Reference: pg. 344

4. Correct Answer: 4 Reference: pg. 346

5. Correct Answer: 1 Reference: pg. 346

6. Correct Answer: 5 Reference: pg. 348

7. Correct Answer: 3 Reference: pg. 348

8. Correct Answer: 4 Reference: pg. 349

9. Correct Answer: 1 Reference: pg. 349

10. Correct Answer: 2 Reference: pg. 349

11. Correct Answer: 5 Reference: pg. 349

12. Correct Answer: 3 Reference: pg. 350

13. Correct Answer: 2 Reference: pg. 351

14. Correct Answer: 4 Reference: pg. 351

15. Correct Answer: 1 Reference: pg. 352

16. Correct Answer: 3 Reference: pg. 352

17. Correct Answer: 4 Reference: pg. 352

18. Correct Answer: 2 Reference: pg. 353

19. Correct Answer: 3 Reference: pg. 354

20. Correct Answer: 1 Reference: pg. 354

21. Correct Answer: 2 Reference: pg. 354

22.	Correct Answer:	4	Reference:	pg. 356
23.	Correct Answer:	5	Reference:	pg. 358
24.	Correct Answer:	1	Reference:	pg. 353
25.	Correct Answer:	5	Reference:	pg. 344
26.	Correct Answer:	3	Reference:	pg. 344
27.	Correct Answer:	4	Reference:	pg. 344
28.	Correct Answer:	2	Reference:	pg. 354
29.	Correct Answer:	3	Reference:	pg. 355
30.	Correct Answer:	1	Reference:	pg. 348

True/False Answers

1.   TRUE   Reference: pg. 343   Topic: Internal Factors Affecting
                                                    Pricing Decisions
2.   FALSE   Reference: pg. 344   Topic: Internal Factors Affecting
                                                    Pricing Decisions
3.   FALSE   Reference: pg. 344   Topic: Internal Factors Affecting
                                                    Pricing Decisions
4.   TRUE   Reference: pg. 345   Topic: Marketing-Mix Strategy

5.   TRUE   Reference: pg. 345   Topic: Marketing-Mix Strategy

6.   FALSE   Reference: pg. 345   Topic: Marketing-Mix Strategy

7.   TRUE   Reference: pg. 346   Topic: Costs

8.   TRUE   Reference: pg. 346   Topic: Costs

9.   FALSE   Reference: pg. 348   Topic: Costs as a Function of
                                                    Production Experience
10. FALSE   Reference: pg. 349   Topic: The Market and Demand

11. FALSE   Reference: pg. 349   Topic: The Market and Demand

12. TRUE   Reference: pg. 351   Topic: The Market and Demand

13. FALSE   Reference: pg. 351   Topic: Consumer Perceptions of
                                                    Price and Value
14. TRUE   Reference: pg. 351   Topic: Analyzing the Price-Demand
                                                    Relationship
15. TRUE   Reference: pg. 351   Topic: Analyzing the Price-Demand
                                                    Relationship
16. TRUE   Reference: pg. 353   Topic: Cost-Plus Pricing

17. FALSE   Reference: pg. 354   Topic: Cost-Plus Pricing

18. FALSE   Reference: pg. 355   Topic: Value-Based Pricing

19. TRUE   Reference: pg. 356   Topic: Value-Based Pricing

20. TRUE   Reference: pg. 356   Topic: Value-Based Pricing

Applying Terms and Concepts Answers

Case #1   Polar Plate:

Question #1
- People who like to tinker with their cars
- People who are looking for convenience
- Baby boomers ages 30 to 52
- Incomes between $25,000 and $50,000

Question #2
- Security
- Prevents extension cord damage
- Convenience and ease of use
- Uniqueness
- Quality materials and construction to withstand harsh winter conditions
- Ease of installation

Question #3
- Unit Cost = $23.61

Question #4
- Breakeven volume = 5715

Question #5
- Value-based pricing is possible
- Consumers will find value in this product therefore manufacturers can price the product at a higher price to ensure that they cover their costs and not hurt sales because consumers are willing to pay more

Case #2   Scoff Refining Company:

1.   C
2.   C
3.   D
4.   C
5.   A

Case #3   Ronica Camera Company:

1. Pure competition

2. Survival

3. Cost-plus

4. Elastic demand curve
   - Industry characterized by many buyers and sellers, with no seller having much influence on the going market price.
   - Customers see the products as being homogeneous.
   - Company operating at/or about breakeven. Customers do not exhibit brand loyalty.
   - Customers are price sensitive.

Case #4   Perfume:

1. The relationship between the price charged for a product and the resulting demand level yields the demand curve. The demand curve shows the number of units customers will buy in a given time period at different prices that might be charged. In the normal case, demand and price are inversely related — that is, the higher the price, the lower the demand. Most demand curves, therefore, are downward sloping.

   Prestige products have a different demand curve, one that slopes upwards and backward (it resembles the letter C written backward). This demand curve suggests that the quantity demanded will actually increase if the price is raised — up to a point. However, if consumers perceive the price as being too high, demand will begin to drop.

   For perfumes perceived as prestige products, a high price actually enhances their image and sales.

2. Under monopolistic competition, the market consists of many buyers and sellers who trade over a range of prices rather than a single market price. A range of prices is possible because sellers can differentiate their offers to buyers; either the physical product can be varied in quality, features, or style, or the accompanying services can be varied. Because buyers see differences in sellers' products, they will pay different prices.

Sellers try to develop differentiated offers for different customer segments and, in addition to price, freely use branding, advertising, and personal selling to set their offers apart. Because there are many competitors, each firm is less affected by competitors' marketing strategies.

3. Price elasticity is related to the change in demand and total revenue resulting from a given change in price.

    If demand is inelastic and the perfume marketer raises the price, demand may drop slightly, but total revenue will either remain the same or increase because although fewer units will be sold, the higher price per unit will preserve or enhance total revenue.

    If demand is elastic and the perfume marketer raises the price, demand will drop dramatically, resulting in a decrease in total revenue. The increased price per unit will not be sufficiently great to offset the decrease in the number of units sold.

    If demand is elastic rather than inelastic, sellers will consider lowering their price. A lower price will produce more total revenue. This makes sense as long as the extra costs of producing and selling more of the product do not exceed the extra revenue.

4. Buyers are less price-sensitive when the product they are buying is unique or when it is high in quality, prestige, or exclusiveness. They are also less price-sensitive when substitute products are hard to find or when they cannot easily compare the quality of substitutes. Finally, buyers are less price-sensitive when the total expenditure for a product is low relative to their income or when the cost is shared by another party. All of these factors are true of perfumes.

Chapter 11

Pricing Strategies

Chapter Overview

Pricing decisions are subject to an incredibly complex array of environmental and competitive forces. A company sets not a single price, but rather a pricing structure that covers different items in its line. This pricing structure changes over time as products move through their life cycles. The company adjusts product prices to reflect changes in costs and demand and to account for variations in buyers and situations. As the competitive environment changes, the company considers when to initiate price changes and when to respond to them.

Chapter Objectives

1. Describe the major strategies for pricing imitative and new products.
2. Explain how companies find a set of prices that maximize the profits from the total product mix.
3. Discuss how companies adjust their prices to take into account different types of customers and situations.
4. Discuss the key issues related to initiating and responding to price changes.

Chapter Topics

New-Product Pricing Strategies
- Market-Skimming Pricing
- Market-Penetration Pricing

Product-Mix Pricing Strategies
- Product Line Pricing
- Optional-Product Pricing
- Captive-Product Pricing
- By-Product Pricing
- Product-Bundle Pricing

Price-Adjustment Strategies
- Discount and Allowance Pricing
- Segmented Pricing
- Psychological Pricing
- Promotional Pricing
- Geographical Pricing
- International Pricing

Price Changes
- Initiating Price Changes
  - Initiating Price Cuts
  - Initiating Price Increases
  - Buyer Reactions to Price Changes
  - Competitor Reactions to Price Changes
- Responding to Price Changes

Chapter Summary

1.   The major strategies of pricing new products.

New products can be either innovative or imitative. There are two strategies for innovative products. Market-skimming pricing sets an initial high price to "skim" revenues layer by layer for the market. Skimming also helps recoup high introduction costs. Market-penetration pricing sets a low price to capture a large market share and dominate the market as the low cost leader. Imitative products seek a price-quality niche.

2.   The five product-mix strategies used to maximize profits from the total product mix.

Product-line pricing sets price steps for successive combinations of features for related products in the product line. Optional-product pricing offers to sell optional or accessory products with main product. Captive-product pricing involves products that must be used with the main product. By-product pricing markets waste from products or packaging. Product-bundle pricing combines several products at a special reduced price.

3.   The major price-adjustment strategies for dealing with different types of customers and situations.

Discount pricing rewards customers for early payment, volume purchases, off-season buying, and promotional activity. Discriminatory pricing adjusts prices for different customer groups but the price is not directly due to different costs. Psychological pricing considers price/quality perceptions. Promotional pricing uses temporary reductions. Value pricing seeks price-feature combinations. Geographical pricing uses location.

4.   The major reasons why companies decide to change prices.

Companies may cut prices if faced with excessive capacity to stimulate demand. Other cuts may come from loss of market share, a strategy of low cost leadership, or competitive moves. Increases may result from inflation or over-demand. All price changes should be weighed carefully and evaluated in terms of customer and competitive reactions.

5.   The conditions appropriate for using segmented pricing strategies.

Segmented pricing sells a product or service at two or more prices even though the difference is not based on different costs. Customer-segment pricing charges different customer groups different prices. Product-form pricing offers different product versions at different prices. Location pricing based different value on the location, such as seat locations in an arena. Time pricing varies by season, month, day, or even hour.

Key Terms

Allowances   (pg. 375)
Basing-point pricing   (pg. 380)
By-product pricing   (pg. 373)
Captive-product pricing   (pg. 371)
Cash discount (pg. 375)
FOB-origin pricing   (pg. 379)
Freight-absorption pricing   (pg. 380)
Functional discount   (pg. 375)
Market-penetration pricing   (pg. 370)
Market-skimming pricing   (pg. 369)
Optional-product pricing   (pg. 371)

Product-bundle pricing   (pg. 374)
Product line pricing   (pg. 371)
Promotional pricing   (pg. 378)
Psychological pricing (pg. 377)
Quantity discount   (pg. 375)
Reference prices   (pg. 377)
Seasonal discount   (pg. 375)
Segmented pricing   (pg. 375)
Uniform delivered pricing   (pg. 379)
Zone pricing   (pg. 380)

Multiple Choice Questions

11-1   Multiple

A new product pricing strategy qualifying as a value strategy has the following characteristics:

1.   High price, high quality
2.   High price, low quality
3.   Low price, high quality
4.   Low price, low quality
5.   Moderate price, high quality

11-2   Multiple

Market skimming is the practice of charging a higher price for a new product to gain higher profits. This pricing strategy only makes sense in all the following situations except:

1.   The producer's image and quality must support the price
2.   The costs of producing a small quantity cannot be so high that they cancel out the benefits of charging a higher price
3.   Competitors should not be able to enter the market to undercut prices
4.   Consumers must want the product to support the price
5.   All of the above

11-3   Multiple

There are many advantages to implementing a low-price market penetration strategy. Among them are all the following except:

1.   The market must be highly price sensitive
2.   The product is not unique but valuable
3.   Production and distribution costs must fall as sales increase
4.   The low price must help keep out the competition
5.   All of the above

11-4　Multiple

Which of the following is not considered a product mix strategy situation?

1.　　Product line pricing
2.　　Optional-product Pricing
3.　　Captivc-product pricing
4.　　By-product pricing
5.　　Packaged pricing

11-5　Multiple

General Motors offers their vehicles in a variety of colours and with a variety of different options. Their cars come with the basic features, however if you desire additional features, you must pay extra for them. This type of pricing strategy is considered:

1.　　Optional-product pricing
2.　　Captive-product pricing
3.　　Product-bundle pricing
4.　　By-product pricing
5.　　Product line pricing

11-6　Multiple

Many camera manufactures and razor manufacturers price their basic products low so they can make their money on the film and razor blades. This type of pricing strategy is considered:

1.　　Optional-product pricing
2.　　Product line pricing
3.　　Captive-product pricing
4.　　Packaged pricing
5.　　Product-bundle pricing

11-7　Multiple

Hotels and amusement parks offer customers special packaged rates. These rates may include room, meals and entertainment, and are cheaper than if the consumer were to purchase the products separately. This pricing strategy is known as:

1.　　Packaged pricing
2.　　Product-bundle pricing
3.　　Optional-product pricing
4.　　Captive-product pricing
5.　　Optional-product pricing

11-8   Multiple

The price adjustment strategy that reduces prices to reward customer responses such as
paying early or promoting the product is:

1.   Discount and allowance pricing
2.   Segmented pricing
3.   Promotional pricing
4.   Value pricing
5.   International pricing

11-9   Multiple

The price adjustment strategy that temporarily reduces prices to increase short-run sales
is:

1.   Segmented marketing
2.   International pricing
3.   Value pricing
4.   Promotional pricing
5.   Discount and allowance pricing

11-10   Multiple

Discount and allowance pricing includes all the following discount strategies except:

1.   Cash
2.   Manufacturing
3.   Quantity
4.   Seasonal
5.   All of the above

11-11   Multiple

A _____ discount provides an incentive for the customer to buy more from one
given seller, rather than from many different sources.

1.   Quantity
2.   Cash
3.   Functional
4.   Seasonal
5.   Manufacturing

11-12 Multiple

Segmented pricing is another form of a price-adjustment strategy. The segmented pricing strategy used by utility companies that vary their prices to commercial users based on the time of day and weekend versus weekday is called:

1. Customer-segment pricing
2. Product-form pricing
3. Location pricing
4. Differentiation pricing
5. Time pricing

11-13 Multiple

Just as market segmentation can be done in a variety of ways, so can price segmentation. However, for a segmented pricing strategy to be effective, it must comply with all the following except:

1. The segment must be substantial
2. The market must be segmentable
3. The segments must show different degrees of demands
4. Competitors should not be able to undersell the firm
5. All the above

11-14 Multiple

Reference pricing – prices that buyers carry in their minds and refer to when looking at a given product, is part of which pricing strategy?

1. Value pricing
2. Geographical pricing
3. Psychological pricing
4. Segmented pricing
5. International pricing

11-15 Multiple

Which of the following is not an example of promotional pricing?

1. Loss leader
2. Price points
3. Special-event pricing
4. Cash rebates
5. All of the above

11-16 Multiple

Geographic pricing can be very difficult to use as not everyone involved will benefit to the same extent. The geographic pricing strategy which charges all customers the freight costs from one specific city to the customer's location is called:

1. Free-on-board
2. Uniform delivered pricing
3. Basing-point pricing
4. Zone pricing
5. Freight-absorption pricing

11-17 Multiple

The geographic pricing strategy where pricing is used for market penetration and to hold onto increasingly competitive markets is called:

1. Free-on-board
2. Uniform delivered pricing
3. Basing-point pricing
4. Zone pricing
5. Freight-absorption pricing

11-18 Multiple

International pricing is the most complex pricing strategy as everything except _____ _____ must be considered before deciding on the price the company should charge.

1. Economic conditions
2. Competitive situations
3. Laws and regulations
4. Development of wholesaling and retaining system
5. All of the above

11-19 Multiple

Initiating price changes can be a very difficult decision for companies to make. Of the following what is the only reason why a company would not initiate a price cut?

1. They had excess capacity
2. They were faced with failing market share
3. The wanted to initiate a drive to dominate the market
4. The company's profits were suffering
5. All of the above

11-20 Multiple

Price increases are resented more than price cuts. Which group is least likely to complain about a price increase?

1.   Customers
2.   Lobbyists
3.   Dealers
4.   Company salesforce
5.   All of the above

11-21 Multiple

The major factor(s) that affect price increases is (are):

1.   Inflation
2.   Interest rates
3.   Overdemand
4.   Only 1 and 3
5.   All of the above

11-22 Multiple

_____ are not affected by the raising or lowering of prices.

1.   Manufacturers
2.   Buyers
3.   Competitors
4.   Distributors
5.   All of the above

11-23 Multiple

Competitors are most likely to react to a price change when:

1.   The number of firms involved are small
2.   The product is uniform
3.   They are experiencing drops in market share
4.   The buyers are well informed
5.   All of the above

11-24 Multiple

There are many questions a company can ask themselves to prepare for a competitor's price change. All the following issues help a company make a broader analysis of its situation except:

1.   The company's intentions and resources for the product
2.   The product's stage in the life cycle
3.   The products importance in the company's product mix
4.   The intentions and resources of the competitor
5.   The possible consumer reactions to price changes

11-25 Multiple

In response to a competitor's change in price, a company may decide that an effective action must be taken. What is one action a company can take?

1.   Reduce its price
2.   Raise the perceived quality of its offer
3.   Improve quality and increase price
4.   Introduce a new low-price "fighting-brand"
5.   All of the above

11-26 Multiple

When IGA uses the waste heat from its refrigeration units to heat its stores, it is really practising a form of:

1.   Product-bundle pricing
2.   Optional-product pricing
3.   Captive-product pricing
4.   By-product pricing
5.   Packaged pricing

11-27 Multiple

One factor firms considering a price cut to deal with overcapacity must weigh is the possibility of:

1.   Customer resentment over lower prices
2.   A weakening of competition
3.   Price wars as competitors respond
4.   Too great an increase in demand as a result
5.   All of the above

11-28 Multiple

What type of pricing strategy is being used when the seller places products at no charge with a carrier and the title and responsibility pass to the customer who pays the freight?

1. FOB-origin pricing
2. FOB-destination pricing
3. CFI pricing
4. Basing-point pricing
5. Freight-absorption pricing

11-29 Multiple

The redesign of existing brands to offer more quality at a given price or the same quality at a lower price is typical of which of the following?

1. Product-form pricing
2. Cash discount pricing
3. Seasonal discount pricing
4. Value pricing
5. Functional pricing

11-30 Multiple

The setting of prices at $29.95 rather than $30.00 under the belief that consumers will perceive the first price as more affordable is part of the basis of:

1. Discount pricing
2. Discriminatory pricing
3. Psychological pricing
4. Promotional pricing
5. Perceptual pricing

True/False Questions

11-1   True/False

Pricing strategies usually change as the product passes through its product life cycle.

11-2   True/False

A company planning to develop an imitative new product faces a product pricing problem.

11-3   True/False

Many companies inventing new products initially set high prices to "skim" revenues layer by layer from the market.

11-4   True/False

The strategy for setting a product's price often remains the same when the product is part of a product mix.

11-5   True/False

If the price difference between two successive products is large, buyers will usually buy the more advanced product.

11-6   True/False

The seller's task is to establish perceived quality differences that support the price differences.

11-7   True/False

Captive-product pricing is similar to a dual pricing strategy for services.

11-8   True/False

Using by-product pricing, the manufacturer seeks a market for these by-products and should accept only a price that covers more than the cost of storing, delivering and processing them.

11-9   True/False

Marketers must be cautious and avoid overbundling services.

11-10 True/False

Seasonal discounts allow the seller to keep production steady during an entire year.

11-11 True/False

Companies often will adjust their cost prices to allow for differences in customer, products and locations.

11-12 True/False

When consumers can judge the quality of products by examining it or by calling on past experience with it, they use price more to judge quality.

11-13 True/False

When marketers use reference pricing, they must ensure they comply only with pricing regulations.

11-14 True/False

The use of misleading comparison prices hurts consumers and makes it difficult to maintain healthy competition.

11-15 True/False

Some psychologists argue that certain digits have symbolic values and visual qualities that should be considered in pricing.

11-16 True/False

With promotional pricing, companies will temporarily price their products below list price and sometimes even below cost.

11-17 True/False

Used too frequently, promotional pricing can create "deal-prone" customers who wait until brands go on sale before buying them.

11-18 True/False

One advantage of FOB pricing is it is fairly easy to administer and it lets the firm advertise its price nationally.

11-19 True/False

If all sellers used the same basing-point city, delivery prices would be the same for all customers and price competition would be eliminated.

11-20 True/False

Price escalations may result from differences in selling strategies or market conditions.

Applying Terms and Concepts

To determine how well you understand the materials in this chapter, read each of the following brief cases and then respond to the questions that follow. Answers are given at the end of this chapter.

Case #1   Maislin Power[1]

Maislin Power produces diesel engines at its manufacturing plant in Montreal, Quebec. Although the basic engine can be modified to perform a variety of functions, it is most often used as the power plant in locomotives, tugboats and ocean going ships. It can also be used as a power generator to supply electricity.

The base price for its most popular engine—the AL1—is $190,000 and it is typically sold F.O.B. origin. Other geographical pricing schemes are used depending upon the pricing strategies of the competition. Maislin has two major competitors in this market including White Motor in Toronto, Ontario, and Connors Diesel in Saskatoon, Saskatchewan.

Recently two customers inquired as to the delivered cost of an AL1 from Maislin. One potential customer, St. Albert Medical Centre (AMC) located in southern Ontario, is interested in purchasing an engine to serve as a back-up generator should the centre lose electrical power. The other potential customer is Marsden Construction, located in Halifax, Nova Scotia. Marsden was recently awarded a contract by Java National Oil to construct an offshore drilling platform. The engine would serve as the primary source of electrical power aboard the rig.

Relevant transportation costs for the AL1 from Montreal to St. Albert are $500, from Montreal to Toronto $1,000, from Montreal to Halifax $2,000, from Toronto to St. Albert $1,500, from Toronto to Halifax $4,000, and from Saskatoon to Halifax $5,000.

Maislin realizes it must be flexible in its pricing to remain competitive. Customers view Maislin, White and Connors engines as roughly equal in capability, dependability, and serviceability. None of the three has a price advantage.

1.   What would the transportation charge be to the St. Albert Medical Centre if Maislin sold an AL1 engines with the following terms:

a. F.O.B. base point Toronto

_____

b. F.O.B. origin

_____

---

[1] *Principles of Marketing*, 3rd Edition, Kotler, Armstrong, Warren (Prentice Hall) – pg. 232.

c. Freight absorption (F.O.B. destination)

_____

2. What would the transportation charges be to Marsden Construction if Maislin sold an AL1 engine with the following terms:
   a. F.O.B. base point Toronto

   _____

   b. F.O.B. origin

   _____

   c. Freight absorption (F.O.B. destination)

   _____

3. If Maislin sold AL1 engines to both St. Albert Medical Centre and Marsden Construction terms F.O.B. base point Toronto, what would the net transportation charge to Maislin? Explain your answer.

   _____

   _____

   _____

   _____

Case #2   Jaffe Computer Company

Clark Jaffe began the Jaffe Computer Company in 1988 in order to produce a portable computer, packing it with useful programs and selling it at a reasonable price. The result was the Jaffe I, a 24-pound machine with a 5 inch diagonal screen and a selling price of less than $2,000.

The machine was designed for the business-person who needed processing at remote locations such as construction sites. The Jaffe I with 512K and high-resolution color/graphics was also designed to serve as a terminal for large computers made by DATADEC. The Jaffe I became the first practical lap-top computer.

The pricing strategy for the Jaffe I was to introduce the machine at $1,895 and when sales dropped off, to gradually lower the price. The machines were produced in Ottawa, Ontario, but sold throughout the United States and Canada; Jaffe charges a common freight cost to each customer regardless of location. Distribution is through independent electronics shops and computer stores.

Sales to date have been outstanding, each retail location averaging 10 computer sales per month. In an effort to further increase company sales and profits, Jaffe instituted a new policy whereby any retailer taking delivery of more than 12 machines per month would receive a 5 percent discount on all machines delivered that month. The discount would be passed along to the customers or used to increase store profits.

Jaffe also instituted two additional changes in the company pricing policy. First, any customer who purchased a Jaffe Special Use Program (beyond those included in the purchase price) would receive $25 back from the Jaffe Computer Company. Second, certain nonprofit agencies, such as schools, were to receive a $200 reduction in the retail price for purchasing the computer. Jaffe would reimburse the retailer upon verification of the customer's purchase and nonprofit status.

_____1. The Jaffe Computer Company appears to be using which pricing policy regarding the Jaffe I?
   A.   market skimming
   B.   penetration pricing
   C.   predatory pricing
   D.   zone pricing
   E.   integrated pricing

_____2. Which geographical pricing policy is this company using regarding freight charges?
   A.   FOB origin
   B.   uniform delivered
   C.   zone pricing
   D.   basing-point pricing
   E.   both (A) and (B)

_____3. When Jaffe authorized a change in company policy to grant a discount of 5 percent to all retailers taking delivery of more than 12 computers per month, he was offering a _____ discount.
   A.   cash
   B.   functional
   C.   seasonal
   D.   quantity
   E.   trade

_____4. When Jaffe modified the base price of the Jaffe I for nonprofit agencies, he was engaging in _____.
   A.   market penetration.
   B.   promotional pricing.
   C.   segmented pricing.
   D.   geographic pricing.
   E.   both (A) and (C)

_____5. The $25 cash refund offer is an example of:

      A.   discriminatory pricing.

      B.   cash rebate.

      C.   promotional pricing.

      D.   by-product pricing.

      E.   both (B) and (C)

Case #3   Axton Corporation

The Axton Corporation has just completed preparation for the introduction of a unique new product, the firm had worked for years before achieving its breakthrough to find a way to convert some of the "waste" materials generated by the production of its existing line of products into a profitable market offering. The product Axton has developed appears to be a dream come true. Not only can it be produced from waste materials, but Axton has developed a series of accessories that can be added to the basic item in order to customize the offering to the tastes of individual customers. Just prior to introduction, Axton management was notified that its new offering had been granted patent protection.

1.   With regard to its introductory pricing strategy, Axton can employ _____ - _____ pricing if it wishes to derive maximum immediate advantage from its unique, patent-protected product.

2.   Should Ax-ton decide to adopt an introductory strategy that is designed to maximize market shale while slowing competitive entry, it will employ _____ _____.

3.   The fact that Axton's new product can be produced from the "waste" material of current products allows the firm to utilize _____ pricing.

4.   Axton's ability to customize its basic offering by offering a wide range of accessories will enable the firm to employ _____ pricing.

5.   The use of products that have formerly been wasted to produce a new product that is expected to be highly profitable should enable Axton to stimulate the sales and profitability of its existing products through lower prices. Such an action would be a form of _____ _____.

Multiple Choice Answers

1. Correct Answer: 3   Reference: pg. 369

2. Correct Answer: 4   Reference: pg. 370

3. Correct Answer: 2   Reference: pg. 370

4. Correct Answer: 5   Reference: pg. 374

5. Correct Answer: 1   Reference: pg. 317

6. Correct Answer: 3   Reference: pg. 371

7. Correct Answer: 2   Reference: pg. 374

8. Correct Answer: 1   Reference: pg. 374 (Table 11-2)

9. Correct Answer: 4   Reference: pg. 374 (Table 11-2)

10. Correct Answer: 2   Reference: pg. 375

11. Correct Answer: 1   Reference: pg. 375

12. Correct Answer: 5   Reference: pg. 376

13. Correct Answer: 1   Reference: pg. 377

14. Correct Answer: 3   Reference: pg. 377

15. Correct Answer: 2   Reference: pg. 378

16. Correct Answer: 3   Reference: pg. 380

17. Correct Answer: 5   Reference: pg. 380

18. Correct Answer: 5   Reference: pg. 380

19. Correct Answer: 4   Reference: pg. 382

20. Correct Answer: 2   Reference: pg. 382

21. Correct Answer: 4   Reference: pg. 382

22.	Correct Answer:	1	Reference:	pg. 382
23.	Correct Answer:	3	Reference:	pg. 383
24.	Correct Answer:	1	Reference:	pg. 383
25.	Correct Answer:	5	Reference:	pg. 386
26.	Correct Answer:	4	Reference:	pg. 372
27.	Correct Answer:	3	Reference:	pg. 382
28.	Correct Answer:	1	Reference:	pg. 379
29.	Correct Answer:	4	Reference:	pg. 374 (Table 11-2)
30.	Correct Answer:	3	Reference:	pg. 377

True/False Answers

1.	TRUE	Reference:	pg. 369	Topic:	New-Product Pricing Strategies
2.	FALSE	Reference:	pg. 369	Topic:	New-Product Pricing Strategies
3.	TRUE	Reference:	pg. 369	Topic:	Market-Skimming Pricing
4.	FALSE	Reference:	pg. 370	Topic:	Product-Mix Pricing Strategies
5.	FALSE	Reference:	pg. 371	Topic:	Product Line Pricing
6.	TRUE	Reference:	pg. 371	Topic:	Product Line Pricing
7.	FALSE	Reference:	pg. 372	Topic:	Captive-Product Pricing
8.	FALSE	Reference:	pg. 373	Topic:	By-Product Pricing
9.	TRUE	Reference:	pg. 374	Topic:	Product-Bundle Pricing
10.	TRUE	Reference:	pg. 375	Topic:	Discount and Allowance Pricing
11.	FALSE	Reference:	pg. 375	Topic:	Segmented Prices
12.	FALSE	Reference:	pg. 377	Topic:	Psychological Pricing
13.	FALSE	Reference:	pg. 377	Topic:	Psychological Pricing
14.	TRUE	Reference:	pg. 377	Topic:	Psychological Pricing
15.	FALSE	Reference:	pg. 378	Topic:	Psychological Pricing
16.	TRUE	Reference:	pg. 378	Topic:	Promotional Pricing
17.	TRUE	Reference:	pg. 379	Topic:	Promotional Pricing
18.	FALSE	Reference:	pg. 379	Topic:	Geographical Pricing
19.	TRUE	Reference:	pg. 380	Topic:	Geographical Pricing
20.	TRUE	Reference:	pg. 381	Topic:	International Pricing

Applying Terms and Concept Answers

<u>Case #1   Maislin Power:</u>

Question #1
a. $1,500
b. $500
c.   0

Question #2
a. $4,000
b. $5,000
c.   0

Question #3
- Zero
- When Maislin sold to Marsden, they actually incurred $5,000 in transportation costs, but only billed Marsden $4,000.
- Yet, when they sold to St. Albert Medical Centre, they actually incurred only $500 in transportation costs (since the engine was shipped directly to St. Albert) but collected $1,500.
- In both cases, transportation was charged as if the engine came from Toronto rather than from Montreal.
- Maislin made $1,000 on a phantom freight charge in the sale to St. Albert Medical Centre but it was cancelled out when they absorbed $1,000 of the freight charge on the sale to Marsden Construction.

<u>Case #2   Jaffe Computer Company:</u>

1.   A

2.   B

3.   D

4.   C

5.   E

<u>Case #3   Axton Corporation:</u>

1.   market-skimming

2.   market-penetration

3.   by-product

4.   optional product

5.   product line

Chapter 12

Distribution Channels and Logistics Management

Chapter Overview

Marketing channel decisions are among the most important decisions management faces. A company's channel decision directly affects every other marketing decisions. Each channel system creates a different segment of target consumers. Management must make channel decisions carefully, incorporating today's needs with tomorrow's likely selling environment. While some companies pay too little attention to their distribution channels, others have used imaginative distribution systems to gain a competitive advantage.

Chapter Objectives

1. Explain why companies use distribution channels and explain the functions these channels perform.
2. Discuss how channel members interact and how they organize to perform the work of the channel.
3. Identify the major channel alternatives open to a company.
4. Explain how companies select, motivate, and evaluate channel members.
5. Discuss the nature and importance of physical distribution and integrated logistics management.

Chapter Topics

The Nature of Distribution Channels
- Why are Marketing Intermediaries Used?
- Distribution Channel Functions
- Number of Channel Levels

Channel Behaviour and Organization
- Channel Behaviour
- Vertical Marketing System
  - Corporate VMS
  - Contractual VMS
  - Administered VMS
- Horizontal Marketing System
- Hybrid Marketing System

Channel Design Decision
- Analyzing Consumer Service Needs
- Setting the Channel Objectives and Constraints
- Identifying Major Alternatives
  - Types of Intermediaries
  - Number of Marketing Intermediaries
  - Responsibilities of Channel Members
- Evaluating the Major Alternatives
- Designing International Distribution Channels

Channel Management Decisions
- Selecting Channel Members
- Motivating Channel Members
- Evaluating Channel Members

Physical Distribution and Logistics Management
- Nature and Importance of Physical Distribution and Marketing Logistics
- Goals of the Logistics System
- Major Logistics Functions
  - Order Processing
  - Warehousing
  - Inventory
  - Transportation
    - Rail
    - Truck
    - Water

- Pipeline
- Air
- Integrated Logistics Management
  - Cross-Functional Teamwork Inside the Corporation
  - Building Channel Partnerships
  - Third-Party Logistics

Chapter Summary

1.   Why companies use distribution channels and the functions they perform. Producers use intermediaries because they may lack the financial resources to carry out direct marketing, for greater efficiency, contacts, and specialization. Intermediaries perform the functions of providing information, promotion, contact, matching, negotiation, physical distribution, financing, and risk taking.

2.   How channel members interact and organize themselves to do the work of the channel.

Channel members interact in mutually interdependent ways. Channels consist of dissimilar firms that band together for the common good. Channel members may experience horizontal or vertical conflict. Types of vertical marketing systems include corporate, contractual, and administered. Corporate are wholly owned. Contractual may be wholesaler-sponsored voluntary, retailer co-operatives, or franchise. A franchise can be either manufacturer sponsored or a service firm.

3.   The major distribution channel alternatives open to a company.

Major alternatives include types of intermediaries (company sales force, manufacturer's agency, or industrial distributors), number of intermediaries (intensive, selective, exclusive distribution), and determining the responsibilities of each channel member.

4.   How companies select, motivate, and evaluate channel members.

Selection involves determining the characteristics that distinguish better intermediaries, years in business, other lines carried, profit record, growth, profitability, cooperativeness, and reputation.

5.   The issues firms face when setting up physical distribution systems.

Firms must consider the nature of physical distribution, the physical distribution objective, order processing, warehousing, inventory, transportation mode to be used, and organizational responsibility for physical distribution.

Key Terms

Administered VMS (pg. 404)

Channel conflict (pg. 400)

Channel level (pg. 398)

Containerization (pg. 429)

Contractual VMS (pg. 403)

Conventional distribution channel (pg. 400)

Corporate VMS (pg. 403)

Direct marketing channel (pg. 395)

Distribution centre (pg. 417)

Distribution channel (pg. 396)

Exclusive distribution (pg. 409)

Franchise organization (pg. 403)

Full-line forcing (pg. 414)

Horizontal marketing systems (pg. 404)

Hybrid marketing channels (pg. 405)

Indirect marketing channel (pg. 398)

Integrated logistics management (pg. 420)

Intensive distribution (pg. 409)

Physical distribution (pg. 413)

Retailer cooperatives (pg. 403)

Selective distribution (pg. 409)

Third-party logistics (pg. 421)

Vertical marketing system (pg. 400)

Wholesaler-sponsored voluntary chains (pg. 403)

Multiple Choice Questions

12-1   Multiple

Caterpillar is a marketing intermediary used by a number of firms. What is the one factor Caterpillar cannot generally perform better than the firm itself?
1.   Contracts
2.   Experiences
3.   Financing
4.   Scale of operation
5.   All of the above

12-2   Multiple

Producers make _____ assortments of products in _____ quantities, but customers want _____ assortments of products in _____ quantities.

1.   Broad, large, narrow, small
2.   Narrow, large, broad, small
3.   Broad, small, Narrow, large
4.   Narrow, small, broad, large
5.   None of the above

12-3   Multiple

A distribution channel overcomes all the following major gaps except _____ that separates goods and services from those who would use them.

1.   Distance
2.   Time
3.   Place
4.   Possession
5.   All of the above

12-4   Multiple

Which of the following functions do members of the marketing channel not perform?

1.   Contract
2.   Physical distribution
3.   Negotiation
4.   Risk taking
5.   They perform all of the above

12-5   Multiple

Which function does not connect the institutions in the marketing channel?

1.   They use up scarce resources
2.   They often can be performed better through specialization
3.   They can be shifted amoung channel members
4.   They need to be performed in a prescribed order
5.   All of the above

12-6   Multiple

Several types of flows connect all of the institutions in the channel. Which of the
following is not one of them?

1.   Physical flow
2.   Creative flow
3.   Flow of ownership
4.   Payment flow
5.   Promotion flow

12-7   Multiple

In the customer marketing channels, channel # _____ involves the manufacturer,
wholesaler, retailer, and consumer.

1.   1
2.   2
3.   3
4.   4
5.   5

12-8   Multiple

In both the consumer and business marketing channels, there are complex systems of
behaviour where people and companies interact to accomplish all of the following goals
except:

1.   Profit
2.   Individual
3.   Company
4.   Channel
5.   All of the above

12-9   Multiple

When Coca-Cola came into conflict with some of its bottlers who agreed to bottle competitor Dr. Pepper, they were experiencing _____ conflict.

1.   Controversial
2.   Horizontal
3.   Vertical
4.   Bi-lateral
5.   Unilateral

12-10 Multiple

The vertical marketing system, which is a unified system, can be dominated by the:

1.   Producer
2.   Wholesaler
3.   Retailer
4.   Only 1 and 2
5.   All of the above

12-11 Multiple

The vertical marketing system is becoming very popular as its users achieve economies through all the following except:

1.   Size
2.   Strong relationships
3.   Bargaining power
4.   Elimination of duplicate services
5.   All of the above

12-12 Multiple

Gallo is one of the world's largest wineries. It participates in every aspect of selling, including the production and marketing of its wines. Gallo practices which type of vertical marketing system?

1.   Contractual
2.   Administered
3.   Corporate
4.   Integrated
5.   Cooperative

12-13 Multiple

Licence bottlers in various markets who buy Coca-Cola syrup concentrate and then carbonate, bottle and sell the finished product to retailers in local market. They are practising which type of vertical marketing system?

1.   Contractual
2.   Administered
3.   Corporate
4.   Integrated
5.   Cooperative

12-14 Multiple

In horizontal marketing systems, two or more companies at one level join together to follow a new marketing opportunity. Companies can combine all the following except _____ to accomplish more together than they could alone.

1.   Capital
2.   Production capabilities
3.   Marketing resources
4.   New product idea
5.   All of the above

12-15 Multiple

Computers have emerged over the last few years as a necessity in today's business and home environment. Three things make up a winning computer product. Which of the following is not one of them?

1.   A product
2.   Customers
3.   Corporate relationships
4.   Distributors
5.   All of the above

12-16 Multiple

Which of the following questions would not be used in analyzing consumer service needs?

1.   Do customers want bargains or good quality?
2.   Do customers want to buy from nearby locations?
3.   Do customers want add-on services?
4.   Would they rather buy over the phone or through the mail?
5.   Do customers value breadth of a product or do they want specialization?

12-17 Multiple

Which of the following channel objective characteristics greatly affect channel design?

1.   Product characteristics
2.   Characteristic of intermediaries
3.   Environmental factors
4.   Only 1 and 3
5.   All of the above

12-18 Multiple

When a company has defined its channel objectives, it should next identify its major channel alternatives in terms of all the following except:

1.   Types of intermediaries
2.   Number of intermediaries
3.   Stability of intermediaries
4.   Responsibility of each channel member
5.   All of the above

12-19 Multiple

Independent firms whose sales forces handle related products for many companies are known as:

1.   Company sales force
2.   Manufacturer's agency
3.   Industrial distributors
4.   Sales agencies
5.   Wholesalers

12-20 Multiple

Producers of common raw materials and convenience products typically seek:

1.   Selective distribution
2.   Exclusive distribution
3.   Expedient distribution
4.   Intensive distribution
5.   Reliable distribution

12-21 Multiple

The responsibilities of channel members are very important to articulate. This is the only item channel members do not need to agree on before entering into a contract.

1. Price policies
2. Conditions of sale
3. Marketing strategies
4. Territorial rights
5. Specific services

12-22 Multiple

A company that wants to keep the channel as flexible as possible would place greater importance on the _____ criteria in evaluating major alternatives.

1. Economic
2. Control
3. Financial
4. Adaptive
5. Replacement

12-23 Multiple

Channel management does not require _____:

1. Selecting channel members
2. Promoting channel members
3. Motivating channel members
4. Evaluating channel member performance
5. All of the above

12-24 Multiple

When selecting intermediaries, a company will want to evaluate its channel members on everything except:

1. Years in business
2. Other lines carried
3. Growth and profit recorded
4. Cooperativeness
5. All of the above

12-25 Multiple

Companies today are placing greater emphasis on logistics for several reasons. Which of the following is not one of them?

1.   To attain total quality management.
2.   Customer service and satisfaction have become the cornerstones of marketing
3.   Logistics is a major cost element for most companies
4.   The explosion in product variety has created a need for improved logistics
5.   Improvements in technology have created opportunities for major gains in distribution efficiency

12-26 Multiple

Shipping and transportation account for _____ % of an average product's price.

1.   20
2.   10
3.   5
4.   15
5.   25

12-27 Multiple

Containerization consists of putting goods in boxes or trailers that are easy to transfer between two transportation modes. _____ describes the use of rail and trucks.

1.   Fishyback
2.   Piggyback
3.   Trainship
4.   Airtruck
5.   None of the above

12-28 Multiple

Which of the following factors are not important in ranking the transportation modes?

1.   Speed
2.   Dependability
3.   Capability
4.   Availability
5.   All of the above

12-29 Multiple

Building channel partnerships is becoming increasingly popular. Which of the following is not considered a form of channel partnership?

1.   Cross-company teams
2.   Shared projects
3.   Bi-lateral teams
4.   Information sharing
5.   Continuous inventory replenishment

12-30 Multiple

Companies may use third-party logistics providers for several reasons. What is one reason they would cite for not using a third party?

1.   Getting product to market is their main focus
2.   Outsourcing logistics frees a company to focus more intensely on its core business
3.   Integrated logistics companies understand the increasingly complex logistics environment
4.   It is always cheaper
5.   All of the above

True/False Questions

12-1   True/False

Giving some of the selling jobs to intermediaries means a company gives up some control over how and to whom products are sold.

12-2   True/False

The role of marketing intermediaries is to transform the assortment of products made by producers into the assortment wanted by consumers.

12-3   True/False

The concept of distribution channels in limited to the distribution of tangible products.

12-4   True/False

Producers, not final consumers, are part of every channel.

12-5   True/False

Channel systems do not stand still, new types of intermediaries surface, and whole new channel systems evolve.

12-6   True/False

Each channel member depends on the others.

12-7   True/False

The channel will be most effective when each member is assigned to the task it can do best.

12-8   True/False

Individual channels are interested in the broad view, therefore are more concerned with the success of the channel than its own short-run goals.

12-9   True/False

No conflict in a channel helps ensure health competition.

12-10 True/False

A vertical marketing system acts as a unified system.

12-11 True/False

The fact most consumers can tell the difference between contractual and corporate vertical marketing systems shows how unsuccessful the contractual organizations compete with corporate chains.

12-12 True/False

Forming successfully horizontal marketing systems is absolutely essential in an era of global business and global travel.

12-13 True/False

Hybrid channels offer few advantages to companies facing large and complex markets.

12-14 True/False

Marketing channels can be thought of as customer value supply systems in which each channel member adds value for the customers.

12-15 True/False

In each segment, the company wants to minimize the total channel cost of meeting customer service requirements.

12-16 True/False

A company need only identify one type of channel member who can carry out its channel work.

12-17 True/False

Three strategies are available with respect to the number of marketing intermediaries used. They are intensive, exclusive, and sequential distribution.

12-18 True/False

Mutual services and duties need to be spelled out carefully, especially in franchise and exclusive distribution channels.

12-19   True/False

The company must not only sell through the intermediaries, but also to them.

12-20   True/False

Logistics addresses the problem of outbound distribution, but fails to address the issue of inbound distribution.

Applying Terms and Concepts

To determine how well you understand the materials in this chapter, read each of the following brief cases and then respond to the questions that follow. Answers are given at the end of this chapter.

Case #1   Pro Image[1]

The marketing of professional and university team sportswear and novelty items is a $3 billion-a-year industry. Since 1985, approximately 300 sports fan shops have opened. Most are independent operations, but franchisers are an increasingly important part of the retailing scene. Pro Image wasn't the first franchiser of the one-stop sports fan shop, but they are battling to lead the pack. In the franchise field, Pro Image competes with such firms as SpectAthlete, Sports Fantasy, Fan Fair, and Sports Arena Ltd.

Fan shops seem to sell just about anything from T-shirts, sweatshirts, sweaters, and caps to coffee mugs, key chains, pennants, bedspreads, and football helmet telephones. While many items are licensed from teams and emblazoned with team logos, most shops also sell authentic merchandise like team jackets and jerseys.

Pro Image was founded in 1985 by Chad and Kevin Olson. Three years later they controlled over 130 stores, with an additional 100 franchised outlets. Each franchise store costs roughly $100,000 approximately $16,000 of which covers the franchise fee with the rest going towards inventory and store improvements.

Since Pro Image recognizes the importance of a good location, it requires franchisees to locate in high-traffic regional malls. Pro Image assists franchisees in site selection, lease negotiation, and advertising. Storeowners must create an upscale image with glass storefronts and wood-slat wall displays. Pro Image requires new owners to attend a four-day training session. They also sponsor an annual convention. Other assistance includes a business hotline and a computerized inventory and sales system. As an added service, they stock hard-to-get items in a 4,500-square-foot warehouse, making them more readily available to franchisees.

Pro Image recognizes consumers want to wear what their sports heroes wear on the field. Therefore, they stock authentic merchandise that comes directly from the same manufacturers that supply leagues and teams. But authentic merchandise carries a relatively high price. Replica merchandise is available for the more price-conscious. Though it's very similar to the authentic merchandise, it's not exactly the same product worn by the pro players.

---

[1] *Principles in Marketing*, 3rd Edition, Kotler, Armstrong, Warren (Prentice Hall) – pg. 253.

The main customer base for Pro Image is men between 18 and 40, although women are becoming increasingly important customers. They purchase the product for themselves, their spouses, or their children.

Competition for the sports fan market is intense. Pro Image must battle not only other franchise operations but also independents, department stores, general retailers, and athletic stores that sell similar merchandise. The latter three constitute the major competition for Pro Image since they control approximately 90 percent of the total licensed merchandise market.

Retailers and their customers aren't the only ones benefiting from the boom in sports wear and novelty item merchandising. Consider NFL Properties, the licensing arm of the National Football League. Since 1980, NFL Properties has seen its souvenir revenues increase by nearly 400 percent to approximately $1.5 billion US. The licensing division of NFL Properties oversees the authorization and sale of more than 700 items.

Team owners love NFL Properties. In the past decade, with two player strikes, relatively stagnant television income, and escalating player salaries, team owners have come to appreciate the approximately $1.5 million US they receive each year from Properties' activities.

Also benefiting are a variety of charities. Each year NFL Properties raises and distributes nearly $700,000US to deserving organizations.

1.   In your opinion, is the sports merchandise "boom" a fad or a trend that will continue to be profitable?

_____

_____

_____

_____

2.   Would a conventional distribution channel work in this industry? Why or why not?

_____

_____

_____

_____

3. Explain why an organization such as NFL Properties might choose to have independent retailers, franchise operations, department stores, mass merchandisers, and athletic stores sell NFL-authorized merchandise to consumers rather than sell the merchandise directly to consumers through their own chain of retail outlets.

_____

_____

_____

_____

4. Discuss the nature of the vertical marketing system employed by Pro Image.

_____

_____

_____

_____

5. Suppose you are interested in opening a sports fan shop. What do you see as the advantages and disadvantages of becoming part of a franchise operation?

_____

_____

_____

_____

Case #2   Ramer Gourmet Popcorn Shop

Cynthia Ramer opened her first Gourmet Popcorn Shop in November 1979, at the Riverside Mall in Victoria, BC. In addition to her fresh-popped popcorn, she sold a full range of popcorn merchandise, including unpopped corn, flavoured oils and salts, and various styles of corn poppers. She has since abandoned most of the Popcorn merchandise and now concentrates on selling her flavoured popcorn and a small selection of flavoured salts.

Ramer's organization had grown by 1983 to include eight outlets in the Victoria and Richmond areas. Four shops were located in shopping malls, two in large hotel complexes, and two in office complexes, each location averaging $200,000 in sales per year.

In a bold venture, Ramer allowed her system of preparing and flavouring popcorn to become a franchise operation. She sold distribution rights to an independent group. The franchise contract set very strict requirements on nearly all facets of the operation, including pricing. Ramer also forced C.R. Purchasing to act as the wholesaler servicing the franchise locations.

After two years, Ramer Gourmet Popcorn Shops were a huge success, with over 30 franchise locations in operation in BC, in addition to their own eight shops. It seemed as if they were everywhere people were likely to congregate — hotels, subways, airports, and hospitals, in addition to shopping malls and office complexes. Ramer was beginning to experience some difficulty with her suppliers of popcorn and thought that if the operation continued to grow, she would consider moving into the farm business to assure a steady supply of popcorn. Ramer had no concern about the long-term viability of her organization. A report released in January by the Morden Manitoba-based Popcorn Institute indicated the popcorn consumption was expected to exceed 15 billion litres annually, up from the 10 billion litres consumed in 1988. Besides, her gourmet popcorn was so chic, it was sometimes purchased as a gift or used as hors d'oeuvre's at parties.

Last month, Ramer began hearing complaints that several of the franchise locations were lowering their prices and/or selling new flavours of popcorn, even though this was clearly in violation of the franchise agreement.

_____1. The marketing strategy of Ramer Gourmet Popcorn Shops is to have _____ distribution.

    A.   intensive

    B.   selective

    C.   exclusive

    D.   market

    E.   blanket

_____2. The type of channel system currently used in marketing Ramer Gourmet Popcorn is:

    A.   conventional marketing system.

    B.   corporate vertical marketing system.

    C.   contractual vertical marketing system.

    D.   both (B) and (C)

    E.   none of the above.

_____3. What is occurring when several of the individual popcorn shop owners begin lowering their prices in violation of the franchise agreement?

    A.   channel cooperation

    B.   channel discommunication

    C.   horizontal channel conflict

    D.   vertical channel conflict

    E.   channel interdependence

_____4. Ramer Gourmet Popcorn is currently sold through a _____-level channel system.
  A.   zero
  B.   one
  C.   two
  D.   direct
  E.   sub

Case #3   Fast Eddie

Fast Eddie is a former race car driver who retired from racing to manufacture equipment specifically designed for the dirt track driver. His twenty years of racing on clay ovals in Manitoba, Saskatchewan, Alberta and BC, as well as his engineering degree from General Motors Institute of Technology (GMIT), provided him with the background necessary to produce some of the finest automotive equipment to be found. His 30,000 square feet plant, located in Gimli, Manitoba, produces conventional carburetors as well as fuel injection systems, turbochargers, a complete line of intake manifolds, high-temperature titanium exhaust valves, and camshafts.

Fast Eddie sells his products directly to independent retailers located throughout the Prairies. He sells to only one retailer in a given area. Rather than suggesting a retail selling price, he allows the retailers to promote and sell his parts as they see fit. Fast Eddie has no formal contract with each retailer. This arrangement works to his advantage and his disadvantage. While he reserves the right to pull his parts from any store at any time, he has very little control over the retailers. Many of them carry a number of lines that directly compete with Fast Eddie parts.

Each retailer is small and sometimes located in a small town. Since inventory in each store is limited, Fast Eddie needs to have his goods delivered quickly and efficiently. It is not unusual for a customer to buy a substitute rather than wait for delivery of another brand.

_____1. Fast Eddie automotive parts are sold utilizing a(n) _____ distribution strategy.
  A.   intensive
  B.   exclusive
  C.   selective
  D.   market
  E.   blanket

_____2. The type of channel system currently used in distributing Fast Eddie automotive parts is a:

A. conventional marketing system.

B. corporate vertical marketing system.

C. contractual vertical marketing system.

D. two-level system.

E. zero-level system.

_____3. If Fast Eddie opened his own retail outlets to sell his automotive parts, he would be establishing a(n) _____ marketing system.

A. horizontal

B. conventional

C. corporate

D. contractual

E. interdependent

_____4. Fast Eddie automotive products are currently sold through a _____ -level channel system.

A. zero

B. one

C. two

D. three

E. sub

_____5. If Fast Eddie, in addition to selling to retailers, also sold his automotive parts directly to companies that build race cars, Fast Eddie would be:

A. operating a multichannel marketing system.

B. operating a hybrid marketing system

C. engaged in direct marketing.

D. all of the above

E. none of the above

6. Which mode of transportation do you believe Fast Eddie should use to transport his goods to his customers, and why?

_____

_____

_____

_____

Multiple Choice Answers

1. Correct Answer: 3   Reference: pg. 396

2. Correct Answer: 2   Reference: pg. 396

3. Correct Answer: 1   Reference: pg. 397

4. Correct Answer: 5   Reference: pg. 397

5. Correct Answer: 4   Reference: pg. 397

6. Correct Answer: 2   Reference: pg. 398

7. Correct Answer: 3   Reference: pg. 399

8. Correct Answer: 1   Reference: pg. 399

9. Correct Answer: 3   Reference: pg. 400

10. Correct Answer: 5   Reference: pg. 400

11. Correct Answer: 2   Reference: pg. 400

12. Correct Answer: 3   Reference: pg. 403

13. Correct Answer: 1   Reference: pg. 403

14. Correct Answer: 4   Reference: pg. 404

15. Correct Answer: 2   Reference: pg. 407

16. Correct Answer: 1   Reference: pg. 407

17. Correct Answer: 5   Reference: pg. 407

18. Correct Answer: 3   Reference: pg. 408

19. Correct Answer: 2   Reference: pg. 408

20. Correct Answer: 4   Reference: pg. 409

21. Correct Answer: 3   Reference: pg. 409

22.	Correct Answer:	4	Reference:	pg. 410
23.	Correct Answer:	2	Reference:	pg. 411
24.	Correct Answer:	5	Reference:	pg. 411
25.	Correct Answer:	1	Reference:	pg. 415
26.	Correct Answer:	4	Reference:	pg. 416
27.	Correct Answer:	2	Reference:	pg. 419
28.	Correct Answer:	5	Reference:	pg. 419 (Table 12-2)
29.	Correct Answer:	3	Reference:	pg. 421
30.	Correct Answer:	4	Reference:	pg. 423

True/False Answers

1. TRUE   Reference: pg. 396   Topic: Why are Marketing
                                                Intermediaries Used?
2. TRUE   Reference: pg. 396   Topic: Why are Marketing
                                                Intermediaries Used?
3. FALSE   Reference: pg. 397   Topic: Why are Marketing
                                                Intermediaries Used?
4. FALSE   Reference: pg. 398   Topic: Number of Channel Levels
5. TRUE   Reference: pg. 399   Topic: Channel Behaviour and
                                                Organization
6. TRUE   Reference: pg. 399   Topic: Channel Behaviour
7. TRUE   Reference: pg. 399   Topic: Channel Behaviour
8. FALSE   Reference: pg. 400   Topic: Channel Behaviour
9. FALSE   Reference: pg. 400   Topic: Channel Behaviour
10. TRUE   Reference: pg. 400   Topic: Vertical Marketing System
11. FALSE   Reference: pg. 404   Topic: Contractual VMS
12. TRUE   Reference: pg. 405   Topic: Horizontal Marketing
                                                Systems
13. FALSE   Reference: pg. 406   Topic: Hybrid Marketing Systems
14. FALSE   Reference: pg. 407   Topic: Analyzing Consumer Service
                                                Needs
15. TRUE   Reference: pg. 407   Topic: Setting the Channel
                                                Objectives and Constraints
16. FALSE   Reference: pg. 408   Topic: Identifying Major
                                                Alternatives
17. FALSE   Reference: pg. 409   Topic: Number of Marketing
                                                Intermediaries
18. TRUE   Reference: pg. 410   Topic: Responsibilities of Channel
                                                Members
19. TRUE   Reference: pg. 411   Topic: Motivating Channel
                                                Members
20. FALSE   Reference: pg. 413   Topic: Nature and Importance of
                                                Physical Distribution and
                                                Marketing Logistics

Applying Terms and Concept Answers

Case#1   Pro Image:

Question #1
- As long as professional and college sports teams continue to produce exciting games and quality entertainment, the sportswear industry will continue to flourish.
- In addition, the high profile of athletes and products also contribute to the sales.

Question #2
- A conventional distribution channel is a channel that consists of one or more independent producers, wholesalers, and retailers.
- Each is a separate business that seeks to maximize its own profits even at the expense of profits for the system as a whole.
- Since sports merchandise is more of a luxury product and carries high prices, a vertically integrated system would be most beneficial for this industry.
- Independent parties in a conventional system would result in higher end prices for the consumer.
- Furthermore, the nature of the product requires that professional teams give permission for the use of their name and logos, thus the use of a vertical distribution system would be more cost-efficient, and less complex.

Question #3
- NFL Properties might choose to use a variety of retailers to reach target markets for several reasons, but two are especially important.
- First, NFL Properties may lack the financial resources to carry out direct marketing activities.
- Second, direct marketing activities would require NFL Properties to become an intermediary, which would not only mean that they would have to develop expertise in retailing and wholesaling activities, but might also mean they would have to carry products from other organizations to sell along with their own merchandise lest their own assortment be viewed as too narrow by target customers.
- The usefulness of intermediaries largely boils down to their greater efficiency in making goods and services available to target markets.
- Through their contacts, experience, specialization, and scale of operation, intermediaries usually offer the firm more than it can achieve on its own.

Question #4
- A conventional distribution channel consists of one or more independent producers, wholesalers, and retailers.
- Each is a separate business seeking to maximize its own profits, even at the expense of profits for the system as a whole.
- No channel member has much control over the other members, and there are no formal means of assigning roles and resolving channel conflict.

- By contrast, a vertical marketing system. (VMS) consists of producers, wholesales, and retailers acting as a unified system.
- One channel member either owns the others, has contracts with them, or wields so much power that all must cooperate.
- The vertical marketing system may be dominated by the producer, the wholesaler, or the retailer.
- VMS's came into being to control channel behaviour and manage channel conflict.
- They achieve economies through size, bargaining power, and elimination of duplicated services.
- Pro Image is a contractual vertical marketing system.
- Specifically, it's a service firm-sponsored retailer franchise organization wherein Pro Image licenses a system of retailers to bring selected products to customers.

Question #5
- The advantages of associating with a franchise organization such as Pro Image include company assistance with site selection, leave negotiation, advertising, financing, purchasing, and inventory control systems, and training; networking through newsletters, meetings and conventions; and a proven store design and layout and pricing strategy.
- There is also a greater likelihood of increased sales and profitability from associating with a franchise operation because of the name recognition.

Case #2   Gourmet Popcorn Shop:

1.   A

2.   D

3.   C

4.   C

Case #3   Fast Eddie:

1.   B

2.   A

3.   C

4.   B

5.   D

6.   Trucks — Fast Eddie's customers are scattered in many locations. He needs a fast, frequent dependable, and flexible delivery system. Trucks will provide these needed services.

Chapter 13

Retailing and Wholesaling

Chapter Overview

Although most retailing is conducted in retail stores, in recent years, non-store retailing has increased enormously. In addition, although many retail stores are independently owned, an increasing number are now banding together under some form of corporate or contractual organization. Wholesalers have also experienced recent environmental changes, most notably mounting competitive pressures. They have faced new sources of competition, more demanding customers, new technologies, and more direct-buying programs on the part of large industrial, institutional, and retail buyers.

Chapter Objectives

1. Explain the roles of retailer and wholesaler in the distribution channel.
2. Describe the major types of retailers and give examples of each.
3. Identify the major types of wholesalers and give examples of each.
4. Explain the marketing decisions facing retailers and wholesalers.

Chapter Topics

Retailing

Store Retailing
- Amount of Service
- Product Line
- Relative Prices
- Control of Outlets

Non-Store Retailing
- Direct Marketing
- Direct Selling
- Automatic Vending

Retailer Marketing Decisions
- Target Market and Positioning Decision
- Product Assortment and Services Decision
- Price Decision
- Promotion Decision
- Place Decision

The Future of Retailing
- New Retail Forms and Shortening Retail Life Cycles
- Growth of Non-Store Retailing
- Increasing Intertype Competition
- The Rise of Mega-Retailers
- Growing Importance of Retail Technology
- Global Expansion of Major Retailers
- Retail Stores as "Communities" or "Hangouts"

Wholesaling

Types of Wholesalers

Wholesaler Marketing Decisions
- Target Market and Positioning Decision
- Marketing-Mix Decisions

Trends in Wholesaling

Chapter Summary

1.   The major types of retailers.

Store retailers can be classified by 5 major types: Amount of service, Product line sold, Relative price emphasis, Control of outlets, Type of store cluster. Non-store retailers include direct marketing, direct selling and automatic vending.

2.   The different types of retailers as distinguished by product line sold.

Speciality stores carry a narrow product line with a deep assortment. Department stores carry a wide variety of product lines; each managed as a separate department with specialist buyers and merchandisers. Supermarkets are large, low-cost, low-margin, high-volume, and self-service. Convenience stores carry a limited line of high-turnover convenience goods. Superstores are giant retailers carrying large assortments of many product lines.

3.   The types of retailers as distinguished by control of outlets.

Corporate chains consist of one or more outlets commonly owned using central buying and merchandising. Voluntary chains are wholesaler sponsored while retailer co-operatives jointly own their wholesaler. Consumer co-operatives are owned by customers. Franchises are contractual agreements between the organizations and independent businesspeople. Merchandising conglomerates combine several different retailing forms and share distribution and management.

4.   The major types of wholesalers.

Merchant wholesalers are independently owned businesses that take title. Two broad types are full service (wholesale merchants and industrial distributors) and limited service (cash-and-carry, truck jobbers, drop shippers, rack jobbers, producer co-ops, mail order). Brokers bring two parties together and negotiate for them. Agents work for one party permanently. Sales branches carry inventory while offices do not.

5.   The marketing decisions faced by retailers and wholesalers.

Retailers and wholesalers both must first make target market decisions, and also decisions about product assortment and services (width, depth, store atmosphere, differentiation), price decisions (markup vs. volume), promotion (including special events, sponsorships, press conferences, and public relations), and place (location, location, location).

Key Terms

Multiple Choice Questions

13-1   Multiple

Retail stores come in all shapes and sizes. Which of the following characteristics is not a common method of classifying retail stores?

1.   Amount of service
2.   Product line
3.   Costs
4.   Relative prices
5.   Control of outlets

13-2   Multiple

Stores such as Wal-Mart and Saan provide sales assistance because they carry more shopping goods about which customers need information. These two stores would be classified as:

1.   Self-service retailers
2.   Limited-service retailers
3.   Full-service retailers
4.   Specialty-service stores
5.   Complementary-service stores

13-3   Multiple

Specialty stores are increasing in popularity for many reasons. Which of the following is not considered one of them?

1.   Increase use of market segmentation
2.   Market targeting
3.   Product specialization
4.   Time poor society
5.   All of the above

13-4   Multiple

Stores with the following characteristics: relatively large, low-cost, low-margin, high-volume, self-service operations, are considered:

1.   Supermarkets
2.   Department stores
3.   Specialty stores
4.   Superstores
5.   Discount stores

13-5   Multiple

Stores selling standard merchandise at lower prices by accepting lower margins and selling higher volumes are:

1.   Supermarkets
2.   Department stores
3.   Specialty stores
4.   Superstores
5.   Discount stores

13-6   Multiple

A store that is owned and operated by manufacturers and normally carries the manufacturer's surplus, discontinued or irregular goods is a (n):

1.   Warehouse club
2.   Factory outlet
3.   Independent off-price retailer
4.   Convenience store
5.   Catalogue Showroom

13-7   Multiple

These stores once sold overpriced emergency goods, but are now offering automated teller and stamp machines, as well as faxes and photocopiers.

1.   Specialty store
2.   Mail office
3.   Convenience store
4.   Supermarkets
5.   Superstores

13-8   Multiple

Hypermarkets are huge superstores that are very popular in Europe. The largest size of a hypermarket would be equivalent to _____ football fields.

1.   4
2.   7
3.   2
4.   6
5.   1

13-9   Multiple

Winners has become very popular in the last few years. They provide designer clothing at affordable prices. They get new stock every week and are able to clear most of it out because of its high quality and low price. Winners is a (n):

1.   Factory outlet
2.   Warehouse club
3.   Independent off-price retailer
4.   Discount store
5.   Specialty store

13-10 Multiple

Corporate chain stores are found in all areas of retailing, but are strongest in this area:

1.   Department stores
2.   Variety stores
3.   Drug stores
4.   Women's clothing
5.   All of the above

13-11 Multiple

Independent Grocers Alliance (IGA) is smaller in comparison to Safeway, but provides comparable services at similar prices. IGA engages in group buying to offer better deals to their consumers. IGA is part of a:

1.   Voluntary chain
2.   Corporate chain
3.   Retailer cooperative
4.   Joint-venture
5.   Collaborative retailing effort

13-12 Multiple

Franchises are very popular, with chains like McDonald's, Shoppers Drug Mart, and Bata Shoes International popping up everywhere. The differences between a franchise and a contractual system is a franchise system is based on everything except:

1.   A unique product or service
2.   A trade name
3.   Goodwill
4.   Popular products
5.   All of the above

13-13 Multiple

_____ is growing in use with consumer markets in response to the increasing fragmentation of the world's mass markets into subsegments with distinct needs and wants.

1.   Direct selling
2.   Direct marketing
3.   Automatic vending
4.   Integrated marketing communications
5.   Advertising

13-14 Multiple

Automatic vending is increasing in frequency and popularity around the world. The only problem with vending machines is the high cost it incurs. Prices of vended goods are often _____ % higher than those in retail stores.

1.   10 to 20
2.   25 to 40
3.   20 to 25
4.   15 to 20
5.   30 to 40

13-15 Multiple

Kiet is opening up a new retail outlet to sell men's grooming products. Which of the following product variables does he not have to consider before opening the store?

1.   Price points
2.   Product assortment
3.   Services mix
4.   Store atmosphere
5.   All of the above

13-16 Multiple

Product assortment must match the target shopper's expectations. Restaurants all have different product assortments, meaning they have different width and depth of products. Which of the following restaurants would have a narrow and deep assortment?

1.   Small lunch counter
2.   Delicatessen
3.   Cafeteria
4.   Larger restaurant
5.   Fast food

13-17 Multiple

A _____ is the largest and most dramatic type of shopping facility with from 40 to 200 stores under its roof.

1.   Central business district
2.   Community shopping centre
3.   Regional shopping centre
4.   Neighbourhood shopping centre
5.   Megamalls

13-18 Multiple

Shopping malls may be very profitable; however, the traffic flow in most malls has decreased over the last few years. All the following are reasons for this phenomenon except:

1.   People have less time to shop
2.   Large malls offer great selection but are less comfortable and convenient
3.   There are more alternatives available to shoppers, such as on-line shopping
4.   People have less disposable income to shop with
5.   None of the above

13-19 Multiple

What is one reason why there has been a huge rise in superpower mega-retailers except:

1.   Vertical marketing systems
2.   Buying alliances
3.   Retail mergers
4.   Acquisitions
5.   All of the above

13-20 Multiple

Wholesaling is composed of all activities involved in selling goods and services to those buying for resale or business use. Which of the following functions would a wholesaler not perform?

1.   Selling and promoting
2.   Bulk-breaking
3.   Contract negotiations
4.   Financing
5.   Transportation

13-21 Multiple

Merchant wholesalers – independently owned businesses that take title to the merchandise they handle, are the largest single group of wholesalers, accounting for roughly _____ % of all wholesaling.

1.   50
2.   40
3.   75
4.   60
5.   90

13-22 Multiple

_____, upon receiving an order, they select a manufacturer, who ships the merchandise directly to the customer.

1.   Wholesale merchant
2.   Drop shipper
3.   Cash-and-carry wholesalers
4.   Producer's co-operatives
5.   Rack jobbers

13-23 Multiple

_____ have a long-term relationship with buyers and make purchases for them, often receiving, inspecting, warehousing and shipping the merchandise to the buyers.

1.   Selling agents
2.   Purchasing offices
3.   Purchasing agents
4.   Commission merchants
5.   Sales branches and offices

13-24 Multiple

Wholesalers must also define their target markets and position themselves effectively – they cannot serve everyone. This is one method not used by wholesalers in selecting target markets.

1.   Size of customer
2.   Type of customer
3.   Need for service
4.   Price range of the customer
5.   All of the above

13-25 Multiple

Costco is an example of a grocery store wholesaler. They have very large stores, with few frills and large purchase quantities. They depend on large volumes to generate enough profit to survive as their average profit margin is often less than ___ %.

1.   5
2.   10
3.   7
4.   3
5.   2

13-26 Multiple

A retail firm owned by its customer would be called a (n):

1.   Volunteer chain
2.   Corporate chain
3.   Merchandising conglomerate
4.   Consumer co-operative
5.   Independent chain

13-27 Multiple

Creating and maintaining a store's atmosphere is part of which marketing decision?

1.   Target market
2.   Product assortment and services
3.   Price
4.   Promotion
5.   Store layout and décor

13-28 Multiple

This statement about retailing is not true.

1.   Retailing involves selling to final consumers
2.   Retailing is a major industry
3.   Manufacturers and wholesalers cannot make retailing decisions
4.   Retail sales may be done by person, mail, telephone, or vending machine
5.   None of the above

13-29 Multiple

A retailing operation that depends on location and long hours to attract customers for its limited line of frequently purchased products is called a:

1.   Convenience store
2.   Supermarket
3.   Specialty store
4.   Department store
5.   Superstore

13-30 Multiple

Which of the following types of retailing combines supermarket, discount and warehouse retailing principles?

1.   Discount operations
2.   Hypermarkets
3.   Self-service stores
4.   Superstores
5.   Both 1 and 3

True/False Questions

13-1   True/False

Today, self-service is the basis of all discount operations and typically is used by sellers of convenience goods.

13-2   True/False

Most supermarkets are facing steady sales growth despite slower population growth and an increase in competition from convenience stores and superstores.

13-3   True/False

Future shop is considered a specialty store known as a "category killer."

13-4   True/False

For some businesses, the "product line" is actually a service.

13-5   True/False

Most retailers charge lower prices and offer normal-quality goods and customer service.

13-6   True/False

Off-price retailers buy at less than regular wholesale prices and charge consumers regular retail prices.

13-7   True/False

Retailing is more concentrated in Canada than it is in the US.

13-8   True/False

Non-store retailing – direct marketing, direct selling and automatic vending – has been growing at the same rate as traditional store retailing.

13-9   True/False

Direct advertising vehicles are used to obtain immediate orders from targeted consumers.

13-10 True/False

The advantages of door-to-door selling are consumer convenience and personal attention.

13-11 True/False

Today's automatic vending machine use space-age and computer technology to sell a variety of convenience and impulse goods such as $100 Armani ties and beer.

13-12 True/False

Large stores such as The Bay and Eaton's do not need to define their target markets because they are such large retailers they can cater to everybody.

13-13 True/False

The service mix is the only tool of non-price competition that sets one store apart from another.

13-14 True/False

Retail stores are not just assortment of goods, they are also environments to be experienced by people who shop in them.

13-15 True/False

All retailers would like to charge high markups and achieve high volume.

13-16 True/False

Retailers often cite three critical factors in retailing success: loyalty, location, and layout.

13-17 True/False

According to the International Council of Shopping Centres, 70% of Canadian retail sales occur in shopping centres.

13-18 True/False

The life cycle of new retailers is becoming shorter. Department stores use to have a life cycle of 100 years, now new retailers like catalogue showrooms have a life cycle of only 10 years.

13-19 True/False

Today's retailers are focusing on a share of particular product-market, rather than a share of wallet.

13-20 True/False

North American retailers are still significantly ahead of Europe and Asia when it comes to global expansion.

Applying Terms and Concepts

To determine how well you understand the materials in this chapter, read each of the following brief cases and then respond to the questions that follow. Answers are given at the end of this chapter.

Case #1   Chan's[1]

Cindy Chan is presently assembling the resources necessary to launch "Chan's," a retail chain designed to meet the clothing need of the professional woman. Her intended customer is twenty-five to forty years old and willing to pay more to acquire the proper look.

Chan is planning to open three outlets in Vancouver. Each outlet will have approximately 5,000 square feet of selling space and feature suits, as well as coordinated separates for the working woman. Casual and sportswear will be limited. However, higher quality professional attire will be offered in a wide range of styles, fabrics, and sizes, in patterns and solids. Clothing accessories will include hats, scarves, belts, and stockings, with a small selection of handbags.

Chan, a former vice president of purchasing for S. Altman Department Stores in Calgary, will function as the buyer while Joan Wilder will be responsible for sales and operations. Each store will have a manager with two assistants and two to four sales associates (depending upon sales and volume.) Each sales associate is expected to offer honest and objective opinions regarding the clothing and accessories that are "right " for the customer. Each sales associate must have prior personal sales experience and demonstrated the ability to provide personalized attention to a client. The sales associates are to be from the same approximate age bracket as the intended target market.

As an extra service, Chan has hired a fashion consultant to service the three stores. She will be available by appointment to meet the fashion needs of individual customers.

1.   What type of retailer is Chan's? Explain.

_____

_____

_____

_____

---

[1] *Principles of Marketing*, 3rd Edition, Kotler, Armstrong, Warren (Prentice Hall) – pg. 274.

2.   Describe Chan's merchandise assortment in terms of depth and selection.

        _____

        _____

        _____

        _____

3.   Where should Chan locate her three stores and why?

        _____

        _____

        _____

        _____

4.   Which type of services do you believe Chan's should offer its customers?

        _____

        _____

        _____

        _____

5.   How would you classify Chan's as a service retailer?

        _____

        _____

        _____

        _____

Case #2   Freed Slack Company

Samuel Freed began the Freed Slack Company in Winnipeg, in December 1981. Over the years his company has served the needs of approximately nine million mail order customers, over half as repeat customers.

Freed's current offering consists of men's double-knit dress slacks available in blue tweed, navy, brown, gray, tan, and green, in waist sizes 30" to 44" and inseam sizes from 28" to 35". The slacks are sold at $11.55 per pair with a minimum order of two pairs. They feature Quatral polyester, Tanalon nonsnag zippers, Bana-roll anti-roll waistline, and reinforced belt loops accommodating belts up to one and a half inches. Freed slacks are sold with a moneyback guarantee; however, returns average less than two percent. Postage of $4.85 per shipment is paid by the customer.

Freed has indicated that the current production run will last approximately two years before it is changed. In the past Freed has featured casual slacks, sportswear, dress shirts, and work clothes. It is his practice to feature a type of menswear for a period of time, allowing him to concentrate his buying, manufacturing, and selling efforts on a limited product line, thereby reducing costs of operation.

Freed's literature boasts that his product's quality is comparable to that of slacks costing two or three times as much. A recent article in *Canadian Consumer* magazine agreed with this claim. Freed will quote the magazine in promoting his next dress slack offering.

Prospective customers receive a flyer which describes the products and includes a small sample of material. Also included for their convenience is a postcard order blank, postage paid by the company. Freed acquires mailing lists of possible customers from the Addresser Company, a mailing list brokerage house in Moncton, New Brunswick.

_____1. The Freed Slack Company should be classified as a(n) _____ service retailer.

    A.   self

    B.   limited

    C.   full

    D.   augmented

    E.   customer

_____2. The textbook would classify the Freed Slack Company on the basis of:

    A.   type of store cluster.

    B.   control of outlets.

    C.   relative price.

    D.   nonstore retailing.

    E.   store retailing.

_____3. Freed's merchandise assortment is best described as _____ and _____.

    A.   wide, deep

    B.   wide, shallow

    C.   narrow, deep

    D.   narrow, shallow

    E.   wide, extensive

_____4. Which type of nonstore retailing is Freed involved in:

    A.   telemarketing.

    B.   direct mail marketing.

    C.   electronic shopping.

    D.   catalog marketing.

    E.   integrated marketing.

_____5. Comment on the pricing policy of the Freed Slack Company.

_____

_____

_____

_____

_____

_____

Case #3   Noisebreakers

The volume of noise in our daily lives is considerable and increasing steadily. Vehicle exhaust systems, power transformers, dishwashers, ventilation systems, vacuum cleaners, heavy equipment and machinery are just a few of the things that continually assault our senses. Too much noise cannot only cause hearing loss but also distraction and anxiety — both of which can affect one's disposition and productivity. While most people simply live with the offending sounds, some have found them to be a debilitating force.

David Martin, an engineer and physicist by training, has developed what he believes is a product whose time has come — a personalized noise abatement system he calls the noise breaker. The Noisebreaker operates by having a microphone pick up incoming sounds and then electronically producing an opposite sound. The mirror image of the sound is broadcast back through a speaker system built into the device. As the competing sounds collide, they partially cancel each other out. While the noise is not eliminated entirely, the Noisebreaker substantially reduces the volume of the offending sounds. While noise abatement systems have long been available and primarily used in the broadcasting and recording industries, this is the first such product aimed at the consumer market.

Martin's initial product looks remarkably like a personal stereo with headphones. It is small enough to be clipped to a belt and worn while one is jogging, driving or simply sitting back relaxing. The Noisebreaker reduces background noise, which in turn reduces distraction and anxiety.

Martin expects the Noisebreaker to retail for $149. Future applications in the industrial and commercial markets will be forthcoming. Martin envisions attaching the device directly to the offending object. He is hoping a commercial version of the Noisebreaker will do for noise pollution what recycling and legislation have done for environmental pollution.

1.   What are the relative advantages of selling the Noisebreaker through each of the
      following:

      A.   Specialty store

      _____

      _____

      _____

      _____

      B.   Discount store

      _____

      _____

      _____

      _____

      C.   Direct marketing

      _____

      _____

      _____

      _____

Multiple Choice Answers

1.   Correct Answer: 3   Reference: pg. 434

2.   Correct Answer: 2   Reference: pg. 434

3.   Correct Answer: 4   Reference: pg. 434

4.   Correct Answer: 1   Reference: pg. 435 (Table 13-1)

5.   Correct Answer: 5   Reference: pg. 435 (Table 13-1)

6.   Correct Answer: 2   Reference: pg. 435 (Table 13-1)

7.   Correct Answer: 3   Reference: pg. 436

8.   Correct Answer: 5   Reference: pg. 437

9.   Correct Answer: 3   Reference: pg. 438

10.   Correct Answer: 5   Reference: pg. 439

11.   Correct Answer: 1   Reference: pg. 439

12.   Correct Answer: 4   Reference: pg. 440

13.   Correct Answer: 2   Reference: pg. 442

14.   Correct Answer: 4   Reference: pg. 443

15.   Correct Answer: 1   Reference: pg. 444

16.   Correct Answer: 2   Reference: pg. 444

17.   Correct Answer: 3   Reference: pg. 448

18.   Correct Answer: 4   Reference: pg. 449

19.   Correct Answer: 5   Reference: pg. 452

20.   Correct Answer: 3   Reference: pg. 454

21.   Correct Answer: 1   Reference: pg. 454

22.	Correct Answer:	2	Reference:	pg. 455 (Table 13-4)
23.	Correct Answer:	3	Reference:	pg. 456
24.	Correct Answer:	4	Reference:	pg. 456
25.	Correct Answer:	5	Reference:	pg. 457
26.	Correct Answer:	4	Reference:	pg. 440
27.	Correct Answer:	2	Reference:	pg. 446
28.	Correct Answer:	3	Reference:	pg. 433
29.	Correct Answer:	1	Reference:	pg. 435 (Table 13-1)
30.	Correct Answer:	2	Reference:	pg. 437

True/False Answers

1.	TRUE	Reference:	pg. 434	Topic:	Amount of Service	
2.	FALSE	Reference:	pg. 436	Topic:	Product Line	
3.	TRUE	Reference:	pg. 436	Topic:	Product Line	
4.	TRUE	Reference:	pg. 437	Topic:	Product Line	
5.	FALSE	Reference:	pg. 437	Topic:	Relative Prices	
6.	FALSE	Reference:	pg. 438	Topic:	Relative Prices	
7.	TRUE	Reference:	pg. 439	Topic:	Control of Outlets	
8.	FALSE	Reference:	pg. 440	Topic:	Non-Store Retailing	
9.	TRUE	Reference:	pg. 442	Topic:	Direct Marketing	
10.	TRUE	Reference:	pg. 443	Topic:	Direct Selling	
11.	TRUE	Reference:	pg. 443	Topic:	Automatic Vending	
12.	FALSE	Reference:	pg. 444	Topic:	Target Market and Positioning Decision	
13.	FALSE	Reference:	pg. 446	Topic:	Product Assortment and Services Decisions	
14.	TRUE	Reference:	pg. 447	Topic:	Product Assortment and Services Decisions	
15.	TRUE	Reference:	pg. 447	Topic:	Price Decisions	
16.	FALSE	Reference:	pg. 448	Topic:	Place Decisions	
17.	FALSE	Reference:	pg. 449	Topic:	Place Decision	
18.	TRUE	Reference:	pg. 450	Topic:	New Retailing Forms and Shortening Retail Life Cycles	
19.	FALSE	Reference:	pg. 450	Topic:	Increasing Intertype Competition	
20.	FALSE	Reference:	pg. 453	Topic:	Global Expansion of Major Retailers	

Applying Terms and Concept Answers

Case #1   Chan's:

Question#1

- Chan's should be classified as a limited line retailer.

Question#2

- Chan's is a specialty store, thus their product assortment is narrow and deep.

Question#3

- Cindy Chan should probably locate in regional and community shopping centres to facilitate comparison shopping with the other specialty and department stores.

Question#4

Possible services include:

- Free alterations
- Evening and weekend hours
- Gift certificates
- Lay-away and credit programs
- Store-sponsored fashion show
- Garment bags with selected purchases
- Merchandise return policy
- Coupons for free dry-cleaning with selected purchases

Question#5

- Chan's is a full service retailer because the focus of the store is geared toward a particular segment of the market.
- Chan's is geared towards working women who want professional attire of superior quality.
- The employees will be trained to pay personal attention to all customers.
- The sales associates will ideally, offer one-on-one service.

Case #2   Freed Slack Company:

1.   A

2.   D

3.   C

4.   B

5.   The Freed Slack Company can charge a relatively low price for its products because of long production runs, volume purchase of materials, specialization of labor, low overhead, and few services offered. The low price encourages customers to buy and try the product and for the low price customers probably do not expect expertly tailored clothing.

<u>Case #3</u>   <u>Noisebreaker:</u>

1.   A   A specialty store carries a narrow product line with a deep assortment within that line. Electronic enthusiasts, who shop in such stores as Radio Shack, are inclined to seek out and purchase electronic wizardry. These innovators are willing to pay a higher price as the product comes on the market. Knowledgeable salespeople serve as a resource for their technically minded customers.

      B.   A discount store sells standard merchandise at lower prices by accepting lower margins and selling higher volume. The Noisebreaker would get considerable exposure in discount stores but would be sold at a reduced price. The purchaser would be those consumers making up the early and late majority who buy items with minimal support from sales personnel.

      C.   Direct marketing uses various advertising media to interact directly with consumers, generally calling for the consumer to make a direct response. Mass advertising typically reaches an unspecified number of people, most of whom are not in the market for a product or will not buy it until some future date. Direct-advertising vehicles are used to obtain immediate orders directly from targeted consumers. Although direct marketing initially consisted mostly of direct mail and mail-order catalogs, it has taken on several additional forms in recent years, including telemarketing, direct radio and television marketing, and online computer shopping.

               Direct marketing has boomed in recent years. All kinds of organizations use direct marketing: manufacturers, retailers, services companies, catalog merchants, and nonprofit organizations, to name a few. Its growing use in consumer marketing is largely a response to the "demassification" of mass markets, which has resulted in an ever-greater number of fragmented market segments with highly individualized needs and wants. Direct marketing allows sellers to focus efficiently on these minimarkets with offers that better match specific consumer needs.

               Thus direct marketing can lead to greater selectivity and messages that can be personalized and customized. This may translate to improved sales and productivity.

Chapter 14

Developing the Marketing Mix

Chapter Overview

Modern marketing calls for more than just developing a good product, pricing it attractively, and making it available to target customers. Companies must also communicate with current and prospective customers, and what they communicate should not be left to chance. For most companies, the question is not whether to communicate, but how much to spend and in what ways.

Chapter Objectives

1. Name and define the four tools of the promotion mix.
2. Outline the steps in developing effective marketing communication.
3. Explain the methods for setting the promotions budget and factors that affect the design of the promotion mix.
4. Identify the major factors that are changing today's marketing communications environment.
5. Discuss the process and advantages of integrated marketing communications.

Chapter Topics

The Marketing Communications Mix
- A View of the Communication Process

Steps in Developing Effective Communication
- Identifying the Target Audience
- Determining the Response Sought
- Designing the Message
  - Message Content
  - Message Structure
  - Message Format
- Choosing Media
  - Personal Communication Channels
  - Non-Personal Communication Channels
- Selecting the Message Source
- Collecting Feedback

Setting the Total Promotion Budget and Mix
- Setting the Total Promotion Budget
  - Affordable Method
  - Percentage-of-Sales Method
  - Competitive-Parity Method
  - Objective-and-Task Method
- Setting the Promotion Mix
  - The Nature of Each Promotional Tool
    - Advertising
    - Personal Selling
    - Sales Promotion
    - Public Relations
    - Direct Marketing
  - Promotion Mix Strategies
    - Type of Product/Market
    - Buyer Readiness Stage
    - Product Life-Cycle Stage

The Changing Face of Marketing Communications
- The Changing Communications Environment
- Integrated Marketing Communications

Socially Responsible Marketing Communications
- Advertising
- Personal Selling

Chapter Summary

1. **The four tools of the promotion mix.**

Advertising is any paid form of non-personal promotion of ideas, goods, or services by an identified sponsor. Personal selling is the oral presentation for the purpose of making a sale. Sales promotion consists of short-term incentives to encourage purchase or sales of a product or service. Public relations involves building good relations with the company's various publics by obtaining favourable publicity, building up a good "corporate image."

2. **The elements of the communication process.**

The nine elements are:

Sender—party sending the message to another

Encoding—putting thought into symbolic form

Message—set of symbols transmitted;

Media—communication channels used

Decoding—receiver assigning meaning to encoded symbols transmitted

Receiver—the target for the message

Response—the receiver's reaction to the message

Feedback—the part of the response returned to the sender

Noise—static or distortion

3. **The methods used for setting the promotion budget.**

The affordable method sets the budget based upon available funds. The percentage-of-sales method bases the budget on a set fraction of current or forecasted sales. The competitive-parity method matches the competition's spending. The objective-and-task method defines goals; determines the tasks necessary to reach them; estimates the cost of the tasks and sets their budget. Only the objective-and-task method is proactive.

4. **The factors that affect the design of the promotion mix.**

Factors used in setting the promotion mix are the type of product and market, the use of a push versus a pull strategy, the buyer readiness state, and the product's stage in the product life cycle.

5.   The buyer readiness states.

Awareness is the state at which the target audience is first aware of the product's existence. Knowledge is their degree of understanding of the product. Liking is the degree of positive or negative affect. Preference is the level at which the product is liked better than the competition. Conviction leads to demanding the product and not accepting substitutes. Purchase is buying. Promotion should be tailored to the appropriate state.

Key Terms

Advertising   (pg. 468)

Affordable method   (pg. 479)

Buyer-readiness stages   (pg. 471)

Direct marketing   (pg. 469)

Emotional appeals   (pg. 473)

Integrated marketing communications (pg. 486)

Marketing communications mix   (pg. 468)

Moral appeals (pg. 474)

Non-personal communication channels (pg. 476)

Objective-and-task method   (pg. 480)

Percentage-of-sales method   (pg. 479)

Personal communication channels   (pg. 475)

Personal selling   (pg. 469)

Public relations   (pg. 469)

Pull strategy   (pg. 482)

Push strategy   (pg. 482)

Rational appeals   (pg. 473)

Sales promotion   (pg. 469)

Word-of-mouth influence   (pg. 475)

Multiple Choice Questions

14-1   Multiple

The Safeway coupon book is full of short-term incentives encouraging the purchase of grocery products. This form of marketing communication would be considered:

1.   Advertising
2.   Personal selling
3.   Sales promotion
4.   Public relations
5.   Direct marketing

14-2   Multiple

The use of mail, telephone, fax, e-mail and other non-personal tools to communicate with specific customers is called:

1.   Advertising
2.   Personal selling
3.   Sales promotion
4.   Public relations
5.   Direct marketing

14-3   Multiple

Sales promotion is a very common sight in many stores. Which of the following is not considered a sales promotion?

1.   Point-of-purchase displays
2.   Premiums
3.   Coupons
4.   Billboards
5.   All of the above

14-4   Multiple

The communication process plays an important part in the consumer buying process. Different strategies are more beneficial at certain stages and less effective at others. Of the following which is not considered part of the customer buying process from the communication process?

1.   Pre-selling
2.   Post-selling
3.   Post-consumption
4.   Consuming
5.   Selling

14-5   Multiple

There are nine elements of communication. The process of putting thought into symbolic form is part of which element?

1.   Feedback
2.   Message
3.   Decoding
4.   Encoding
5.   Response

14-6   Multiple

The communication element where the consumer is more aware of the attributes of a product, and may actually make a purchase is:

1.   Response
2.   Feedback
3.   Decoding
4.   Noise
5.   Message

14-7 Multiple

Communication is very important in marketing. Senders are probably the most important elements in the communication process, because without them, there would be no message. The following are all required characteristics of a good message sender except:

1. Senders need to know what audiences they wish to reach and what responses they want
2. The must be good at encoding messages
3. They must send messages through media that reach target audiences
4. They must develop feedback channels so that they can assess the audiences response to the message
5. All of the above are required

14-8 Multiple

There are many steps involved in developing an effective communication strategy. What is the one item the marketing communicator is not required to do?

1. Identify the target audience
2. Develop the product idea
3. Choose a message
4. Select the message source
5. Collect feedback

14-9 Multiple

Which of the following is not part of the buyer-readiness stages?

1. Awareness
2. Linking
3. Feeling
4. Preference
5. Conviction

14-10 Multiple

Enchantress Travel is trying out a new travel package for its loyal customers. This is a new concept and therefore in the marketing process, once the consumers feel favourable about the package, and learn to associate Enchantress with this great new travel package, Enchantress has reached the _____ stage in the buyer-readiness model.

1.   Linking
2.   Knowledge
3.   Preference
4.   Conviction
5.   None of the above

14-11 Multiple

Designing a message is a complex process. Many marketers use the AIDA model as a framework to help them with this step. Which of the following is not part of this model?

1.   Attention
2.   Desire
3.   Interest
4.   Idea
5.   Action

14-12 Multiple

Buckley's Mixture's advertising campaign has been very effective for the company. They have used the slogan "It tastes awful. And it works." This type of marketing approach would be considered a (n) _____ appeal.

1.   Emotional
2.   Moral
3.   Rational
4.   Reverse
5.   Controversial

14-13 Multiple

The message structure of a marketing communications mix is hard to establish. There are many different angles a company can take with the message they are trying to send. A one-sided argument is most effective in every case except when:

1.   The audience is highly educated
2.   The audience is young and easily influenced
3.   The audience is negatively disposed
4.   The audience is likely to hear opposing claims
5.   All of the above

14-14 Multiple

A marketer who decides to use print ads as their medium of communication does not need to consider?

1.   Eye-catching pictures
2.   Message size and position
3.   Message content
4.   Distinctive formats
5.   All of the above

14-15 Multiple

There are two different channels of communication: personal and non-personal. In which of the following scenarios does personal communication not carry much weight?

1.   Weekly groceries
2.   A Rolls Royce
3.   The stock markets
4.   A prom dress
5.   None of the above

14-16 Multiple

When a company starts with total revenues, deducts operating expenses and capital outlays, and then devotes some portion of the remaining funds to advertising, they are using the _____ method of calculating the promotion budget.

1.   Objective and task
2.   Competitive-parity
3.   Percentage-of-sales
4.   Affordable
5.   Simplistic

14-17 Multiple

The _____ method of calculating the promotion budget views sales as the cause of promotions rather than as the result.

1. Objective and task
2. Competitive-parity
3. Percentage-of-sales
4. Affordable
5. Simplistic

14-18 Multiple

The objective-and-task method of calculating the promotion budget involves everything except:

1. Determining the tasks needed to achieve these objectives
2. Estimating the sales expected
3. Defining specific promotion objectives
4. Estimating the costs of performing these tasks
5. All of the above

14-19 Multiple

_____ can reach masses of geographically dispersed buyers at a low cost per exposure.

1. Advertising
2. Personal selling
3. Sales promotions
4. Public relations
5. Direct marketing

14-20 Multiple

North American firms spend up to _____ times as much on personal selling as they do on advertising.

1. Two
2. Four
3. Six
4. Five
5. Three

14-21 Multiple

Direct marketing can be described by all the following items except:

1. Non-public
2. Immediate
3. Simplistic
4. Customized
5. Interactive

14-22 Multiple

Using a _____ strategy, the producer directs its marketing activities toward the final consumers to induce them to buy the product.

1. Sales promotion
2. Pull
3. Direct marketing
4. Push
5. Intense advertising

14-23 Multiple

In the _____ stage of the product life cycle, sales promotion becomes important relative to advertising.

1. Introduction
2. Early adoption
3. Growth
4. Maturity
5. Decline

14-24 Multiple

In an integrated marketing communication system, a company must keep track of its promotional expenditures by:

1. Product
2. Promotional tool
3. Product life cycle
4. Observed effect
5. All of the above

368

14-25 Multiple

Sellers must avoid the _____ advertising that attracts buyers under false pretenses, because governments in North America are cracking down on these practices.

1.   Pull-and-tug
2.   Bait-and-switch
3.   Foot-in-the-door
4.   Come-and-see
5.   None of the above

14-26 Multiple

In selling to businesses, this tactic is not used as part of the communication process.

1.   Offer bribes to purchasing agents
2.   Use technical or trade secrets of competition through bribery or industrial espionage
3.   Use false advertising with respect to competitors
4.   Copy competitors products and marketing ideas
5.   None of the above

14-27 Multiple

The "learn-feel-do" sequence of the buyer readiness states corresponds to:

1.   Cognitive, affective, behavioural
2.   Affective, behavioural, cognitive
3.   Behavioural, cognitive, affective
4.   Affective, cognitive, behavioural
5.   None of the above

14-28 Multiple

Using sales promotion to encourage early product trail emphasizes this factor in the promotion mix.

1.   Type of product/market
2.   Push versus pull strategy
3.   Buyer readiness state
4.   Product life cycle
5.   Both 1 and 4

14-29 Multiple

When advertising is primarily used to remind buyers already familiar with the brand, its features and availability, the marketer is emphasizing which factor in setting the promotion mix?

1.　　Buyer readiness state
2.　　Product life cycle stage
3.　　Push versus pull strategy
4.　　Type of product/market
5.　　Both 1 and 3

14-30 Multiple

The concept by which a company carefully coordinates its communication channels to deliver a clear, consistent, and compelling message about the organization and its product is called:

1.　　Integrated direct marketing
2.　　The marketing mix
3.　　Integrated marketing communications
4.　　Direct marketing communications
5.　　Coordinated marketing communications

True/False Questions

14-1   True/False

New technologies have encouraged more companies to move from mass communication to more targeted communication and one-on-one dialogue.

14-2   True/False

Too often, marketing communications has a short-term outlook.

14-3   True/False

The communication process should start with an audit of all the interactions target consumers have with the product and company.

14-4   True/False

A marketing communicator starts with a broad target audience in mind.

14-5   True/False

Marketing alone can create positive feelings and purchases for a company.

14-6   True/False

The marketing communicator must solve three problems: what to say; how to say it logically; and how to say it symbolically.

14-7   True/False

It has become accepted for a company not to draw conclusions in an advertisement but rather to leave it up to the consumer.

14-8   True/False

There are two broad types of communication channels—personal and industrial.

14-9   True/False

Personal communication channels are effective because they allow for personal addressing and feedback.

14-10 True/False

Non-personal communication affects buyers directly.

14-11 True/False

Mass communications should aim their messages directly at the public, and allow them to hear and see the messages for themselves.

14-12 True/False

Feedback on marketing communications can suggest changes in the promotion program or in the product offer itself.

14-13 True/False

There is sufficient evidence budgets based on competitive parity prevent promotion wars.

14-14 True/False

Companies within the same industry have similar designs in the promotion mix.

14-15 True/False

Advertising can be used to build a long-term image for a product or trigger quick sales.

14-16 True/False

Personal selling is the most effective tool at the buyers' preference, convictions and actions stage of the buying process.

14-17 True/False

Industrial companies tend to use a "pull" strategy more frequently and therefore put most of their funds into personal selling, followed by sales promotion.

14-18 True/False

Television, magazines and other mass media's dominance is declining and has been for the past few years.

14-19 True/False

Customers do not distinguish between message sources the way marketers do.

14-20 True/False

To integrate its internal communications effectively, the company must first integrate its external communication activities.

Applying Terms and Concepts

To determine how well you understand the materials in this chapter, read each of the following brief cases and then respond to the questions that follow. Answers are given at the end of this chapter.

Case#1   Bagelicious[1]

According to the AIDA concept, effective advertisements must get the Attention, hold the Interest, arouse consumer Desire and result in Action. The specific action is the purchase of the advertised product or service. This is difficult to accomplish when consumers are bombarded with over 1,500 advertisements per day. To accomplish this action marketers must use promotional methods that make them stand out.

Aaron Kaura is an articling student and part owner of Cafe Asante in Winnipeg. One day Aaron noticed that unlike the neighbouring cities of Regina and Minneapolis, Winnipeg did not have a restaurant specializing in bagels. Aaron saw this as a tremendous opportunity because of the increasing consumption of bagels by North Americans. Health conscious consumers were turning to bagels as a quick, healthy and nutritious substitute for doughnuts and bread product. Aaron, therefor, decided to create Bagelicious, Winnipeg's first restaurant specializing in bagels. The menu at Bagelicious consisted of 12 different types of bagels ranging from plain to one made from a combination of flax and bran. Bagels could be purchased to takeout or eat-in. Aaron planned to offer a wide selection of cream cheese spreads for use with the bagels and a selection of deli sandwiches made with the bagels.

To reach the largest possible market, Aaron planned a phased roll-out out of his concept. His first step was to build a restaurant in the southern section of Winnipeg close to the site of the new Jewish Congress Centre. This restaurant would have an oversized kitchen commissary area that would be fully utilized in the next phase. Phase Two called for Aaron to introduce kiosks and food carts in the downtown area, the Universities of Winnipeg and Manitoba and at Winnipeg's most popular tourist destination, The Forks. Aaron wanted six satellite locations in operation by the end of his second month of operation. A competitive analysis revealed there were currently no direct competitors, but that the Great Canadian Bagel was close to leasing space in Winnipeg. This analysis also revealed the existence of several small indirect competitors. None of these is a threat to Bagelicious due to their small size and out of the way locations.

Aaron needed to find a way to stand out from the competition. He decided the best way to do this was through a promotional campaign targeted to health conscious consumers. He built his plan around the name Bagelicious and the fact it contained information about the

---

[1] *Principles of Marketing*, 3rd Edition, Kotler, Armstrong, Warren (Prentice Hall) – pg. 300.

product and its taste. Aaron also decided to team up with the local "adult contemporary" radio station, for a series of promotions. This included becoming the lunch sponsor for the station's "Office of the Day" and sponsoring a series of remote broadcasts by the hosts of the drive-in program. Finally, Aaron decided to team up with a community group to display his social responsibility.

1. Describe how Aaron's plan uses the AIDA model to get consumers to buy his products.

    _____

    _____

    _____

    _____

2. Aaron decides sales might improve if he had a spokesperson for his product. Describe the factors that make a spokesperson or source credible.

    _____

    _____

    _____

    _____

3. Aaron decides to hire former Winnipeger and current CNN anchor Lyndon Soles as his spokesperson. Does Mr. Soles meet the criteria described earlier?

    _____

    _____

    _____

    _____

4. Who do you think would be an appropriate spokesperson for Bagelicious?

    _____

    _____

    _____

    _____

5. Aaron plans on doing radio spots to promote Bagelicious. What is the media? What is the message?

    _____

    _____

    _____

    _____

Case #2   Shock Cola

Larry Clark, a successful bottler of soft drinks, quietly introduced a cola last year which is taking the industry by storm. Shock, short for "The Shock Treatment," defies the trend of reducing the sugar and caffeine in colas. Clark maintains that soft drinks were meant to be a treat--not a health food. And what a treat Shock is. It contains 6.0 milligrams of caffeine per ounce--twice what Coke and Pepsi offer and the maximum allowed by the Food and Drug Administration. And it is made with the highest quality beet and cane sugar, not the cheaper corn sweetener found in off-brand soft drinks. Clark has found that the combination of caffeine and sugar can give people a buzz unlike that of any other colas on the market.

Shock at $2.29 per six-pack and $1.19 for the two-litre bottle, is less expensive than name-brand colas. In fact, Clark views Shock as a premium cola at a popular price. And the public seems to agree. Last year Clark shipped only 60,000 cases of Shock; current sales projections are for 450,000. Interestingly, he spends very little on advertising as earnings are reinvested to improve bottling capacity and the distribution system. Any money left is then spent on newspaper advertising. Included in each ad is a coupon good for $.25 off the retail price of a six-pack or two-litre bottle.

Clark doesn't advertise very much because Shock's virtues are mostly spread by its aficionados. The messages, especially among younger drinkers include "It's cheap and it's legal," and "Get the treatment." Clark only smiles when he hears one of these lines.

_____1. Clark sets the promotional budget for Shock Cola using the _____ method.

    A.   affordable

    B.   percentage-of-sales

    C.   competitive-parity

    D.   objective and task

    E.   none of the above

_____2. The coupon included in the newspaper advertisement is an example of a(n) _____.

    A.   advertisement

    B.   personal selling

    C.   publicity

    D.   sales promotion

    E.   public relations

3.   Clark is using the coupon as a _____ (pushing, pulling) promotional
      strategy.

_____4. Clark's belief that Shock is an inexpensive treat suggests that a promotional
      campaign should stress a(n) _____ and _____ appeal.
      A.   emotional and rational
      B.   emotional and moral
      C.   rational and moral
      D.   sociological and psychological
      E.   emotional and moral

_____5. The word of mouth advertising used by the cola's fans, is an example of a(n)
      _____ communication channel.
      A.   personal
      B.   nonpersonal
      C.   suprapersonal
      D.   superpersonal
      E.   extrapersonal

Case #3   Angela Brown

Angela Brown had been interested in purchasing a portable radio/cassette player/recorder for some time. She was confused, however, by the wide variety of portables on the market. Prices ranged from $129 for a basic portable to $349 for the most elaborate models. Many possessed features she would probably not use, but she was unsure which features were the most desirable.

Brown's friend, Anna Henry, had purchased a Toshiba SR 100 portable while she was attending McGill University. When Henry returned home over the semester break, she shared her experience with her friend.

Henry said that she believed the best features included: automatic reverse, automatic replay, music selection system, AM filter, battery condition metre, sleep switch, 3-way power mode. She indicated that her Toshiba did not have all these features, but that an Aiwa CZ101 did and it cost $180.

Brown went to her library and found that the December issue of *Canadian Consumer Product Reports* magazine had an article which rated portable radio-cassette player/recorders. The article indicated that the Aiwa CZ101 was an excellent value because it possessed features not found on more expensive models. The article also indicated that the Aiwa possessed minimal flutter and excellent sensitivity and tone quality.

_____1. The article in *Canadian Consumer Product Reports* magazine indicating that the Aiwa CZ101 was an excellent value for the money could be promoted by Aiwa as a(n) _____ reason for buying the CZ 101.

A.   rational

B.   moral

C.   emotional

D.   none of the above

E.   all of the above

_____2. When Henry told her friend about the attributes of the Aiwa CZ101, this was an example of a(n) _____ channel.

A.   personal

B.   nonpersonal

C.   moral

D.   emotional

E.   social

_____3. The article in the magazine about the portable radio/cassette player/recorder is an example of:

A.   sales promotion.

B.   publicity.

C.   advertising.

D.   personal selling.

E.   corporate communications.

_____4. The product review by *Canadian Consumer Product Reports*, magazine which is a nonprofit publication and which accepts no advertising, is a credible source because of its:

A.   expertise.

B.   trustworthiness.

C.   likability.

D.   clientele.

E.   both (A) and (B)

378

Multiple Choice Answers

1. Correct Answer: 3   Reference: pg. 469

2. Correct Answer: 5   Reference: pg. 469

3. Correct Answer: 4   Reference: pg. 469

4. Correct Answer: 2   Reference: pg. 469

5. Correct Answer: 4   Reference: pg. 470

6. Correct Answer: 1   Reference: pg. 470

7. Correct Answer: 5   Reference: pg. 471

8. Correct Answer: 2   Reference: pg. 471

9. Correct Answer: 3   Reference: pg. 471

10. Correct Answer: 1   Reference: pg. 473

11. Correct Answer: 4   Reference: pg. 473

12. Correct Answer: 3   Reference: pg. 473

13. Correct Answer: 2   Reference: pg. 474

14. Correct Answer: 3   Reference: pg. 474

15. Correct Answer: 1   Reference: pg. 475

16. Correct Answer: 4   Reference: pg. 479

17. Correct Answer: 3   Reference: pg. 479

18. Correct Answer: 2   Reference: pg. 480

19. Correct Answer: 1   Reference: pg. 482

20. Correct Answer: 5   Reference: pg. 481

21. Correct Answer: 3   Reference: pg. 482

22.	Correct Answer:	2	Reference:	pg. 482
23.	Correct Answer:	4	Reference:	pg. 484
24.	Correct Answer:	5	Reference:	pg. 486
25.	Correct Answer:	2	Reference:	pg. 488
26.	Correct Answer:	4	Reference:	pg. 489
27.	Correct Answer:	1	Reference:	pg. 471
28.	Correct Answer:	4	Reference:	pg. 483
29.	Correct Answer:	2	Reference:	pg. 483
30.	Correct Answer:	3	Reference:	pg. 486

True/False Answers

1. TRUE   Reference: pg. 469   Topic: The Marketing Communications Mix

2. TRUE   Reference: pg. 469   Topic: The View of the Communication Process

3. FALSE   Reference: pg. 469   Topic: A View of the Communication Process

4. FALSE   Reference: pg. 471   Topic: Identifying the Target Audience

5. FALSE   Reference: pg. 473   Topic: Determining the Response Sought

6. TRUE   Reference: pg. 473   Topic: Designing the Message

7. TRUE   Reference: pg. 474   Topic: Message Structure

8. FALSE   Reference: pg. 475   Topic: Choosing Media

9. TRUE   Reference: pg. 475   Topic: Personal Communication Channels

10. TRUE   Reference: pg. 476   Topic: Non-Personal Communication Channels

11. FALSE   Reference: pg. 476   Topic: Non-Personal Communication Channels

12. TRUE   Reference: pg. 478   Topic: Collecting Feedback

13. FALSE   Reference: pg. 480   Topic: Competitive-Parity Method

14. FALSE   Reference: pg. 480   Topic: Setting the Promotion Mix

15. TRUE   Reference: pg. 481   Topic: Advertising

16. TRUE   Reference: pg. 481   Topic: Personal Selling

17. FALSE   Reference: pg. 483   Topic: Type of Product/Market

18. TRUE   Reference: pg. 485   Topic: The Changing Communications Environment

19. TRUE   Reference: pg. 486   Topic: Integrated Marketing Communications

20. FALSE   Reference: pg. 486   Topic: Integrated Marketing Communications

Applying Terms and Concept Answers

Case#1   Bagelicious:

Question#1

- Attention: By teaming with the local "adult contemporary" station, Aaron will reach a large number of consumers in his target group. More importantly, by taking part in the station's promotions he will gain the attention of this group.

- Interest: Hearing the Bagelicious name and a description of its unique product offerings will attract the interest of consumers.

- Desire: Wanting to take part in a popular trend, eating bagels, and visiting a new restaurant will raise consumers' desire.

- Action: Once in the restaurant people will want to buy a bagel or bagel sandwich.

Question#2:
An effective spokesperson should have the following characteristics:

Expertise: The source is seen as having experience in the area.

Trustworthiness: This refers to how objective and honest consumers think the source is.

Likability: The audience wants a source they consider attractive in terms of being open, humorous and natural.

Question #3
Mr. Soles would have problems in the expertise area because the audience would see him as news anchor and not a bagel expert. His position and reputation as a fair and honest person makes him a trustworthy source. Mr. Soles is very likable because people in Winnipeg remember him as a good-natured, friendly person.

Question #4
Aaron needs someone who is an expert in the field of bagels. Sadly, bagel experts are hard to come by unless you hire some unknown, obscure dietitian. However, a local radio or TV personality should do the trick. They may not be a bagel expert, but they can profess to the good taste and fine quality of the Bagelicious products.

Question#5

- The media is radio, and the message is "these bagels rock."

<u>Case #2   Shock Cola:</u>

1.   A

2.   D

3.   pulling

4.   A

5.   A

<u>Case #3   Angela Brown:</u>

1.   A

2.   A

3.   B

4.   E

Chapter 15

Advertising, Sales Promotion, and Public Relations

Chapter Overview

Companies must do more than make good products – they must inform consumers about product benefits and carefully position products in consumers' minds. To do this, they must skilfully use three mass-promotion tools in addition to personal selling, which targets specific buyers. The three mass-promotion tools are advertising, sales promotion, and public relations.

Chapter Objectives

1. Define the roles of advertising, sales promotion, and public relations in the promotion mix.
2. Describe the major decisions involved in developing an advertising program.
3. Explain how sales promotion campaigns are developed and implemented.
4. Explain how companies use public relations to communicate with their publics.

Chapter Topics

Advertising

Major Decisions in Advertising
- Setting Objectives
- Setting the Advertising Budget
- Advertising Strategy
    - Creating the Advertising Message
        - The Changing Message Environment
        - Message Strategy
        - Message Execution
    - Selecting Advertising Media
        - Deciding on Reach, Frequently, and Impact
        - Choose Among Major Media Types
- Advertising Evaluation
- Organizing for Advertising
- International Advertising Decisions

Sales Promotion

- Rapid Growth of Sales Promotion
- Purpose of Sales Promotion
- Setting Sales-Promotion Objectives
- Selecting Sales-Promotion Tools
    - Consumer-Promotion Tools
    - Trade-Promotion Tools
    - Business-Promotion Tools
- Developing the Sales-Promotion Program

Public Relations

- Major Public Relations Tools
- Major Public Relations Decisions
    - Setting Public Relations Objectives
    - Choose Public Relations Messages and Vehicles
    - Implementing the Public Relations Plan
    - Evaluating Public Relations Results

Chapter Summary

1.   The roles of advertising, sales promotion, and public relations in the promotion mix.

Each is part of the tools for mass-production. Advertising helps build awareness, interest, and brand loyalty. Sales promotion provides short-term incentives to buy now. Public relations is used to create a favourable image. Effective promotion strategy considers the strengths and limitations of each mass-promotion tool and assigns specific, coordinated objectives for each in support of an overall corporate objective.

2.   The major decisions involved in developing an advertising program.

Major decisions include setting objectives (communication, sales); setting the budget (affordable, percent of sales, comparative parity, objective-and-task); message decisions (generation, evaluation/selection, execution); media decisions (reach, frequency, impact, type, vehicles, timing); and campaign evaluation (communication and sales impact).

3.   How sales promotion campaigns are developed and implemented.

Sales promotion campaigns must determine the size of the incentive, the conditions for participation, how to promote and distribute the promotion, the length of time it is to run, the budget for the promotion, and whether or not to pretest the program. Following implementation, the company should evaluate the results by objective criteria as possible linked to sales and profit.

4.   How companies use public relations to communicate with their publics.

Public relations seeks to manage the presentation of the corporate image through press relations, product publicity, corporate communications, and lobbying efforts. Major tools for reaching various publics include news, speeches, special events, written materials, audio-visual materials, corporate identity materials, and public service activities.

5.   The different types of advertising used to meet advertising objectives.

Advertising objectives can be classified by purpose. Informative advertising is used heavily when introducing a new product category. Persuasive advertising becomes important as competition increases and the company seeks to build selective demand. Remainder advertising keeps consumers thinking about the product and is important for mature products.

Key Terms

Multiple Choice Questions

15-1   Multiple

Advertising is a significant industry in Canada, employing more than 196,000 people. It is almost as important to the Canadian economy as the _____ industry.

1.   Agricultural
2.   Car manufacturing
3.   Tourism
4.   Government
5.   Natural resources

15-2   Multiple

Advertising is such a large industry, that in Canada we spend more than $8 billion annually on it while the US spends more than $250 billion and the worldwide advertising spending is approximately:

1. $600 billion
2. $900 billion
3. $500 billion
4. $ 1 trillion
5. $750 billion

15-3   Multiple

Each industry does not spend the same amount of money on advertising. Which of the following in not one of the top 5 advertising industries?

1.   Retailing
2.   Automotive
3.   Business equipment and services
4.   Entertainment
5.   Tourism

15-4   Multiple

Which of the following is not an important decision management has to make with regards to advertising?

1.   Setting objectives
2.   Setting and advertising budget
3.   Choosing an advertising agency
4.   Setting an advertising strategy
5.   Performing an advertising evaluation

15-5   Multiple

Kar-Wai has been in business for just over 8 years. She owns and operates a speciality herbal shop, selling herbal remedies and the like. Lately more people have realized that the "herbal" craze is getting larger and therefore she is facing much more competition than before. It is in Kar-Wai's interest to use _____ advertising at this stage in the game.

1.   Informative
2.   Persuasive
3.   Comparison
4.   Comparative
5.   Unique

15-6   Multiple

Before one can set the advertising budget, one must consider all the following factors except:

1.   Stage in the product life cycle
2.   Competition and clutter
3   Product differentiation
4.   Cost of different advertising mediums
5.   None of the above

15-7   Multiple

Advertising strategy consists of which of the following:

1.   Advertising messages
2.   Advertising market
3.   Advertising media
4.   Only 1 and 3
5.   All of the above

15-8   Multiple

In today's fast paced, over cluttered media society, consumers are not interested in sitting through commercials. They feel it is a waste of their time; therefore when commercials are on, they either fast-forward through them, or they channel surf. To combat these problems, today's advertising messages must be:

1.   Better quality
2.   Better planned
3.   More rewarding
4.   More imaginative
5.   All of the above

15-9   Multiple

When most TV viewers are armed with remote controls, a commercial has to cut through the clutter and seize the viewer's attention in:

1. 4-5 seconds
2. 1-2 seconds
3. 1-3 seconds
4. 3-6 seconds
5. None of the above

15-10 Multiple

The message portion of the advertising strategy is very important. Developing an effective message strategy begins with identifying consumer _____ that can be used as advertising appeals.

1. Preferences
2. Needs
3. Wants
4. Benefits
5. All of the above

15-11 Multiple

Sherry is the advertising manger for Sabre Industries. From the following list, what is the one item Sherry does NOT need to consider in setting an advertising appeal?

1. Compatible
2. Meaningful
3. Believable
4. Distinctive
5. All of the above are required

15-12 Multiple

Any message can be presented in different execution styles. A series of ads showing young Canadians with their faces painted, ready to attend Molson's Hockey Night in Canada, is an example of which advertising execution styles?

1. Technical expertise
2. Fantasy
3. Slice of life
4. Lifestyle
5. Mood or image

15-13 Multiple

When Maxwell House shows one of its buyers carefully selecting the coffee beans, they are using which advertising execution style?

1.	Testimonial evidence
2.	Technical expertise
3.	Scientific evidence
4.	Personality symbol
5.	Mood or image

15-14 Multiple

Which of the following is not a major step in the media selection process?

1.	Deciding on the reach, frequency and impact
2.	Choosing among the major media types
3.	Selecting specific media vehicles
4.	Deciding on media timing
5.	None of the above

15-15 Multiple

Media planners consider many factors when making their media choices. These factors include all the following except:

1.	Media habits of target consumers
2.	Spending habits of target consumers
3.	The nature of the product
4.	Cost
5.	All the following are factors

15-16 Multiple

What media type is limited by high absolute cost, high clutter, fleeting exposure and less audience selectivity?

1.	Newspaper
2.	Direct mail
3.	Magazines
4.	Television
5.	Radio

15-17 Multiple

The media type whose advantages include high geographic and demographic selectivity, credibility and prestige, high-quality reproduction, a long life and good pass-along relationship is:

1.   Newspaper
2.   Direct mail
3.   Magazines
4.   Television
5.   Radio

15-18 Multiple

In selecting media vehicles, the media planner must balance media cost measures against the media impact factors. Which of the following is not an impact factor?

1.   Audience creativity
2.   Audience quality
3.   Audience attention
4.   Editorial quality
5.   None of the above

15-19 Multiple

Most large advertising agencies have the staff and resources to handle all phases of an advertising campaign for their clients. Agencies usually have four departments. Which of the following is not one of them?

1.   Media departments
2.   Creative departments
3.   Research departments
4.   Business departments
5.   None of the above

15-20 Multiple

_____ produces many benefits – lower advertising costs, greater coordination of global advertising efforts, and a more consistent worldwide company or product image.

1.   Globalization
2.   Standardization
3.   Media cooperation
4.   Integrated marketing communication
5.   None of the above

15-21 Multiple

Not all countries have an open media market like North America. In fact, many countries heavily regulate the media and advertising. From the following list, select the item least likely to be regulated.

1.   How much a company can spend on advertising
2.   The media used
3.   The people used in the advertising campaigns
4.   The nature of the advertising claims
5.   All of the above are regulated

15-22 Multiple

In many consumer packaged-goods companies, sales promotion accounts for _____ % or more of all marketing expenditures.

1.   50
2.   30
3.   90
4.   75
5.   65

15-23 Multiple

Sales promotion has grown immensely in the last few years. Which of the following is not one of the reasons?

1.   Product managers inside the company face greater pressures to increase their current sales
2.   Externally companies face more competition
3.   Advertising efficiency has declined due to rising costs and media clutter
4.   Retailers are demanding more deals from manufacturers
5.   Rise in the time-poor consumer

15-24 Multiple

Kraft Canada started a magazine called *What's Cooking*. This magazine contains letters from consumers, cooking tips, information on maintaining a healthy diet and recipes based on Kraft products. This magazine is used to meet which criteria of a good sales promotion strategy?

1.   Consumer promotions
2.   Customer relationship building
3.   Trade promotions
4.   Loyalty programs
5.   None of the above

15-25 Multiple

Goods offered either for free or at low cost as an incentive to buy – for example a bottle of hair spray with a bonus 50ml for the price of a regular bottle – would be considered:

1.   A price pack
2.   An advertising speciality
3.   A premium
4.   A patronage reward
5.   A point-of-purchase promotion

15-26 Multiple

A _____ calls for consumers to submit their names for a drawing.

1.   Sweepstake
2.   Game
3.   Contest
4.   Silent auction
5.   All of the above

15-27 Multiple

In developing a sales promotion program, a marketer must consider all the following except:

1.   Size of the incentive
2.   Conditions for participation
3.   Length of promotion
4.   Sales-promotion budget
5.   All the above must be considered

15-28 Multiple

Public relations departments in many companies are growing in importance and need. The following function performed by the pubic relations department, helps build relations with donors or members of non-profit organizations to gain financial or volunteer support.

1.   Press relations of press agentry
2.   Lobbying
3.   Investor relations
4.   Development
5.   Product publicity

15-29 Multiple

Evaluating public relations results can be very difficult, as public relations is usually accompanied by other means of marketing. However, a good measure of the effectiveness of a public relations campaign would be a change in all the following except:

1.   Product awareness
2.   Product consumption
3.   Product knowledge
4.   Product attitude
5.   Changes in all the above would be good

15-30 Multiple

The advantages of flexibility, timeliness, good local market coverage, broad acceptance, and high believability apply to which media type?

1.   Television
2.   Direct mail
3.   Radio
4.   Newspaper
5.   Magazines

True/False Questions

15-1   True/False

Advertising can be traced back to about the 1300s.

15-2   True/False

The sixth largest advertising spender is a non-profit organization – the Canadian government.

15-3   True/False

The Competition Act stipulates an advertisement using competitive claims must be based on adequate and proper tests that support it.

15-4   True/False

The role of advertising is to affect demand for a product.

15-5   True/False

Some critics charge large consumer packaged-goods companies tend to underspend on advertising and business-to-business marketers generally overspend on advertising.

15-6   True/False

A large advertising budget guarantees a successful advertising campaign.

15-7   True/False

The first step in creating effective advertising messages is to decide what general message will be communicated to consumers.

15-8   True/False

The impact of the message depends only on what is said, not on how it is said.

15-9   True/False

A small change in ad design really makes no significant change in its effect.

15-10   True/False

The media planner ultimately decides which vehicles give the best reach frequency, and impact for the money.

15-11 True/False

Some companies do only seasonal advertising.

15-12 True/False

The sales effect of advertising is often easier to measure than the communication effect.

15-13 True/False

Many Canadian viewers believe they are able to tell whether or not a commercial is Canadian-made.

15-14 True/False

Most international advertisers think globally but act locally.

15-15 True/False

Consumers are increasingly accepting sales promotions, therefore strengthening their ability to trigger immediate purchase.

15-16 Truc/False

If properly designed, every sales promotion tool has consumer-relationship-building potential.

15-17 True/False

An increasing number of manufacturers believe that coupons are costly and inefficient.

15-18 True/False

Companies only spend a small amount of money, maybe a few million, each year on promotion to industrial customers.

15-19 True/False

In emerging countries like Russia, trade fairs are the only means of reaching potential buyers.

15-20 True/False

Public relations can have a strong impact on public awareness at a much lower cost than advertising.

Applying Terms and Concepts

To determine how well you understand the materials in this chapter, read each of the following brief cases and then respond to the questions that follow. Answers are given at the end of this chapter.

Case#1   Skin So Soft[1]

Is Skin So Soft a bath oil or an insect repellent? Avon, the makers of Skin So Soft (SSS), insists it is a bath oil. But while the company appreciates the revenue from sales to sports enthusiasts, pet owners, outdoorsmen, and even the military, Avon knows that those customers are purchasing Skin So Soft for a reason other than to smell nice. Some people believe that the product, when mixed with equal parts of water and applied to the skin, is an effective insect repellent.

Avon officials claim to be baffled why mosquitoes, fleas, and other bugs don't like their product. Scientists say there is no ingredient in SSS that should make it act like a repellent, but speculate the fragrance, a proven people pleaser is offensive to the keen sense of smell of some insects. SSS clearly doesn't ward off all bugs, and some research suggests it is effective on only one strain of mosquito. The research also suggests its effectiveness is short-lived. But that hasn't slowed the sales of SSS. Even pet owners are getting in on the act. According to one study, the flea count on dogs can be cut by one-third in just two days after a sponge bath with a mixture of SSS and water, and fleas seem to stay off longer than when regular flea dips are used alone. An added benefit is that the mixture leaves the dog's coat shinier and more pleasant-smelling. Unfortunately, the treatment doesn't work for cats; it seems their skin is too sensitive for the chemicals in the mixture. Horses, however, benefit from the treatment.

Law prohibits Avon from touting SSS as an insect repellent. But advertisements such as "Millions of People Know the Secret of Skin So Soft, Do You?" are beginning to bug Avon's competitors, the makes of traditional insect repellents. They believe Avon should register the product with the EPA and subject it to the safety and effectiveness testing required by law. Avon professes innocence and maintains any benefits from secondary usage are spread by word-of-mouth among its devotees.

Recent findings some traditional insect repellents contain chemicals suspected of being hazardous to health have enhanced the sales of Skin So Soft, currently in the tens of millions of dollar—prompting one to wonder if SSS should really be translated as Sweet Smell of Success.

---

[1] *Principles of Marketing*, 3rd Edition, Kotler, Armstrong, Warren (Prentice Hall) – pg. 322.

1.   Explain how Avon could use each of the following consumer promotion tools to increase the short-term sales of Skin So Soft and to help build long-tem market share. Sample

    _____

    _____

    _____

    _____

2.   Coupons

    _____

    _____

    _____

    _____

3.   Cash refund offers

    _____

    _____

    _____

    _____

4.   Price packs

    _____

    _____

    _____

    _____

5.   Law prohibits Avon from advertising SSS as an insect repellent, so word of its effectiveness as a repellent is primarily spread by devotees. What are the relative advantages and disadvantages of this word-of-mouth advertising?

    _____

    _____

    _____

    _____

Case #2   Safeway Coupon Book

The Safeway coupon book was a monthly coupon book filled with reduced prices on a number of items, ranging from milk and dairy products to hair and beauty care products. The book was very popular and many people actually traded the coupons they did not want with their friends for ones they did want. The savings in each book totalled over $500 per month. The coupon book was used in an attempt to draw people into the stores and purchase items that they would not normally buy, but now were on sale. The book was also used to convince people that shopping at Safeway with the coupon book was almost as cheap as SuperValu, but the quality was better. The Safeway coupon book was delivered by Canada Post to all residents of an area and was a very successful venture for Safeway.

1.   What was the major marketing objective of Safeway's coupon book?

_____

_____

_____

_____

2.   How could Safeway tabulate and analyze the results of the coupon books' use?

_____

_____

_____

_____

3.   Could Safeway charge its suppliers a fee to place their coupons in their book? Why or Why not? Do you believe they are doing it now?

_____

_____

_____

_____

4.   Do you believe samples are more effective in selling new products than coupons? Why do you say that?

_____

_____

_____

_____

5.   What did you think of the Safeway coupon book? Do you believe it is an effective marketing tool?

_____

_____

_____

_____

Case #3   Barone Wine

Marlo Barone opened his new winery in the Tuscany district of Italy with pageantry rivaling that of the opening ceremonies of the modern Olympic Games. Tuscan standard bearers hurled their flags into the air as the music of Nanini, Vivaldi, and Goldoni, Italy's renowned composers, was performed by the symphony orchestra of Milan. White doves were released to announce arrival of the Cardinal of Siena, who bestowed his blessing on the winery and vineyards. Italian dignitaries looked on as a parade marched through town. Fireworks lit the evening sky, with Barone's winery, housed in a medieval castle, looming in the background.

The event last November, which was covered by media representatives from 12 countries writing for 32 different publications, signaled a major undertaking for Barone. The $100 million winery was built in the heart of Arezzo, Tuscany's most respected wine district. The winery, surrounded by 7,000 hectares of prime grape-growing land, was capable of producing 5.0 million litres of wine annually.

Barone had made his fortune by importing table wines such as Lambrusco and Sangria and bottling them under a variety of now popular brand names. Barone wines, based in Toronto, had sales last year of $260 million.

The opening of the Arezzo Winery was a bold move not only because it would mark the first time Barone produced its own wines, but also because the winery would be Barone's entry into the high-quality premium wine market.

Barone hoped to break into the fast-growing market for fine wines now dominated by Californian and French vintners. A recent article in *Vintner*, the prestigious newsletter from the union of international oenologists, indicated that the worldwide market for premium wines had been growing by 15 percent annually, compared to only a 2.6 percent growth in the table wine market.

Barone's promotional campaign will be designed to build selective demand for the wine. One of the company's promotions is a magazine advertisement that shows an apparently wealthy couple leaning against a Rolls-Royce Silver Shadow on which has been placed a bottle of Barone's wine. (Starch Readership scores indicated the advertisement to be extremely effective.) This particular advertisement will be run in three consecutive issues of *Macleans*, *Canadian Business*, *Saturday Night* and *Psychology Today* magazines.

_____1. The winery's magazine promotion campaign would fall under which class of advertising objectives?

      A.   persuasive

      B.   comparison

      C.   information

      D.   reinforcement

      E.   remind

_____2. Which style of message execution is used by the magazine ad?

      A.   slice-of-life

      B.   life style

      C   personality symbol

      D.   testimonial

      E.   fantasy

_____3. The communication-effect research on the magazine advertisement (Starch Readership scores) is an example of:

      A.   a consumer panel.

      B.   direct ratings.

      C.   testimonial evidence.

      D.   a recognition test.

      E.   technical expertise.

_____4. Scheduling the magazine advertisement in three consecutive issues is an example of _____ (continuity/pulsing).

_____5. Which major promotional tool was Barone using to announce the opening of his winery?

    A.   advertisement

    B.   personal selling

    C.   public relations

    D.   sales promotion

    E.   trade promotion

Case #4 Tyco Car Wax

The Tyco Car Wax Company is planning to sponsor a sales promotion activity from October 1 to December 31 of this year. Tyco is allowing any resident of Canada who is 18 years of age with a valid driver's license to enter the activity. Each individual must complete an entry form and send it to Tyco's headquarters in Goose Bay, Labrador. No purchase is necessary, and each person may enter as many times as he or she wishes.

Tyco is providing retailers with signs and cardboard displays to call attention to the promotion. Each display will contain a packet of entry forms which individuals may tear off, complete, and send to Tyco headquarters.

The prizes for this activity include:

	# of Prizes	Prize
First Prize	1	a vehicle of the winner's choice, value not to exceed $25,000
Second Prize	10	free gasoline for one year, value per prize not to exceed $1,000
Third Prize	1,000	Tyco Car Wax t-shirt, value per prize $5
Fourth Prize	2,000	can of Tyco Car Wax, value per prize $1.50

In addition to the prizes listed above, each entrant receives a certificate entitling the bearer to a certain savings on the purchase of any Tyco car care product.

Each winner is responsible for the GST and any provincial sales tax. The activity is void where prohibited and all entries must be postmarked by December 31 of this year. Winners will be selected by the independent certified public accounting firm of Hartley and Sanger, whose decisions are final. Tyco car wax employees and their immediate families are restricted from participating in this activity.

_____1. This Tyco Car Wax sales promotion activity is best described as a:

    A.   contest.

    B.   sweepstakes.

    C.   game.

    D.   sales contest.

    E.   trade promotion.

_____2. The main tool of the Tyco sales promotion activity is for _____ (consumer/trade) promotion.

_____3. When Tyco prepared cardboard signs and displays for use in stores to call attention to the sales promotion activity, Tyco was using:

    A.   trade promotion.

    B.   advertising allowances.

    C.   point-of-purchase displays.

    D.   premiums.

    E.   advertising specialties.

_____4. When Tyco sent each individual who participated in the sales promotion activity a certificate entitling the bearer to a stated saving on the next purchase of any Tyco car care product. Tyco was distributing:

    A.   samples.

    B.   coupons.

    C.   price packs.

    D.   premiums.

    E.   advertising specialty.

_____5. When Tyco decided that the first, second, third, and fourth prizes would not exceed $25,000, $10,000, $5,000, and $3,000, respectively, Tyco was deciding on:

A.   conditions of participation.

B.   distribution vehicle for promotion.

C.   size of the incentive.

D.   timing of promotion.

E.   reach, frequency and impact.

Multiple Choice Answers

1.	Correct Answer:	3	Reference:	pg. 499
2.	Correct Answer:	1	Reference:	pg. 499
3.	Correct Answer:	5	Reference:	pg. 499
4.	Correct Answer:	3	Reference:	pg. 501
5.	Correct Answer:	2	Reference:	pg. 501
6.	Correct Answer:	4	Reference:	pg. 502
7.	Correct Answer:	4	Reference:	pg. 503
8.	Correct Answer:	1	Reference:	pg. 505
9.	Correct Answer:	3	Reference:	pg. 506
10.	Correct Answer:	4	Reference:	pg. 506
11.	Correct Answer:	1	Reference:	pg. 506
12.	Correct Answer:	3	Reference:	pg. 507
13.	Correct Answer:	2	Reference:	pg. 507
14.	Correct Answer:	5	Reference:	pg. 508
15.	Correct Answer:	2	Reference:	pg. 508
16.	Correct Answer:	4	Reference:	pg. 509
17.	Correct Answer:	3	Reference:	pg. 509
18.	Correct Answer:	1	Reference:	pg. 511
19.	Correct Answer:	5	Reference:	pg. 512
20.	Correct Answer:	2	Reference:	pg. 513
21.	Correct Answer:	3	Reference:	pg. 514

22.	Correct Answer:	4	Reference:	pg. 515
23.	Correct Answer:	5	Reference:	pg. 515
24.	Correct Answer:	2	Reference:	pg. 516
25.	Correct Answer:	3	Reference:	pg. 518
26.	Correct Answer:	1	Reference:	pg. 519
27.	Correct Answer:	5	Reference:	pg. 520
28.	Correct Answer:	4	Reference:	pg. 521
29.	Correct Answer:	2	Reference:	pg. 525
30.	Correct Answer:	4	Reference:	pg. 509

True/False Answers

1.	FALSE	Reference:	pg. 498	Topic:	Advertising	
2.	TRUE	Reference:	pg. 499	Topic:	Advertising	
3.	TRUE	Reference:	pg. 502	Topic:	Setting Objectives	
4.	TRUE	Reference:	pg. 502	Topic:	Setting the Advertising Budget	
5.	FALSE	Reference:	pg. 502	Topic:	Setting the Advertising Budget	
6.	FALSE	Reference:	pg. 504	Topic:	Creating the Advertising Message	
7.	TRUE	Reference:	pg. 506	Topic:	Message Strategy	
8.	FALSE	Reference:	pg. 506	Topic:	Message Execution	
9.	FALSE	Reference:	pg. 508	Topic:	Message Execution	
10.	TRUE	Reference:	pg. 511	Topic:	Selecting Specific Media Vehicles	
11.	TRUE	Reference:	pg. 511	Topic:	Selecting Specific Media Vehicles	
12.	FALSE	Reference:	pg. 511	Topic:	Advertising Evaluation	
13.	TRUE	Reference:	pg. 512	Topic:	Organizing for Advertising	
14.	TRUE	Reference:	pg. 513	Topic:	Organizing for Advertising	
15.	FALSE	Reference:	pg. 515	Topic:	Rapid Growth of Sales Promotion	
16.	TRUE	Reference:	pg. 516	Topic:	Setting Sales Promotion Objectives	
17.	TRUE	Reference:	pg. 517	Topic:	Consumer-Promotion Tools	
18.	FALSE	Reference:	pg. 519	Topic:	Business-Promotion Tools	
19.	TRUE	Reference:	pg. 520	Topic:	Business-Promotion Tools	
20.	TRUE	Reference:	pg. 521	Topic:	Public Relations	

Applying Terms and Concepts Answers

Case#1   Skin So Soft:

Question #1
- Samples: Samplers are offers of a trial amount of a product.
- A small container of Skin So Soft could be included free of charge along with each Avon order delivered to a customer.

Question #2
- Coupons: Coupons are certificates that give buyers savings when they purchase specified products.
- A coupon for specified savings off the regular price of Skin So Soft could be included in each Avon catalogue or distributed by the Avon salesperson when servicing customers.

Question #3
- Cash refund offers: Rebates are price reductions given after the purchase rather than at the time of sale.
- Avon could allow the consumer to receive a portion of the retail price back, after the consumer sends a "proof-of-purchase" to them.

Question #4
- Price packs: Price packs offer consumers savings off the regular price of a product, Skin So Soft could be sold as a single item at a reduced price, or it could be bundled with another product and sold at a price below that which both would cost if sold separately.

Question #5
- Personal communication channels involve two or more persons communicating directly with one another.
- They might communicate face-to-face, person-to-person, over the telephone, or through the mail.
- Personal communication channels are effective because they individualize presentation and feedback.
- There are three types of personal communication channels: advocate channels, consisting of company salespeople contacting buyers in the marketplace; expert channels, consisting of independent persons with expertise making claims to target buyers; and social channels, consisting of neighbours, friend, family members, and associates talking to target buyers.
- This last channel, known as word-of-mouth influence, is the most persuasive in many product areas.

- Word-of-mouth has the advantage of being more believable in that acquaintances have nothing to gain financially from the advice they are giving to potential buyers.
- Most of the time, they are simply trying to provide assistance.
- The disadvantages of word-of-mouth are that it may be inaccurate and biased.
- The product's supporters may be well intentioned but ill informed, and therefore impart poor information.
- Personal influence is especially important when the product is expensive, risky, purchased infrequently, or has significant social status.
- But even with a product as "simple" as Skin So Soft, personal influence can greatly impact sales.

Case #2   Safeway's Coupon Book:

Question #1
- To get people to buy products they would not normally buy if they weren't on sale
- To get people to buy more products than normal since they are on sale
- To increase sales of slower moving products
- To get rid of ageing merchandise before it becomes outdated

Question #2
- They can compare sales of the products before, after and during the promotion to see if there was any effect – for example brand loyalty as a result of trying the product on sale
- They can compare the number of the same items purchased and see if the coupons influenced people to buy more than what they really needed

Question #3
- Yes, if the results of the coupon book was positive – people buy more of the products that are in the book – then Safeway could charge the company a fee to place their products in the book
- The book is not just a coupon book, it also allows companies to advertise their products so consumers will see and buy, therefore this is a form of promotion, therefore Safeway can charge a fee

Question #4
- For new products, sampling is more effective as people are not familiar with the product, therefore if they can form an educated opinion about it before they buy, they are more likely to buy it

Coupons are good for repeat purchases where people are really indifferent about the different brands and are price sensitive

Case #3   Barone Wines:

1.   A

2.   B

3.   D

4.   continuity

5.   C

Case #4   Tyco Car Wash:

1.   B

2.   consumer

3.   C

4.   B

5.   C

Chapter 16

Personal Selling and Sales Management

Chapter Overview

Selling is one of the world's oldest professions. People that sell are known by a variety of names including salespeople, sales representatives, account executives, sales consultants, sales engineers, agents, district managers, and marketing representatives. Regardless of their titles, members of the sales force play a key role in modern marketing organizations.

The term salesperson covers a wide spectrum of positions. Salespeople may be order takers, such as the department-store salespeople who stand behind the counter. Or they may be order getters – salespeople engaged in the creative selling of products and services such as appliances, industrial equipment, advertising, or consulting services. Other salespeople perform missionary selling, in which they are not involved in taking an order but in building goodwill or educating buyers. To be successful in these more creative forms of selling, a company must first build and manage an effective sales force.

Chapter Objectives

1. Discuss the role of a company's salespeople in creating value for customers and building customer relationships.
2. Identify the six major sales-force management steps.
3. Explain how companies design sales-force strategy and structure.
4. Explain how companies recruit, select, and train salespeople.
5. Describe how companies compensate and supervise salespeople, and how they evaluate sales-force effectiveness.
6. Discuss the personal selling process, distinguishing between transaction-oriented marketing and relationship marketing.

412

Chapter Topics

The Role of Personal Selling
- The Nature of Personal Selling
- The Role of the Sales Force

Managing the Sales Force
- Designing Sales-Force Strategy and Structure
  - Sales-Force Structure
    - Territorial Sales-Force Structure
    - Product Sales-Force Structure
    - Customer Sales-Force Structure
    - Pyramid Structures
    - Complex Sales-Force Structures
  - Sales-Force Size
  - Other Sales-Force Strategy and Structure Issues
    - Outside and Inside Sales Forces
    - Team Selling
- Recruiting and Selecting Salespeople
  - What Makes a Good Salesperson?
  - Recruiting Procedures
  - Selecting Salespeople
- Training Salespeople
- Compensating Salespeople
- Supervising Salespeople
  - Directing Salespeople
  - Motivating Salespeople
- Evaluating Salespeople
  - Sources of Information
  - Formal Evaluation of Performance
    - Comparing Salespeople's Performance
    - Comparing Current Sales with Past Sales
    - Qualitative Evaluation of Salespeople

Principles of Personal Selling
- The Personal Selling Process
- Steps in the Selling Process
  - Prospecting and Qualifying
  - Preapproach
  - Approach
  - Presentation and Demonstration
  - Handling Objections
  - Closing
  - Follow-up
- Relationship Marketing

Chapter Summary

1.   The steps in the selling process.

There are seven major steps in the selling process. Prospecting involves identifying qualified potential customers. Preapproach involves learning about the target customer. Approach meets the buyer and gets things off to a good start. Presentation tells the story to the buyer. Handling objections solves logical and psychological problems. Closing asks for the order. Follow-up ensures contact for satisfaction and repeat business.

2.   The six major sales-force management steps.

Major steps are: designing sales-force strategy and structure; recruiting and selecting salespeople; training salespeople; compensating salespeople; supervising salespeople; evaluating salespeople.

3.   How companies design sales-force strategy and structure.

Companies set different strategic goals for sales forces. Some use general guidelines such as "sell, maintain, develop, serve" while others provide specific instructions on time/activity allocation. Designing sales-force strategy involves determining the type of selling (individual, team, conference, seminar), the structure (territorial, product, customer, complex), and size.

4.   The companies recruit, select, and train salespeople.

Recruitment and selection are based upon the company's perception about what type of person will be successful representing the company. Personnel look at applications, prospects from employees, places ads, interview college students. Training is increasingly seen as an investment and may run several months, even more than a year, with planned continuing development during the saleperson's tenure with the company.

5.   How companies supervise salespeople and evaluate their effectiveness.

Supervision involves developing customer targets and call norms, using sales time efficiently and motivating salespeople through organizational climate, sales quotas, and positive incentives. Evaluating salespeople relies on sources of information such as sales reports (work plan, annual territory marketing plans, expense reports, call reports) and formal procedures such as current to past sales comparison and qualitative evaluations.

414

Key Terms

Approach   (pg. 554)
Closing   (pg. 555)
Complex sales-force structure(pg. 541)
Customer sales-force structure
         (pg. 540)
Follow-up   (pg. 555)
Handling objections   (pg. 555)
Inside sales force   (pg. 542)
Outside sales force   (pg. 542)
Preapproach   (pg. 554)
Presentation   (pg. 555)
Product sales-force structure (pg. 540)

Prospecting   (pg. 554)
Pyramid sales-force structure (pg. 541)
Relationship marketing   (pg. 557)
Sales-force management   (pg. 539)
Salesperson   (pg. 538)
Sales quotas   (pg. 550)
Selling process   (pg. 554)
Team selling   (pg. 543)
Telemarketing (pg. 542)
Territorial sales-force structure
         (pg. 540)
Workload approach   (pg. 542)

Multiple Choice Questions

16-1   Multiple

Modern salespeople are a far cry from the stereotypes of the past. Today sales people are:

1.   Well-educated professionals
2.   Well-trained professionals
3.   Well-dressed professional
4.   Only 1 and 2
5.   All of the above

16-2   Multiple

Personal selling today is much more than closing a sale. Salespeople must ensure the following is (are) done.

1.   Satisfy customer needs
2.   Listen to their customers
3.   Solve their customers problems
4.   Only 1 and 2
5.   All of the above

16-3   Multiple

Salespeople whose positions demands the creative selling of products and services are considered:

1.   Order takers
2.   Order getters
3.   Missionary sellers
4.   Aggressive sellers
5.   None of the above

16-4   Multiple

Salespeople should be more concerned with more than just _____. They must also know how to produce _____ and _____.

1.   Sales, customer satisfaction, company profit
2.   Company profit, sales, customer satisfaction
3.   Company profits, customer satisfaction, customer loyalty
4.   Sales, company profits, customer loyalty
5.   None of the above

16-5   Multiple

The definition of sales-force management includes all the following except:

1.   Analyzing
2.   Financing
3.   Implementing
4.   Planning
5.   All the following

16-6   Multiple

Sales-force management includes designing sales-force strategy and structure. It also includes all the following except _____ with respect to the sales force.

1.   Training
2.   Evaluating
3.   Surveying
4.   Recruiting
5.   Compensating

16-7   Multiple

Which of the following descriptions of sales-force structure clearly defines the salesperson's job and improves selling effectiveness.

1.   Pyramid
2.   Complex
3.   Customer
4.   Territorial
5.   Product

16-8   Multiple

IBM Canada recently reorganized its sales force so its 1,000-plus members could become specialists in selling computers, software, and services to narrow industry sectors such as banks, insurance companies and resource-based firms. They are using which sales-force structure?

1.   Pyramid
2.   Complex
3.   Customer
4.   Territorial
5.   Product

16-9   Multiple

These sales forces are often composed of people with different skills, who are employed to accomplish different tasks ranging from merchandisers who help retailers, to telemarketers, to information managers.

1.   Pyramid
2.   Complex
3.   Customer
4.   Territorial
5.   Product

16-10   Multiple

A company has 1000 Type-A accounts and 2000 Type-B accounts. Type A accounts require 36 calls a year and Type B accounts require 12 calls per year. In this case, the sales-force's workload – the number of calls it must make per year – is:

1.   60,000
2.   84,000
3.   194
4.   138
5.   None of the above

16-11   Multiple

Inside sales force include all the following except:

1.   Technical support people
2.   Sales assistants
3.   Telemarketers
4.   Managers
5.   All of the above

16-12   Multiple

Sales teams are becoming more popular in larger companies. Which of the following divisions would not be part of a sales team?

1   Engineering
2   Finance
3   Upper management
4   Technical support
5   All of the above would participate

418

16-13 Multiple

In a typical sales force, the top _____ % of the salespeople might bring in _____ % of the sales.

1. 25, 75
2. 30,60
3. 40,50
4. 20,80
5. 15,60

16-14 Multiple

Selecting salespeople is often hard for a company, as there is not a set list of traits which qualify someone as an excellent salesperson. Which of the following would definitely NOT be a qualifying trait for a good salesperson?

1. Outgoing
2. Aggressive
3. Energetic
4. Soft-spoken
5. All of the above are good traits

16-15 Multiple

Selecting salespeople is quite a challenge. Most companies administer a series of tests, either prior to all interviews, or after the first interview. These formal tests can measure all the following except:

1. Sales aptitude
2. Education level
3. Analytical skills
4. Personality traits
5. All of the above can be measured

16-16 Multiple

There are many different compensation packages offered to salespeople. Packages can include base salary, commission, bonuses, and fringe benefits. The average plan consists of about _____ % salary and _____ % incentive pay.

1. 60,40
2. 50,50
3. 70,30
4. 55,45
5. 30,70

16-17 Multiple

The relationship between overall marketing strategy and sales-force compensation is very important and easily identifiable. Which strategic goal would a company be trying to achieve if its ideal salesperson was a competitive problem-solver, the sales focus was consultative selling and its compensation role was to reward new and existing accounts sales?

1.   To rapidly gain market share
2.   To maximize profitability
3.   To solidify market share
4.   To solidify market leadership
5.   To maximize shareholder wealth

16-18 Multiple

Not all a salesperson's time is spent selling. Come other activities may include service calls, administrative tasks, telephone selling and waiting/travelling. On average a salesperson only spends _____ % of their time engaged in face-to-face selling.

1.   40
2.   50
3.   30
4.   20
5.   15

16-19 Multiple

_____ is the motivation tool, which helps salespeople have a positive view about their opportunities, values, and regards for a good performance within the company.

1.   Sales quotas
2.   Positive incentives
3.   Performance based reward system
4.   Organizational climate
5.   None of the above

16-20 Multiple

There are many sources of information companies use to evaluate salespeople. _____ outlines salespeople's plans for building new accounts and increasing sales from existing accounts.

1. Work plan
2. Expense reports
3. Annual territory marketing plans
4. Call reports
5. Projected sales reports

16-21 Multiple

Formal evaluation produces many benefits. Which of the following is not one of them?

1. Management must develop and communicate clear standards for judging performance
2. Management must gather well-rounded information about salespeople
3. Salespeople receive constructive feedback that helps them to improve future performance
4. Salespeople are motivated to perform well because they know they will have to sit down with the sales manager and explain their performance
5. All the above are benefits

16-22 Multiple

Salespeople cannot make sales calls to every company in their territory. They must carefully select companies according to certain criteria. During the prospecting and qualifying stage, salespeople evaluate and qualify potential companies on all the following except:

1. Competitive take-over possibilities
2. Financial ability
3. Volume of business
4. Special needs
5. All of the above are used for qualifying potential companies

16-23 Multiple

Companies who are interested in just making the sales are _____.

1. Profit oriented
2. Transaction oriented
3. Relationship oriented
4. Product oriented
5. Customer oriented

16-24 Multiple

Companies that are good prospects for a relationship-marketing program have all the following characteristics except:

1. That they prefer suppliers who can sell and deliver a coordinated set of products and services to many locations
2. That they want suppliers who can quickly solve problems
3. That want suppliers who can work closely with customer teams to improve products and processes
4. That they want suppliers who emphasize service over technical support
5. All the above are characteristics

16-25 Multiple

Which of the following tasks involves the identification and cultivation of new customers?

1. Prospecting
2. Communications
3. Selling
4. Information gathering
5. Presentation and demonstration

16-26 Multiple

Which of the following involves the most creative form of selling?

1. Order taking
2. Technical specialist
3. Selling intangible products
4. Selling tangible products
5. Detailing

16-27 Multiple

When a sales representative brings resource people from the company to meet with one or more buyers to discuss problems and mutual opportunities, the firm is engaged in _____ _____ selling.

1. Sales representative to buyer group
2. Conference
3. Seminal
4. Sales team to buyer group
5. Group

16-28 Multiple

Many companies determine the size of the sales force by using:

1.   Industry averages
2.   The build-up approach
3.   The customer-contact approach
4.   The relationship marketing approach
5.   The workload approach

16-29 Multiple

Which of the following elements in a compensation package provides the greatest incentive for sales representatives?

1.   Salary
2.   Fringe benefits
3.   Expense allowances
4.   Commissions
5.   Use of company vehicles

16-30 Multiple

Which of the following has not been identified as a desirable trait of a sales representative?

1.   Sympathy
2.   Enthusiasm
3.   Self-confidence
4.   Initiative
5.   All of the above are good traits

True/False Questions

16-1   True/False

Selling is the oldest profession in the world.

16-2   True/False

Personal selling can be more effective than advertising in more complex selling situations.

16-3   True/False

All companies have some salespeople.

16-4   True/False

Salespeople constitute one of the company's most productive – and most expensive – assets.

16-5   True/False

Increasing the number of salespeople in a company will increase both costs but not sales.

16-6   True/False

Outside salespeople travel to call on customers, while inside salespeople conduct business from their offices.

16-7   True/False

Companies realize they must emphasize the importance of teamwork in their training programs and at the same time they must diminish the importance of individual initiative.

16-8   True/False

According to one study, sales superstars sell an average of 2-4 times more than the average salesperson.

16-9   True/False

Companies still find it difficult to convince university students a career in selling is a lucrative and rewarding one.

16-10 True/False

To attract salespeople, a company must have an appealing compensation plan.

16-11 True/False

The sales-force plan can only be used to motivate salespeople, but cannot be used to direct their activities.

16-12 True/False

Companies are now designing compensation plans that reward salespeople for building customer relationships and growing the long-run value of each customer and not so much the short-term sales.

16-13 True/False

Sales-force automation not only lowers sales force costs and improves productivity, but it also improves the quantity of sales management decisions.

16-14 True/False

Some salespeople will do their best without any special urging from management.

16-15 True/False

Generally sales quotas are set equal to sales forecasts to encourage sales managers and salespeople to give their best effort.

16-16 True/False

Sales reports are divided into summaries for future activities and plans of completed activities.

16-17 True/False

Sales are usually the best indicator of achievement.

16-18 True/False

The problem-solver salesperson fits better with the marketing concept than does the hard-seller salesperson.

16-19 True/False

The last step in the selling process – follow-up – is necessary if the salesperson wants to ensure customer satisfaction and repeat business.

16-20 True/False

Companies are realizing that when operating in maturing markets and facing stiffer competition, it costs more to keep a current customer than to secure new customers.

Applying Terms and Concepts

To determine how well you understand the materials in this chapter, read each of the following brief cases and then respond to the questions that follow. Answers are given at the end of this chapter.

Case#1   Goodwin Publishing Co.[1]

Nikki Lawson was sales manager for Goodwin Publishing Company, a small firm located in Charlottetown, PEI. Goodwin specializes in business texts used at both the undergraduate and graduate levels. Cathy Goodwin, founder of the company, focused on business texts because she had been a professor of marketing at Mount Allison College. Goodwin was dissatisfied with the quality of available books so she wrote her own, *Marketing in Canada*. The text sold well—so well in fact that she left teaching to devote herself to the publishing business. Goodwin's book is still in print, now co-authored by two of Goodwin's colleagues at Mount Allison. Goodwin controls 23 other titles, several of which are industry standards selling in excess of 20,000 copies per year. Sales for the company totalled $14 million last year and returned a respectable profit.

There had been considerable consolidation in the publishing business the last few years. The industry is now dominated by a few firms. Individual company names still appear as publishers but most are now subsidiaries of some conglomerate. Goodwin is still one of the few true independents and she wanted to stay that way.

Goodwin decided the company needed to increase profits. The profits would be used to increase the stockholder dividend and to begin buying back company stock. There was little indication of stockholder discontent and Goodwin wanted that to continue. And what better way than to increase the value of their holdings and their dividends. Sales projections were flat so the only way to increase profits was to reduce costs.

Goodwin had always treated her employees well. Her 20 sales representatives enjoyed privileges that were the envy of the industry. The sales staff was paid a straight salary and enjoyed generous fringe benefits including a company car and a liberal expense account. Goodwin thought that perhaps the company was too generous. Goodwin asked Carlson to review several aspects of the sales department operation. Company records indicated that approximately 10,200 sales calls to college faculty were made last year, with each sales representative averaging 17 visitations per week, over a 30-week academic year. Carlson was also asked to review the compensation program and general role of the sales force.

---

[1] *Principles of Marketing*, 3rd Edition, Kotler, Armstrong, Warren (Prentice Hall) – pg. 345.

1. Using workload analysis, calculate how many sales representatives could be terminated, if Goodwin instructed Carlson to increase the average number of sales calls per representative from 17 to 19 per week holding the total number of calls constant.

   _____

   _____

   _____

   _____

2. Discuss the relative merits of each of the following compensation programs for a sales representative: Straight salary

   _____

   _____

   _____

3. Straight commission

   _____

   _____

   _____

   _____

4. Salary plus bonus

   _____

   _____

   _____

   _____

5. Salary plus commission

   _____

   _____

   _____

   _____

Case #2 Hemphill Industries

Guy Bovi was a May graduate of St. Paul's College in Quebec City, who accepted a position with Hemphill Industries of Vancouver. Bovi was hired as a sales representative and would be assigned, after training, to the Pacific region of BC, Washington and Oregon, currently staffed by Elana Watt who was retiring in six months.

Hemphill Industries manufactures and distributes industrial machine tools (lathes and milling machines) under the Hemphill brand name throughout the United States and Canada. Its products are handled by sales representatives employed by Hemphill Industries, with each representative concentrating on a given geographic location.

When Bovi was hired, he was told that in the coming year he was expected to increase sales to existing Hemphill customers by 15 percent and sales to new customers in the region by 5 percent. For his efforts, he would earn a base salary of $21,000 plus a commission of 2 percent on all sales exceeding $500,000. The $500,000 figure was considered modest and would be increased in subsequent years, as several of the computerized machine tools manufactured by Hemphill had a selling price in excess of $80,000. In addition to this salary, Bovi would have use of a company vehicle and an expense account to a limit of $300 per month.

Bovi would report to the district sales manager, Claude Caron, who would also supervise his training program. The training program consisted of twelve weeks of in-house training, followed by several months of field training with an experienced sales representative

The in-house training was designed to familiarize the sales representative with company policies and procedures. Approximately six weeks of the training was devoted to machine setup and operation. The balance of the program included training the representative to identify customer needs and then propose solutions to the problems utilizing Hemphill machine tools.

Hemphill sales representatives were responsible for making their own contact with customers and concentrating on speaking with a single purchasing agent or buying committee. It was stressed that sales representatives are expected to answer all questions posed by the customer.

_____1. When Bovi was assigned to the Pacific region to be the exclusive sales representative of Hamphill Machine Tools in that area, Mephill appeared to use which sales-force structure?

    A.   territorial-structured

    B.   product-structured

    C.   customer-structured

    D.   market-structured

    E.   matrix-structured

_____2. When Bovi was told to increase sales to existing customers by 15 percent and sales to new customers by 5 percent, he was in essence being given:

    A.   a salesforce strategy.

    B.   a salesforce structure.

    C.   an objective.

    D.   an annual call schedule.

    E.   workload analysis.

_____3. Bovi, as a sales representative, will probably find that the _____ approach to selling will be most effective.

    A.   supporting sales

    B.   order taker

    C.   sales oriented

    D.   customer problem solving

    E.   product-oriented

_____4. Hemphill's strategy of speaking to an individual purchasing an example of which sales agent or buying committee is approach strategy?

    A.   sales representative to buyer

    B.   sales representative to buyer group

    C.   conference selling

    D.   seminar selling

    E.   both (A) and (B)

_____5. As a seller of expensive machine tools, Bovi is faced with a position requiring:

    A.   little product knowledge.

    B.   little customer knowledge.

    C.   very creative selling.

    D.   routine order taking.

    E.   routine problem solving skills.

Case #3   Nonverbal Communication

In recent years marketers have begun to pay close attention to the role of nonverbal factors in the communication process. Communication is a complex process composed of many elements with signals, both verbal and nonverbal, continually flowing back and forth between the communicators. Studies have indicated that such wordless signals as the vocal element (tone, pitch, volume, resonance), the facial element (expression, eye contact), the proximity element (physical distance between communicators), the kinetic element (body and limb movements), the physical element (grooming, dress), and general deportment all play a role in the communication process. Nonverbal clues may actually alter what the receiver has "heard." Receivers tend to search out such cues to determine the "real" message.

1.   Explain the significance of such findings for a salesperson.

    _____

    _____

    _____

_____2. Nonverbal skills would be *most* useful to salespeople in which of the following sales positions?

    A.   inside order takers

    B.   outside order takers

    C.   sales engineers

    D.   creative sales

    E.   detailers

_____3. The adept use of nonverbal communication would be evidence of which of the following traits of a successful salesperson?

    A.   empathy

    B.   ego drive

    C.   aggressiveness

    D.   deceptiveness

    E.   perseverance

_____4. A salesperson who believes in the usefulness of nonverbal behavior would be most likely to use which of the following types of sales presentations?

    A.   canned approach

    B.   formulated approach

    C.   need-dissatisfaction approach

    D.   AIDA approach

    E.   none of the above

Multiple Choice Answers

1. Correct Answer: 4   Reference: pg. 537

2. Correct Answer: 5   Reference: pg. 537

3. Correct Answer: 2   Reference: pg. 538

4. Correct Answer: 1   Reference: pg. 539

5. Correct Answer: 2   Reference: pg. 539

6. Correct Answer: 3   Reference: pg. 539

7. Correct Answer: 4   Reference: pg. 540

8. Correct Answer: 3   Reference: pg. 540

9. Correct Answer: 2   Reference: pg. 541

10. Correct Answer: 1   Reference: pg. 542

11. Correct Answer: 4   Reference: pg. 542

12. Correct Answer: 5   Reference: pg. 543

13. Correct Answer: 2   Reference: pg. 543

14. Correct Answer: 5   Reference: pg. 543

15. Correct Answer: 2   Reference: pg. 545

16. Correct Answer: 1   Reference: pg. 547

17. Correct Answer: 4   Reference: pg. 547 (Table 16-1)

18. Correct Answer: 3   Reference: pg. 549 (Figure 16-2)

19. Correct Answer: 4   Reference: pg. 550

20. Correct Answer: 3   Reference: pg. 551

21. Correct Answer: 5   Reference: pg. 552

22. Correct Answer: 1   Reference: pg. 554

23.	Correct Answer:	2	Reference:	pg. 556
24.	Correct Answer:	4	Reference:	pg. 557
25.	Correct Answer:	1	Reference:	pg. 554
26.	Correct Answer:	3	Reference:	pg. 538
27.	Correct Answer:	2	Reference:	pg. 539
28.	Correct Answer:	5	Reference:	pg. 542
29.	Correct Answer:	4	Reference:	pg. 547
30.	Correct Answer:	1	Reference:	pg. 543

True/False Answers

1. TRUE   Reference: pg. 537   Topic: The Nature of Personal
                                                  Selling
2. TRUE   Reference: pg. 538   Topic: The Role of the Sales Force

3. FALSE   Reference: pg. 538   Topic: The Role of the Sales Force

4. TRUE   Reference: pg. 541   Topic: Sales-Force Size

5. FALSE   Reference: pg. 541   Topic: Sales-Force Size

6. TRUE   Reference: pg. 542   Topic: Other Sales-Force Strategy
                                                  and Structure Issues
7. FALSE   Reference: pg. 543   Topic: Team Selling

8. FASLE   Reference: pg. 543   Topic: Recruiting and Selective
                                                  Salespeople
9. FALSE   Reference: pg. 544   Topic: What Makes a Good
                                                  Salesperson
10. TRUE   Reference: pg. 546   Topic: Compensating Salespeople

11. FALSE   Reference: pg. 547   Topic: Compensating Salespeople

12. TRUE   Reference: pg. 547   Topic: Compensating Salespeople

13. FALSE   Reference: pg. 549   Topic: Directing Salespeople

14. TRUE   Reference: pg. 550   Topic: Motivating Salespeople

15. FALSE   Reference: pg. 550   Topic: Motivating Salespeople

16. FALSE   Reference: pg. 551   Topic: Sources of Information

17. FALSE   Reference: pg. 552   Topic: Comparing Salespeople's
                                                  Performance
18. TRUE   Reference: pg. 553   Topic: The Personal Selling Process

19. TRUE   Reference: pg. 555   Topic: Follow-Up

20. FALSE   Reference: pg. 557   Topic: Relationship Marketing

Applying Terms and Concept Answers

Case#1   Goodwin Publishing Company:

Question #1
- Carlson currently supervises 20 sales representatives who average 17 visitations per week.
- Given Goodwin's directive, the number of sales representatives could be reduced by 2.
- The calculations are as follows: 10, 200 calls divided by 30 weeks equals 340 calls per week.
- 340 divided by 19 calls per sales representative equals (approximately) 18 sales representatives.
- A relatively modest increase in the required number of sales calls per week per sales representative, reduced the sales force by 2.

Question #2
Straight salary provides maximum security for the sales representative. Their earnings are guaranteed regardless of sales. There may be minimal incentive for the sales representative to make additional calls to generate additional sales.

Question #3
Straight commission provides maximum incentive for the sales representative since their earnings are based on how much they sell. While there is relatively little security for the sales representative; the company only pays a commission when sales are generated.

Question #4
Salary plus bonus provides some security for the sales representative but also provides an incentive. The incentive is based on the bonus to be received after other goals and objectives have been met. The bonus may be paid based on such goals and objectives as an increase in sales, increase in profitability, reduction of costs, increase in new accounts, or sales of certain products.

Question #5
Salary plus commission provides some security for the sales representatives but also provides an incentive. The incentive is based on the commission earned from the generation of sales.

Case #2   Hemphill Industries:

1.   A

2.   C

3.   D

4.   E

5.   C

Case #3   Nonverbal Communication:

1.   The salesperson must communicate effectively to sell effectively. Insights into nonverbal communication can assist a sales representative in better preparing the sales presentation to be more effective in dealing with a client. These insights also allow the sales representative to better understand the customer's responses and attitudes and can help the salesperson frame, tailor, and adjust the sales presentation.

2.   D

3.   A

4.   D

Chapter 17

Direct and Online Marketing

Chapter Overview

Mass marketers typically try to reach millions of buyers with a single product and a standard message communicated via the mass media. Consequently, most mass marketing communications are one-way communications directed at consumers rather than two-way communications with consumers. Today, many companies are turning to direct marketing in an effort to reach carefully targeted customers more efficiently and to build stronger, more personal, one-to-one relationships with them.

Chapter Objectives

1. Discuss the benefits of direct marketing to customers and companies and the trends fuelling its rapid growth.
2. Define a customer database and list the four ways companies use databases in direct marketing.
3. Identify the major forms of direct marketing.
4. Compare the two types of online marketing channels and explain the effect of the Internet on electronic commerce.
5. Identify the benefits of online marketing to consumers and marketers and the four ways that marketers can conduct online marketing.
6. Discuss the public policy and ethical issues facing direct marketers.

Chapter Topics

What is Direct Marketing?

Growth and Benefits of Direct Marketing
- The Benefits of Direct Marketing
- The Growth of Direct Marketing

Customer Databases and Direct Marketing

Forms of Direct Marketing Communication
- Face-to-Face Selling
- Direct-Mail Marketing
- Catalogue Marketing
- Telemarketing
- Direct-Response Television Marketing
- Kiosk Marketing

Window on the Future: Online Marketing and Electronic Commerce
- Rapid Growth of Online Marketing

Understanding Empowered Consumers
- Who Uses the Net?
- The Benefits of Online Marketing
  - Benefits to Consumers
  - Benefits to Marketers
- Online Marketing Channels
  - Creating an Electronic Storefront
  - Placing Advertisements Online
  - Participating in Forums, Newsgroups, and Web Communities
  - Using E-mail and Webcasting
- The Promise and Challenges of Online Marketing

Integrated Direct Marketing

Public Policy and Ethical Issues in Direct Marketing
- Irritation, Unfairness, Deception, and Fraud
- Invasion of Privacy

Key Terms

Multiple Choice Questions

17-1   Multiple

Consumers report home shopping is all the following except:

1.   Fun
2.   Convenient
3.   Offers a large selection of merchandise
4.   Offers everyday low prices
5.   All of the above

17-2   Multiple

Direct marketing has surpassed mass marketing in the 1990s. Which of the following is not an advantage of direct marketing?

1.   Marketers are able to measure the type and rate of response
2.   Marketers are able to compile databases
3.   Direct marketing provides security
4.   Only 2 and 3
5.   All of the above

17-3   Multiple

While retail sales are growing at a rate of 3% per year, catalogue and direct-mail sales are growing at around ___ % per year.

1.   5
2.   7
3.   9
4.   11
5.   15

17-4   Multiple

Sue has had it with shopping centres and retail stores. She does all of her shopping over the phone, through the mail or over the Internet. This is one reason that would not lead Sue to this extreme.

1.   Less disposable income
2.   Higher costs of driving
3.   Shortage of sales retail help
4.   Lack of time
5.   Lines at checkout counters

17-5   Multiple

Companies that know about individual customer needs and characteristics cannot customize this area to maximize customer value and satisfaction.

1.   Offers
2.   Messages
3.   Structure
4.   Delivery modes
5.   Payment methods

17-6   Multiple

Customer databases are becoming a necessity to compete in the markets today. Customer databases collect data on all the following except:

1.   Demographic
2.   Physiological
3.   Behavioural
4.   Geographic
5.   All of the above

17-7   Multiple

A business-to-business database or a salesperson's customer profile will probably not contain data on this subject.

1.   Products and services a customer has bought
2.   Status of current contracts
3.   An assessment of competitive strengths and weaknesses
4.   Financial stability
5.   Competitive suppliers

17-8   Multiple

Which of the following groups most frequently uses databases?

1.   Non-profit organizations
2.   Commodity product producers
3.   Service retailers
4.   1 and 3
5.   All of the above

17-9　Multiple

Companies use their databases in four ways. Which of the following is not one of those ways?

1. Identifying prospects
2. Deciding which customers should receive a particular offer
3. Deepening customer loyalty
4. Reactivating customer purchases
5. All of the above are used

17-10　Multiple

Like many other marketing tools, database marketing requires a special investment. Companies must invest in all the following except _____ to have an efficient and productive database.

1. Skilled personnel
2. Proper Internet links
3. Hardware
4. Analytical programs
5. All of the above

17-11　Multiple

Today most business-to-business marketers rely heavily on a professional sales force to locate prospects, develop them into customers, build lasting relationships and grow a business. These activities comprise _____.

1. Face-to-face selling
2. Direct-mail marketing
3. Catalogue marketing
4. Telemarketing
5. Direct-response television marketing

17-12　Multiple

Direct mail marketing has evolved immensely over the last few years. All the following except _____ are new forms of direct mail marketing.

1. Fax mail
2. E-mail
3. Snail mail
4. Voice mail
5. 3 and 4

17-13 Multiple

While catalogue sales represent _____ % of retail sales in the United Sates, they represent _____ % of sales in Canada.

1.   4,6
2.   5,8
3.   2,1
4.   8,3
5.   10,15

17-14 Multiple

George runs a catalogue publishing firm. He receives many orders to make catalogues for different businesses that wish to market directly to other businesses. He tells them all the following except _____ are different types of catalogues for business-to-business marketing.

1.   Brochures
2.   Three-ring binders
3.   Encoded video tapes
4.   Encoded computer disks
5.   All of the above are forms of catalogues

17-15 Multiple

Infomercials are also growing in popularity along with direct marketing. However, few companies use infomercials to:

1.   Sell their wares over the phone
2.   Collect information from callers to compile company databases
3.   Refer customers to retailers
4.   Send out coupons and product information
5.   All of the above

17-16 Multiple

Online marketing has taken off at an enormously fast pace. Every day hundreds of new companies put their services on line in an attempt to increase their market share. Which of the following is not part of these new online services?

1.   Provide subscribers with new information
2.   Provide entertainment
3.   Provide dialogue opportunities
4.   Provide e-mail
5.   All of the above are services

17-17 Multiple

The Internet is a vast and flourishing global web of computer networks. The Internet was created by:

1.   The Russian Government
2.   IBM
3.   The US Government
4.   The US Defense Department
5.   Microsoft

17-18 Multiple

Dilbert has a computer at home and just purchased the necessary software to be hooked up to the Internet 5 weeks ago. He has made a routine of surfing the Net every Wednesday night for about 3 hours. He looks for information on different topics, and likes to download some of the different games offered. Dilbert would be considered a (n):

1.   Casual user
2.   Heavy user
3.   Frequent user
4.   Intermittent user
5.   Compulsory user

17-19 Multiple

Internet users come in all shapes and sizes; however, the typical Internet user is probably not _____:

1.   Young
2.   Wealthy
3.   Well educated
4.   French-speaking
5.   Professional

17-20 Multiple

Because of its one-to-one interactive nature, online marketing is a good tool for building:

1.   Customer relationships
2.   Brand loyalty
3.   Product knowledge
4.   Short-term sales
5.   Long-term sales

17-21 Multiple

The reason online marketing has become so popular over the last few years is not because
_____.

1.   It reduces costs
2.   It is a fad
3.   It increases efficiency
4.   It is flexible
5.   None of the above

17-22 Multiple

_____ web sites are designed to handle interactive communication initiated by
the consumer.

1.   Advertising
2.   Product placement
3.   Corporate
4.   Independent
5.   Customer-oriented

17-23 Multiple

One of the major problems with online marketing are privacy and security issues. To
solve these problems, companies are now using _____extensions of their internal
computer networks that allow them to link with their suppliers, members of their
distribution channels and corporate customers.

1.   Intranets
2.   Supportnets
3.   Transnets
4.   Extranets
5.   Conglomernets

17-24 Multiple

_____ provide a place where members can congregate online and exchange
views on issues of common interest.

1.   Web communities
2.   Newsgroups
3.   Bulletin board systems
4.   Forums
5.   All of the above

17-25 Multiple

Webcasting, also known as _____ programming, provides an attractive channel for online marketers to deliver their Internet advertising or other information content.

1.   Pull
2.   Direct web
3.   Market
4.   Online
5.   Push

17-26 Multiple

One study found a site must capture web surfers' attention within _ seconds or lose them to another site.

1.   3
2.   6
3.   8
4.   10
5.   2

17-27 Multiple

Irritation, unfairness, deception and fraud are becoming associated more and more with online marketing and markets. All the following except _____ are reasons why fraudulent direct marketers are hard to catch.

1.   Customers often respond quickly
2.   Customers usually do not understand all they see and read on their screen
3.   Customers do not interact personally with the sellers
4.   Customers usually expect to wait for delivery
5.   All of the above are reasons

17-28 Multiple

The direct marketing industry is addressing issues of ethics and public policy because they know if these issues are left unattended everything except _____ is likely to happen.

1.   Increasing negative consumer attitudes
2.   Lower response rates
3.   Increase in company liability
4.   Increase in more restrictive provincial and federal legislation
5.   All of the above are bound to happen

17-29 Multiple

The creation of the "information superhighway" promises to revolutionize commerce. Today more than ____ % of the 11.6 million Canadian households have a personal computer.

1.   15
2.   52
3.   24
4.   36
5.   48

17-30 Multiple

A database can help a company make attractive offers of product replacements, upgrades, or complementary products just when customers might be ready to act. This capability would qualify as which of the following uses of databases?

1.   Reactivating customer purchases
2.   Deepening customer loyalty
3.   Deciding which customers should receive a particular offer
4.   Identifying prospects
5.   None of the above

True/False Questions

17-1 True/False

Most marketing communications consist of two-way communication with consumers, not directed at them.

17-2 True/False

Direct marketers can build closer relationships with their customers.

17-3 True/False

No Canadian university offers a degree or certificate in direct marketing, despite it being a rapidly growing trend.

17-4 True/False

The growth of affordable computer power and customer databases has enabled direct marketers to single out the best prospects for a limited number of items that they wish to sell.

17-5 True/False

A recent survey found that almost two-thirds of all large consumer-products companies currently use or build databases for targeting their marketing efforts.

17-6 True/False

A well-managed database always leads to sales gains that will more than cover its costs.

17-7 True/False

As people begin to receive more e-mail messages, including unimportant ones, they may look for an "agent" software program to sort out the more important messages from those that can be ignored or discarded.

17-8 True/False

Sears Canada, which has 1,700 catalogue stores across the country, traditionally used their catalogues as a speciality products merchandising tactic.

17-9 True/False

Marketers use inbound telephone marketing to sell directly to consumers and businesses.

17-10 True/False

Many experts think that advances in two-way, interactive television and linkages with Internet technology will eventually make video shopping one of the major forms of direct marketing.

17-11 True/False

The Internet is being overtaken by the commercial online services as the primary online marketing channel.

17-12 True/False

Electronic markets are "marketspaces" in which sellers offer their products and services electronically.

17-13 True/False

The fundamental principle that businesses must understand when considering marketing on the Internet is consumers have greater control over the marketing process than ever before.

17-14 True/False

Buyers will increasingly become consumers of product information, not creators of it.

17-15 True/False

Rather than just being another communication tool, online marketing helps companies reinforce their core strategy.

17-16 True/False

With a marketing web site, the consumer initiates communication and interaction.

17-17 True/False

Barriers to growth for online business commerce include the belief that firms are not offering the right products or services and that there are security and privacy issues.

17-18 True/False

Although web advertising is on the increase, many marketers still question its values as an effective advertising tool.

17-19 True/False

There is a very clear line between adding value and the consumer feeling that you are being intrusive.

17-20 True/False

In an integrated direct marketing campaign, the marketer seeks to improve response rates and profits by adding media and stages that contribute more to additional sales than to additional costs.

Applying Terms and Concepts

To determine how well you understand the materials in this chapter, read each of the following brief cases and then respond to the questions that follow. Answers are given at the end of this chapter.

Case #1   Quenching Small Businesses' Thirst[1]

Coca-Cola USA's research found there are approximately 1 million American workplaces, employing less than fifty people that do not have soft drinks available on - site. For this market, Coca-Cola developed a small fountain-drink dispenser that it called the BreakMate. To promote the new machine to small businesses, Coke mailed to office managers and presidents of small businesses a direct mail piece that focused on the convenience of having an in-house soda dispenser. Coca-Cola now has about 60,000 BreakMate machines pumping more than 1 million gallons of syrups in workplaces.

1.   What was the measurable response Coca-Cola was seeking with this mailing?

_____

_____

_____

_____

2.   By using direct mail as its primary advertising medium to reach prospective customers, what advantage(s) of direct marketing is Coca-Cola using?

_____

_____

_____

_____

3.   Why is Coca-Cola gathering information from those who respond to its mailing for a database?

_____

_____

_____

_____

_____

[1] *Marketing*, 5th Edition, Schoell, Guilitinan (Allyn and Bacon) – pg. 168.

452

4. Who would consider this mailing to be junk mail?

_____

_____

_____

5. Besides direct mail, identify other forms of direct marketing.

_____

_____

_____

_____

Case #2   Infomercials[2]

What would life be like without such necessities as a Vege-Matic or a complete set of Ginzu knives? Producers of infomercials don't intend to let us find out. Their extended commercials, often masquerading as talk shows or news programs, continue to bombard our airwaves. While many of the products on direct-response television in the early days made dubious claims about their ability to promote weight loss or make long-lost hair grow back, the industry is evolving as mainstream corporations begin to get into the act.

Still pitfalls remain. One pitfall is infomercials may dupe consumers into changing their attitudes towards advertised items by making them believe the information they are receiving is more credible and objective than is really the case. By presenting product information in a news or talk show format, receivers of these pervasive communications may not counter-argue as heavily as if they message were clearly identified as coming from a commercial sponsor. For example, in a controversial campaign for Maxwell House coffee, TV newscaster Linda Ellerbee and Willard Scott plugged the product in a setting resembling a news show. This format attempted to capitalize on the actors' backgrounds to produce the inference that their reports were news rather than commercials. So look carefully next time you are channel surfing and happen to land on an adoring crowd applauding a demonstration of the latest juicer, glass maker or other "must have" product. The money you save may be your own.

---

[2] *Consumer Behaviour*, 3rd Edition, Michael Solomon (Prentice Hall) – pg. 218.

1.   What are the benefits of direct-response television?

_____

_____

_____

_____

2.   What are disadvantages of direct-response television?

_____

_____

_____

_____

3.   Do you believe direct-response marketing is replacing door-to-door selling? Why or why not?

_____

_____

_____

_____

4.   Would infomercials be as (more) effective if they went online?

_____

_____

_____

_____

5.   Do you watch infomercials? What do you think of them?

_____

_____

_____

_____

Case #3 You Can't Hide[3]

For years Lisa Tomaino kept her address secret. She and her husband, Jim, a police office, wanted to make it as hard as possible for the crooks he put away to find out where they lived. But last year Lisa had a baby. So much for her big secret. Within six weeks she was inundated with junk mail aimed at new mothers. The hospital had sold her name and address to a direct-marketing company, and soon she was on dozens of other lists. Efforts to get their names removed from these lists proved fruitless. "It was a complete violation of our right to privacy," she declares.

Private citizens, private watchdogs, and a handful of lawmakers have railed for years about Big Brotherism by business. But when politicians balance industry's interest in reaching markets against the customer's right to privacy, marketing usually wins. "Existing laws regulating privacy simply aren't effective," gripes Robert Bulmash, president of Private Citizen, Inc., a public advocacy group.

Marketers are keenly aware of the public's reaction to their unwanted attention. After all, it's their job to stay in touch with the preferences of consumers. Vendors of marketing data argue that any intrusion on privacy from selling lists is offset "by the significant potential gain to consumers from the special offers and products offered by direct marketers."

The industry has largely staved off regulation by convincing the federal government that it can police itself. The Information Monitoring Association (IMA), for example, runs a phone number for people who want their names removed from mailing lists. Or, you can register with the Mail Preference Service (MPS), at the following address: Mail Preference Service, Direct Marketing Association, P.O. Box 9008, Farmingdale, New York, 11735-9008.

But relatively few consumers use it, and those who do contend their names come off some, but no all, lists. Even long-standing laws, such as the 1970 Fair Credit Reporting Act, aren't effective. The statute is supposed to prevent credit agencies such as TRW, Equifax, and TransUnion from releasing financial information about a person except for "legitimate" business needs, such as a credit check. Unfortunately, it doesn't always do so.

As marketing techniques become more sophisticated, the privacy of the Lisa Tomainos of the world will grow increasingly difficult to protect.

---

[3] *Introduction to Marketing Communications*, Burnett, Moriarty, pg. 390.

1. As a direct marketer, how would you justify this perceived invasion of privacy?

   _____

   _____

   _____

   _____

2. Suppose the Tomainos started receiving threats from a criminal that Officer Tomaino had apprehended. Suppose also that the criminal had found their personal phone number and address through access to a direct-marketing database. Do you think the Tomainos should have any recourse against the hospital?

   _____

   _____

   _____

   _____

3. Now assume that you are the director of a non-profit hospital. Direct marketers offer hundreds of thousands of dollars for the database you maintain of those who recently had a baby in the hospital. By accepting the money for selling your database, you can lower your delivery and newborn care costs and upgrade medical equipment. However, you're worried about privacy issues. Can you suggest a data collection process that does not violate a patient's right to privacy?

   _____

   _____

   _____

   _____

4. What inconveniences can consumers be subjected to regarding direct marketing?

   _____

   _____

   _____

   _____

5. Discuss the public policy and ethical issues facing direct marketers.

   _____

   _____

   _____

   _____

Multiple Choice Answers

1. Correct Answer: 4 Reference: pg. 568

2. Correct Answer: 5 Reference: pg. 568

3. Correct Answer: 2 Reference: pg. 569

4. Correct Answer: 1 Reference: pg. 569

5. Correct Answer: 3 Reference: pg. 570

6. Correct Answer: 2 Reference: pg. 570

7. Correct Answer: 4 Reference: pg. 571

8. Correct Answer: 4 Reference: pg. 571

9. Correct Answer: 5 Reference: pg. 571

10. Correct Answer: 2 Reference: pg. 573

11. Correct Answer: 1 Reference: pg. 573

12. Correct Answer: 3 Reference: pg. 574

13. Correct Answer: 1 Reference: pg. 575

14. Correct Answer: 5 Reference: pg. 576

15. Correct Answer: 2 Reference: pg. 577

16. Correct Answer: 5 Reference: pg. 578

17. Correct Answer: 4 Reference: pg. 578

18. Correct Answer: 3 Reference: pg. 582

19. Correct Answer: 4 Reference: pg. 582

20. Correct Answer: 1 Reference: pg. 583

21. Correct Answer: 2 Reference: pg. 584

22. Correct Answer: 3 Reference: pg. 584

23.	Correct Answer:	4	Reference:	pg. 586
24.	Correct Answer:	1	Reference:	pg. 587
25.	Correct Answer:	5	Reference:	pg. 588
26.	Correct Answer:	3	Reference:	pg. 589
27.	Correct Answer:	2	Reference:	pg. 590
28.	Correct Answer:	3	Reference:	pg. 593
29.	Correct Answer:	4	Reference:	pg. 569
30.	Correct Answer:	1	Reference:	pg. 573

True/False Answers

1. FALSE   Reference: pg. 567   Topic: What is Direct Marketing

2. TRUE   Reference: pg. 568   Topic: The Benefits of Direct
                                                          Marketing
3. TRUE   Reference: pg. 569   Topic: The Growth of Direct
                                                          Marketing
4. FALSE   Reference: pg. 570   Topic: The Growth of Direct
                                                          Marketing
5. TRUE   Reference: pg. 571   Topic: Customer Databases and
                                                          Direct Marketing
6. FALSE   Reference: pg. 573   Topic: Customer Databases and
                                                          Direct Marketing
7. TRUE   Reference: pg. 574   Topic: Direct-Mail Marketing

8. FALSE   Reference: pg. 575   Topic: Catalogue Marketing

9. FALSE   Reference: pg. 576   Topic: Telemarketing

10. TRUE   Reference: pg. 577   Topic: Direct-Response Television
                                                          Marketing
11. FALSE   Reference: pg. 578   Topic: Window on the Future:
                                                          Online Marketing and
                                                          Electronic Commerce
12. TRUE   Reference: pg. 580   Topic: Rapid Growth of Online
                                                          Marketing
13. TRUE   Reference: pg. 581   Topic: Understanding Empowered
                                                          Consumers
14. FALSE   Reference: pg. 581   Topic: Understanding Empowered
                                                          Consumers
15. TRUE   Reference: pg. 583   Topic: Benefits to Marketers

16. FALSE   Reference: pg. 584   Topic: Creating Electronic
                                                          Storefront
17. TRUE   Reference: pg. 586   Topic: Creating Electronic
                                                          Storefront
18. TRUE   Reference: pg. 587   Topic: Placing Advertisements
                                                          Online
19. FALSE   Reference: pg. 588   Topic: Using E-mail and
                                                          Webcasting
20. TRUE   Reference: pg. 590   Topic: Integrated Direct Marketing

Applying Terms and Concept Answers

Case #1   Quenching Small Businesses' Thirst:

Question #1
- The measurable response was calls to Coke's 800 number.

Question #2
- Coke is enjoying the following advantages: selectivity, precise targeting of prospects, measurement of results with possible adjustments to the strategy based on these results, demonstration of size of product and how easily it will fit into the prospect's office, less expensive than face-to-face personal sales calls.

Question #3
- Coke is creating a database in order to better target future promotions.

Question #4
- Executives and office managers would receive this mail as junk mail who were not interested in providing soft drinks for their employees or who already have soda vending machines.

Question #5
- Telemarketing (over the telephone)
- Television marketing
- Online shopping

Case #2   Infomercials:

Question #1
- They can go in-depth
- You can have various different visual demonstrations of the product
- You can get well-known people on your infomercials at most likely a reduced cost
- You can give the customer a lot of additional information if they are interested

Question #2
- Not face-to-face
- People can easily flip the channel and not listen
- It may be too long and people will not watch the whole thing
- It may be expensive and overdone

Question #3
- Yes, door-to-door selling is becoming harder and harder as many households have both partners working therefore there is no one at home
- Infomercials are on usually at night when they know people are home
- They are able to give the same amount of information in the infomercial as they would face-to-face

Question #4
- It may not be as effective if the Internet site is not well developed
- There are limitations with the Internet, not enough visual appeal etc.
- More people have TVs than PCs

Case #3   You Can't Hide:

Question #1
- As a direct marketer, I would claim that I was informing potential customers and the general public of goods and services that I have to offer.
- They may learn of products through my mailing that they otherwise, would be unaware of.

Question #2
- The Tomainos could be old-fashioned Americans and sue the hospital for millions.

Question #3
- The hospital could ask the patients if they minded their names being given out.
- Or, the hospital could maybe have a sign-up or registration for patients who are interested in new products.

Question #4
- Consumers are irritated, let's talk about dinner-time phone calls
- Unfairness, smooth talking sales representatives can take advantage of people
- Deception, mail designed to mislead buyers
- Fraud, crooked direct marketers

Question #5
- Invasion of privacy
- Too much financial information
        Access to information that most people would not disclose

Chapter 18

Competitive Strategies: Building Lasting Customer Relationships

Chapter Overview

Today's companies face their toughest competition ever. To survive, a company must win customers and outperform competitors, often by moving from a product and selling philosophy. Winning companies in today's marketplace have become adept at developing and implementing strategies for building customers, not merely building products.

Chapter Objectives

1. Define customer value and satisfaction, and discuss how companies attract new customers and retain current ones through relationship marketing.
2. Explain the role of a company value chain and the value delivery network in meeting customer needs.
3. Clarify the concept of total quality marketing and its relationship to customer value and satisfaction.
4. Discuss the need to understand competitors as well as customers through competitor analysis.
5. Explain the fundamentals of competitive marketing strategies based on creating value for customers.
6. Illustrate the need for balancing customer and competitor orientations in becoming a truly market-centred organization.

Chapter Topics

Defining Customer Value and Satisfaction
- Customer Value
- Customer Satisfaction

Retaining Customers
- Customer Satisfaction and Customer Loyalty
- The Need for Customer Retention
- The Key: Customer Relationship Marketing

Delivering Customer Value and Satisfaction
- Value Chain
- Value Delivery Network

Implementing Total Quality Marketing
- Total Quality Management
- Marketing's Role in Total Quality

Competitive Marketing Strategies

Competitor Analysis
- Identifying Competitors
- Assessing Competitors
- Selecting Competitors to Attack and Avoid

Competitive Strategies
- Basic Competitive Strategies
- Competitive Positions
- Market-Leader Strategies
- Market-Challenger Strategies
  - Choosing an Attack Strategy
- Market-Follower Strategies
- Market-Nicher Strategies

Balancing Customer and Competitor Orientations

Chapter Summary

1. The definition and descriptions of value chains and value delivery systems.

Value chains consist of nine activities. Primary activities are inbound logistics, operations, outbound logistics, marketing and sales, and service. Support activities are firm infrastructure, human resource management, technology development, and procurement. Value delivery systems extend the value chain concept beyond a single company to partnerships between other channel members to improve overall customer satisfaction.

2. Customer relationship marketing.

Relationship marketing involves creating, maintaining, and enhancing strong relationships with customers and other stakeholders. Five levels are basic, reactive, accountable, proactive, and partnership. To develop stronger customer bonding and satisfaction, the company can adopt any of three customer value-building approaches: financial, social, or structural.

3. The major competitive positions used to develop competitive advantage.

Strong competitive advantage can be developed from one of four competitive strategies. Market leaders have the largest market share and often lead in price changes, introductions, distribution, and promotion. Market challengers fight to increase share from either leaders or smaller firms. Market followers try to avoid leader retaliations and pattern programs after leaders. Market nichers serve small segments overlooked by larger firms.

4. The steps companies go through in analyzing competitors.

Competitor analysis consists of 6 steps:
(1) Identifying the company's competitors;
(2) Determining competitors' objectives;
(3) Identifying competitors' strategies;
(4) Assessing competitors' strengths and weaknesses;
(5) Estimating competitors' reaction patterns;
(6) Selecting competitors to attack and to avoid.

464

5. The competitive strategies that market leaders use to expand the market and to protect and expand their market shares.

Market leaders seek to expand the total market by finding new users, new uses, and more usage. Protecting share strategies include position, flanking, pre-emptive, counteroffensive, mobile, and contraction defences. Expanding share in non- or slow-growth markets is most effective when a business gains share relative to competitors in its served market.

Key Terms

Benchmarking (pg. 621)
Competitive advantage   (pg. 620)
Competitive marketing strategies (pg. 620)
Competitor analysis   (pg. 620)
Competitor-centred company (pg. 633)
Customer-centred company   (pg. 634)
Customer delivered value   (pg. 605)
Customer value delivery system   (pg. 614)
Market-oriented company   (pg. 634)
Market challenger   (pg. 626)
Market follower   (pg. 626)
Market leader (pg. 626)
Market nicher (pg. 626)
Market orientation   (pg. 620)
Relationship marketing   (pg. 611)
Strategic group   (pg. 621)
Total customer cost   (pg. 605)
Total customer value (pg. 605)

Multiple Choice Questions

18-1   Multiple

Consumers buy from the firm they believe offers the highest consumer delivered value which is the difference between:

1.   Total customer value and total customer benefits
2.   Total customer cost and total customer benefits
3.   Total customer benefits and total customer satisfaction
4.   Total customer value and total customer costs
5.   None of the above

18-2   Multiple

Which of the following is not a source which adds to total customer value?

1.   Product
2.   Service
3.   Location
4.   Personnel
5.   Image

18-3   Multiple

Russ is going to buy a car. He has come down to two choices, a Chrysler Daytona and a Chevrolet Cavalier. The level of total customer value for both cars are the same, therefore the determining factor will be on total customer cost. Which of the following is not considered a customer cost?

1.   Time costs
2.   Leisure costs
3.   Energy costs
4.   Psychic costs
5.   All of the above are customer costs

18-4   Multiple

This factor does not help buyers form expectations.

1.   Past buying experiences
2.   The opinions of friends and associates
3.   The marketers information and promises
4.   The competitors information and promises
5.   All of the above help

466

18-5   Multiple

Today's most successful companies are _____ expectations and delivering performances to _____ them.

1.   Raising, match
2.   Raising, exceed
3.   Lowering, match
4.   Lowering, exceed
5.   Neutralizing, match

18-6   Multiple

Which of the following is not a benefit associated with highly satisfied customers?

1.   They are less price sensitive
2.   They do not expect more of the company than they get
3.   They remain customers for a longer period
4.   They speak favourably about the company to other people
5.   None of the above

18-7   Multiple

The need for customer retention is growing rapidly. Companies today are facing new marketing realities that cause them to focus more on their consumer. Which of the following would not be considered a new marketing reality?

1.   Changing demographics
2.   A slow-growth economy
3.   More sophisticated competitors
4.   Increase use in technology
5.   Overcapacity

18-8   Multiple

The key to customer retention is:

1.   Customer satisfaction and customer loyalty
2.   Customer loyalty and customer value
3.   Customer value and customer satisfaction
4.   Customer satisfaction and customer awareness
5.   Customer awareness and customer loyalty

18-9 Multiple

There is not one specific key to building customer relationships. Many different
relationships must be built at many different levels. Which of the following is not
considered one of those levels?

1. Economic
2. Social
3. Technical
4. Legal
5. None of the above

18-10 Multiple

Marketers can use a number of specific marketing tools to develop stronger bonds with
customers. Which of the following is not one of those tools?

1. By adding psychological benefits
2. By adding financial benefits
3. By adding social benefits
4. By adding structural ties
5. All of the above are viable tools

18-11 Multiple

Each department in a company can be thought of as a link in the company's value chain.
That is each department carries out value-creating activities on the firm's products. From
the following list, select the one option not generally considered to be part of this value
chain.

1. Produce
2. Design
3. Deliver
4. Finance
5. None of the above

18-12 Multiple

The value delivery network is a very important link in the value chain. Many companies
have their suppliers on an EDI system for delivering inventory and to ensure their stock
never runs out, so their consumers are satisfied. This quick response system is also known
as a _____ system.

1. Pushed by supply
2. Pulled by demand
3. Pushed by demand
4. Pulled by supply
5. None of the above

468

18-13 Multiple

Which of the following ensures consistency in product performance level?

1.   Performance quality
2.   Consistent quality
3.   Conformance quality
4.   Total quality
5.   Product quality

18-14 Multiple

Marketers play several major roles in helping their companies define and deliver high-quality goods and services to target consumers. Which of the following is not one of those roles?

1.   Marketers bear the major responsibility for correctly identifying the customers needs and requirements
2.   Marketers must endure that the customer's orders are filled correctly and on time
3.   Marketers must stay in contact with customers after the sale to ensure that they remain satisfied
4.   Marketers must gather and convey customer ideas for product and service improvement to the appropriate company departments.
5.   All of the above are marketing roles

18-15 Multiple

To plan an effective competitive marketing strategy, a company needs to find out all it can about its competitors. This item is generally not compared when planning an effective strategy.

1.   Products
2.   Place
3.   Prices
4.   Channels
5.   Promotion

18-16 Multiple

Companies usually learn about their competitor's strengths and weaknesses through every method except:

1.   Personal experience
2.   Secondary data
3.   Hearsay
4.   Suppliers
5.   None of the above

18-17 Multiple

Scooter bike shop's major competitor is Sports Traders, located about 5 km away. They sell the same products and offer the same services. Scooter's did not react quickly or strongly to Sports Traders latest competitors marketing campaign. What's one reason why they didn't react quickly?

1.   They may lack the experience to know how to react
2.   They may feel their customers are loyal
3.   They may have been slow in noticing the move
4.   They may lack the funds to react
5.   All of the above are reasons

18-18 Multiple

Companies which engage in the _____ competitive strategy, serve few market segments well rather than going after the whole market.

1.   Cost leadership
2.   Differentiation
3.   Focus
4.   Concentrated
5.   Narrow

18-19 Multiple

A company which provides superior value by leading its industry in price and convenience is practising:

1.   Product leadership
2.   Customer intimacy
3.   Customer excellence
4.   Operational excellence
5.   Operational leadership

470

18-20 Multiple

A market _____ wants to hold its share without rocking the boat.

1.   Leader
2.   Challenger
3.   Follower
4.   Nichers
5.   Stabilizer

18-21 Multiple

Market leaders like Coca-Cola ad Campbell's do not have an easy road. They must
constantly ensure the competition does not creep up and take over their market share. In
order to remain a leader, these firms can take all the following actions except:

1.   Find ways to expand total demand
2.   They can change their product to be perceived as unique
3.   Protect their current market share through good defensive and offensive actions
4.   They can try to expand their market share further
5.   All of the above are possible

18-22 Multiple

In a _____ the challenger matches the competitor's product, advertising,
price, and distribution efforts.

1.   Guerrilla attack
2.   Encirclement attack
3.   Flanking attack
4.   Bypass attack
5.   Frontal attack

18-23 Multiple

The _____ makes sense when the challenger has superior resources and
believes that it can break the competitor's hold on the market quickly.

1.   Flanking attack
2.   Bypass attack
3.   Encirclement attack
4.   Frontal attack
5.   Guerrilla attack

18-24 Multiple

The market _____ is often a major target for attacks. For that reason they must keep manufacturing costs low and its product quality and services high.

1.   Follower
2.   Leader
3.   Challenger
4.   Nicher
5.   All of the above

18-25 Multiple

Whereas a mass marketer achieves _____, the niche marketer achieves _____.

1.   High margins, high profits
2.   High volumes, low profits
3.   Low profits, high profits
4.   High volume, high margins
5.   Low margins, low volume

18-26 Multiple

A company which is not customer-centred and not competition-centred is:

1.   Competitor oriented
2.   Product oriented
3.   Customer oriented
4.   Market oriented
5.   Service oriented

18-27 Multiple

The ISO 9000 internationally accepted standards for quality systems includes which of the following?

1.   It established standards and systems for quality management within a firm
2.   It sets quality assurance benchmarks against which customers can evaluate a suppliers quality system
3.   It helps companies effectively implement environmental management systems
4.   Only 1 & 2
5.   All of the above

472

18-28 Multiple

The two dimensions determining the company's likely relationship marketing strategy are:

1.   Size purchase and profit margin
2.   Number of customers and marketing expenditures
3.   Number of customers and profit margin
4.   Size of sales force and profit marketing
5.   None of the above

18-29 Multiple

Amy Anderson just purchased a new car. Her selection, a Mustang convertible cost a bit more than the others but she felt it offered her the most car for her dollar. Two other cars were nice, and less expensive, but Amy liked the Mustang. For Amy, the Mustang provides:

1.   The highest delivered value
2.   An average amount of total customer value
3.   The least total customer cost
4.   Prestige feelings
5.   All of the above

18-30 Multiple

Donna Watt loves her sales job. She worked hard to identify customers—clients she called them—and stayed in touch with them after the sale to build strong personal ties as their representative in the firms. In her approach to sales, Donna practises:

1.   Traditional marketing
2.   Relationship marketing
3.   Radical marketing
4.   Traditional sales
5.   Reinforcement marketing

True/False Questions

18-1 True/False

Customers choose the marketing offer giving them the most satisfaction.

18-2 True/False

The real price of everything is the toil and trouble of acquiring it.

18-3 True/False

Buyers operate under various constraints and sometimes make choices that give more weight to their personal benefits than to the company benefit.

18-4 True/False

Although the customer-centred firm seeks to deliver high customer satisfaction relative to competitors, it also attempts to maximize customer satisfaction.

18-5 True/False

The relationship between customer satisfaction and loyalty varies greatly across industries and competitive situations.

18-6 True/False

Traditional marketing theory and practice have focused on attracting new customers rather than retaining existent ones.

18-7 True/False

It costs eight times more to attract a new customer than it does to keep a current customer satisfied.

18-8 True/False

Relationship marketing means marketers must focus on managing their customers, not their products.

18-9 True/False

Marketing is only a partner in attracting and keeping new companies, not the be all and end all.

474

18-10 True/False

A company's value chain in only as strong as its strongest link.

18-11 True/False

ISO is an acronym for the International Organization for Standardization.

18-12 True/False

Marketing must deliver marketing quality as well as production quality.

18-13 True/False

Companies gain competitive advantages by designing offers that satisfy customer needs better than the competitor's offers.

18-14 True/False

Knowing a competitor's mix of objectives reveals whether the competitor is satisfied with its current situation, but does not reveal how it might react to different competitive actions.

18-15 True/False

Marketers need to carefully assess each competitor's opportunities and threats in order to answer the question: What can our competitors do?

18-16 True/False

A company selects its major competitors through prior decisions, such as target customers, distribution channels and marketing-mix strategies.

18-17 True/False

Middle-of-the-roaders try to be good on all strategic counts, but end up only being good in one of them.

18-18 True/False

Competitors focus on the leader as a company to challenge, imitate or avoid.

18-19 True/False

In many markets, small market share increases mean very large sales increases.

18-20 True/False

Flanking attacks are small, periodic attacks to harass and demoralize the competitor, with the goal of eventually establishing permanent footholds.

Applying Terms and Concepts

To determine how well you understand the materials in this chapter, read each of the following brief cases and then respond to the questions that follow. Answers are given at the end of this chapter.

Case #1   Chiropractic Care[1]

Dr. Carole Babiak graduated two years ago from the London College of Chiropractic in London, Ontario. Dr. Babiak would eventually open her own office, but upon graduation, she needed two things—an income to support herself and to begin paying off her $80,000 in school loans, and experience. Experience, not in how to provide appropriate chiropractic and patient care, but experience in how to run a business and have a successful practice.

Upon graduation, Dr. Babiak accepted a position as associate in Cranberry Chiropractic, a practice owned by Dr. Tim Darrow, located in Sudbury, Ontario. Dr. Babiak's salary was a modest $40,000 per year and her primary task was performing spinal adjustment. Dr. Babiak averaged seven adjustments per hour. At seven patients an hour, there was hardly enough time to review the patient's file and perform the adjustment before the receptionist was calling to say the next patient had arrived. Dr. Babiak was dismayed there was no time to get to know the patient. No time to discuss patient care, preventative measure, exercise or nutrition. At $40 per session, Dr. Babiak thought the patient deserved better. She thought she deserved better as well. She hadn't spent the equivalent of nine years in college to work for a taskmaster whose only apparent interest was in making money. "Where was the concern for the patient?" Dr. Babiak decided when she opened her own practice, she would run her office with the patient in mind first and foremost.

Two years of Dr. Darrow were enough. After arranging the needed financing, Dr. Babiak's own practice in Sudbury would open in July.

1. When Dr. Babiak opens her own chiropractic office, she intends to engage in customer relationship making. What is the intent of customer relationship marketing?

_____

_____

_____

_____

---

[1] Principles of Marketing, 3rd Edition, Kotler, Armstrong, Warren (Prentice Hall) – pg. 364.

2.   Explain the five different levels of relationship that can be formed between the patient and the chiropractor.   Basic

_____

_____

_____

_____

3.   Reactive

_____

_____

_____

_____

4.   Accountable

_____

_____

_____

_____

5.   Proactive

_____

_____

_____

_____

6.   Partnership

_____

_____

_____

_____

Case #2 Eastern Townships University

Eastern Townships University is a midsized institution located in Quebec. Eastern offers baccalaureate degree programs in a variety of areas including anthropology, art, biology, business administration, chemistry, computer science, economics, education, English, French, history, linguistics, mathematics, music, philosophy, sociology, and theatre. The university also offers graduate degree programs in art, biology, economics, education, linguistics, mathematics, and philosophy. Eastern is a widely respected institution but one whose enrollment has declined slightly over the last few years. The university is also faced with increasing costs and declining financial support from the province. In a recent session, the provincial legislature ruled that Eastern may raise its tuition and fees, as needed, to offset its declining support.

Michelle Romuld, President of the University, is concerned about these trends and recognizes the need to more effectively market the university. In support of this concept, President Romuld has created the position of Vice President for Enrollment, Marketing and Development. Reporting to the Vice President will be the Dean of Student Services as well as the Directors of Admissions, Financial Aid, Publications and Communication, Alumni Affairs and Placement.

Dr. Romuld recognizes the importance of these various areas as they impact enrollment, retention and student satisfaction. In the coming years, she wishes them to work in a more coordinated and synergistic fashion. President Romuld has scheduled a meeting for next week and the new vice president will be on the agenda to discuss enrollment, retention and student satisfaction at Eastern Townships University.

1.   How might a prospective student use the concept of customer delivered value
      when making a decision to attend Eastern Townships University?

      _____

      _____

      _____

      _____

2. How can Eastern Townships University use the concept of customer delivered value to attract new students, and/or improve the retention rate of current students?

_____

_____

_____

_____

Case #3   Saturn Corporation

On October 25, 1990, the first Saturn automobiles were made available for sale to the general public. In eight short years, Saturn went from an idea to reality. In part, what makes this accomplishment so remarkable is that Saturn is a revolutionary new automobile constructed and sold in a revolutionary new way.

To combat the growing presence of Japanese automobiles, to breathe new life into General Motors-the parent of Saturn Corporation-and to bring the Saturn to market; new relationships had to be forged. New relationships between General Motors and the United Auto Workers, between engineers and designers and production personnel, between (potential) buyers and marketing personnel, and between the company and its suppliers, dealers and the community of Spring Hill, Tennessee-where the Saturn is built. There was a spirit of cooperation and shared commitment and of renewal.

The results of these new relationships have been astounding, with the company, its people, and its products winning a stunning array of awards. Trade groups, publishers, professional associations and government agencies have bestowed recognition on Saturn for its efforts to recruit women and minorities, for excellence in communications and community relations, for preservation of the environment, for innovative marketing techniques, for innovative engineering and product design, and for commitment to customer sovereignty.

480

Customers, when surveyed by J. D. Power and Associates, consistently rank Saturn Automobiles as having fewer problems and higher quality and higher overall customer satisfaction than many other brands including such prestigious nameplates as Lincoln, Mercedes-Benz, Volvo and BMW. The surveys suggest that Saturn has set standards for product quality that others must strive to match if they wish to compete.

1.   What has Saturn Corporation done that suggests a deviation from classic marketing theory?

_____

_____

_____

2.   Explain how Saturn Corporation appears to be practicing relationship marketing.

_____

_____

_____

3.   Discuss how Saturn Corporation appears to have adopted the concept of total quality management.

_____

_____

_____

Case #4 MBA Cologne

William Lovell, a Vancouver-based entrepreneur, was proud of the MBA he earned at Simon Fraser University. He was also proud of his accomplishments to date and comfortable with his dreams of successes yet to come. Lovell had learned to set goals and pursue them in quiet dignity. He learned to respect others, and to be a man of his word. Lovell recognized that while he did not always agree with the actions of others, he knew that such diversity often provided strength for an organization. He also learned the arts of diplomacy and compromise and of strength through knowledge and perseverance.

Lovell had made his mark in the trucking industry and slowly branched out to other fields. His latest venture was distribution of a men's cologne called MBA.

MBA is imported by Lovell from Michaels' of Milan, Ltd., an Italian based cosmetic manufacturer.

Lovell reasoned that if a man aspired to a position of authority and responsibility, he should act, look, and dress the part. So he developed MBA cologne to complement the executive's image.

With such a commanding name and price--$100 an ounce--one might think the fragrance would be equally forceful. Not so--it has a subtlety that only hints at the potential that lies within. As Lovell explains, "The man distinguishes his possessions, position, and accomplishments, not the other way around." With each bottle comes a booklet containing thoughtful prescriptions for success from the likes of Drucker, Townsend, Waterman and Peters, Austin, and Kotler.

The cologne is already selling in better department stores in Alberta and BC. Sales have been brisk, but have been mainly to more mature buyers. Preliminary research indicates that many would-be executives (recent graduates of MBA programs) do not know the product exists. To inform potential customers, Lovell will advertise his cologne in *MBA Magazine*, a professional group publication distributed free to recent graduates. Lovell also intends to sell MBA cologne in bookstores at schools that have graduate programs in business.

Sales to date have returned a respectable 28 percent on investment, Lovell currently controls considerably less than 1 percent of the men's cologne market. Mainstream colognes such as Old Spice and Brut generate sales many times that of MBA, CEO, Wall Street, and Preferred Stock combined. (The latter colognes are MBA's competition in the premium cologne market.)

With the success of the men's cologne, Lovell expects to introduce Ms. MBA later this year.

1.　　Identify Lovell's competitive strategy for MBA cologne.

　　　_____

2.　　Explain the key to Lovell's success from the strategy identified above.

　　　_____

　　　_____

　　　_____

3.　　Discuss the potential risk to MBA cologne with the pursuit of the competitive strategy identified above.

　　　_____

　　　_____

　　　_____

　　　_____

　　　_____

Case #5   Griffin Industries

Sixteen months ago, Griffin Industries, a diversified plastic manufacturer, announced that it had developed a new material which makes fabrics water repellent, yet breathable. The coated fabric would be ideal for products that not only need to shed water, but also release moisture vapor rapidly. This announcement caused a commotion in the textile business because Griffin would be taking on Herman and Associates, whose HERTRON II has allowed them to become the leading manufacturer of water-repellent and breathable clothing for skiers, joggers, mountain climbers, and other sports enthusiasts.

Perry Humphrey is the man behind the new Griffin coating, called OXFORD IX. He named it OXFORD IX because he received his chemical engineering degree from Oxford University and because he worked nine months to develop the material. Humphrey explained that the coating was developed by modifying a polyurethane film so that when water vapor pressure built up on one side 'of the film, it would begin seeping through the minute openings between the molecular gaps instead of actual holes, therefore, OXFORD IX remains impervious to liquid water. Thus, through the diffusion process, the product breathes yet remains a barrier to water.

OXFORD IX differs from HERTRON II in that the Griffin product can be sprayed onto any fabric, even single-thickness fabrics, whereas HERTRON II is an ultrathin sheet of material which must be sewn between two fabrics. The sprayability of OXFORD IX gives it several advantages over HERTRON II, including a wider variety of uses and a less expensive method of incorporation into the fabric.

Both companies have since become embroiled in a battle for market share and dominance. Herman and Associates has lowered the price of HERTRON II garments and began promoting itself as the innovator in the industry. It has also mounted a promotional campaign which claims that HERTRON II is the most effective breathable, water-repellent material on the market. Griffin has successfully introduced its own line of clothing for skiers, joggers, and other amateur and professional athletes. It has also begun to market a line of camping tents and sleeping bags. Griffin's latest use of OXFORD IX is for the medical community as a bandage for cuts, burns, and surgical incisions. Herman, not to be outmarketed, is reportedly negotiating with the department of defense to produce foul weather gear for the U.S. Navy.

_____1. Griffin Industries initiated a _____ attack on Herman and Associates when it began to produce athletic clothing to compete with HERTRON II sportswear.

   A.   bypass

   B.   flank

   C.   frontal

   D.   guerrilla

   E.   preemptive

_____2. When Herman and Associates lowered the price of HERTRON II clothing and began promoting itself as the innovator in the industry, it was engaged in a _____ defense.

   A.   preemptive

   B.   mobile

   C.   contraction

   D.   counteroffensive

   E.   bypass

_____3. Griffin's diversification into the medical products market is an example of a _____ attack on Herman and Associates.

   A.   bypass

   B.   flank

   C.   frontal

   D.   guerrilla

   E.   preemptive

_____4. If Griffin Industries initiated a lawsuit against Herman and Associates challenging the claim that HERTRON II is the most effective breathable, water-repellent material on the market, Griffin would be engaging in a _____ attack on Herman and Associates.

   A.   position

   B.   guerrilla

   C.   preemptive

   D.   frontal

   E.   flank

_____5.   Griffin Industries is best described as a:

    A.   challenger in the sportswear market.

    B.   leader in the medical applications market.

    C.   follower in the military applications market.

    D.   only (A) and (B)

    E.   all of the above

Case #6   Reebok vs. Nike

Sneakers have become an international obsession. Everyone seems to have them and everyone likes them--from the sports enthusiast and the health conscious to the junior executive, the fashion conscious, and the active homemaker. Indeed, according to one analyst, one-third of all shoes sold in Canada are sneakers.

Two giants dominate the athletic shoe industry: Nike from Oregon and Reebok from Boston control approximately 50 percent of the sneaker business. Nike's success was based on creating a performance shoe for the fitness boom, specifically for the jogging craze of the 1970s, while Reebok made it on the new relaxed lifestyle of the 1980s, recognizing that 80 percent of all sneakers sold are for leisure use. Now both companies make hundreds of styles for both performance and recreational use.

Today in the battle to be number one, it has become Nike substance versus Reebok style. In the mid-1980s, by focusing on a special shoe for women, Reebok roared past Nike, unseating them from their position atop the athletic shoe industry. It was the aerobic shoe that propelled Reebok to number one. although the wrinkled leather was originally a production mistake, management loved it and so did the consumer.

Paul Fireman, Reebok's CEO and founder of Reebok in the United States, was a salesman who once ran a small family sporting goods business. Because of the success of Reebok, he has become one of the highest-paid executives in the nation. Even he is surprised by the success of the business. But Fireman concedes that it is consumers who have made his company number one. Therefore, Reebok will continue to focus its efforts on satisfying the customer. A recent example of this customer orientation is the introduction of hand-painted sneakers for the masses.

Nike was founded by Phil Knight, a runner from the University of Oregon. Knight and his former track coach, Bill Baumann, started the company and rue the running boom to instant success. Knight is the driving force, and remains immensely competitive. While Nike has made concessions to fashion, it is technology the company is counting on to win the war against Reebok. A recent innovation is the Air Revolution, a plastic airbag in the heel of the shoe that is visible. Reebok has developed its own system, called Energy Return, which involves the placement of plastic tubes in the shoes. It may ultimately include a window so that the tubes would be visible.

The competition never ceases. An upstart company called L.A. Gear sneers at research, development, and technology-simply letting people wear their sneakers and then listen to what is said about them. L.A. Gear came from nowhere in 1987 to capture an 11 percent share of the market in the early 1990s.

The industry is cyclical. Today's leaders could easily go the way of Keds, Converse, and Adidas--popular in the 1950s, 60s, and 70s, respectively, and still on the market, but nowhere near number one today.

1.   Explain how Reebok has been both a market leader and a market challenger.

_____

_____

_____

_____

2.   Explain why Nike should properly be classified as a market-centred company.

_____

_____

_____

_____

3.   Discuss market-expansion strategies that Nike either has used or could use to enhance its market position.

_____

_____

_____

_____

_____

_____

Sources: "Sneaker Attack," *Advertising Age,* June 20, 1988, p. 2; "Treading on Air," *Business Month,* January 1984, pp. 29-34; "Foot's Parade," *Time,* August 28, 1989, pp. 54-55; "L.A. Gear is Going Where the boys Are," *Business Week,* June 19, 1989, p. 54; and "Reebok on the Rebound," *New* York, October 16, 1989, "Sneaker Wars." *ABC News Broadcast,* August 19, 1988.

Multiple Choice Answers

1. Correct Answer: 4   Reference: pg. 605

2. Correct Answer: 3   Reference: pg. 605

3. Correct Answer: 2   Reference: pg. 606

4. Correct Answer: 5   Reference: pg. 607

5. Correct Answer: 1   Reference: pg. 607

6. Correct Answer: 2   Reference: pg. 607

7. Correct Answer: 4   Reference: pg. 610

8. Correct Answer: 3   Reference: pg. 611

9. Correct Answer: 5   Reference: pg. 611

10. Correct Answer: 1   Reference: pg. 612

11. Correct Answer: 4   Reference: pg. 613

12. Correct Answer: 2   Reference: pg. 614

13. Correct Answer: 3   Reference: pg. 617

14. Correct Answer: 5   Reference: pg. 618

15. Correct Answer: 2   Reference: pg. 620

16. Correct Answer: 5   Reference: pg. 621

17. Correct Answer: 1   Reference: pg. 622

18. Correct Answer: 3   Reference: pg. 624

19. Correct Answer: 4   Reference: pg. 625

20. Correct Answer: 3   Reference: pg. 626

21. Correct Answer: 2   Reference: pg. 627

22.	Correct Answer:	5	Reference:	pg. 629
23.	Correct Answer:	3	Reference:	pg. 630
24.	Correct Answer:	1	Reference:	pg. 631
25.	Correct Answer:	4	Reference:	pg. 631
26.	Correct Answer:	2	Reference:	pg. 634 (Figure 18-7)
27.	Correct Answer:	4	Reference:	pg. 618
28.	Correct Answer:	3	Reference:	pg. 613
29.	Correct Answer:	1	Reference:	pg. 605
30.	Correct Answer:	2	Reference:	pg. 611

True/False Answers

1. FALSE   Reference: pg. 605   Topic: Defining Customer Value and Satisfaction

2. TRUE   Reference: pg. 605   Topic: Customer Value

3. TRUE   Reference: pg. 606   Topic: Customer Value

4. FALSE   Reference: pg. 607   Topic: Customer Satisfaction

5. TRUE   Reference: pg. 608   Topic: Retaining Customers

6. TRUE   Reference: pg. 610   Topic: Customer Satisfaction and Customer Loyalty

7. FALSE   Reference: pg. 611   Topic: The Need for Customer Retention

8. FALSE   Reference: pg. 612   Topic: The Key: Customer Relationship Marketing

9. TRUE   Reference: pg. 613   Topic: Delivering Customer Value and Satisfaction

10. FALSE   Reference: pg. 614   Topic: Value Chain

11. TRUE   Reference: pg. 617   Topic: Total Quality Management

12. TRUE   Reference: pg. 618   Topic: Marketing's Role in Total Quality

13. TRUE   Reference: pg. 620   Topic: Competitive Marketing Strategies

14. FALSE   Reference: pg. 621   Topic: Assessing Competitors

15. FALSE   Reference: pg. 621   Topic: Assessing Competitors

16. TRUE   Reference: pg. 622   Topic: Selecting Competitors to Attack and Avoid

17. FALSE   Reference: pg. 625   Topic: Basic Competitive Strategies

18. TRUE   Reference: pg. 626   Topic: Market-Leader Strategies

19. TRUE   Reference: pg. 628   Topic: Expanding Market Share

20. FALSE   Reference: pg. 630   Topic: Choosing an Attacking Strategy.

Applying Terms and Concepts Answers

Case #1   Chiropractic Care:

Question #1
- Relationship marketing involves creating, maintaining, and enhancing strong relationships with customers and other stakeholders.
- Increasingly, marketing is moving away from a focus on individual transactions and toward a focus on building value-laden relationships and value delivery networks.
- Relationship marketing is oriented more toward the long term.
- The goal is to deliver long-term value to customers, and the measure of success is long-term customer satisfaction.
- Relationship marketing requires that all of the company's departments work together with marketing as a team to serve the customer.
- It involves building relationships at many levels—economic, social, technical, and legal—resulting in high customer loyalty.

Question #2
- Basic – The doctor performs the spinal adjustment and does not follow up the office visit in any way.

Question #3
- Reactive – The doctor performs the spinal adjustment and encourages the patient to call whenever he or she has any questions or problems.

Question #4
- Accountable – The doctor or others in the practice phones the patient a short time after the office visit to determine how the patient is responding to the treatment.
- The doctor may also solicit any suggested improvements or enhancements to the care (massage therapy, exercise consultation, referral, x-rays, etc.) and any specific disappointments. This information helps the practice to continuously improve its patient care.

Question #5
- Proactive – The doctor occasionally telephones the patient with suggestions for improved health care and/or to inform them of new services offered.

Question #6
- Partnership – The doctor works continuously with the patients and others to discover ways to deliver better value.

This may include informational brochures, seminars at schools, hospitals, athletic clubs, and area companies, public service demonstrations, patient newsletter, in office health care lectures, developing relationships with pharmacists, attorneys and allied health professionals, more convenient office hours, improved billing procedures new services such as massage therapy and advice on exercise, diet and nutrition and so on.

492

Case #2   Eastern Townships University:

1.   Generally, a prospective student will choose to attend the university which they
      believe offers the highest delivered value. To evaluate competing universities, the
      student will consider the differences between two factors. The first would be the
      values associated with a university including its product (courses of study and
      degrees offered), services (financial aid, counseling, health, placement, housing,
      etc.), personnel (reputation, quality, and helpfulness of instructional and support
      staff), and image, next, the prospective student will consider the total cost
      associated with attending a particular university. Included in the analysis of costs
      will be monetary costs such as tuition, fees, housing and transportation as well as
      nonmonetary costs such as time, energy and any physical costs.

2.   Eastern Townships University should consider conducting a customer value
      assessment as well as an image assessment. These assessments will provide
      information about how the various publics (prospective students, current students,
      parents, alumni employers, high school guidance counselors, community colleges,
      transfer counselors, among others) view Eastern Townships University. University
      personnel could then evaluate the information and develop strategies to increase
      customer value. This would be accomplished by emphasizing identified strengths
      while minimizing the impact of perceived weaknesses. The University could also
      develop strategies to reduce both monetary and nonmonetary costs. Depending
      upon the information gained from the assessment studies, the university might
      develop any number of strategies including developing new courses or programs
      of study, reducing class size, improving scheduling, opening a branch campus,
      streamlining the registration process, developing internships, scheduling a greater
      number and wider variety of social activities, and developing creative tuition
      payment plans to name just a few. The exact strategies developed should be those
      that serve to increase customer value.

Case #3   Saturn Corporation:

1.   Classic marketing theory and practice has traditionally centred on the art of attracting new customers and creating transactions while discussion was focused on presale and Sale activity. Saturn on the other hand, appears to be focused not only on attracting new customers, but retaining them as well. They are relationship oriented and engage in considerable postsale activity. Saturn is interested in developing and maintaining long-term, mutually beneficial relationships with their customers.

2.   Relationship marketing involves creating, maintaining, and enhancing strong relationships with customers and other stakeholders. Increasingly, marketing is moving away from a marketing mix focus to a relationship focus--from a focus on individual transactions and toward a focus on building value-laden relationships and marketing networks. Relationship marketing is more long-term oriented. The goal is to deliver long-term value to customers and the measure of success is long-term customer satisfaction. Relationship marketing requires that all of the company's departments work together with marketing as a team to serve the customer. It involves building relationships at many levels--economic, social, technical, and legal-resulting in high customer loyalty. And as the case indicated, Saturn has established new relationships with its employees, suppliers, dealers, and customers which have resulted in extremely high levels of customer satisfaction.

3.   The American Society for Quality Control defines quality as the totality of features and characteristics of a product or service that bear on its ability to satisfy stated or implied needs. This is clearly a customer-centered definition of quality. It suggests that a company has delivered quality whenever its product and service meet or exceed customers needs, requirements, and expectations. A company that satisfies most of its customers' needs most of the time is a quality company. And given the high levels of customer satisfaction, as demonstrated by the J. D. Power and Associate Surveys, it appears that Saturn has embraced the concept of total quality management.

<u>Case #4   MBA Cologne:</u>

1.   Market-nicher strategy

2.   The key to the Cologne's success is specialization among customer and marketing mix lines.

3.   Market niching carries the risk that the market may disappear (if the product is perceived as a fad) or that the market may be more aggressively attacked by either existing competitors or new competitors such as the mainstreamers who develop a new product and position it against existing competitors.

<u>Case #5   Griffin Industries:</u>

1.   C   4.   B

2.   D   5.   D

3.   A

<u>Case #6   Reebok vs. Nike:</u>

1.   A market leader is the firm that has the largest market share in the industry. It usually leads the other firms in price changes, new-product introductions, distribution coverage, and promotion spending. The leader may or may not be admired or respected, but other firms concede its dominance. The leader is a focal point for competition to challenge, imitate, or avoid.

Reebok was an innovator when it introduced the aerobic shoe. It was the aerobic shoe that propelled Reebok into the number-one position in the market. Hence, they were the leader in this instance.

A market challenger is a runner-up firm that is fighting hard to increase its market share. A market challenger must first define its strategic objective. Most market challengers seek to increase their profitability by increasing their market shares. But the strategic objective chosen depends on who the competitor is. In most cases, the company can choose which competitors it will challenge.

The challenger can attack the market leader--a high-risk but potentially high-gain strategy that makes good sense if the leader is not serving the market well. To succeed with such an attack, a company must have some sustainable competitive advantage over the leader--a cost advantage leading to lower prices or the ability to provide better value at a premium price. When attacking the leader, a challenger must also find a way to minimize the leader's response. Otherwise its gains may be short-lived.

The challenger can avoid the leader and instead attack firms its own size or smaller local and regional firms. Many of these firms are underfinanced and are not serving their customers well.

Reebok became a market challenger when they developed the Energy Return air system for sneakers. This product introduction positioned them directly against Nike, the leader in this aspect of the industry.

It should be emphasized that a firm might be a market leader in one aspect of the industry, a market challenger in another, a follower in yet another aspect of the industry, and even a nicher in still another aspect.

2.   *A competitor-centred company* is one whose moves are based mainly on competitors actions and reactions. The company spends most of its time tracking competitors' moves and market shares and trying to find strategies to counter them.

A customer-centred company, in contrast, focuses more on customer developments in designing its strategies. Clearly, the customer-centred company is in a better position to identify new opportunities and set a strategy that makes long-run sense. By watching customer needs evolve, it can decide what customer groups and what emerging needs are the most important to serve, given its resources and objectives.

Nike is properly classified as a market-centered company because their market strategy planning considers not only the competition--Reebok, L.A. Gear, Adidas, and so on--but also consumers--for example, in the development of the Air Revolution sneaker line.

3.   Leading firms want to remain number one. This calls for action on three fronts. First, the firm must find ways to expand total demand. Second, the firm must protect its current market share through good defensive and offensive actions. Third, the firm can try to expand its market share further, even if market size remains constant.

Nike has sought to increase total demand of athletic shoes by attracting new users of the footwear as well as by promoting new uses for it, while also encouraging more usage of the footwear. As a result, people who had never before purchased athletic shoes began to buy several pairs for the various activities they are involved in.

Chapter 19

The Global Marketplace

Chapter Overview

In the past, North American companies paid little attention to international trade. If they could pick up some extra sales through exporting, that was fine. But the big market was at home, and it teemed with opportunities. Companies today can no longer afford to focus only on their domestic market, regardless of its size. Many industries are global industries, and firms that operate globally achieve lower costs and higher brand awareness. At the same time, global marketing is risky because of variable exchange rates, unstable governments, protectionist tariffs and trade barriers, and several other factors. Given the potential gains and risks of international marketing, companies need a systematic way to make their international marketing decisions.

Chapter Objectives

1. Discuss how the international trade system, economic, political-legal and cultural environment affects a company's international marketing decisions.
2. Describe three key approaches to entering international markets.
3. Explain how companies adapt their marketing mixes for international markets.
4. Identify the three major forms of international marketing organization.

Chapter Topics

Global Marketing into the Twenty-First Century

Looking at the Global Marketing Environment
- The International Trade System
  - The World Trade Organization and GATT
  - Regional Free Trade Zones
- Economic Environment
- Political-Legal and Ethical Environment
- Cultural Environment

Deciding Whether to Go International

Deciding Which Markets to Enter

Deciding How to Enter the Market
- Exporting
- Joint Venture
  - Licensing
  - Contract Manufacturing
  - Management Contracting
  - Joint Ownership
- Direct Investment

Deciding on the Global Marketing Program
- Product
- Promotion
- Price
- Distribution Channels

Chapter Summary

1.   The elements of the international trade system.

International trade is regulated and restricted by various governments. A tariff is a tax levied by a foreign government on certain products. A quota sets limits on the amount of goods that an importing company will accept. An embargo totally bans some imports. Exchange controls limit the amount of foreign exchange and the exchange rate against other currencies. Non-tariff barriers include bias against firms and unfair product standards.

2.   The major forces operating in the economic, political, legal, and cultural environments that affect international marketing decisions.

Foreign economies may be subsistence, raw material exporting, industrializing, or industrial. Income distribution may be mostly low incomes, very-low/very-high, low/medium/high, and mostly medium family incomes. Political-legal environments vary on attitudes toward international buying, political stability, monetary regulations, and government bureaucracy. Cultural factors include differences in values, proxemics, and symbolism.

3.   The three key approaches to entering international markets.

International markets entry strategies include exporting (indirect, direct), joint venture (licensing, contract manufacturing, management contracting, and joint ownership), and direct investment (assembly facilities, manufacturing facilities). Each form varies in the amount of commitment, risk, control, and profit potential.

4.   How companies might adapt their marketing mixes for international markets.

Mix variations include standardized marketing mix with virtually no adaptation and several adaptation strategies. Product adaptation includes straight product extension, product adaptation, and product invention. Promotion adaptation involves language, symbolism, and value translations and message modifications. Price adaptation must consider economic and cultural differences. Distribution must take a whole-channel approach.

5.   The three major forms of international marketing organizations.

Export departments simply ship out the goods. International divisions manage the different forms of international marketing for each foreign country the company is in. Global organizations no longer view themselves as belonging to one or another domestic market as a primary or host country and plan, promote, and market according to worldwide organizational needs.

Key Terms

Adapted marketing mix   (pg. 664)
Communication adaptation   (pg. 666)
Contract manufacturing   (pg. 663)
Counter-trade (pg. 655)
Direct investment   (pg. 663)
Economic community (pg. 650)
Embargo   (pg. 648)
Exchange controls   (pg. 648)
Exporting   (pg. 661)
Global firm   (pg. 647)
Global industry   (pg. 647)
Joint ownership   (pg. 663)
Joint venturing   (pg. 662)
Licensing   (pg. 662)
Management contracting   (pg. 663)
Non-tariff trade barriers   (pg. 648)
Product adaptation   (pg. 665)
Product invention   (pg. 665)
Quota (pg. 648)
Standardized marketing mix (pg. 664)
Straight product extension   (pg. 665)
Tariff (pg. 648)
Whole-channel view (pg. 668)

Multiple Choice Questions

19-1   Multiple

The world is shrinking rapidly as a result of everything except:

1.   Faster communications
2.   Faster transportation
3.   Faster financial flows
4.   Faster cultural adaptations
5.   All of the above

19-2   Multiple

Companies that go global confront every problem except this one.

1.   High debt, inflation and unemployment in many countries
2.   Oversaturation
3.   Governments are placing more regulations on foreign firms
4.   Corruption
5.   None of the above

19-3   Multiple

A global firm is one that, by operating in more than one country, gains every advantage except:

1.   Marketing
2.   Production
3.   R&D
4.   Financial
5.   None of the above

19-4   Multiple

International trade restrictions that allow countries to be biased against bids or restrictive towards product standards, are considered:

1.   Non-tariff trade barriers
2.   Tariffs
3.   Quotas
4.   Embargoes
5.   Exchange controls

19-5   Multiple

The General Agreement on Tariffs and Trade (GATT) is a treaty designed to promote world trade by reducing tariffs and other international trade barriers. The date of its inception is:

1.   1930
2.   1948
3.   1964
4.   1952
5.   1976

19-6   Multiple

The GATT agreement went through several rounds of negotiations before coming to a consensus. The first seven rounds of negotiations reduced average worldwide tariffs on manufactured goods from _____ % to just _____ %.

1.   80, 25
2.   75, 10
3.   45, 5
4.   50, 7
5.   30, 2

19-7   Multiple

Certain countries have formed free trade zones. The countries included in these free trade zones are known as:

1.   Trading communities
2.   Partnership counties
3.   Trade cooperatives
4.   Economic communities
5.   None of the above

19-8   Multiple

In January 1994, the North America Free Trade Agreement was signed between Canada, Mexico and the US. This agreement created a single market of _____ million people.

1.   120
2.   190
3.   260
4.   300
5.   360

19-9   Multiple

The Asian-Pacific Economic Cooperation is composed of 18 member counties and accounts for
_____ % of world trade.

1.   80
2.   30
3.   45
4.   65
5.   15

19-10 Multiple

Other free trade areas are forming in Latin and South America. For example, MERCOSUL now
links all the following counties except _____, to free trade zones.

1.   Brazil
2.   Chile
3.   Columbia
4.   Mexico
5.   All of the above are linked

19-11 Multiple

Despite NAFTA's many successes, a number of challenges are posed to maintaining the smooth
trade relations between Canada and the US. All the following except _____ explain
why these relationships are hurting.

1.   Salmon fishing rights along the shores of Vancouver Island
2.   Canada's protection of its dairy and poultry industries
3.   Canada's insistence of protection for its cultural industries
4.   Canada's trading status with Cuba
5.   All of the above are causing problems

19-12 Multiple

Countries that are good markets for large equipment, tools and supplies, and trucks, are:

1.   Industrial economies
2.   Industrializing economies
3.   Raw-material-exporting economies
4.   Subsistence economies
5.   None of the above

19-13 Multiple

In a (n) _____ economy, manufacturing accounts for 10 to 20% of the country's economy.

1. Industrial
2. Industrializing
3. Raw-material-exporting
4. Subsistence
5. 2 and 3

19-14 Multiple

At least four political-legal factors should be considered in deciding whether or not to do business in a given country. Which of the following is not one of these factors?

1. Attitudes towards international buying
2. Government bureaucracy
3. Political stability
4. Ethical standards
5. Monetary regulations

19-15 Multiple

The counter-trade form whereby the seller sells a plant, equipment or technology to another country and agrees to take payment in the resulting products is called:

1. Compensation
2. Counter purchase
3. Barter
4. Delayed payment
5. Reciprocity

19-16 Multiple

The average _____ man uses almost twice as many cosmetic and beauty aids as his wife.

1. German
2. Japanese
3. Canadian
4. Russian
5. French

19-17 Multiple

Which of the following is not a reason for a firm to go international?

1. Global competitors might attack the company's domestic market
2. Government regulations may force companies to globalize
3. The company might want to counter-attack these competitors
4. The company might want to reduce its risk by depending too much on one country
5. All of the above are reasons

19-18 Multiple

Not all global markets are equally attractive. Westsun Communications is thinking about expanding its operation to some countries in the Pacific Rim. Which of the following were not important factors in their assessment?

1. Market growth
2. Competitive advantage
3. Cost of doing business
4. Financing opportunities
5. Risk level

19-19 Multiple

_____ is the simplest way for a manufacturer to enter international markets.

1. Licensing
2. Exporting
3. Contract manufacturing
4. Joint ownership
5. Management contracting

19-20 Multiple

_____ prevents a company from setting up its own operations for a period of time.

1. Licensing
2. Exporting
3. Contract manufacturing
4. Joint ownership
5. Management contracting

506

19-21 Multiple

The biggest involvement in a foreign market comes through:

1.   Joint ownership
2.   Joint ventures
3.   Direct investment
4.   Exporting
5.   Integrated marketing efforts

19-22 Multiple

The philosophy to "take the product as is and find customers for it" is:

1.   Product invention
2.   Product adaptation
3.   Communication adaptation
4.   Straight product extension
5.   None of the above

19-23 Multiple

If a company decides not to change the product but to adapt their promotion when entering new markets, they are performing:

1.   Product invention
2.   Product adaptation
3.   Communication adaptation
4.   Straight product extension
5.   Integrated marketing strategy

19-24 Multiple

The channel concept for international marketing includes everything except:

1.   Seller's headquarters
2.   Marketing intermediaries
3.   Channels between nations
4.   Channels within nations
5.   Final users or buyers

19-25 Multiple

The international divisions corporate staff includes all the following except:

1.   Marketing
2.   Research
3.   Personnel
4.   Finance
5.   None of the above

19-26 Multiple

The European Community Free Trade zone was founded in:

1.   1947
2.   1957
3.   1967
4.   1977
5.   1987

19-27 Multiple

Which of the following factors helped draw Canadian companies to enter international markets?

1.   The weakening of domestic marketing opportunities
2.   A very strong dollar compared to other currencies
3.   Growing opportunities for their products in other countries
4.   Both 1 and 3
5.   All of the above

19-28 Multiple

The Canadian government has been considering the adoption of safety and emission standards that must be met by all companies wishing to sell automobiles in Canada. Such an action is an example of a (n):

1.   Revenue tariff
2.   Non-tariff barrier
3.   Quota
4.   Embargo
5.   Constrictive tariff

508

19-29 Multiple

Economic communities usually strive to do which of the following?

1.   Raise tariffs within the community
2.   Expand employment and investment
3.   Reduce prices
4.   Only 1 and 2
5.   Only 2 and 3

19-30 Multiple

Which of the following is not a component of a country's industrial structure?

1.   Product and service requirements
2.   Employment levels
3.   Values and norms
4.   Income levels
5.   Both 1 and 2

True/False Questions

19-1   True/False

Companies who stay at home and play it safe not only lose their chance to enter other markets, but also risk losing their home market.

19-2   True/False

You must be an industry giant to venture into international markets.

19-3   True/False

The global company sees the world as many different markets.

19-4   True/False

The dominant position of North American firms has been declining over the last few years in the international arena.

19-5   True/False

The financial tariff is the strongest of the quotas.

19-6   True/False

As a result of increased unification, European companies will grow bigger and more competitive.

19-7   True/False

Canadian exports to the US have grown faster than imports from the US.

19-8   True/False

Two economic factors reflect a country's attractiveness as a market: the country's industrial structure and its political distribution.

19-9   True/False

Industrialization usually creates a new rich class and a large and growing middle class, both demanding more goods.

19-10 True/False

International marketers never find it profitable to do business in an unstable country.

19-11 True/False

Most international trade involves cash transactions.

19-12 True/False

Many local firms must be increasingly aware of the globalization of competition even if they never plan to go overseas themselves.

19-13 True/False

Because of the risks and difficulties of entering international markets, most companies do not act until some situation or event thrusts them into the global arena.

19-14 True/False

Direct exporting involves less investment because the firm does not require an overseas sales force or set of contacts.

19-15 True/False

Coca-Cola markets internationally by contract manufacturing its bottlers around the world and supplying them with the syrup to produce the product.

19-16 True/False

In direct investment, a firm usually develops deeper relationships with local government and suppliers than any other form of international trade.

19-17 True/False

Global standardization is an all-or-nothing proposition.

19-18 True/False

Product invention might mean reintroducing earlier product forms that happen to be well adapted to the needs of a given country.

19-19 True/False

The media used by a company also needs to be adapted internationally because its availability varies from country to country.

19-20 True/False

The global operating units report to the head of the international division, not directly to the CEO or executive committee of the organization.

Applying Terms and Concepts

To determine how well you understand the materials in this chapter, read each of the following brief cases and respond to the questions that follow. Answers are given at the end of this chapter.

Case #1   Modern-Day Pirates[1]

You're traveling in Southeast Asia and have an opportunity to visit the outdoor market in Chinatown in Kuala Lumpur, Malaysia. Covering many city blocks, the market is a shopper's fantasy with stalls selling everything from Calvin Klein T-shirts and jeans to Ralph Lauren's signature Polo shirts, Coach bags, and Rolex watches. The question is: Would you buy? The problem is that many of these products are counterfeit.

Marketers with big brands, worried more about their loss of image than monetary loss, are battling with international pirates who steal their logos, packages, and sometimes counterfeit their products. In negotiations with the Chinese, the U.S. trade representative held up two boxes of Microsoft Word—one legitimate, one a copy. There was no way to tell the difference, other than the price.

China has been indifferent to its citizens' unauthorized copyright and trademark use of international marketers' software, music, film, apparel, and sporting goods. However, it agreed to enforce its own laws against piracy and undertook a nationwide crackdown in 1995 in order to be awarded the 1996 Olympiad trademark licenses. The Chinese are not the only marketing pirates. The International Intellectual Property Alliance (IIPA) also cites Turkey, Bulgaria, and Indonesia on its list of priority-watch countries.

The IIPA also estimates that Japan and Germany were the leading sources of monetary loss to piracy. The Software Publishers Association (SPA), representing 1,200 business, education, and consumer software marketers, estimates that the Singapore market cost U.S. software marketers $33 million last year, small potatoes compared to markets like German with an estimated $1.1 billion loss and Japan where the SPA estimates U.S. industry losses at $1.3 billion a year, the world's highest rate. And that's only one industry. Germany, as concerned as the United States about the piracy problem, has passed a tough new law called the Brand Law that enables marketers to protect not only their brand logo but also the logo's colors and the product's packaging design.

As piracy has escalated, marketers and industry trade associations worldwide have increased their vigilance in lobbying lawmakers, instigating local police seizures, and even ad campaigns. International marketers, such as Reebok and Levi-Strauss, are fighting their battles with public relations campaigns. Reebok, fighting piracy in China and South Korea, reaches its trade audience with its message about supporting legitimate brands through articles in business and trade publications.

---

[1] *Advertising Principles & Practice*, 4th Edition, Wells, Burnett, Moriarty, pg.672.

512

The Motion Picture Association is running an ongoing cinema and videocassette trailer campaign in Belgium, Germany, Italy, and the United Kingdom. In Latin America the group has targeted Venezuela, a growing piracy market, for an antipiracy poster campaign. A spokesperson for the association said, "The video trailer in Europe is working very well, with a toll-free hot line [for consumers reporting piracy]."

Washington-based Software Publishers Association this month broke a Singapore antipiracy campaign in both Singapore and Malaysia. The education-and-enforcement campaign is the association's first outside the United States. Previously the association has distributed ads in Spanish for Mexico and Costa Rica, in Portuguese for Brazil, and in Hebrew for Israel.

The bottom line is that piracy hurts brands and consumers of brands. If Ralph Lauren's Polo brand gets copied so much that the original brand is unrecognizable, then why buy Polo? As the marketplace becomes more and more international, the problem only becomes greater. Regardless of where you live, the money you invest in buying a brand is wasted if the brand loses it cachet. How can that message be communicated through advertising and other forms of marketing communication? What message makes that point?

So go back to you imaginary trip through the marketplace in Kuala Lumpur (or walk down a street in New York City). Would you buy that incredibly cheap Rolex watch?

1.   Why would it be difficult for companies to prosecute pirates in a foreign country?

_____

_____

_____

_____

2.   How can companies persuade and motivate consumers to help eliminate piracy?

_____

_____

_____

_____

3.   How can companies persuade foreign governments to implement laws against piracy?

_____

_____

_____

_____

4. Why would the Chinese government be indifferent to the piracy that occurs in their country?

_____

_____

_____

_____

5. Germany has passed the Brand Law, but will this be effective to prosecute pirates in other countries?

_____

_____

_____

_____

Case #2   PepsiCo: Swapping Pepsi for Chickens and Tomato Paste[2]

Pepsi-Cola was the first foreign consumer product to be sold in the USSR and it took the firm's chairman David Kendall many years to ensure PepsiCo's long-term presence there. With the fall of the Berlin Wall, many firms expected large financial returns on relatively little investment in market extension activities. These companies ignore the lesson the PepsiCo had learned "the hard way." Democracy has a difficult job moving East Europeans toward Western-style capitalism and consumption.

Just as the sociocultural environment made it difficult to enter the new markets, so did its lack of technology. East European factories are antiquated; they are not competitive. But, they are the major source of employment. In addition the political environment did not welcome foreign marketers. It is now obvious that many of the predictions about Eastern European economic growth were overly optimistic for most companies. PepsiCo, however, having learned its lessons from its dealings with the Soviet Union has been able to make substantial inroads into the new markets.

1. It took more than a decade for PepsiCo to execute its plan to enter the Soviet market. Discuss some possible ways in which PepsiCo managers may have (1) assured goal-directed actions, (2) assigned resources, and (3) built interpersonal relationships and informal networks.

_____

_____

_____

_____

2. What unanticipated environmental changes are more likely to affect marketers doing business in the Soviet Union and Eastern Europe than Western marketers who confine themselves to domestic marketers? What are the implications for marketers?

_____

_____

_____

_____

3. How successful do you think PepsiCo's counter-trade strategy has been?

_____

_____

_____

_____

4. Many Western marketers initially assumed that Eastern European consumers would be essentially equivalent to Western European consumers once they were allowed to access a free market. How may Eastern Europeans differ from their Western cousins?

_____

_____

_____

_____

5. How could a company successfully enter the Eastern European market?

_____

_____

_____

_____

_____

[2] *Marketing* 5th Edition (resource manual), Schoell, Guiltinan; pg. 232-234.

Multiple Choice Answers

1.   Correct Answer: 4   Reference: pg. 645

2.   Correct Answer: 2   Reference: pg. 547

3.   Correct Answer: 5   Reference: pg. 647

4.   Correct Answer: 1   Reference: pg. 648

5.   Correct Answer: 2   Reference: pg. 648

6.   Correct Answer: 3   Reference: pg. 650

7.   Correct Answer: 4   Reference: pg. 650

8.   Correct Answer: 5   Reference: pg. 651

9.   Correct Answer: 3   Reference: pg. 651

10. Correct Answer: 2   Reference: pg. 651

11. Correct Answer: 5   Reference: pg. 653

12. Correct Answer: 3   Reference: pg. 654

13. Correct Answer: 2   Reference: pg. 654

14. Correct Answer: 4   Reference: pg. 655

15. Correct Answer: 1   Reference: pg. 655

16. Correct Answer: 5   Reference: pg. 657

17. Correct Answer: 2   Reference: pg. 658

18. Correct Answer: 4   Reference: pg. 659

19. Correct Answer: 1   Reference: pg. 662

20. Correct Answer: 5   Reference: pg. 663

21.	Correct Answer:	3	Reference:	pg. 663
22.	Correct Answer:	4	Reference:	pg. 665
23.	Correct Answer:	3	Reference:	pg. 665
24.	Correct Answer:	2	Reference:	pg. 668
25.	Correct Answer:	5	Reference:	pg. 669
26.	Correct Answer:	2	Reference:	pg.650
27.	Correct Answer:	4	Reference:	pg. 646
28.	Correct Answer:	2	Reference:	pg.648
29.	Correct Answer:	5	Reference:	pg. 650
30.	Correct Answer:	3	Reference:	pg. 662

True/False Answers

1. TRUE   Reference: pg. 645   Topic: Global Marketing into the Twenty-First Century

2. FALSE   Reference: pg. 646   Topic: Global Marketing into the Twenty-First Century

3. FALSE   Reference: pg. 647   Topic: Global Marketing into the Twenty-First Century

4. TRUE   Reference: pg. 648   Topic: Looking at the Global Marketing Environment.

5. FALSE   Reference: pg. 648   Topic: The International Trade System

6. TRUE   Reference: pg. 650   Topic: Regional Free Trade Zones

7. TRUE   Reference: pg. 653   Topic: Regional Free Trade Zones

8. FALSE   Reference: pg. 653   Topic: Economic Environment

9. FALSE   Reference: pg. 654   Topic: Economic Environment

10. FALSE   Reference: pg. 655   Topic: Political-Legal and Ethical Environment

11. TRUE   Reference: pg. 655   Topic: Political-Legal and Ethical Environment

12. TRUE   Reference: pg. 658   Topic: Deciding Whether to Go International

13. TRUE   Reference: pg. 658   Topic: Deciding Whether to Go International

14. FALSE   Reference: pg. 661   Topic: Exporting

15. FALSE   Reference: pg. 662   Topic: Licensing

16. TRUE   Reference: pg. 664   Topic: Direct Investment

17. FALSE   Reference: pg. 664   Topic: Deciding on the Global Marketing Program

18. TRUE   Reference: pg. 665   Topic: Product

19. TRUE   Reference: pg. 666   Topic: Promotion

20. FALSE   Reference: pg. 669   Topic: Deciding on the Global Marketing Organization

Applying Terms and Concepts Answers

Case #1   Modern-Day Pirates:

Question #1
- Companies may have a hard time prosecuting pirates due to foreign governments, who may not realize the severity of the problem. In addition, foreign governments may not have sufficient nor adequate laws to properly reprimand the pirates.
- Furthermore, other countries may have different standards and perceptions regarding piracy.

Question #2
- 1-800 telephone numbers that are open 24 hours a day would facilitate the process for consumers.
- In addition, offering incentives such as large sums of money would motivate the ordinary, average Joe.
- Companies could also try to appeal to society's moral side, and try to educate the public with ads and publicity spots on television.
- The key is to educate foreign populations where the piracy occurs.

Question #3
- Companies have to appeal to the foreign governments' morals. Is piracy fair?
- How would they feel if their country were being cheated out of billions of dollars?
- US/German/and Japanese governments could also help foreign governments create anti-piracy laws.
- The key to upholding the law is to have a strict enforcement and a severe penalty.

Question #4
- It could be that the Chinese government is pre-occupied with Asian gangs and they are too busy to deal with small annoyances like piracy.
- However, it is more realistic that the Chinese government realizes that their country is profiting in millions and billions from piracy and unauthorized rip-offs.
- If you were the Chinese government, what would be a priority—satisfying the demands of already prosperous companies, or grabbing a few bucks for your people?

Question #5
- The German law could have minimal impact on foreign pirates.
- Can the Germans even prosecute pirates in another country?
- What are the penalties for violating these laws?
- Can the German companies and the German government really make an impact with their local policies when pirates in Venezuela, Turkey, china, Indonesia, and so forth are copying merchandise like rabbits? I think not.

Case #2   PepsiCo: Swapping Pepsi for Chickens and Tomato Paste:

Question #1
Managers should ensure goal-directed actions by:
(1) making sure that those involved understand that the ultimate goal is beating Coke into the Soviet and Soviet-satellite markets rather than short-term sales figures and
(2) making sure managers are rewarded for advancing relations with Soviets and not penalized for being in a group that does not bring in sales for many years.

They should assign resources to make sure that those involved:
(1) have the resources to pay for the time of translators, lawyers, and consultants on Soviet culture and politics, and
(2) have the equipment and money for taking it to the USSR for demonstrations.

They should make sure that those involved are willing to and are interested in developing relationships with their Soviet counterpart and with all the many people in the home office who will need to be involved.

Question #2
Some environmental changes that affect marketers include
(1) basic political instability and uncertainty,
(2) sudden changes in regime that have a more profound effect than political changes in the West,
(3) sudden changes in the currency, and
(4) the possibilities of civil unrest. The implications for marketers are that they should:
   a. construct crisis control plans in anticipation of such event
   b. assess the balance of such risks against the possible gains in assets
   c. make sure that business in other parts of the world will offset the possible loss of business in the areas.

Question #3
PepsiCo's counter-trade strategy has been very successful. It has allowed PepsiCo to
(1) establish strong market positions in countries where it would have been impossible to do business otherwise,
(2) obtain a steady supply of products that it needs in its other businesses—tomato paste, chickens, etc.—at prices that are lower than in the West,
(3) work out long-term relationships that create goodwill with foreign governments because it helps them to gain credibility for their own products overseas, and

520

(4) establish relationships that are deeper than simple cash-purchase relationships—it would be hard, for instance, for Hungarians to find another such large purchaser for its tomato paste (which provide agricultural and industrial jobs) whereas it might be fairly easy to find another Western marketer who could offer the equivalent amount of cash.

Question #4

- Although many Eastern Europeans crave Western products, their attitudes toward products and marketing may be very different because they were cut off from the West before the great boom of the post-war marketing era.
- First, it may take many years if not decades before they are equally affluent.
- Second, it seems that many do not want to abandon socialist ideas entirely—they may turn out to be just as materialistic but many need different advertising and promoting campaigns.
- Also, many people in Eastern Europe are not "European" in the cultural sense, but rather come from Eurasian, Turkish, or other traditions.

Question #5

- Research and investigate whether there is a need or demand for a product
- Ensure that the marketing and packaging meet local tastes and standards
- Be familiar with local culture

Investigate the economic and political environment, is it feasible to expand into this country?

Chapter 20

Marketing and Society

Chapter Overview

Responsible marketers discover what consumers want and respond with the right products, priced to give good value to buyers and profit to the producer. A marketing system should sense, serve, and satisfy consumer needs and improve the quality of consumers' lives. In working to meet consumer needs, marketers may take some actions that are not to everyone's liking or benefit. Marketing managers should be aware of the main criticisms of marketing.

Chapter Objectives

1. Identify the major social criticisms of marketing.
2. Define consumerism and environmentalism and explain how they affect marketing strategies.
3. Describe the principles of socially responsible marketing.
4. Explain the role of ethics in marketing.
5. List the major principles for public policy toward marketing.

Chapter Topics

Social Criticisms of Marketing
- Marketing's Impact on Individual Consumers
  - High Prices
    - High Costs of Distribution
    - High Advertising and Promotion Costs
    - Excessive Markups
  - Deceptive Practices
  - High Pressure Selling
  - Shoddy or Unsafe Products
  - Planned Obsolescence
  - Poor Service to Disadvantaged Consumers
- Marketing's Impact on Society as a Whole
  - False Wants and Too Much Materialism
  - Too Few Social Goods
  - Cultural Pollution
  - Too Much Political Power
- Marketing's Impact on Other Businesses

Citizen and Public Actions to Regulate Marketing
- Consumerism
- Environmentalism
- Public Actions to Regulate Marketing

Business Actions Toward Socially Responsible Marketing
- Enlightened Marketing
  - Consumer-Oriented Marketing
  - Innovative Marketing
  - Value Marketing
  - Sense-of-Mission Marketing
  - Societal Marketing
- Marketing Ethics

Principles for Public Policy Toward Marketing

Chapter Summary

1.   The social criticisms of marketing's impact on individuals.

Criticisms of marketing include its impact on individual consumers for high prices, high advertising, promotion, and distribution costs, excessive markups, deceptive practices, high pressure selling, unsafe products, planned obsolescence and poor service to disadvantaged consumers.

2.   The social criticisms of marketing's impact on society as a whole.

Marketing is accused of fostering several societal "evils" including false wants and too much materialism, too few social goods, cultural pollution and too much political power.

3.   Defining consumerism and environmentalism and explaining how they affect marketing strategies.

Consumerism is an organized movement of citizens and government agencies to improve the rights and powers of buyers in relation to sellers. Environmentalism is an organized movement of concerned citizens and government agencies to protect and improve people's living environment. Marketing strategies often seek to position the company as more consumer-oriented and/or environmentally responsible (green marketing).

4.   The principles of socially responsible marketing.

Socially responsible or enlightened marketing consists of five principles. Consumer-oriented marketing organizes marketing activities from the consumer's viewpoint. Innovative marketing seeks continuous real product and marketing improvements. Value marketing puts resources into value-building marketing investments. Sense-of-marketing defines the company mission in broad social terms. Societal marketing blends social, company and consumer needs.

5.   The role of ethics in marketing.

Enlightened companies realize that marketing ethics are an important component of a long-term consumer orientation. Ethics much be an integral part of the corporate culture with the full and active participation of upper management to succeed.

Key Terms

Multiple Choice Questions

20-1   Multiple

Many critics charge the marketing system causes prices to be higher than they would be under more "sensible" systems. All the following factors are attributed to this fact except:

1.   High costs of distribution
2.   High advertising and promotion costs
3.   High levels of competition
4.   Excessive markups
5.   All of the above

20-2   Multiple

Companies are defending themselves against allegations they are raising their prices to make more of a profit. Which of the following would not be considered a good statement of defence?

1.   Intermediaries do the work that would otherwise be done by manufacturers or consumers
2.   Markups reflect services that consumers themselves want
3.   Costs of operating stores keep rising, forcing retailers to raise their prices
4.   Retail competition is so intense margins are actually quite low
5.   None of the above

20-3   Multiple

Companies must also defend themselves against critics who insist companies are spending too much on advertising and promotion, which is increasing the price of goods unnecessarily. From the following list, choose the one option that does not explain why companies have such large advertising budgets.

1.   Heavy advertising is needed to establish companies as Fortune 500 companies
2.   Heavy advertising is needed to make consumers feel wealthy, beautiful, or special, which is what they want
3.   Heavy advertising is necessary to create branding, which gives buyers confidence
4.   Heavy advertising is needed to inform millions of potential buyers of the merits of a brand
5.   Heavy advertising and promotion may be necessary for a firm to match competitor's efforts

20-4   Multiple

Deceptive practices fall into all the following groups except:

1.   Deceptive pricing
2.   Deceptive placing
3.   Deceptive promotion
4.   Deceptive packaging
5.   All of the above are deceptive

20-5   Multiple

Consumers feel companies are out to deceive them in an effort to sell more products.
Many consumer complaints are filed every year with the Better Business Bureau, and
other agencies. Which of the following is not a common complaint received by the Better
Business Bureau?

1.   Many products are not made well or services did not perform well
2.   Many products deliver little benefit
3.   Many products are not safe to use
4.   Many products are too expensive
5.   All of the above are common complaints

20-6   Multiple

_____ is a type of economic discrimination in which major chain retailers
avoid placing stores in disadvantaged neighbourhoods.

1.   Streamlining
2.   Embargoing
3.   Redlining
4.   Price-lining
5.   Location-lining

20-7   Multiple

Marya is doing a paper on factors influencing people's wants and needs. She knows
marketers do not have the ultimate influence. Which of the following does not have an
influence on people's wants and needs?

1.   Peer groups
2.   Income
3.   Religion
4.   Ethnic background
5.   Education

20-8   Multiple

"Cultural pollution is becoming more of a problem," claim many critics of marketing systems. Cultural pollution continuously pollutes people's minds with messages about everything except:

1.   Materialism
2.   Sex
3.   Power
4.   Status
5.   All of the above messages lead to pollution

20-9   Multiple

Critics charge a company's marketing practices can harm other companies and reduce competition. What is one factor that does not contribute to this allegation?

1.   Acquisition of competitors
2.   Marketing practices that create barriers to entry
3.   Only large companies can afford to compete
4.   Unfair competitive marketing practices
5.   All of the above are problems

20-10 Multiple

Consumerism is an organized movement of citizens and government agencies to improve the rights and power of buyers in relation to sellers. Consumerism has outlined all the following fundamental consumer rights except:

1.   The right to safety
2.   The right to be informed
3.   The right to be heard
4.   The right to everyday low prices
5.   The right to consumer education

20-11 Multiple

Which of the following is not included in the fundamental right to be informed?

1.   The true intention of advertising
2.   The true interest on a loan
3.   The true cost per unit of a brand
4.   The ingredients in a product
5.   The true benefits of a product

20-12 Multiple

The marketing system's goal should not be to maximize consumption, consumer choice or consumer satisfaction, but rather to maximize:

1.   Consumer quality
2.   Service quality
3.   Societal quality
4.   Product quality
5.   Life quality

20-13 Multiple

_____ minimizes not only pollution from production, but also all environmental impacts throughout the full product life cycle.

1.   Environmental sustainability
2.   Product stewardship
3.   Environmental technologies
4.   Sustainability vision
5.   Sustainable development

20-14 Multiple

Many new regional agreements such as NAFTA and the EC have posed complex environmental problems for many countries. Environmental policies vary widely from country to country and uniform worldwide standards are not expected for another _____ years or more.

1.   5
2.   10
3.   15
4.   20
5.   25

20-15 Multiple

Legal issues facing marketing managers include everything except:

1.   Selling decisions
2.   Packaging decisions
3.   Competitive relations decisions
4.   Financing decisions
5.   Product decisions

20-16 Multiple

Customer-oriented marketing means the company should view and organize its marketing activities from the consumer's point of view. This is the one thing a company does not have to do for the needs of a defined group of customers.

1.   Solidify
2.   Sense
3.   Serve
4.   Satisfy
5.   The must do all of the above

20-17 Multiple

Value marketing is a principle of enlightened marketing that holds a company should put most of its resources into value-building marketing investment. Which of the following is not considered a value-adding strategy?

1.   Lowering costs and prices
2.   Advertising effectively
3.   Improving product quality
4.   Making services more convenient
5.   None of the above

20-18 Multiple

A product, which possesses high immediate satisfaction but low long-run consumer benefits, is a _____ in the societal classification of products scale.

1.   Salutary product
2.   Desirable product
3.   Impulse product
4.   Deficient product
5.   Pleasing product

20-19 Multiple

Under the _____, companies and mangers must look beyond what is legal and allowed and develop standards based on personal integrity, corporate conscience, and long-run consumer welfare.

1. Marketing ethics standard
2. Integrated marketing concept
3. Social marketing concept
4. Environmentalism concept
5. Consumerism concept

20-20 Multiple

The principles for public policy toward marketing reflect certain assumptions that underlie much of modern marketing theory and practice. Which of the following is not one of these principles?

1. The principle of consumer and producer freedom
2. The principle of curbing potential harm
3. The principle of economic efficiency
4. The principle of innovation
5. All of the above are principles

20-21 Multiple

When marketers answer charges that they generate undesired "commercial noise" by pointing out that ads help reduce the cost of magazines and newspapers, it is responding to which of the following criticisms?

1. Marketing emphasizes too much materialism
2. Marketing spreads cultural pollution
3. Marketing creates too few social goods
4. Marketing exercises too much political power
5. All of the above

20-22 Multiple

When large companies use patents and heavy promotion spending to prevent new competitors entering their markets, then marketing is sometimes criticized for its:

1.   Impact on other businesses
2.   Impact on the economy
3.   Impact on the individual
4.   Impact on society as a whole
5.   Impact on fair marketing practices

20-23 Multiple

All the following relate to proposals on consumer protection except:

1.   Strengthening consumer rights in cases of business fraud
2.   Reducing the level of advertising noise
3.   Requiring greater product safety
4.   Giving more power to government agencies
5.   None of the above

20-24 Multiple

From a societal marketing perspective, dental floss is a:

1.   Desirable product
2.   Pleasing product
3.   Deficient product
4.   Salutary product
5.   None of the above

20-25 Multiple

From a societal marketing perspective, a candy bar is a:

1.   Desirable product
2.   Pleasing product
3.   Deficient product
4.   Salutary product
5.   All of the above

20-26 Multiple

From a societal marketing perspective, bad-tasting mouthwash that doesn't work is a:

1.   Desirable product
2.   Pleasing product
3.   Deficient product
4.   Salutary product
5.   Rejected product

20-27 Multiple

In order to be truly effective, ethics and societal responsibility in business:

1.   Must be a component of the overall corporate culture
2.   Must be written into codes
3.   Should be left to the individual's sense of right and wrong
4.   And be determined on a case-by-case basis
5.   Only 1 and 2

20-28 Multiple

Corporate marketing ethics policies are broad guidelines everyone in the organization must follow. These policies should cover everything except:

1.   Distributor relations
2.   Advertising standards
3.   Product development
4.   Supplier contracts
5.   All of the above are covered

20-29 Multiple

Environmental sustainability means developing strategies both _____ the environment and produce _____ for the company.

1.   protect, customers
2.   protect, profits
3.   sustain, customers
4.   sustain, benefits
5.   sustain, profits

20-30 Multiple

Differentiated products like cosmetics, detergents, toiletries, include promotion and packaging costs that can amount to _____ % or more of the manufacturer's price to the retailer.

1. 30
2. 40
3. 50
4. 60
5. 70

True/False Questions

20-1   True/False

Surveys usually show consumers hold mixed or even slightly unfavourable attitudes toward marketing practices.

20-2   True/False

Consumers usually can buy functional versions of products at lower prices but often are willing to pay more for products providing desired psychological benefits.

20-3   True/False

Deceptive practices have led to legislation and other consumer protection actions, but not to industry self-regulation standards.

20-4   True/False

Marketers argue most companies avoid deceptive practices because such practices harm their business in the long run.

20-5   True/False

Much of the so-called planned obsolescence is not the working of the competitive and technological forces, but rather companies wanting to sell more products to make better profit margins.

20-6   True/False

Marketing is seen as creating false wants that benefit consumers more than they benefit the industry.

20-7   True/False

Marketers are most effective when they create new wants rather than appealing to existing ones.

20-8   True/False

Advertisers are accused of holding too much power over the mass media, limiting their freedom to report independently and objectively.

20-9   True/False

The two major movements in citizen and public action groups have been commercialism and environmentalism.

20-10 True/False

Consumers have not only the right but also the responsibility to protect themselves instead of leaving this function to someone else.

20-11 True/False

Pollution control means eliminating or minimizing waste before it is created.

20-12 True/False

Design for environment (DFE) practices not only help to sustain the environment, but they can also be highly profitable.

20-13 True/False

Most companies today invest heavily in pollution prevention.

20-14 True/False

Sense-of-mission marketing means the company should define its mission in narrow social terms rather than broad product terms.

20-15 True/False

Alert companies view societal problems as threats.

20-16 True/False

The challenge posed by pleasing products is they sell very well, but may end up hurting the consumer.

20-17 True/False

Managers need a set of principles to help them determine the moral importance of each situation and decide how far they can go in good conscience.

20-18 True/False

While it is both illegal and unethical for a Canadian firm to bribe a Canadian government official, Canada currently does not have a law preventing firms from paying bribes when they operate overseas.

20-19 True/False

Canada's charities and not-for-profit organizations use marketing extensively for two purposes: working toward rectifying a pressing social problem and getting their name known and respected.

20-20 True/False

The seven principles for public policy toward marketing are based on the assumption marketing's job is to maximize company profits and total consumption and consumer choice, not to maximize life quality.

Applying Terms and Concepts

<u>Case#1</u>   <u>Biodegradable Diapers</u>[1]

Some marketers have been criticized for being so concerned about their own interest they ignore all others. High prices, deceptive practices, high-pressure selling and poor service to disadvantaged customers are some of the practices critics bring up when charging some firms are socially irresponsible. But now several firms have developed what appears to be the correct product for the 1990s—biodegradable disposable diapers.

Over a half million babies are born each year in Canada. They are part of the "baby boom echo"—children of the postwar baby boomers. A baby in the house means bottles, baby food, and lots and lots of diapers. The average baby goes through between 8,000 and 10,000 diapers between birth and toilet training. For the country, that means 1.8 billion used diapers a year, which converts to a half million tonnes of waste filling up landfills and taking 2 to 500 years to dissolve. Concern about the impact of all these diapers has led to a different kind of boom—biodegradable diapers.

Biodegradable diapers are made with advanced plastics, most involving the binding of cornstarch polymers—molecules made up of repeating, identical subunits—with plastic molecules. The newly formed plastic is supposed to be readily broken down in the soil by a variety of microorganisms, such as fungi and bacteria that feed on the starch. As the cornstarch is eaten, the plastic's polymeric chains are broken down into smaller and smaller units, leaving behind only a plastic dust.

The condition of the nation's landfills has also contributed to the growth in the demand for biodegradable diapers. Many municipalities are finding their existing landfills must soon be closed because they do not meet federal guidelines for pollution control. Permits to construct new landfills are difficult to obtain and modern environmentally sound landfills are extremely expensive to build, maintain and monitor.

So far, most of the new diapers have been sold to well-educated parents who are willing to help the environment by paying an extra 5 to10 percent for a disposable diaper that actually does dispose of itself. Even though the industry is still in its infancy, brands such as Rocky Mountain, Tender Cares, DoveTails, Nappies, and Bunnies are starting to challenge major brands for supermarket shelf space.

But recently, some people have begun to question just how much disposable biodegradable diapers will do to alleviate the landfill problem. One researcher found the average landfill contains 36 percent paper, 20 percent yard wastes, 9 percent metal, 9 percent food, 8 percent glass, 7 percent plastic, and 11 percent other materials. And these proportions of materials do not change appreciably over time. Research also indicates

---

[1] Principles of Marketing, 3rd Edition, Kotler, Armstrong, Warren (Prentice Hall) – pg. 442.

once material is placed in a landfill, it remains virtually unchanged. Decades after it was buried, paper, metal, glass, and plastic remain. Even yard waste and food do no easily decay. It seems that in order for biodegradation to take place, water, oxygen, and sunlight must be present so that the microorganisms can break down the materials. Unfortunately, these conditions are not typically present in modern landfills. Also, the problem with landfills is not so much the type of material placed in them as the volume of that material. Some researchers suggest that the benefits of biodegradable plastics are illusory and that the solution to our waste problem is a combination of recycling, incineration, composition, and landfills.

1. What is the philosophy of society marketing?

_____

_____

_____

_____

2. Explain why firms that make biodegradable disposable diapers could be said to be following a philosophy of society marketing.

_____

_____

_____

_____

3. What impact, if any will biodegradable disposable diapers have on landfills?

_____

_____

_____

_____

4. How are environmentalists likely to view biodegradable disposable diapers?

_____

_____

_____

_____

5. Discuss any feasible alternatives to disposable diapers.

_____

_____

_____

_____

Case #2   Brown's Department Stores

Helen Mahon is the vice-president of security for Halifax-based Brown's Department Stores. She has become increasingly alarmed at the high rate of shoplifting and employee theft within Brown's store system. The current rate of loss is estimated at $2,600,000 per year.

Mahon is particularly upset because she realizes that everyone is hurt by the losses. Shoplifters, when caught, are prosecuted. Customers must pay higher prices to cover the loss, and cost of the security systems, and store managers are faced with an unpleasant, time-consuming activity that reduces the profitability of the organization.

Mahon was recently approached by Todd Roy Hill, the president of Hill Communications, Inc., with a proposal that has left her in a quandary. Hill Communications produces cassette tapes that contain subliminal messages designed to alter the behaviour of listeners. The listener hears music or "pink" noise such as ocean waves or rushing wind, while the subconscious hears the message (in this situation) "Do not shoplift." Hill explained that the message (any message) is recorded at about 5 decibels below the audible range. In time, the message embeds itself in the listener's mind, thereby affecting behaviour.

Hill produced evidence (studies he had conducted) indicating that losses were reduced by an average of 39 percent in similar settings. With a projected loss reduction of over $1,000,000, Mahon was interested, but she was uneasy because she wondered if it was right to manipulate people in this fashion. She also asked herself: "If subliminal messages can be used to reduce shoplifting, why not use it to stimulate sales at Brown's Stores?"

That evening Mahon came across an article in the magazine Psychology In Action by McGill University psychology professor Rene Alphonse, a specialist in the study of perception, who maintained that subliminal messages do not alter behaviour. Alphonse also went on to state that studies conducted to prove that they do were often flawed and unscientific.

The cost of the system proposed by Hill Communications is essentially what Brown now pays for background music in its stores. Hill has documentation from the provincial government that the practice is perfectly legal in Nova Scotia. He also stated that Brown's would be the first chain of department stores to use the service.

1. What would Mahon decide if she believed that issues of morality, ethics, responsibility and conscience should be made according to the free market or legal system?

   _____

   _____

   _____

2. What would Mahon decide if she believed that issues of morality, ethics, responsibility and conscience should be made according to managers "social conscience?"

   _____

   _____

   _____

Case #3   Palmer Industries

Carl Palmer, President of Palmer Industries, recently startled the beverage industry with the introduction of a self-cooling can. The technology, pioneered by Palmer, allows a slightly modified can to cool itself within 20 seconds of opening. Cooling is accomplished by a carbon dioxide cartridge encased in an aluminum sheath surrounding the beverage container. When the container is opened, the carbon dioxide cartridge is pierced. As the carbon dioxide escapes from the cartridge, it freezes the outer sheath, thereby cooling the beverage. Variations in temperature can be achieved by increasing or decreasing the volume of carbon dioxide in the cartridge. Beer will chill to 3 degrees and soft drinks to 5 degrees, the ideal temperature.

The self-cooling can will have the same outer dimensions as a standard can. However, there will be approximately a 75 mL liquid displacement to accommodate the cooling mechanism. The outer sheath will be bonded to the top and bottom of the can with the inner container wall 2 mm from the outer wall. The carbon dioxide will escape through the aperture created when the can is opened. The self-cooling can will cost approximately $.05 more per unit than a conventional can.

The technology is protected by 16 Canadian and US patents, foreign patents pending. Palmer Industries will license manufacturers to produce the containers and sell them to various bottling companies. Bay Street responded enthusiastically; with Palmer Industries--posting a 12% gain. An additional 6% was posted when the Consumer and Corporate and Agriculture Canada approved the technology as safe for sale.

Palmer plans to start with the beverage industry, but sees this technology applied to any packaged food consumers prefer chilled prior to consumption, including canned fruits, vegetables, desserts and meats. To date, the only group to express doubt about the new technology is the manufacturers of refrigerated soft drink vending machines, who will find demand for their machines declining as the self-cooling cans gain wide-spread distribution.

_____1. Critics may charge that development of a self-cooling can to replace regular cans is an example of _____.

    A.   unfair competition

    B.   planned obsolescence

    C.   deceptive packaging

    D.   high pressure selling

    E.   price gouging

_____2. Palmer Industries has utilized patent protection as a(n):

    A.   barrier to entry.

    B.   unfair competition.

    C.   unfair political protection.

    D.   high pressure selling.

    E.   planned obsolescence.

____3. Consumers may view Palmer Industries as practicing _____ marketing.

     A.   antisocial

     B.   enlightened

     C.   production oriented

     D.   sales oriented

     E.   product oriented

____4. If. in a promotional campaign, Palmer Industries advertised the self-cooling can would chill soft drinks to 5 degrees when it would only chill them to 14 degrees, Palmer would be engaged in _____.

     A.   high pressure selling

     B.   puffery

     C.   deceptive advertising

     D.   creating false wants

     E.   deceptive pricing

____5. The self-cooling can is best classified as a _____ product.

     A.   deficient

     B.   decadent

     C.   desirable

     D.   pleasing

     E.   salutary

Multiple Choice Answers

1.	Correct Answer:	3	Reference:	pg. 680
2.	Correct Answer:	5	Reference:	pg. 680
3.	Correct Answer:	1	Reference:	pg. 681
4.	Correct Answer:	2	Reference:	pg. 681
5.	Correct Answer:	4	Reference:	pg. 683
6.	Correct Answer:	3	Reference:	pg. 683
7.	Correct Answer:	2	Reference:	pg. 685
8.	Correct Answer:	5	Reference:	pg. 686
9.	Correct Answer:	3	Reference:	pg. 687
10.	Correct Answer:	4	Reference:	pg. 688
11.	Correct Answer:	1	Reference:	pg. 688
12.	Correct Answer:	5	Reference:	pg. 689
13.	Correct Answer:	2	Reference:	pg. 692
14.	Correct Answer:	3	Reference:	pg. 694
15.	Correct Answer:	4	Reference:	pg. 695
16.	Correct Answer:	1	Reference:	pg. 695
17.	Correct Answer:	2	Reference:	pg. 696
18.	Correct Answer:	5	Reference:	pg. 698
19.	Correct Answer:	3	Reference:	pg. 699
20.	Correct Answer:	5	Reference:	pg. 704

21.	Correct Answer:	2	Reference:	pg. 686
22.	Correct Answer:	1	Reference:	pg. 687
23.	Correct Answer:	2	Reference:	pg. 689
24.	Correct Answer:	4	Reference:	pg. 698
25.	Correct Answer:	2	Reference:	pg. 698
26.	Correct Answer:	3	Reference:	pg. 698
27.	Correct Answer:	1	Reference:	pg. 697
28.	Correct Answer:	4	Reference:	pg. 698
29.	Correct Answer:	5	Reference:	pg. 691
30.	Correct Answer:	2	Reference:	pg. 680

True/False Answers

1.   TRUE   Reference: pg. 680   Topic: Marketing's Impact on Individual Consumers

2.   TRUE   Reference: pg. 680   Topic: Marketing's Impact on Individual Consumers

3.   FALSE   Reference: pg. 681   Topic: Deceptive Practices

4.   TRUE   Reference: pg. 682   Topic: Deceptive Practices

5.   FALSE   Reference: pg. 683   Topic: Planned Obsolescence

6.   FALSE   Reference: pg. 685   Topic: False Wants and Too Much Materialism

7.   FALSE   Reference: pg. 685   Topic: False Wants and Too Much Materialism

8.   TRUE   Reference: pg. 686   Topic: Too Much Political Power

9.   FALSE   Reference: pg. 687   Topic: Citizen and Public Action to Regulate Marketing

10.   TRUE   Reference: pg. 689   Topic: Consumerism

11.   FALSE   Reference: pg. 691   Topic: Environmentalism

12.   TRUE   Reference: pg. 692   Topic: Environmentalism

13.   TRUE   Reference: pg. 694   Topic: Environmentalism

14.   FALSE   Reference: pg. 697   Topic: Sense-of-Mission Marketing

15.   FALSE   Reference: pg. 697   Topic: Societal Marketing

16.   TRUE   Reference: pg. 698   Topic: Societal Marketing

17.   TRUE   Reference: pg. 698   Topic: Marketing Ethics

18.   TRUE   Reference: pg. 701   Topic: Marketing Ethics

19.   FALSE   Reference: pg. 703   Topic: Marketing Ethics

20.   FALSE   Reference: pg. 704   Topic: Principles for Public Policy Toward Marketing

Applying Terms and Concept Answers

<u>Case#1</u>   <u>Biodegradable Diapers:</u>

Question #1
- An enlightened company following the principle of societal marketing makes marketing decisions by considering consumers' wants, the company's requirements, consumers' long-run interests, and society's long-run interests.
- The company is aware that neglecting the last two factors is a disservice to consumers and to society.
- Alert companies view societal problems as opportunities.
- A socially oriented marketer wants to design products that are not only pleasing but also beneficial.
- Therefore products can be classified according to their degree of immediate consumer satisfaction and long-run consumer benefit.
- Desirable products give both high immediate satisfaction and long-run benefits.

Question #2
- Biodegradable disposable diapers could be seen as a product that meets both of these criteria.
- Disposable diaper producers were responding to the consumers' environmental interests.
- The disposables are still completely functional and more beneficial to the environment.
- In addition, parents and consumers feel at ease knowing that the diaper won't be around in 100 years.

Question #3
- The impact will likely be negligible. In order for a substance to biodegrade, sunlight, water, and oxygen must be present, and these elements are typically absent in modern landfills.
- Researchers like Dr. William Rathje, an anthropologist at the University of Arizona, have found that most material put into a landfill dos not decay.
- Decades after it was buried, paper, metal, glass and plastic remain. Even yard waste and food do not easily decay.
- This is because biodegradation is accomplished by microorganisms that need sunlight, moisture, and oxygen to do the job.
- The problem with landfills is not so much the type of material placed in them as the volume of that material.
- Some researchers suggest that the benefits of biodegradable plastics are illusory and that our waste problem will only be solved by a combination of recycling, incineration, composting, and landfills.

Question #4

- While consumer advocates look at whether the marketing system is efficiently serving consumer wants, environmentalists look at how marketing affects the environment and at the costs of serving consumer needs and wants.
- Environmentalism is an organized movement of concerned citizens and government agencies out to protect and improve people's living environment.
- Environmentalists are concerned about damage to the ecosystem caused by strip mining forest depletion, acid rain, loss of the ozone layer in the atmosphere, toxic wastes, and litter; about the loss of recreational areas; and about the increase in health problems caused by bad air, polluted water, and chemically treated food.
- Environmentalists are not against marketing and consumption; they simply want people and organizations to operate with more care for the environment.
- The marketing system's goal should not be to maximize consumption, consumer choice, or consumer satisfaction. Rather, it should be to maximize life quality.
- And "life quality" means not only the quality of consumer goods and services, but also the quality of the environment.
- Environmentalists want environmental costs included in producer and consumer decision making.
- Environmentalists are likely to endorse the marketing of biodegradable disposable diapers over regular disposables since the former are more compatible with their views.

Question #5

- There is always good old-fashioned cloth diapers.
- However, cloth diapers are not as convenient and simple to use. An alternative could be a cloth diaper service or business that would drop off clean diapers and pick up dirty diapers daily.
- This business would also clean and sterilize the diapers before their next use.
- Another alternative could be the production of the absorbing pads in diapers.
- Diapers are made up of the absorbing pads and the plastic outside shell.
- Diaper manufacturers could sell the absorbing pads and produce a re-useable plastic panty.
- This alternative would be less detrimental to the environment versus traditional diapers.

Case #2   Brown's Department Store:

1.   The "Free Market and "Legal Systemö philosophies suggest that it is the responsibility of :the firm to obey the law as it pursues rational and economic objectives and that the common good is best served when a business pursues its own competitive advantage. Therefore, it is Mahon's obligation to use the subliminal messages as a loss prevention mechanism to legally enhance Brown's competitive advantage and increase Brown's profitability.

2. The "Social Conscience" philosophy suggests that corporations exercise independent, noneconomic judgment in deciding what is morally and ethically right. It also calls for management to apply individual morality to corporate decision. If Mahon was convinced that the system was legal and worked, she could decide to implement it because (a) the potential shoplifter is spared prosecution; (b) the cost of theft does not have to be passed on to the customers in the form of higher prices; and (c) store managers and owners avoid unpleasant situations and enjoy greater profitability. In this decision, her reasoning would be that manipulation of the would-be criminal through the use of subliminal messages is a small price to pay, given the benefits. In essence, the end justifies the means.

However, Mahon might also decide that subliminal messages should not be included in the background music because it is an act of manipulation and subconscious behavior modification.- Even though the act of shoplifting is wrong, the would-be criminal would not be acting of his or her own free will, therefore, the end, no matter how well intentioned, does not justify the means. In essence, it is morally wrong to engage in manipulation and subconscious behavior modification.

Case #3   Palmer Industries:

1.   B

2.   A

3.   B

4.   C

5.   C

Appendix 4

Measuring and Forecasting Demand

Applying Terms and Concepts

To determine how well you understand the materials in this chapter, read each of the following brief cases and then respond to the questions that follow Answers are given at the end of this chapter

Case #1 Clark Motors

Larry Clark is the president of Clark Motors, a network of six automotive dealerships in New Brunswick. Clark operates Chevrolet dealerships in Moncton, Riverview, and Sackville, a Pontiac/Buick dealership in Fredericton, and Toyota dealerships in Amherst and Oromacto. Each dealership operates in the black, although profits at the Toyota dealerships were limited because new automobiles were in short supply. Prior to 1990, the Toyota dealerships chronically sold out their allotment of automobiles because import quotas limited the availability of vehicles. However, with the increased availability of Toyotas, Clark estimates that he now receives approximately 150 additional Toyotas per dealership, per year.

Clark, while visiting relatives in Sydney, noticed that the community had no Toyota dealership. In fact, the majority of dealerships ignored imports, with the exception of the local Chevrolet dealership, which also sold Subarus. Clark, ever vigilant for an opportunity to make money, also noticed that an attractive building was available for sale or lease on the upper east side of Sydney located near Highway 4. It had formerly housed a Dodge dealership which had gone bankrupt in the sales slump of 1983. Clark reasoned that with minimal effort, the facility Could become a Toyota dealership.

Upon returning to his base of operations in Oromacto, Clark contacted Bobby Thompson, Toyota's zone manager, about the possibility of opening a dealership if the need could be justified. Thompson indicated that Toyota would support Clark not only with automobiles, but also with advertising allowances if he (Clark) would open a Toyota dealership in the area. Clark was especially pleased to hear of the advertising allowances because past experience showed that considerable consumer demand was generated by local, as well as, regional advertising.

Clark quickly hired the market research firm of Gauthier and Nault to assess the needs for another dealership in the Sydney area and to determine the residents' interest in purchasing an imported automobile. Two weeks later, Clark also sent two of his dealership managers, three sales managers, and one business manager to the area to assess the attractiveness of the market.

Upon their return he gave them the report generated by the research firm and additional market information supplied by Toyota. He then instructed each manager to develop an estimate of sales potential for a dealership in Sydney.

Two weeks after the managers returned from Sydney, Clark brought them to Oromacto for a meeting. He instructed each manager to offer his/her estimate of sales potential and supporting rationale. Estimates of auto sales ranged from 600 to 900 vehicles per year, averaging 775. After each manager had offered their opinion. Clark instructed them to consider what the others had said. He also said he would reconvene the group in three days, when each manager would be expected to offer a revised sales estimate. During the next meeting, the estimates ranged from 640 to 830 vehicles per year, with an average of 750. Six weeks later, after financing had been arranged, a decision was made to open what eventually became Cindy Toyota (named after Clark"s wife), the seventh addition to Clark's Motors.

_____1. Identify the factor that served to reduce Toyota sales prior to 1990.

      A.   consumer interest

      B.   access barrier

      C.   qualified buyers

      D.   available income

      E.   qualified available market

2.   From the evidence presented in the case, it is clear that Toyota faced a(n) _____ (expandable/nonexpandable) market.

_____3. Identify the approach used by Clark in forecasting the demand for automobiles in Sydney.

      A.   survey of buyers intentions

      B.   expert opinion

      C.   Delphi method

      D.   composite of salesforce opinions

      E.   both (B) and (C)

_____4. The average estimate of 750 automobiles is an example of:

      A.   industry sales forecast.

      B.   economic forecast.

      C.   company sales forecast.

      D.   market potential.

      E.   time-series analysis.

5. Comment on the process used by Clark in arriving at an average sales potential estimate of 750. Include in your comments, why the sales potential range of 600 to 900 with an average of 775 vehicles changed to a range of 640 to 830 vehicles with an average of 750.

_____

_____

_____

_____

_____

Case #2   Xenephon Corporation

The Xenephon Corporation of Saskatchewan has just developed a radical new Concept in competition dune buggies. A new suspension system and drive chain provide much better acceleration and stability, while a special alloy frame gives the machine greater strength and lighter weight. Xenephon plans to charge a premium price for its offering.

The company believes that it can obtain immediate distribution in Canada, Mexico, and the US. Surveys indicate strong interest in an improved competition machine among residents of all three countries -- because of the popularity of the sport of dune buggy racing. The countries have stringent age and licensing requirements for competition machines.

1. Keeping in mind that potential buyers for a product or service have four characteristics: interest, income, access and qualifications, define each of the following:

   A. Potential market

   _____

   _____

   _____

   _____

552

B.   Available market

_____

_____

_____

_____

C.   Qualified Available market

_____

_____

_____

_____

D.   Penetrated market

_____

_____

_____

_____

Case #3   Automobili Lamborghini USA

It has been said, "If you have to ask the price, you can't afford it." While that may have been true in the past, it is probably less so now. Exotic sports cars like the Lamborghini, Vector, Ferrari, Bugatti and McLaren priced to sell at 400 thousand dollars (CDN) or more are not as immune to the economy as they once were. Even the wealthy are becoming more value conscious. True, exotic sports cars are not bought for transportation, they are bought because they fit the lifestyle of the owner. They project a certain image with their seductive design and mesmerizing power.

Very few people will ever see a Lamborghini on the road and only a handful will ever purchase one. In fact, this partly adds to their mystique. But Megatech, the Indonesian investment group who recently purchased Lamborghini from Chrysler wants to change that. Lamborghini only sold 33 cars in the US in 1993, 89 in 1994 and approximately 100 in 1995. Megatech's plans are to eventually sell 1500 to 2000 units per year in the US. These ambitious sales goals will be achieved by a expanding the product line to include a sport utility vehicle in the 100 to 140 thousand dollar range and a sports sedan priced below 280 thousand dollars. Aggressive marketing techniques designed to promote customer awareness are also planned. The activities include advertising in upscale business, travel and lifestyle publications, strategic partnerships with equally upscale products and organizations and allowing auto journalists to test drive a Lamborghini for review in their publications. Lamborghini is also planning appearances at the PPG Indy Car races where prospective buyers can take one out for a test drive and perhaps run a few hot laps on the race track.

A new dealership network and lease program touted in both an advertising and direct mail program will complement other sales efforts.

1. Explain what is meant by the concept of total market demand as it applies to exotic sports cars.

    _____

    _____

    _____

2. What is the difference between primary demand and selective demand?

    _____

    _____

    _____

3.   Explain why the market for Lamborghini automobiles is expandable.

_____

_____

_____

Sources: "Even Lamborghini Must Think Marketing" *Advertising Age,* May 7, 1995, p. 4. "1995 New Cars" *Motor Trend,* October 94, p. 41. *Vector Aeromotive Corporation Annual Report,* 1995.

Answers

Applying Terms and Concepts

Case #1   Clark Motors:

1.   B (Import Quotas)   3.   E

2.   expandable   4.   C

5.   Clark used the expert opinion method to obtain the average sales estimate of 750 vehicles. In particular, he used the Delphi method when he brought the managers in for a second meeting where the managers offered their revised sales estimates. It is probable that the sales range converged during the second meeting because each manager had the opportunity to reflect on the opinions offered by the other managers. In essence, each manager now had a broader base of information on which to base the estimate.

Case #2   Xenephon Corporation:

1.   a.   Xenephon's potential market consists of those consumers who have expressed a strong interest in their dune buggy.

      b.   Xenephon's available market consists of those consumers who live in the company's three-country coverage area, are interested in a high performance dune buggy and are willing to pay Xenephon's price.

c.   Xenephon's qualified available market consists of those consumers who have expressed an interest, possess the necessary purchasing power and who can meet the legal requirements for purchase.

d.   Xenephon's penetrated market consists of those consumer who have all four characteristics. That is they are interested in the dune buggies, have the income to purchase them, have access to the dealership network and who also meet the age and licensing requirements.

Case #3   Automobile Lamborqhini USA:

1.   The total market demand for a product or service is the total volume that would be bought by a defined consumer group in a defined geographic area in a defined time period in a defined marketing environment under a defined level and mix of industry marketing effort. Total market demand is not a fixed number but a function of given conditions including elements of the micro and macro environments. As these elements and others such as the level and types of competitive marketing activity change, so too will the level of demand.

2.   Primary demand is the total demand for all brands of exotic sports cars while selective demand is the demand for one brand such as the demand for Lamborghinis.

3.   Lamborghini has had a fairly steady increase in the sale of automobiles since Megatech purchased the company from Chrysler Corporation in 1994. The increase in selective demand for Lamborghini Automobiles can be attributed at least in pan to an increase in marketing expenditures. Therefore, as Lamborghini and the other exotic sports car manufacturers increase their marketing expenditures, the total market demand can be expected to increase. Whether it will increase to the level that would allow Lamborghini to realize its eventual goal of selling 1,500 to 2,000 units a year in the US is debatable and remains to be seen.